ADOBE® ILLUSTRATOR® CS
DESIGN PROFESSIONAL

Chris Botello

THOMSON
COURSE TECHNOLOGY

Adobe® Illustrator® CS—Design Professional

Chris Botello

Executive Editor:
Nicole Jones Pinard

Product Manager:
Jane Hosie-Bounar

Associate Product Manager:
Emilie Perreault

Editorial Assistant:
Shana Rosenthal

Production Editor:
Summer Hughes

Developmental Editor:
Ann Fisher

Composition House:
GEX Publishing Services

QA Manuscript Reviewers:
John Freitas, Ashlee Welz,
Jeffrey Schwartz, Danielle Shaw

Text Designer:
Ann Small

Illustrator:
Philip Brooker

Cover Design:
Philip Brooker

ISBN 0-619-18835-9

Design Professional Series Vision

The Design Professional Series is your guide to today's hottest multimedia applications. These comprehensive books teach the skills behind the application, showing you how to apply smart design principles to multimedia products such as dynamic graphics, animation, Web sites, software authoring tools, and video.

A team of design professionals including multimedia instructors, students, authors, and editors worked together to create this series. We recognized the unique learning environment of the multimedia classroom and created a series that:

- Gives you comprehensive step-by-step instructions
- Offers in-depth explanation of the "why" behind a skill
- Includes creative projects for additional practice
- Explains concepts clearly using full-color visuals

It was our goal to create a book that speaks directly to the multimedia and design community—one of the most rapidly growing computer fields today.

We would like to thank Philip Brooker for developing the inspirational artwork found on each chapter opener and book cover. We would also like to give special thanks to Ann Small of A Small Design Studio for developing a sophisticated and instructive book design.

—The Design Professional Series

Author's Vision

Hands-on is the best way to explore any software application. You can study every chapter of an instruction manual, but reading about Adobe Illustrator and drawing in Adobe Illustrator are two very different things indeed.

This book is a series of exercises that will take you on a fully guided tour of Illustrator CS—from basic concepts to advanced techniques—all with a hands-on approach. You will learn by doing, and you'll have fun, which is an essential skill not covered in any instruction manual.

I had fun writing this, and that was possible because of the focus and hard work of my editor and long-time friend Ann Fisher. Ann kept the project on track but left me enough room to bounce around the application and share with you some of my favorite tips and tricks. Her dedication—combined with a great capacity for laughter—brought out the best in both of us. Special thanks also go to Nicole Pinard, Executive Editor for this series and others, and Jane Hosie-Bounar, the Product Manager.

I also want to acknowledge the QA manuscript reviewers for their input: John Freitas, Ashlee Welz, Jeff Schwartz, and Danielle Shaw. Thanks also to our table of contents reviewers: Susan Oakes and Max Dutton of Briarcliffe College, Mary Malinconico of Gloucester County College, and Patrick Miller of Mississippi State University. Mary Malinconico, Patrick Miller, and Susan Oakes also reviewed the new material in Chapter K.

iii

Introduction to Adobe Illustrator CS

Welcome to *Adobe Illustrator CS—Design Professional*. This book offers creative projects, concise instructions, and complete coverage of basic to advanced Illustrator skills, helping you to create polished, professional-looking illustrations. Use this book both in the classroom and as your own reference guide.

This text is organized into thirteen chapters. In these chapters you will learn many skills, including how to draw illustrations, transform objects, work with layers, patterns, brushes, and filters, use effects, create graphics for the Web, create graphs, work in 3D, and prepare files for print production.

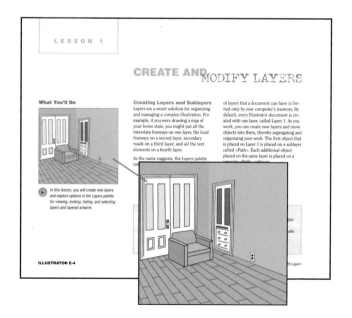

What You'll Do

A What You'll Do figure begins every lesson. This figure gives you an at-a-glance look at what you'll do in the chapter, either by showing you a page or pages from the current project or a tool you'll be using.

Comprehensive Conceptual Lessons

Before jumping into instructions, in-depth conceptual information tells you "why" skills are applied. This book provides the "how" and "why" through the use of professional examples. Also included in the text are tips and sidebars to help you work more efficiently and creatively, or to teach you a bit about the history or design philosophy behind the skill you are using.

Step-by-Step Instructions

This book combines in-depth conceptual information with concise steps to help you learn Illustrator CS. Each set of steps guides you through a lesson where you will create, modify, or enhance an Illustrator CS file. Step references to large colorful images and quick step summaries round out the lessons.

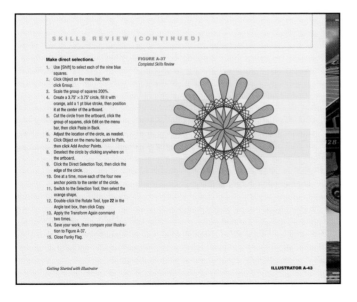

Projects

This book contains a variety of end-of-chapter materials for additional practice and reinforcement. The Skills Review contains hands-on practice exercises that mirror the progressive nature of the lesson material. The chapter concludes with four projects: two Project Builders, one Design Project, and one Group Project. The Project Builders and the Design Project require you to apply the skills you've learned in the chapter. Group Projects encourage group activity as students use the resources of a team to address and solve challenges based on the content explored in the chapter.

What Instructor Resources Are Available with this Book?

The Instructor Resources CD-ROM is Course Technology's way of putting the resources and information needed to teach and learn effectively into your hands. All the resources are available for both Macintosh and Windows operating systems, and many of the resources can be downloaded from *www.course.com*.

Instructor's Manual

Available as an electronic file, the Instructor's Manual is quality-assurance tested and includes chapter overviews and detailed lecture topics for each chapter, with teaching tips. The Instructor's Manual is available on the Instructor Resources CD-ROM, or you can download it from *www.course.com*.

Syllabus

Prepare and customize your course easily using this sample course outline (available on the Instructor Resources CD-ROM).

PowerPoint Presentations

Each chapter has a corresponding PowerPoint presentation that you can use in lectures, distribute to your students, or customize to suit your course.

Figure Files

Figure Files contain all the figures from the book in bitmap format. Use the figure files to create transparency masters or use them in a PowerPoint presentation.

Data Files for Students

To complete most of the chapters in this book, your students will need Data Files. The Data Files are available on the CD at the back of this text book. Instruct students to use the Data Files List at the end of this book. This list gives instructions on organizing files.

30-Day Tryout Software

On the CD at the back of this book, you will also find a 30-day tryout version of Adobe® Illustrator® CS software for both Macintosh and Windows operating systems. Students can use this software to gain additional practice away from the classroom. *Note*: The tryout software will expire after 30 days. Check the Read Me file on the CD-ROM for more information.

Solutions to Exercises

Solution Files are Data Files completed with comprehensive sample answers. Use these files to evaluate your students' work. Or distribute them electronically so students can verify their work. Sample solutions to all lessons and end-of-chapter material are provided.

Test Bank and Test Engine

ExamView is a powerful testing software package that allows instructors to create and administer printed, computer (LAN-based), and Internet exams. ExamView includes hundreds of questions that correspond to the topics covered in this text, enabling students to generate detailed study guides that include page references for further review. The computer-based and Internet testing components allow students to take exams at their computers, and also save the instructor time by grading each exam automatically.

CHAPTER C   DRAWING AND COMPOSING AN ILLUSTRATION

CHAPTER D   TRANSFORMING AND DISTORTING OBJECTS

CHAPTER F — WORKING WITH PATTERNS AND BRUSHES

CHAPTER G — WORKING WITH FILTERS, GRADIENT MESHES, ENVELOPES, AND BLENDS

CHAPTER J   DRAWING WITH SYMBOLS

CHAPTER K   CREATING 3D OBJECTS

Measurements

Measurements on the artboard and measurements referring to an object are given in inches, not points or picas. In order to follow the exercises, it's important that the General Units Preference in the Preferences dialog box be set to Inches. To set this preference, click Edit on the menu bar, point to Preferences, then click Units & Undo.

Text attributes are given in points.

You may or may not prefer to work with rulers showing. You can make rulers visible by clicking View on the menu bar, then clicking Show Rulers, or by pressing [Ctrl][R] (Win) or ⌘[R] (Mac). You can hide visible rulers by clicking View on the menu bar, then clicking Hide Rulers or by pressing [Ctrl][R] (Win) or ⌘[R] (Mac).

Document Color Mode

Documents in Adobe Illustrator CS can be created in one of two color modes—RGB or CMYK. You can determine the color mode in the New dialog box when you create a document. You can also change a document's color mode by clicking File on the menu bar, then clicking Document Color Mode.

The color mode for each document is identified in the title bar at the top of the Illustrator window.

Whenever you are asked to create a new document, the color mode will be specified. Many menu commands, such as those under the Effect menu, are available only in RGB mode. If you run into a situation in which a specified menu command is not available, first check the color mode.

Specifying Colors

Default color swatches in the Swatches palette of Illustrator CS are named. If you position your cursor over a swatch, the color's name will appear. Note, however, that there may be differences in swatch names when the same document is opened on a Mac or a PC. Therefore, when an exercise calls for you to fill or stroke an object with a default color from the Swatches palette, the exercise will refer to the color by a generic name, such as "red" or "light green."

Fonts

Whenever fonts are used in Data and Solution Files, they are chosen from a set of very common typefaces that you will most likely have available on your computer. If any of the fonts in use are not available on your computer, please make a substitution.

For variety and typographic appeal, we have used other typefaces in Data and Solution Files that are not standard; however, we have converted those fonts to outlines. When a font is converted to an outline, the letterform is simply a vector graphic, like all other vector graphics.

Quick Keys

Quick keys are keyboard shortcuts that can be used in place of clicking the command on the menu. [Ctrl][X], for example, is the quick key for Cut on the PC platform. Mastering basic quick keys is essential for a smooth work flow in Illustrator. It's a good idea to start with the commands on the Edit and Object menus as candidates for quick keys.

GETTING STARTED WITH ILLUSTRATOR

1. Create a new document.

2. Explore the Illustrator window.

3. Create basic shapes.

4. Apply fill and stroke colors to objects.

5. Select, move, and align objects.

6. Transform objects.

7. Make direct selections.

CHAPTER A
GETTING STARTED WITH ILLUSTRATOR

Getting to Know Illustrator

Adobe Illustrator CS is a professional illustration software application created by the Adobe Systems Incorporated. If this name is familiar to you, it's because Adobe is a leading producer of graphics software for the personal computer. Along with Illustrator, Adobe produces an entire suite of applications, including InDesign, Acrobat, Type Manager, GoLive, and, of course, the revolutionary and award-winning Photoshop.

With Illustrator, you can create everything from simple graphics, icons, and text to complex and multilayered illustrations, all of which can be used within a page layout, in a multimedia presentation, or on the Web.

Adobe Illustrator offers dozens of essential tools. Using them in combination with various menu commands, you have the potential to create any illustration that your imagination can dream up. With experience, you will find that your ability to create complex graphics rests on your ability to master simple, basic operations.

Tools You'll Use

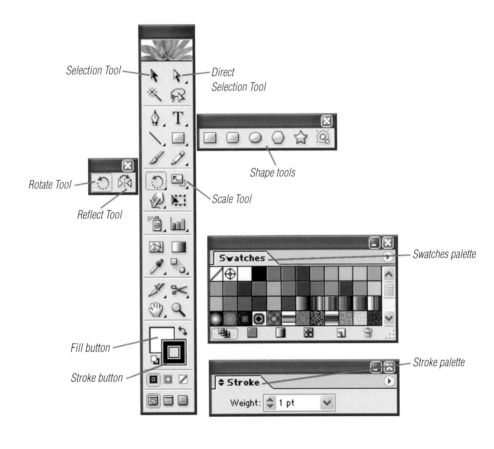

Selection Tool

Direct Selection Tool

Shape tools

Rotate Tool

Scale Tool

Reflect Tool

Swatches palette

Fill button

Stroke button

Stroke palette

CREATE A NEW DOCUMENT

What You'll Do

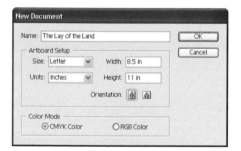

 In this lesson, you will start Adobe Illustrator and create a new document.

Creating a New Document

When you are ready to create a new document in Illustrator, you begin in the New Document dialog box. In the New document dialog box, you specify the name of the document, which appears in the title bar when you close the New Document dialog box. You also specify the document size—the width and height of the finished document. In addition, you can choose the page orientation, landscape or portrait, and the unit of measure you would like the rulers to display. Some designers like to work with inches; others prefer points or picas. Finally, you can choose whether you want to work in CMYK Color or RGB Color by clicking the appropriate option button.

Choosing Color Modes and Document Size

Generally, CMYK Color (Cyan, Magenta, Yellow, and Black) is the color mode used for print projects, and RGB Color (Red, Green, and Blue) is the color mode used for

Understanding native file types

The "native" Illustrator file format is noted as an .ai suffix. Native Illustrator files can be opened and placed by other Adobe software packages, such as Photoshop and InDesign. If you want to save an Illustrator file for use in QuarkXPress, save the file as an Illustrator EPS (Encapsulated PostScript). QuarkXPress does not recognize nor does it import Illustrator files in the native .ai format.

projects that will appear on a screen, such as a monitor or television. Once a document is created, you may change the size and color mode settings by clicking File on the menu bar, then clicking Document Setup and Document Color Mode, respectively.

Choosing a Unit of Measure

Precision is often a key to good design, and many designers choose points and picas as units of measure. A point is $\frac{1}{72}$ of an inch. A pica is 12 points, or $\frac{1}{6}$ of an inch. Defining your artboard in points and picas versus inches is a matter of personal preference. As a designer, you're probably familiar with points and picas, but would you really refer to a letter-size page as 612×792 points? Using measurements such as $\frac{29}{32}$ of an inch gets a bit ridiculous. Working with a combination of the two is the best bet for most people.

You can use more than one unit of measure when working in Illustrator. To set your measurement preferences, click Edit on the menu bar, point to Preferences, then click Units & Display Performance. Click the General, Stroke, and Type list arrows to choose your preferred unit of measure. You'll certainly want to measure your strokes and type in points. Imagine setting type in $\frac{3}{4}$" Garamond!

QUICKTIP

If you are using Macintosh OS 10, you will find your preference settings under the Illustrator menu.

Saving files in legacy format

When you save a file in Illustrator CS, it cannot be opened by older versions of Illustrator, such as Illustrator 9 or Illustrator 10. Earlier versions of the Illustrator file format are called "legacy Illustrator formats." If you want to save a file in Illustrator CS as an older legacy format, you must use the Export command, which allows you to choose which legacy format—which older version of Illustrator— you want to save in. Remember that older versions of the Illustrator file format may not support certain features such as layers, gradients, and transparency.

Create a new document (Windows)

1. Click the **Start button** ![start] on the taskbar, point to **All Programs**, then click **Adobe Illustrator CS**.

2. Click **File** on the menu bar, then click **New**.

3. Type **The Lay of the Land** in the New Document dialog box.

   TIP Note that you have *named* the file in the New Document dialog box, but you have not yet *saved* it.

4. Click the **Size list arrow** in the Artboard Setup section to view the available sizes, then click **Letter**, if necessary.

5. Click the **Units list arrow**, then click **Inches**, if necessary.

   The size of your artboard will be 8.5" × 11".

6. Click the **left icon** next to Orientation (Portrait as opposed to Landscape) as the page orientation.

7. Click the **CMYK Color option button** as the color mode for your document.

   Your New Document dialog box should resemble Figure A-1.

8. Click **OK** to create a new document with these settings.

9. Click **File** on the menu bar, click **Close**, and don't save the document.

You started Illustrator in Windows, then created a new document.

FIGURE A-1

New Document dialog box (Windows)

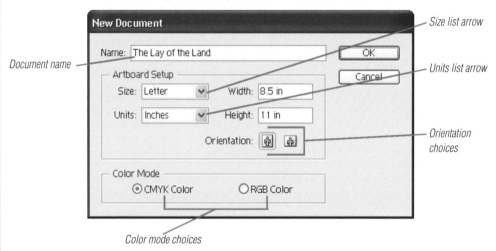

Document name

Size list arrow

Units list arrow

Orientation choices

Color mode choices

FIGURE A-2

New Document dialog box (Macintosh)

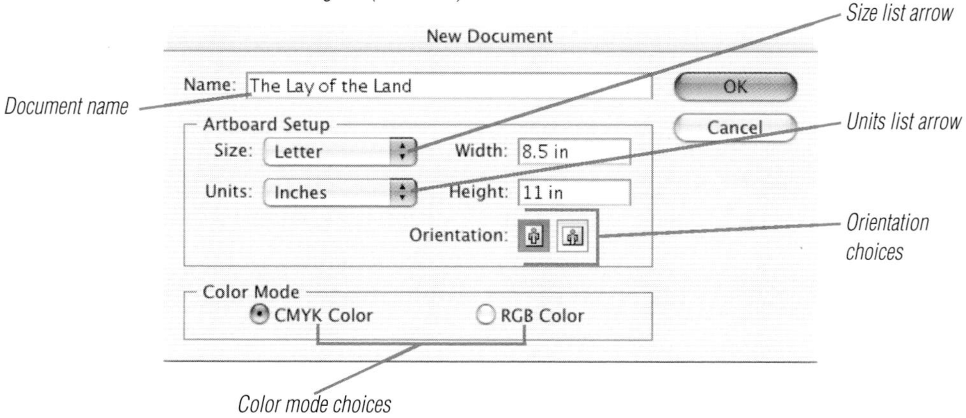

Document name

Size list arrow

Units list arrow

Orientation choices

Color mode choices

1. Double-click the **hard drive icon**, then navigate to and double-click the **Adobe Illustrator CS folder**.

2. Double-click the **Adobe Illustrator CS program icon**.

3. Click **File** on the menu bar, then click **New**.

4. Type **The Lay of the Land** in the New Document dialog box, as shown in Figure A-2.

   TIP Note that you have *named* the file in the New Document dialog box, but you have not yet *saved* it.

5. Click the **Size list arrow** in the Artboard Setup section to view the available sizes, then click **Letter**.

6. Click the **Units list arrow**, then click **Inches**, if necessary.

   The size of your artboard will be 8.5" × 11".

7. Click the **left icon** next to Orientation (Portrait as opposed to Landscape) as the page orientation.

8. Click the **CMYK Color option button** as the color mode for your document.

   Your New Document window should resemble Figure A-2.

9. Click **OK** to create a new document with these settings.

10. Click **File** on the menu bar, click **Close**, and don't save the document.

You started Illustrator in Macintosh, then created a new document.

EXPLORE THE ILLUSTRATOR WINDOW

What You'll Do

 In this lesson, you will learn about the key architecture of the Illustrator window and practice some basic Illustrator skills.

Touring the Illustrator Window

Let's take a few quick minutes to get the lay of the land. It all starts here. If you want to get really good at Illustrator, it's critical that you understand the workspace and learn to how to manage it. Nothing will slow down your work—and dull your creativity—like wrestling with the application. Moving around the window should become second nature.

The Illustrator window includes the artboard, scratch area, toolbox, and "floating" palettes, all of which are described below. Figure A-3 shows some of the more commonly used palettes.

The **title bar** contains the name of your document, magnification level, and color mode; it also contains the Minimize, Maximize, and Close buttons.

The **menu bar** includes all of the Illustrator menus. If a menu item leads to a submenu, a black triangle will be positioned to the right. If a menu item requires you to enter information into a dialog box, it is followed by an ellipsis.

The **artboard** is the area, bound by a solid line, in which you create your artwork; the size of the artboard can be set as large as 227" × 227".

The **imageable area** is the area inside the dotted line on the artboard, which is intended to represent the portion of the page that your default printer can print. Most designers find this dotted line annoying and irrelevant. It can be made invisible by clicking Hide Page Tiling on the View menu.

The **scratch area** is the area outside the artboard where you can store objects before placing them on the artboard; objects on the scratch area will not print.

The **toolbox** is a palette containing tools that let you create, select, and manipulate objects in Illustrator. A tiny black triangle beside a tool indicates "hidden" tools behind that tool. Press and hold a tool to expose the palette of hidden tools behind it. Click the tearoff tab (the tiny black triangle next to the last tool in the palette) to create a floating toolbar.

The **Zoom text box** in the lower-left corner of the Illustrator window displays the current magnification level. To the right of the Zoom text box is the Zoom menu, which you access by clicking the Zoom list arrow. The Zoom menu lets you choose another magnification level to work in.

The **status bar** contains a list arrow menu from which you can choose a status line with information about the current tool, the date and time, the number of undo operations, or the document color profile.

Scroll bars run along the bottom and right sides of the window; dragging the scroll boxes, clicking in a scroll bar, or clicking the scroll arrows changes the portion of the document displayed in the Illustrator window.

Palettes are windows containing features for modifying and manipulating Illustrator objects.

FIGURE A-3
Illustrator window

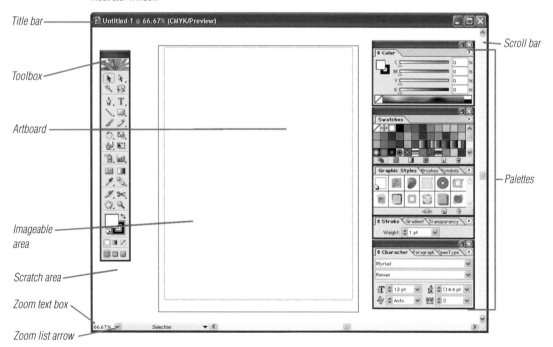

Title bar
Toolbox
Artboard
Imageable area
Scratch area
Zoom text box
Zoom list arrow
Scroll bar
Palettes

Using Quick Keys in Illustrator

Along with the various tools in the toolbox, the commands on the menu bar are essential for performing both basic and complex operations in Illustrator. Many of the menu commands execute operations that you will use over and over again. For that reason, it is a smart idea to memorize the quick keys associated with the basic menu commands. When a quick key is available, it is listed beside the command in the menu.

Many make the mistake of associating quick keys with speed. True, using quick keys will speed up your work, but the real benefit of them is that they help your work flow with fewer disruptions. Leaving your keyboard, moving your mouse, and clicking on a menu command all disrupt the essential flow of your work. Quick keys allow you to quickly execute a command without taking your hands off the keyboard or your eyes off the monitor.

Quick keys are not for 'power users' only; anybody working in Illustrator can use them beneficially. Make learning quick keys a fun part of your work; test yourself along the way. They are so intuitively assigned that you may even find yourself guessing correctly!

In Illustrator, the best place to start memorizing quick keys is with commands in the File, Edit, and Object menus, especially for Open, Close, Save, Copy, Paste, Paste in Front, Paste in Back, Bring to Front, Send to Back, Hide, Show All, Lock, and Unlock All. When you have mastered those commands, keep going. Memorize the keys you use often, and know when to stop. There's no need to memorize the quick key for Clear Guides, unless you find yourself doing it often. Table A-1 and Table A-2 list essential quick keys for Windows and Macintosh.

QUICKTIP

If a menu item can be accessed by a quick key, the quick key is identified to the right of the item. Don't ignore them. Learning basic quick keys will greatly improve the fluidity of your work.

QUICKTIP

Illustrator automatically positions crop marks at the artboard size that you choose. Although the crop marks may be turned on or off, Illustrator regards your artboard size as your trim size.

QUICKTIP

If you understand the concept of trim, bleed, and type safety, feel free to get rid of the imageable area guide, which can be distracting, especially on odd-sized artboards. To hide the imageable area guide, click View on the menu bar, then click Hide Page Tiling.

TABLE A-1: Essential Illustrator Quick Keys (Windows)

command	Windows	command	Windows
Outline	[Ctrl][Y]	Deselect	[Ctrl][Shift][A]
Preview	[Ctrl][Y]	Cut	[Ctrl][X]
Fit in Window	[Ctrl][0]	Copy	[Ctrl][C]
Zoom In	[Ctrl][+]	Paste	[Ctrl][V]
Zoom Out	[Ctrl][-]	Paste in Front	[Ctrl][F]
Access Hand Tool	[Spacebar]	Paste in Back	[Ctrl][B]
Access the Zoom In Tool	[Ctrl][Spacebar]	Undo	[Ctrl][Z]
Access the Zoom Out Tool	[Ctrl][Spacebar][Alt]	Redo	[Ctrl][Shift][Z]
Select All	[Ctrl][A]		

TABLE A-2: Essential Illustrator Quick Keys (Macintosh)

command	Macintosh	command	Macintosh
Outline	⌘[Y]	Deselect	⌘[Shift][A]
Preview	⌘[Y]	Cut	⌘[X]
Fit in Window	⌘[0]	Copy	⌘[C]
Zoom In	⌘[+]	Paste	⌘[V]
Zoom Out	⌘[-]	Paste in Front	⌘[F]
Access Hand Tool	[Spacebar]	Paste in Back	⌘[B]
Access the Zoom In Tool	⌘[Spacebar]	Undo	⌘[Z]
Access the Zoom Out Tool	⌘[Spacebar][option]	Redo	⌘[Shift][Z]
Select All	⌘[A]		

Navigate the Illustrator artboard

1. Click **File** on the menu bar, click **Open**, navigate to the drive and folder where your Data Files are stored, click **AI A-1.ai**, then click **Open**.

2. Click **File** on the menu bar, click **Save As**, type **Window Workout** in the File name text box (Win) or the Save As text box (Mac), navigate to the drive and folder where your Data Files are stored, click **Save**, then click **OK** to close the Illustrator Options dialog box.

3. Click **View** on the menu bar, note the quick key for Outline, then click **Outline**.

   As shown in Figure A-4, outline mode shows the skeleton of your work—the lines and curves that you have drawn. Outline mode can be useful for making very specific selections.

4. Click **View** on the menu bar, note the quick key for Preview, then click **Preview**.

   Preview mode shows your work complete with the colors and styles you used.

5. Toggle between outline and preview modes using the quick key, then return to preview mode.

6. Click the **Zoom Tool** 🔍 in the toolbox, then click the **circle** four times.

7. Click the **Selection Tool** ↖ in the toolbox.

8. Click **View** on the menu bar, then click **Fit in Window**.

(continued)

FIGURE A-4
Viewing the document in outline mode

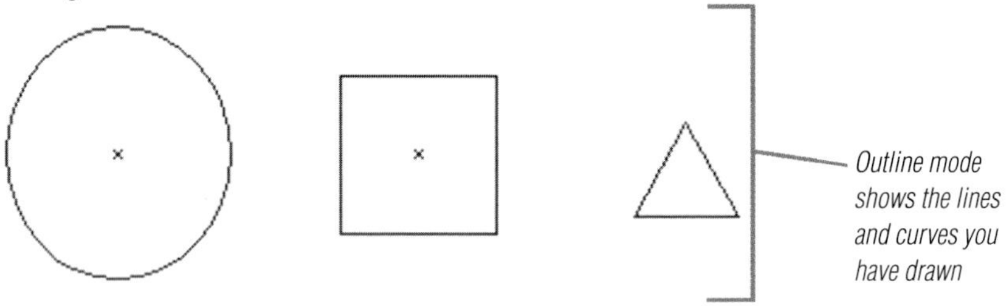

Outline mode shows the lines and curves you have drawn

9. Click **View** on the menu bar, note the quick keys for Zoom In and Zoom Out, then release the menu.

10. Use the quick key to zoom in to 200%.

> TIP The current magnification level appears in the title bar and the Zoom text box in the lower-left corner.

11. Use the quick key to zoom out to 66.67%.

12. Press and hold **[Spacebar]**, notice that the pointer changes to the Hand Tool , then click and drag the **artboard** with the Hand Tool, as shown in Figure A-5.

The Hand Tool allows you to move the artboard in the window; it's a great alternative to using the scroll arrows. Always press [Spacebar] to access the Hand Tool, so as not to interrupt the flow of your work.

You opened an Illustrator document, saved it with a new name, and used menu commands and the Zoom Tool to change the view size of the artboard. You then used the Hand Tool to move the artboard around.

FIGURE A-5
Moving the artboard with the Hand Tool

Work with objects

1. Click **Select** on the menu bar, then click **All**.

2. Click **View** on the menu bar, then click **Show Bounding Box**.

   The bounding box is a box with eight hollow white squares that appears around an object or objects when selected.

   | TIP If you see Hide Bounding Box on the View menu, the bounding box is already showing.

3. Click **View** on the menu bar, then click **Hide Bounding Box**.

4. Click **Select** on the menu bar, then click **Deselect**.

5. Click the **Selection Tool** ▸ in the toolbox, then move each shape—one at a time—to the bottom of the page.

6. Click **Edit** on the menu bar, then click **Undo Move**.

   The last object you moved returns to its original position, as shown in Figure A-6.

7. Undo your last two steps.

8. Click **Edit** on the menu bar, then click **Redo Move**.

9. Redo your last two steps.

10. Click the **artboard** to deselect, click the **red triangle**, click **Edit** on the menu bar, then click **Copy**.

11. Click **Edit** on the menu bar, then click **Paste**.

(continued)

FIGURE A-6
Undoing your last step

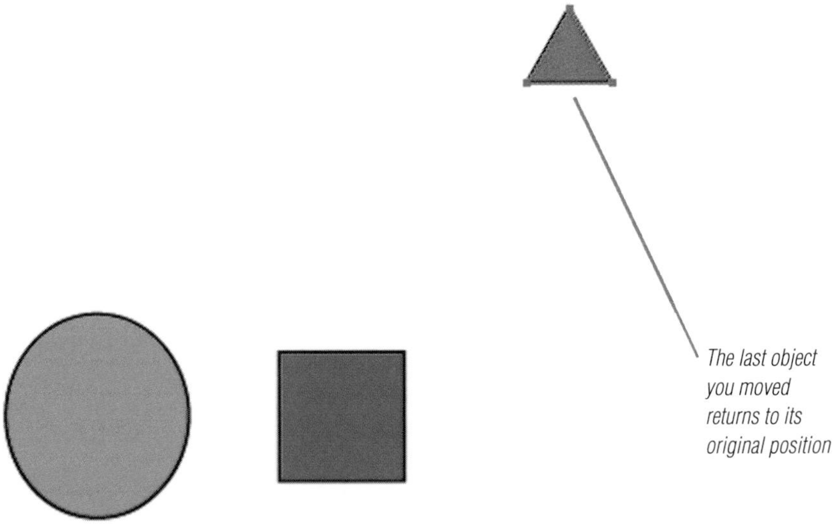

The last object you moved returns to its original position

FIGURE A-7

Copying and pasting the triangle

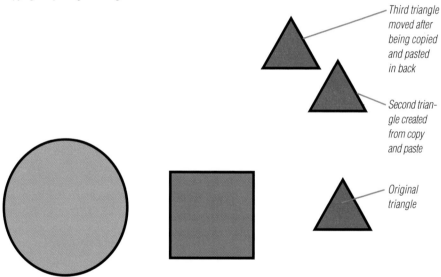

Third triangle
moved after
being copied
and pasted
in back

Second trian-
gle created
from copy
and paste

Original
triangle

12. Copy the new triangle, click **Edit** on the menu bar, then click **Paste in Back**.

The Paste in Front and Paste in Back commands paste the copied object from the clipboard in front or in back of a selected object. If you select an object, copy it, and then choose Paste in Front; the copy will be pasted above the original in exactly the same location.

13. Move the top red triangle to expose the copied triangle pasted behind it, as shown in Figure A-7.

14. Save your work, then close Window Workout.

You moved objects on the artboard and used the Undo and Redo commands on the Edit menu. You selected and copied objects, then applied the Paste in Back command to position a copy precisely in back of its original.

CREATE BASIC SHAPES

What You'll Do

In this lesson, you will examine the differences between bitmap and vector graphics. Then you will use the Rectangle Tool to examine Illustrator's various options for creating simple vector graphics.

Getting Ready to Draw

Are you eager to start drawing? Do you want to create complex shapes, special effects, and original art? Perhaps you are a self-taught user of Adobe Illustrator, and your main interest is to graduate to advanced techniques and add a few of those cool special effects to your skill set. Good for you! Enthusiasm is priceless, and no book can teach it. So maintain that enthusiasm for this first exercise, where you'll start by creating a square. That's right . . . a square.

Consider for a moment that Mozart's sublime opera Don Giovanni is based primarily on eight notes, or that the great American novel can be reduced to 26 letters. Illustrator's foundation is basic geometric shapes, so let's start at square one . . . with one square.

Don't rush. As you work, keep in mind that the lessons you will learn here are the foundation of every great illustration.

Understanding Bitmap Images and Vector Graphics

Computer graphics fall into two main categories—bitmap images and vector graphics. To create effective artwork, you need to understand some basic concepts about the two.

Bitmap images are created using a square or rectangular grid of colored squares called **pixels**. Because pixels (a contraction of "picture elements") can render subtle gradations of tone, they are the most common medium for continuous-tone images—what you perceive as a photograph. All scanned images are composed of pixels. All "digital" images are composed of pixels. Adobe Photoshop is the leading graphics application for working with digital "photos." Figure A-8 shows an example of a bitmap image. The number of pixels in a given inch is referred to as the image's **resolution**. To be effective, pixels must be small enough to create an image with the illusion of continuous tone. Thus, bitmap images are termed **resolution-dependent**.

The important thing to remember about bitmap images is that any magnification—resizing the image to be bigger—essentially means that fewer pixels are available per inch (the same number of pixels is now spread out over a larger area). This decrease in resolution will have a negative impact on the quality of the image. The greater the magnification, the greater the negative impact.

Graphics that you create in Adobe Illustrator are vector graphics. **Vector graphics** are created with lines and curves and are defined by mathematical objects called vectors. Vectors use geometric characteristics to define the object. Vector graphics consist of **anchor points** and **line segments**, together referred to as **paths**.

For example, if you use Illustrator to render a person's face, the software will identify the iris of the eye using the mathematical definition of a circle with a specific radius and a specific location in respect to other graphics. It will then fill that circle with the color you have specified. Figure A-9 shows an example of a vector graphic.

Computer graphics rely on vectors to render bold graphics that must retain clean, crisp lines when scaled to various sizes. Vectors are often used to create logos or "line art," and they are the best choice for typographical work, especially small and italic type.

As mathematical objects, vector graphics can be scaled to any size. Because they are not created with pixels, there is no inherent resolution. Thus, vector graphics are termed **resolution-independent**. This means that any graphic that you create in Illustrator can be output to fit on a postage stamp or on a billboard!

FIGURE A-8
Bitmap graphics

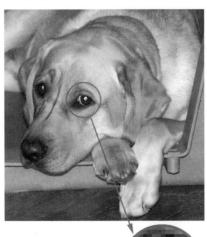

FIGURE A-9
Vector graphics

Use the Rectangle Tool

1. Click **File** on the menu bar, click **New**, create a new document that is 8" wide by 8" in height, name the file **Basic Shapes**, then click **OK**.

2. Click **File** on the menu bar, click **Save As**, navigate to the drive and folder where your Data Files are stored, click **Save**, then click **OK** to close the Illustrator Options dialog box.

3. Click **View** on the menu bar, then click **Hide Page Tiling**, if necessary.

4. Click the **Swap Fill and Stroke button** ↰ in the toolbox to reverse the default colors.

   Your fill color should now be black and your stroke color white. The **fill color** is the inside color of an object. The **stroke color** is the color of the object's border or frame.

5. Click the **Rectangle Tool** ▫. in the toolbox.

6. Click and drag the **Rectangle Tool pointer** on the artboard, then release the mouse to make a rectangle of any size.

7. Press and hold **[Shift]** while you create a second rectangle.

   Pressing and holding [Shift] while you create a rectangle constrains the shape to a perfect square, as shown in Figure A-10.

8. Create a third rectangle drawn from its center point by pressing and holding **[Alt]** (Win) or **[option]** (Mac) as you drag the **Rectangle Tool pointer**.

   TIP Use [Shift] in combination with [Alt] (Win) or [option] (Mac) to draw a perfect shape from its center.

You created a freeform rectangle, then you created a perfect square. Finally you drew a square from its center point.

FIGURE A-10
Creating a rectangle and a square

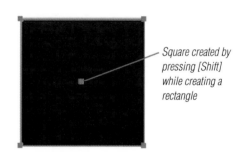

Square created by pressing [Shift] while creating a rectangle

Use the Rectangle dialog box

1. Click **Select** on the menu bar, then click **All** to select all of the objects.
2. Click **Edit** on the menu bar, then click **Cut** to remove the objects from the artboard.
3. Click anywhere on the artboard.

   When a shape tool is selected, clicking once on the artboard opens a dialog box, which allows you to enter precise information for creating the object. In this case, it opens the Rectangle dialog box.
4. Type **4** in the Width text box, type **4** in the Height text box, as shown in Figure A-11, then click **OK**.
5. Save your work.

Using the Rectangle Tool, you clicked the artboard, which opened the Rectangle dialog box. You entered a specific width and height to create a perfect 4" square.

FIGURE A-11
Rectangle dialog box

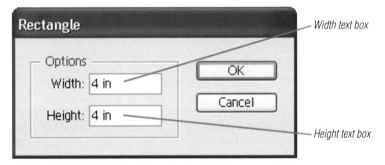

Width text box

Height text box

APPLY FILL AND STROKE COLORS TO OBJECTS

What You'll Do

▶ In this lesson you will use the Swatches palette to add a color fill to an object and apply a stroke as a border. Then you will use the Stroke palette to change the size of the default stroke.

Activating the Fill or Stroke

The Fill and Stroke buttons are at the bottom of the toolbox. To apply a fill or stroke color to an object, you must first activate the appropriate button. You activate either icon by clicking it, which moves it in front of the other. When the Fill button is in front of the Stroke button, the fill is activated, as shown in Figure A-12. The Stroke button is activated when it is in front of the Fill button.

As you work, you will often switch back and forth, activating the fill and the stroke. Rather than using your mouse to activate the fill or the stroke each time, simply press [X] to switch between the two modes.

FIGURE A-12
Fill and Stroke buttons

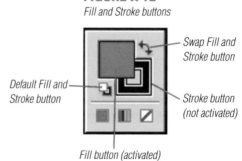

Swap Fill and Stroke button

Default Fill and Stroke button

Stroke button (not activated)

Fill button (activated)

Applying Color with the Swatches Palette

The Swatches palette, as shown in Figure A-13, is central to color management in the application and a simple resource for applying fills and strokes to objects.

The palette has 36 preset colors, along with gradients and patterns. The swatch with the red line through it is the None swatch. "None" is a color in Illustrator, used as a fill for a "hollow" object. Any object without a stroke will always have None as its stroke color.

When an object is selected, clicking a swatch in the palette will apply that color as a fill or a stroke, depending on which of the two is activated in the toolbox. You can also drag and drop swatches onto unselected objects. Dragging a swatch to an unselected object will change the color of its fill or stroke, depending upon which of the two is activated.

FIGURE A-13
Swatches palette

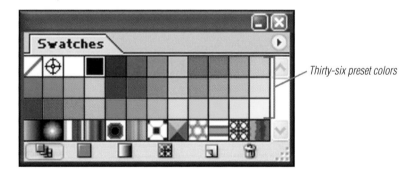

Thirty-six preset colors

Apply fill and stroke colors

1. Verify that the new square is still selected.

2. Click **Window** on the menu bar, then click **Swatches**.

   Your Swatches palette may already be available.

3. Click any blue swatch in the Swatches palette to fill the square.

   Note that the Fill button in the toolbox is now also blue.

   > TIP When you position your pointer over a color swatch in the Swatches palette, a tooltip appears that shows the name of that swatch.

4. Click the **Selection Tool** ▶, then click anywhere on the artboard to deselect the blue square.

5. Drag and drop a **yellow swatch** onto the blue square.

   The fill color changes to yellow because the Fill button is activated in the toolbox. Your colors may vary from the colors shown in the figures.

6. Press **[X]** to activate the Stroke button in the toolbox.

7. Drag and drop the **red swatch** in the Swatches palette onto the yellow square.

   As shown in Figure A-14, a red stroke is added to the square because the Stroke button is activated in the toolbox.

8. Click **Window** on the menu bar, then click **Stroke** to display the Stroke palette.

   Your Stroke palette may already be available.

   (continued)

Red stroke is added to the yellow square

Getting Started with Illustrator

Yellow square without a stroke

9. Select the square, click the **Weight list arrow** in the Stroke palette, then click **8 pt**.

   TIP Illustrator positions a stroke equally inside and outside an object. Thus, an 8 pt stroke is rendered with 4 pts inside the object and 4 pts outside.

10. Click **[None]** ▱ in the Swatches palette to remove the stroke from the square.

   Your screen should resemble Figure A-15.

11. Save your work.

You filled the square with blue by clicking a blue swatch in the Swatches palette. You then changed the fill and stroke colors to yellow and red by dragging and dropping swatches onto the square. You used the Stroke palette to increase the weight of the stroke, then removed the stroke by choosing [None] from the Swatches palette.

SELECT, MOVE AND ALIGN OBJECTS

What You'll Do

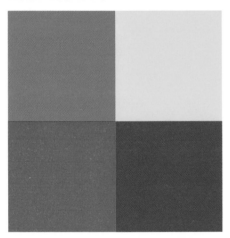

In this lesson, you will use the Selection Tool in combination with Smart Guides to move, copy, and align four squares.

Selecting and Moving Objects

When it comes to accuracy, consider that Illustrator can move objects incrementally by fractions of a point—which itself is a tiny fraction of an inch! That level of precision is key when moving and positioning objects.

Before you can move or modify an Illustrator object, you must identify it by selecting it with a selection tool, menu item, or command key. When working with simple illustrations that contain few objects, selecting is usually simple, but it can become very tricky in complex illustrations, especially those containing a large number of small objects positioned closely together.

Two very basic ways to move objects are by clicking and dragging or by using the arrow keys on the keyboard, which by default move a selected item by 1-pt increments. Pressing [Shift] when dragging an object constrains the movement to the horizontal, the vertical, and 45° diagonals. Pressing [Alt] (Win) or [option] (Mac) when moving creates a copy of the object.

Grouping Objects

Many of the illustrations you create will be composed of a number of small objects. Once you have established the relationships among those objects, grouping them allows you to select them all with one click of the Selection Tool and then move or modify them simultaneously. To group objects, select them, select Object on the menu bar, then click Group.

Making a Marquee Selection with the Selection Tool

By now, you're familiar with using the Selection Tool to select objects. You can also use the Selection Tool to create a marquee selection, a dotted rectangle that disappears as soon as you release the mouse. Any object that the marquee touches before you release the mouse will be selected. Marquee selections are very useful for both quick selections and precise selections. Practice, and make this part of your skill set.

Working with Smart Guides

Smart Guides are temporary guides that can be turned on and off on the View menu. Smart Guides help you move and align objects in relation to other objects or in relation to the artboard. With Smart Guides turned on, you will see words, called Smart Guides, that identify visible or invisible objects, page boundaries, intersections, anchor points, paths, and center points as you move your mouse along the objects on the artboard. When you move an object, Smart Guides give you a visual reference for precise alignment, as shown in Figure A-16. For example, if you want to align two squares exactly side by side, Smart Guides will signal you when the two items come into contact, using the word "intersect."

FIGURE A-16
Using Smart Guides

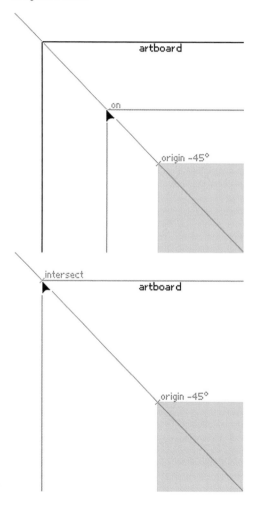

Select and move an object using Smart Guides

1. Click **View** on the menu bar, then click **Fit in Window**.

2. Click **View** on the menu bar, then verify that both Smart Guides and Snap to Point are checked by verifying that there is a check mark to the left of each menu item.

   TIP If you do not see a check mark next to Smart Guides or Snap to Point, click View on the menu bar, then click each item, one at a time, to turn these two features on.

   Snap to Point automatically aligns points when they get close together. When dragging an object, you'll see it "snap" to align itself with a nearby object (or guide).

3. Click the **Selection Tool** in the toolbox, then click the **yellow square**.

4. Identify the anchor points, line segments, and center point, as shown in Figure A-17.

5. Move the Selection Tool pointer over the anchor points, over the line segments that connect the points, and over the center point.

6. Position the pointer over the top-left anchor point, click and drag so that the anchor point aligns with the top-left corner of the artboard, as shown in Figure A-18, then release the mouse.

   The Smart Guide changes from "anchor" to "intersect" when the two corners are aligned.

You used the Selection Tool in combination with Smart Guides to position an object exactly at the top-left corner of the artboard.

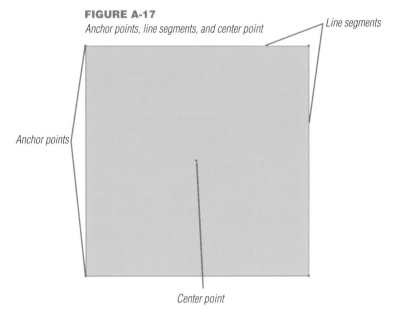

FIGURE A-17
Anchor points, line segments, and center point

Line segments

Anchor points

Center point

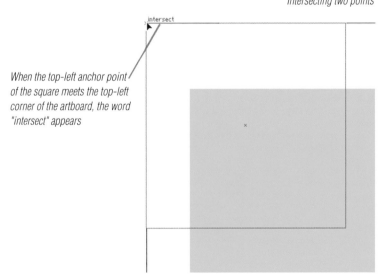

FIGURE A-18
Intersecting two points

intersect

When the top-left anchor point of the square meets the top-left corner of the artboard, the word "intersect" appears

FIGURE A-19

Duplicating the square

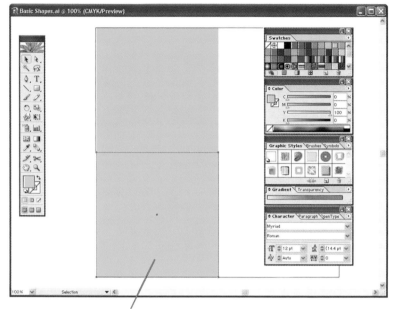

A copy of the original square

FIGURE A-20

Four squares created using drag and drop

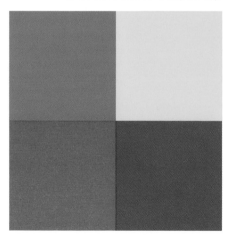

1. Click the **top-left anchor point**, press and hold **[Shift][Alt]** (Win) or **[Shift][option]** (Mac), drag straight down until the top-left anchor point touches the bottom-left anchor point (the "on" Smart Guide will appear), then release the mouse.

   When moving an object, pressing and holding [Shift] constrains the movement vertically, horizontally, or on 45° diagonals. Pressing [Alt] (Win) or [option] (Mac) while dragging an object creates a copy of the object, as shown in Figure A-19.

   > **TIP** When you press [Alt] (Win) or [option] (Mac) while dragging an object, the pointer becomes a double-arrow pointer. When two anchor points are directly on top of each other, the Selection Tool pointer turns from black to white.

2. With the bottom square still selected, press and hold **[Shift]**, then click the **top square** to select both items.

3. Click the **top-left anchor point** of the top square, press and hold **[Shift][Alt]** (Win) or **[Shift][option]** (Mac), drag to the right until the top-left anchor point touches the top-right anchor point, then release the mouse.

4. Change the fill color of each square to match the colors shown in Figure A-20.

5. Save your work.

You moved and duplicated the yellow square using [Shift] to constrain the movement and [Alt] (Win) or [option] (Mac) to duplicate or "drag and drop" copies of the square.

TRANSFORM OBJECTS

What You'll Do

 In this lesson, you will scale, rotate, and reflect objects, using the basic transform tools. You will also create a star and a triangle.

Transforming Objects

The Scale, Rotate, and Reflect Tools are the fundamental transform tools. As their names make clear, the Scale and Rotate Tools resize and rotate objects, respectively. Double-click a transform tool to open the tool's dialog box. When you use the tool's dialog box, the objects are transformed from their centerpoints. This can be a useful choice, because the object's position essentially doesn't change on the artboard or in relation to other objects.

Use the Reflect Tool to "flip" an object over an imaginary axis. The best way to understand the Reflect Tool is to imagine positioning a mirror perpendicular to a sheet of paper with a word written on it. The angle at which you position the mirror in relation to the word is the reflection axis. The reflection of the word in the mirror is the end result of what the Reflect Tool does. For example, text reflected across a horizontal axis would appear upside down and inverted. Text reflected across a vertical axis would appear to be inverted and running backwards, as shown in Figure A-21.

You can transform an object using the desired tool or its dialog box. Each transform tool has a dialog box where you can enter precise numbers to execute the transformation on a selected object. You can access a tool's dialog box by double-clicking the tool. Click the Copy button in the dialog box to create a transformed copy of the selected object. Figure A-22 shows the Scale dialog box.

Repeating Transformations
One of the most powerful commands relating to the transform tools is Transform Again, found on the Object menu. Unfortunately, it is a command often overlooked by new users. Whenever you transform an object, selecting Transform Again repeats the transformation. For example, if you scale a circle 50%, the Transform Again command will scale the circle 50% again.

The power of the command comes in combination with copying transformations. For example, if you rotate a square 10° and copy it at the same time, the Transform Again command will create a second square, rotated another 10° from the first copy. Applying Transform Again repeatedly is very handy for creating complex geometric shapes from basic objects.

FIGURE A-21
Reflected text

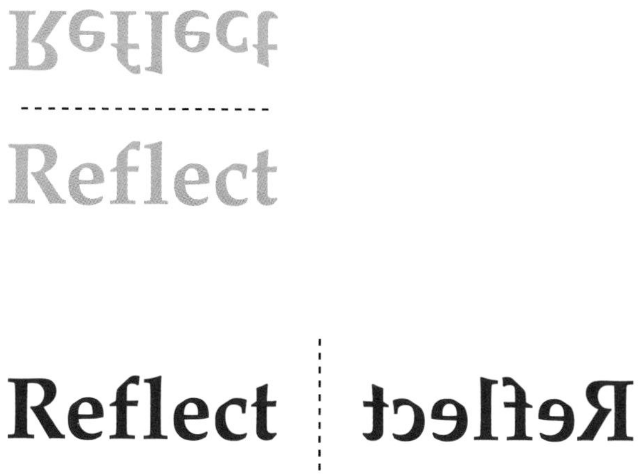

Reflect

Reflect

Reflect | Reflect

FIGURE A-22
Scale dialog box

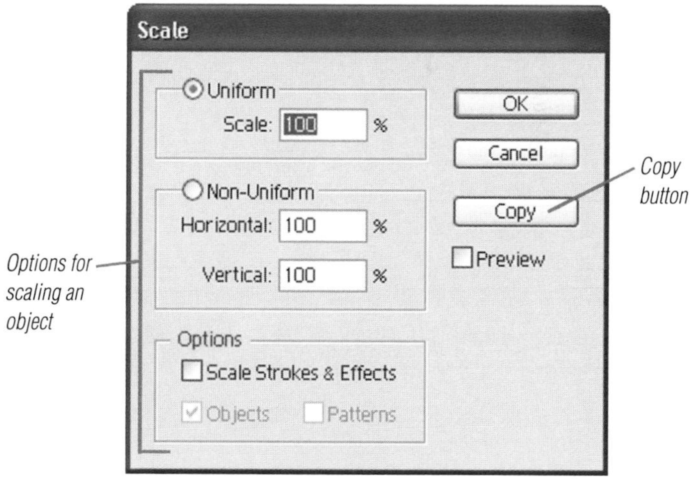

Options for scaling an object

Copy button

Scale

Uniform
Scale: 100 %

Non-Uniform
Horizontal: 100 %
Vertical: 100 %

OK
Cancel
Copy
Preview

Options
Scale Strokes & Effects
Objects   Patterns

Use the Scale and Rotate Tools

1. Select the **green square**, double-click the **Scale Tool** , type **50** in the Scale text box, then click **OK**.

2. Click **Edit** on the menu bar, then click **Undo Scale**.

   TIP You can also undo your last step by pressing [Ctrl][Z] (Win) or ⌘ [Z] (Mac).

3. Double-click the **Scale Tool** again, type **50** in the Scale text box, then click **Copy**.

   The transformation is executed from the center point; the center points of the original and the copy are aligned.

4. Fill the new square created in Step 3 with blue.

5. Double-click the **Rotate Tool**, type **45** in the Angle text box, then click **OK**.

6. Apply a 22 pt, yellow stroke to the rotated square, deselect, then compare your screen to Figure A-23.

You used the Scale Tool to create a 50% copy of the square, then filled the copy with blue. You rotated the copy 45°. You then applied a 22 pt, yellow stroke.

FIGURE A-23
Scaling and rotating a square

FIGURE A-24

Using the Transform Again command

1. Click the **Ellipse Tool** 🔵 in the toolbox.

   TIP   To access the Ellipse Tool, press and hold the Rectangle Tool until a toolbar of shape tools appears, then click the Ellipse Tool.

2. Click the **artboard**, type **3** in the Width text box and **.5** in the Height text box, then click **OK**.

3. Change the fill color to [None], the stroke color to blue, and the stroke weight to 3 pt.

4. Click the **Selection Tool** ▶, click the **center point** of the ellipse, then drag it to the center point of the yellow square. (*Hint*: The center Smart Guide appears when the two centers meet.)

5. Double-click the **Rotate Tool** 🔄, type **45** in the Angle text box, then click **Copy**.

6. Click **Object** on the menu bar, point to **Transform**, then click **Transform Again**.

   TIP   You can also access the Transform Again command by pressing [Ctrl][D] (Win) or ⌘ [D] (Mac).

7. Repeat Step 6 to create a fourth ellipse using the Transform Again command.

   Your screen should resemble Figure A-24.

8. Select the four ellipses, click **Object** on the menu bar, then click **Group**.

You created an ellipse, filled and stroked it, and aligned it with the yellow square. You then created a copy rotated at 45°. With the second copy still selected, you used the Transform Again command twice, thus creating two more rotated copies. You then grouped the four ellipses.

Create a star and a triangle, and use the Reflect Tool

1. Select the **Star Tool** ☆, then click anywhere on the artboard.

   The Star Tool is hidden beneath the current shape tool.

2. Type **1** in the Radius 1 text box, type **5** in the Radius 2 text box, type **5** in the Points text box, as shown in Figure A-25, then click **OK**.

   A star has two radii; the first is from the center to the outer point, and the second is from the center to the inner point. The **radius** is a measurement from the center point of the star to either point.

3. Double-click the **Scale Tool** 🔄, type **25** in the Scale text box, then click **OK**.

   When you create a star using the Star dialog box, the star is drawn upside down.

4. Fill the star with white, then apply a 5 pt blue stroke to it.

5. Click the **Selection Tool** ▶, then move the star so that it is completely within the red square.

6. Double-click the **Reflect Tool** 🔃, click the **Horizontal option button**, as shown in Figure A-26, then click **OK**.

   The star "flips" over an imaginary horizontal axis.

   ｜ TIP The Reflect Tool is hidden beneath the Rotate Tool.

   (continued)

FIGURE A-25
Star dialog box

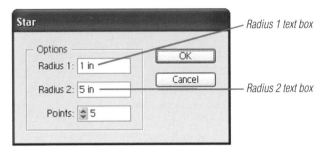

Radius 1 text box

Radius 2 text box

FIGURE A-26
Reflect dialog box

Horizontal option button

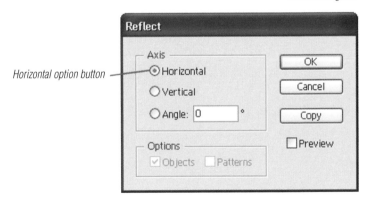

ILLUSTRATOR A-32

Getting Started with Illustrator

Reflecting the star horizontally

FIGURE A-28
The finished project

7. Use the Selection Tool ▶ or the arrow keys on your keyboard to position the star roughly in the center of the red square.

   Your work should resemble Figure A-27.

   > TIP Arrow keys move a selected item in 1 pt increments, known as the Keyboard Increment. You can change this amount by clicking Edit (Win) or Illustrator (Mac) on the menu bar, pointing to Preferences, clicking General, then typing a new value in the Keyboard Increment text box.

8. Click the **Polygon Tool** ⬡ in the toolbox.

   The Polygon Tool is hidden beneath the current shape tool in the toolbox.

9. Click anywhere on the blue square.

10. Type **1.5** in the Radius text box, type **3** in the Sides text box, then click **OK**.

11. Fill the triangle with red.

12. Change the stroke color to yellow and the stroke weight to 22 pt.

13. Position the triangle so that it is centered within the blue square.

    Your completed project should resemble Figure A-28.

14. Save your work, then close Basic Shapes.

You used the shape tools to create a star and a triangle and used the Reflect Tool to "flip" the star over an imaginary horizontal axis.

Selecting

The Select menu offers some powerful selection commands under the Same submenu. There you have commands to select by the same fill, the same fill and stroke, the same stroke color, and the same stroke weight, among others. When it comes to selecting multiple objects, using the Select menu is much faster than Shift-clicking!

MAKE DIRECT SELECTIONS

What You'll Do

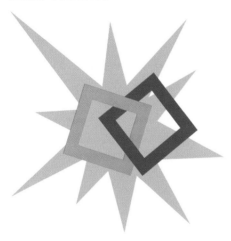

Using the Direct Selection Tool

The Direct Selection Tool selects individual anchor points or single paths of an object. Using [Shift], you can select multiple anchor points or multiple paths. You can also select multiple points or paths by dragging a direct selection marquee. The tool also selects individual objects within a group, which can be very useful for modifying just one object in a complex group. Figure A-29 demonstrates the Direct Selection Tool selecting one piece of a grouped object.

Clicking the center of an object with the Direct Selection Tool selects the entire object. Clicking the edge selects the path only. You will know you have made this direct selection successfully if the anchor points on the object all appear white. A white anchor point is not selected.

The Direct Selection Tool gives you the power to distort simple objects such as squares and circles into unique shapes. Don't underestimate its significance. While the Selection Tool is no more than a means to an end for selecting and moving objects, the Direct Selection Tool is in itself a drawing tool. You will use it over and over again to modify and perfect your artwork.

Adding Anchor Points

As you distort basic shapes with the Direct Selection Tool, you will often find that to create more complex shapes, you will need additional anchor points to work with.

The Add Anchor Points command creates new anchor points without distorting the object. To add anchor points to an object, click the Object menu, point to Path, then click Add Anchor Points. The new points are automatically positioned exactly between the original anchor points. You can create as many additional points as you wish to use.

Turning Objects into Guides

Guides are one of Illustrator's many features that help you to work with precision. Any object you create can be turned into a guide. With the object selected, click the View menu, point to Guides, then click Make Guides. Guides can be locked or unlocked in the same location. It is a good idea to work with locked guides so that they don't interfere with your artwork. Unlock guides only when you want to select them or delete them.

When an object is turned into a guide, it loses its attributes, such as its fill, stroke, and stroke weight. However, Illustrator remembers the original attributes for each guide. To transform a guide back to its original object, first unlock, then select the guide. Click the View menu, point to Guides, then click Release Guides.

FIGURE A-29
Using the Direct Selection Tool

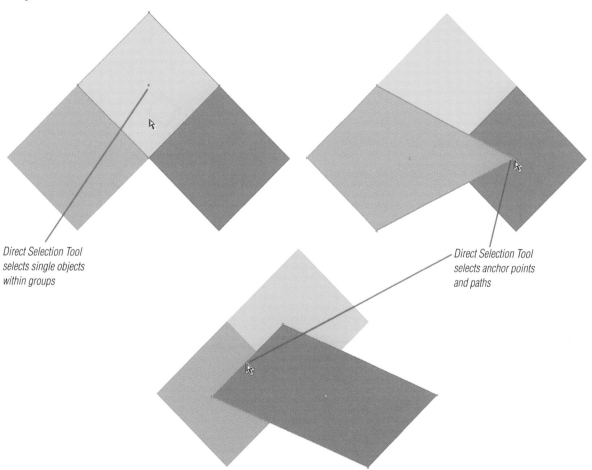

Direct Selection Tool selects single objects within groups

Direct Selection Tool selects anchor points and paths

Make guides and direct selections

1. Open AI A-2.ai, then save it as **Direct Selections**.

   > TIP Each time you save a Data File, click OK to close the Illustrator Options dialog box.

2. Click **View** on the menu bar, then click **Smart Guides** to turn this feature off.

3. Select the **green polygon**.

4. Click **View** on the menu bar, point to **Guides**, then click **Make Guides**.

   The polygon is converted to a guide.

   > TIP If you do not see the polygon-shaped guide, click View on the menu bar, point to Guides, then click Show Guides.

5. Convert the purple starburst to a guide.

6. Click **View** on the menu bar, point to **Guides**, verify that there is a check mark to the left of Lock Guides, then release the mouse.

7. Click the **Direct Selection Tool** ![arrow] , then click the edge of the red square.

   The four anchor points turn white, as shown in Figure A-30.

8. Click and drag the anchor points to the four corners of the guide to distort the square.

   Your work should resemble Figure A-31.

You converted two objects into guides. You then used the Direct Selection Tool to create a new shape from a square by moving anchor points independently.

FIGURE A-30
Red square selected with the Direct Selection Tool

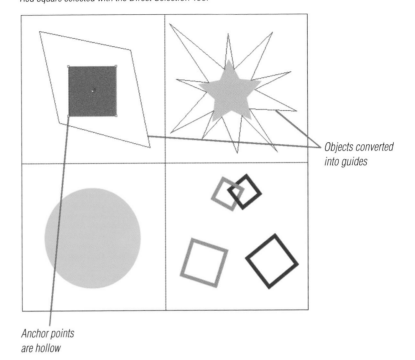

Objects converted into guides

Anchor points are hollow

FIGURE A-31
Red square distorted

Getting Started with Illustrator

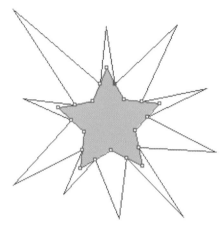

Add anchor points

1. Click the **Direct Selection Tool** in the center of the light blue star, and note the anchor points used to define the shape.

2. Click **Object** on the menu bar, point to **Path**, then click **Add Anchor Points**.

3. Click the **artboard** to deselect the star, then click the edge of the star.

   All the anchor points turn white and are available to be selected independently, as shown in Figure A-32.

4. Move the top anchor point on the star to align with the top point of the guide that you made earlier.

5. Working clockwise, move every other anchor point outward to align with the guide, creating a ten-point starburst.

   Your work should resemble Figure A-33.

6. Select and move any of the inner anchor points to modify the starburst to your liking.

You used the Add Anchor Points command and the Direct Selection Tool to create an original ten-point starburst from a generic five-point star.

FIGURE A-33
Completed starburst

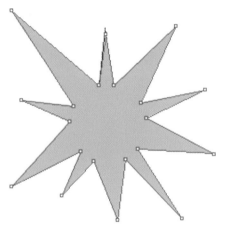

Making a direct selection marquee

When you create a marquee selection with the Selection Tool, any object the marquee touches is selected in its entirety. You can also use the Direct Selection Tool to create selection marquees. A Direct Selection Tool marquee selects only the anchor points and the paths that it touches. A Direct Selection Tool marquee is very useful for selecting multiple points or paths in one step.

Select paths

1. Click the edge of the yellow circle with the Direct Selection Tool ▶.

   The yellow circle is comprised of four anchor points and four line segments, as shown in Figure A-34. Clicking the edge selects one of the four segments.

2. Copy the segment.

3. Click **Edit** on the menu bar, then click **Paste in Front**.

   A copy is pasted directly on top of the selected segment.

4. Change the fill color to [None].

5. Change the stroke color to dark blue and the stroke weight to 14 pt.

6. Moving clockwise, repeat Steps 1, 2, 3, and 4 for the next three line segments, choosing different colors for each.

   Your finished circle should resemble Figure A-35.

You selected individual segments of a circle, copied them, and then pasted them in front. You then created a special effect by stroking the four new segments with different colors.

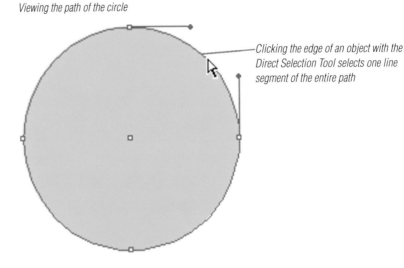

FIGURE A-34
Viewing the path of the circle

Clicking the edge of an object with the Direct Selection Tool selects one line segment of the entire path

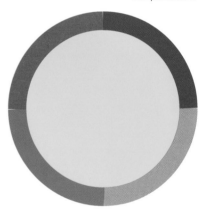

FIGURE A-35
Completed circle

FIGURE A-36
Completed linked squares

1. Using the Selection Tool ▶, overlap the large orange and blue squares so that they resemble the small orange and blue squares, then deselect.

2. Using the Direct Selection Tool ▶, select the top path of the orange square.

3. Copy the path.

4. Select the intersecting path on the blue square.

5. Paste in front, then save your work.

   Your work should resemble Figure A-36.

6. Close the document.

You learned a classic Illustrator trick. Selecting only a path, you copied it and pasted it in front of an intersecting object to create the illusion that the two objects were linked.

Start Illustrator and create a new document.

1. Create a new document and name it **Funky Flag**.
2. Make the size of the document 6" × 4".
3. Select Inches for the type of units, and CMYK Color for the color mode, then click OK.
4. Click File on the menu bar, click Save As, navigate to the drive and folder where you store your Data Files, then click Save.
5. Click View on the menu bar, then click Hide Page Tiling, if necessary.
6. Create a circle at the center of the artboard.
7. Click the Selection Tool.

Explore the Illustrator window.

1. Click View on the menu bar, then click Outline.
2. Click View on the menu bar, then click Preview.
3. Click View on the menu bar, then click Zoom In.
4. Click View on the menu bar, then click Zoom Out.
5. Press and hold [Spacebar] to access the Hand Tool, then move the artboard.
6. Click View on the menu bar, then click Fit in Window.
7. Select the circle, click Edit on the menu bar, then click Copy.

8. Click Edit on the menu bar, then click Paste in Front.
9. Move the new circle to the bottom of the artboard.
10. Click Edit on the menu bar, then click Undo Move.
11. Click Edit on the menu bar, then click Redo Move.
12. Click Select on the menu bar, then click All.
13. Click Select on the menu bar, then click Deselect.
14. Select all of the objects, click Edit on the menu bar, then click Cut.
15. Save your work.

Create basic shapes and apply fill and stroke colors.

1. Set the Fill and Stroke buttons in the toolbox to black and [None], respectively.
2. Create a rectangle that is 3" × 1".
3. Show the Swatches palette, if necessary.
4. Fill the rectangle with a light yellow.

Select, move, and align objects.

1. Click View on the menu bar, then click Smart Guides, if necessary.
2. Move the rectangle so that its top-left anchor point intersects with the top-left corner of the artboard.
3. Click the top-left anchor point, press and hold [Shift][Alt] (Win) or [Shift][option] (Mac), drag straight down until the top-left anchor point touches the bottom-left anchor

point (the "on" Smart Guide appears), then release the mouse.
4. Click Object on the menu bar, point to Transform, then click Transform Again.
5. Repeat Step 4.
6. Change the fill color of the second and fourth rectangles to a darker yellow.
7. Save your work.

Transform objects.

1. Select the four rectangles.
2. Double-click the Reflect Tool, click the Horizontal option button, then click Copy. The four rectangles are copied on top of the original rectangles.
3. Move the four new rectangles to the right so that they align with the right side of the artboard.
4. Click the Rectangle Tool, click the artboard, and create a square that is .75" × .75".
5. Apply a 1 pt blue stroke to the square and no fill.
6. Click the Selection Tool, click the edge of the square, then position it at the center of the artboard.
7. Use the Rotate dialog box to create a copy of the square rotated at 10°.
8. Apply the Transform Again command seven times.
9. Save your work.

Make direct selections.

1. Use [Shift] to select each of the nine blue squares.
2. Click Object on the menu bar, then click Group.
3. Scale the group of squares 200%.
4. Create a 3.75" × 3.75" circle, fill it with orange, add a 1 pt blue stroke, then position it at the center of the artboard.
5. Cut the circle from the artboard, click the group of squares, click Edit on the menu bar, then click Paste in Back.
6. Adjust the location of the circle, as needed.
7. Click Object on the menu bar, point to Path, then click Add Anchor Points.
8. Deselect the circle by clicking anywhere on the artboard.
9. Click the Direct Selection Tool, then click the edge of the circle.
10. One at a time, move each of the four new anchor points to the center of the circle.
11. Switch to the Selection Tool, then select the orange shape.
12. Double-click the Rotate Tool, type **22** in the Angle text box, then click Copy.
13. Apply the Transform Again command two times.
14. Save your work, then compare your illustration to Figure A-37.
15. Close Funky Flag.

FIGURE A-37
Completed Skills Review

The lady who owns the breakfast shop that you frequent knows that you are a designer and asks for your help. Her nephew has designed a sign for her store window, but she confides in you that she doesn't like it. She thinks that it's "boring" and "flat." She wants to redesign the sign with something that is "original" and feels "more like a starburst."

1. Open AI A-3.ai, then save it as **Star Sign**.
2. Click the Direct Selection Tool, then click the edge of the star.
3. Move three of the outer anchor points of the star farther from its center.
4. Move three of the inner points toward the center.
5. Select the entire star.
6. Reflect a copy of the star across the horizontal axis.
7. Fill the new star with orange and reposition it to your liking.
8. Group the two stars.
9. Copy the group, then paste in back.
10. Fill the copies with black.
11. Using your arrow keys, move the black copies five points to the right and five points down.

12. Select only the orange star.
13. Copy the orange star, then paste in back.
14. Fill the new copy with black.
15. Rotate the black copy 7°.

FIGURE A-38
Completed Project Builder 1

16. Apply a yellow fill to the orange star, then apply a 1pt. black stroke to both yellow stars.
17. Save your work, then compare your illustration to Figure A-38.
18. Close Star Sign.

ILLUSTRATOR A-42

Iris Vision Labs has contracted with your design firm to bid on a design for their logo. Researching the company, you learn that they are a biotech firm whose mission is to develop cures for genetic blindness and vision problems. You decide to build your design around the idea of an iris.

1. Create a new document that is 6" × 6".
2. Save the document as **Iris Vision Bid**.
3. Create an ellipse that is 1" wide × 4" in height, and position it at the center of the artboard.
4. Fill the ellipse with [None], and add a 1 pt blue stroke.
5. Create a copy of the ellipse rotated at 15°.
6. Apply the Transform Again command 10 times.
7. Select all and group the ellipses.
8. Create a copy of the group rotated at 5°.
9. Apply a red stroke to the new group.
10. Transform again.
11. Apply a bright blue stroke to the new group.
12. Select all.
13. Rotate a copy of the ellipses 2.5°.
14. Create a black circle that is 2" × 2".
15. Remove the stroke from the black circle.
16. Position the black circle in the center of the ellipses.

17. Cut the black circle.
18. Select all.
19. Paste in back.

FIGURE A-39
Completed Project Builder 2

20. Save your work, then compare your illustration to Figure A-39.
21. Close Iris Vision Bid.

The owner of Emerald Design Studios has hired you to design an original logo for her new company. She's a beginner with Illustrator, but she's created a simple illustration of what she has in mind. She tells you to create something "more sophisticated." The only other information that she offers about her company is that they plan to specialize in precise, geometric design.

1. Open AI A-4.ai, then save it as **Emerald Design**.
2. Select all four diamonds and group them.
3. Select the group of diamonds on the artboard, then create a 75% copy.
4. Use the Transform Again command five times.
5. Use Smart Guides to help you identify each of the seven groups.
6. Rotate one of the groups 90°.
7. Select the other groups and repeat the last transformation, using the Transform Again command.
8. Apply a dark green stroke to all groups. Figure A-40 shows one possible result of multiple transformations. Your illustration may differ.
9. Save your work, then close Emerald Design.

FIGURE A-40
Completed Design Project

You attend a design school, and you're part of a team that is responsible for the artwork placed throughout the common areas of the school. One of the most admired professors brings you a file that he created in Illustrator, admitting that he's a beginner. Your team opens the file and notices that the file is poorly built—everything is misaligned and uneven. After consulting with the professor, your team decides that the file needs to be rebuilt from scratch.

1. Open AI A-5.ai, then save it as **Rings N Things**.
2. Distribute copies of the file to the members of your group.
3. Discuss with the group the areas of the file that are misaligned and poorly constructed.
4. Assign one member the task of pulling apart the file, object by object, to see how the effect was achieved.
5. Have the group create a "game plan" for reproducing the artwork with precision. Where's the best place to start? What's the best methodology for recreating the professor's design?
6. Have a group discussion about the art itself. If the professor is open to new ideas, how would the group suggest that the design could be improved?
7. Have one member work on the original Illustrator file.
8. Work as a group to rebuild the file, using precise methods.
9. Save your work, then compare your illustration to Figure A-41.
10. Close Rings N Things.

FIGURE A-41
Completed Group Project

CHAPTER B

CREATING TEXT AND GRADIENTS

1. Create and format text.

2. Flow text into an object.

3. Position text on a path.

4. Create colors and gradients.

5. Apply colors and gradients to text.

6. Adjust a gradient and create a drop shadow.

CHAPTER B
CREATING TEXT AND GRADIENTS

Working with Text

When it comes to creating compelling and dramatic display text, no other software package offers the graphic sophistication that you'll find with Adobe Illustrator. You can quickly change fonts, font size, leading, and other text attributes in the Character palette. You can make tracking and kerning measurements with a level of precision that would satisfy even the most meticulous typographer. For the designer, Illustrator is the preeminent choice for typography. Powerful type tools offer the ability to fill objects with text, position text on lines—curved or straight—and set type vertically, one letter on top of the next. Once the text is positioned, the Create Outlines command changes the fonts to vector graphics that you can manipulate as you would any other object. For example, you can apply a gradient fill to letter outlines for stunning effects.

Creating and Applying Gradient Fills

A **gradient** is a graduated blend between two or more colors used to fill an object or multiple objects. Illustrator's sophistication for creating gradients and its ease of use for applying them to objects are a dream come true for today's designers. You can create linear or radial gradients between multiple colors, then control the way they fill an object. Moreover, a single gradient can be used to fill multiple objects simultaneously! The unique gradient fills that you create can be saved with descriptive names, then imported into other Illustrator documents to be used again.

Tools You'll Use

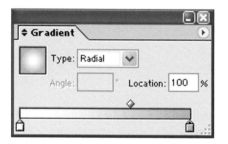

Type tools

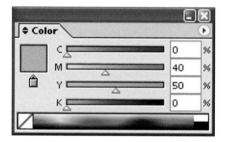

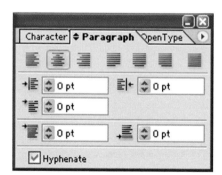

CREATE AND FORMAT TEXT

What You'll Do

 In this lesson, you will use the Type Tool to create the word BERRY as display text. You will use the Character palette to format the text and perfect its appearance. You will also create a vertical version of the text.

Creating Type

You can create text anywhere on the artboard simply by selecting one of the type tools, then clicking the artboard to start typing. You can enter text horizontally or vertically. The ability to type vertically is rather unusual; most text-based applications don't offer this option.

Text generated by the Type Tool is positioned on a blue path called the **baseline**. You can select text simply by clicking anywhere on the text. This feature is a preference that you can turn on or off. Click Edit on the menu bar, point to Preferences, click Type & Auto Tracing, then remove the check mark in the Type Object Selection by Path Only check box, if necessary. When this feature is checked, you must click the baseline to select text.

Formatting Text

The Character and Paragraph palettes neatly contain all of the classic commands for formatting text. Use the Character palette to modify text attributes such as font and type size, tracking, and kerning. You can adjust the **leading**, which is the vertical space between baselines, or apply a horizontal or vertical scale, which compresses or expands selected type. The Paragraph palette applies itself to more global concerns, such as text alignment, paragraph indents, and vertical spaces between paragraphs. Figure B-1 shows examples of formatting that you can apply to text.

Tracking and kerning are essential (and often overlooked) typographic operations. **Tracking** inserts uniform spaces between characters to affect the width of selected words or entire blocks of text. **Kerning** is used to affect the space between any two characters; it is particularly useful for improving the appearance of headlines and other display text. Positive tracking or kerning values move characters farther apart; negative values move them closer together.

Illustrator can track and kern type down to $1/1000$ of a standard em space. The width of an em space is dependent on the current type size. In a 1-point font, the em space is 1 point. In a 10-point font, the em space is 10 points. With kerning units that are $1/1000$ of an em, Illustrator can manipulate a 10-point font at increments of $1/1000$ of 1 point! Figure B-2 shows examples of kerning and tracking values.

Hiding Objects

Two factors contribute to difficulty in selecting text and other objects: the number of objects in the document and proximity of objects. Multiple objects positioned closely together can make selections difficult and impede productivity.

Hiding an object is one simple solution. Hidden objects are safe; they won't be deleted from the document when you quit.

Also, they won't print. Just don't forget that they're there!

The Hide Selection command is under the Object menu, as is Show All, which reveals all hidden objects. When hidden objects are revealed, they are all selected; you can use this to your advantage. Simply press [Shift] as you click to deselect the object you want to see, then hide the remaining objects.

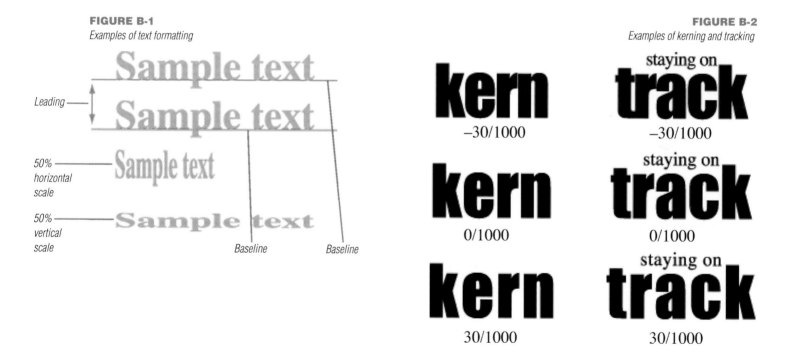

FIGURE B-1
Examples of text formatting

Leading

50% horizontal scale

50% vertical scale

Baseline   Baseline

FIGURE B-2
Examples of kerning and tracking

−30/1000

0/1000

30/1000

−30/1000

0/1000

30/1000

Create text

1. Open AI B-1.ai, then save it as **Berry Symposium**.
2. Click **View** on the menu bar, then click **Hide Bounding Box**, if necessary.
3. Click the **Type Tool** T., then click anywhere on the artboard.
4. Type **BERRY** using all capital letters.

   | TIP By default, new text is generated with a black fill and no stroke.

5. Click the **Selection Tool** , then drag the **text** to the center of the artboard.

   | TIP Hide Smart Guides, if necessary.

6. Click **Window** on the menu bar, point to **Type**, then click **Character** to show the Character palette.
7. Click the **Character palette list arrow**, then click **Show Options** to view the entire palette as shown in Figure B-3.

You used the Type Tool to create the word BERRY, showed the Character palette, then expanded the view of the Character palette.

FIGURE B-3
Character palette

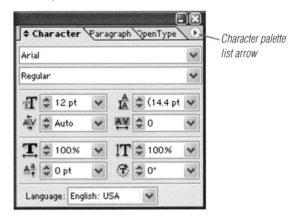

Character palette
list arrow

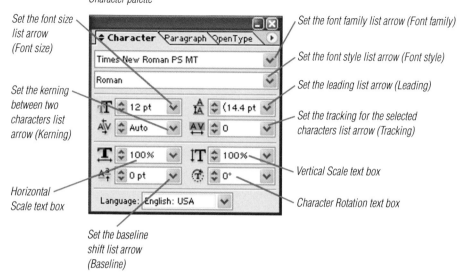

Set the font size list arrow (Font size)

Set the kerning between two characters list arrow (Kerning)

Horizontal Scale text box

Set the baseline shift list arrow (Baseline)

Set the font family list arrow (Font family)

Set the font style list arrow (Font style)

Set the leading list arrow (Leading)

Set the tracking for the selected characters list arrow (Tracking)

Vertical Scale text box

Character Rotation text box

Format text

1. Click the **Font family** (Win) or **Font menu** (Mac) **list arrow**, then click **Times New Roman PS MT**, as shown in Figure B-4.

   TIP Figure B-4 shows the full name of each setting in the Character palette. The steps in this chapter refer to the shorter name provided in parentheses.

2. Click the **Font size text box**, type **150**, then press **[Enter]** (Win) or **[return]** (Mac).

3. Click the **Horizontal Scale text box**, type **90**, then press **[Enter]** (Win) or **[return]** (Mac).

4. Deselect all.

5. Compare your text to Figure B-5.

You used the Character palette to modify the font, the font size, and the horizontal scaling of the word BERRY.

FIGURE B-5
Formatted text

BERRY

Track and kern text

1. Select the text, if necessary.
2. Using the Character palette, click the **Tracking text box**, then type **-30**.

   TIP Click the Character palette list arrow, then click Show Options, if necessary.

3. Click the **Type Tool** T, then click the cursor between the B and the E.
4. Using the Character palette, click the **up and down arrows** in the Kerning text box to experiment with higher and lower kerning values, then change the kerning value to -40.
5. Using Figure B-6 as a guide, change the kerning to -20, 0, and -20 between the next three letter pairs.
6. Click the **Selection Tool**, click the **Paragraph palette name tab**, then click the **Align center button**, as shown in Figure B-7.

   When text is center-aligned, its anchor point doubles as its center point, which is handy for aligning it with other objects.

   TIP If you do not see the Paragraph palette, click Window on the menu bar, point to Type, then click Paragraph.

7. Click **Object** on the menu bar, point to **Hide**, then click **Selection**.

You used the Character palette to change the tracking of the word BERRY, then you entered different kerning values to affect the spacing between the four letter pairs. You center-aligned the text, then hid the text.

FIGURE B-6
Kerning and tracking applied to text

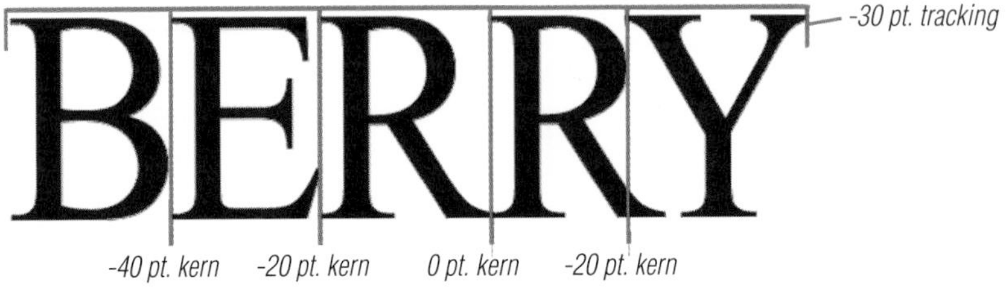

BERRY
-30 pt. tracking
-40 pt. kern
-20 pt. kern
0 pt. kern
-20 pt. kern

FIGURE B-7
Paragraph palette

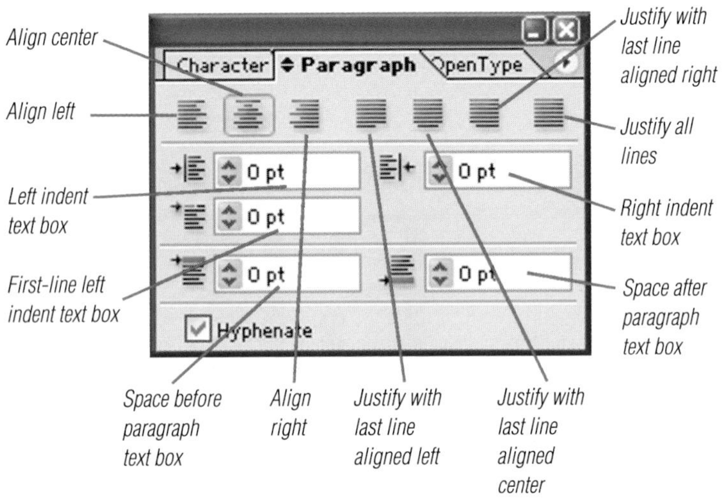

Character
Paragraph
OpenType
0 pt
0 pt
0 pt
0 pt
0 pt
Hyphenate
Align center
Align left
Left indent text box
First-line left indent text box
Space before paragraph text box
Align right
Justify with last line aligned left
Justify with last line aligned center
Justify with last line aligned right
Justify all lines
Right indent text box
Space after paragraph text box

FIGURE B-8

Vertical text

B
E
R
R
Y

Using the Glyphs palette

The Glyphs palette contains various type characters that aren't necessarily available on your keyboard. Examples of these characters include trademarks, copyright marks, accented letters, and numbers expressed as fractions. Click Window on the menu bar, point to Type, then click Glyphs to display the Glyphs palette. To access a glyph, click the Type Tool, click the artboard as you would to type any character, then double-click the glyph in the Glyph palette that you wish to use.

Create vertical type

1. Click the **Vertical Type Tool** !T, then click anywhere on the artboard.

   TIP   The Vertical Type Tool is hidden beneath the Type Tool.

2. Type the word **BERRY** using all capital letters.

   TIP   The type tools retain the formatting attributes that were previously chosen.

3. Click the **Selection Tool** ↖, select the text, then move it to the center of the artboard.

   TIP   When any tool other than the Selection Tool is selected in the toolbox, you can press [Ctrl] (Win) or ⌘ (Mac) to switch to the Selection Tool. When you release [Ctrl] (Win) or ⌘ (Mac), the last chosen tool will be active again.

4. Change the font size to 84 pt.

5. Change the tracking value to -160.

6. Set both the horizontal and vertical scales to 100%, then deselect the text.

   Your screen should resemble Figure B-8.

7. Delete the vertical text, then save your work.

You used the Vertical Type Tool to create a vertical alternative to the first word you typed. You adjusted the tracking and kerning to better suit a vertical orientation, and then deleted the text.

FLOW TEXT INTO AN OBJECT

What You'll Do

rasp
straw blue
cran straw tea
straw checker cran
blue boysen black tea straw
blue boysen checker cran tea rasp
boysen blue black straw tea boysen
checker cran rasp boysen blue black rasp straw
blue black straw tea boysen checker cran rasp straw
blue tea black rasp straw blue black straw tea
boysen checker cran rasp straw blue black
rasp straw blue cran straw tea straw
checker cran straw boysen
black tea straw blue
boysen checker
cran tea
rasp

 In this lesson, you will use the Area Type Tool to flow text into an object.

Filling an Object with Text

Using the Area Type Tool and the Vertical Area Type Tool, you can flow text into any shape you can create, from circles to birds to bumblebees! Text in an object can be formatted as usual. You can change fonts, font size, alignment, etc., and the text will be reflowed in the object as you format it.

When text is flowed into an object, you can manipulate the object as you would any

other object. Apply fills and strokes and transformations; use the Rotate Tool, or the Scale or Reflect Tools. You can even use the Direct Selection Tool to distort the shape. Best of all, you can apply those operations to the text or to the text object independently! Figure B-9 shows an example of an object, in this case a star, filled with text.

Locking Objects

Working in tandem with the Hide command, the Lock Selection command on the Object menu allows you to exempt an object from selections and affix its position on the artboard. The Lock Selection command is useful simply as a device to protect objects from accidental modifications.

Locked objects can be selected only after they are unlocked by choosing the Unlock All command on the Object menu. The Unlock All command unlocks every locked object on the artboard. When locked objects are unlocked, they are all selected. Simply press [Shift] while you click to deselect the object you want to work with, and relock the remaining objects.

Making Guides

Guides are one of Illustrator's many features that help you to work with precision. You can select any object and make it into a guide with the Make Guides command on the View menu. You can also create guides by clicking and dragging the mouse pointer from each ruler to the artboard.

FIGURE B-9
An object filled with text

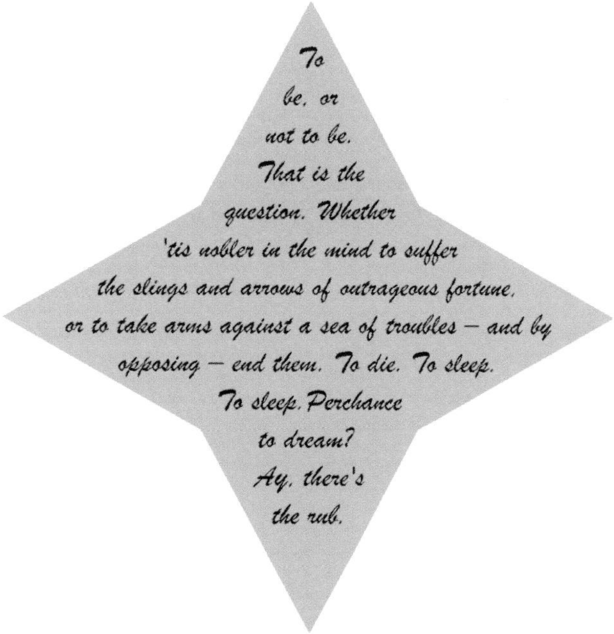

To
be, or
not to be.
That is the
question. Whether
'tis nobler in the mind to suffer
the slings and arrows of outrageous fortune,
or to take arms against a sea of troubles — and by
opposing — end them. To die. To sleep.
To sleep. Perchance
to dream?
Ay, there's
the rub.

Fill an object with text

1. Open AI B-2.ai, then save it as **Diamond Text**.

2. Select the yellow square, double-click the **Rotate Tool** 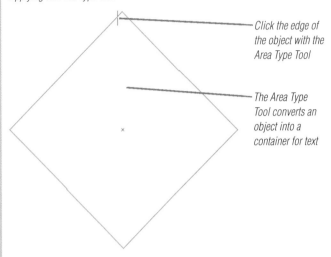, type **45** in the Angle text box, then click **OK**.

3. Click the **Area Type Tool** ⊤, then click the block of text.

   | TIP   The Area Type Tool is hidden beneath the current type tool.

4. Click **Select** on the menu bar, then click **All**.

   | TIP   When you click a type tool cursor on text and apply the Select All command, all the text is selected—not the object that contains the text, and not any other text or objects on the page.

5. Copy the text.

6. Click the **Selection Tool** ▶, select the yellow square, then change the font size to 12 using the Character palette.

   | TIP   When you are working with a Type Tool, you can press [Ctrl] (Win) or ⌘ (Mac) to access the Selection Tool temporarily and remain in Area Type Tool mode.

7. Click the **Area Type Tool** ⊤, if necessary, then click the edge of the yellow square.

   A flashing cursor appears, and the square loses its fill color, as shown in Figure B-10.

8. Paste the copied text into the square.

   Your work should resemble Figure B-11.

You rotated the yellow square, then filled it with text by first copying text from another object, then clicking the edge of the square with the Area Type Tool before you pasted the text into the square.

FIGURE B-10
Applying the Area Type Tool

Click the edge of the object with the Area Type Tool

The Area Type Tool converts an object into a container for text

FIGURE B-11
Text pasted into an object

Objects loses its fill color

Indicates overflow text

rasp
straw blue
cran straw tea
straw checker cran
blue boysen black tea
straw blue boysen checker cran
tea rasp boysen blue black straw tea
boysen checker cran rasp boysen blue
black rasp straw blue black straw
tea boysen checker cran rasp
straw blue tea black
rasp straw blue
black straw
tea
b

FIGURE B-12

Centered text in an object

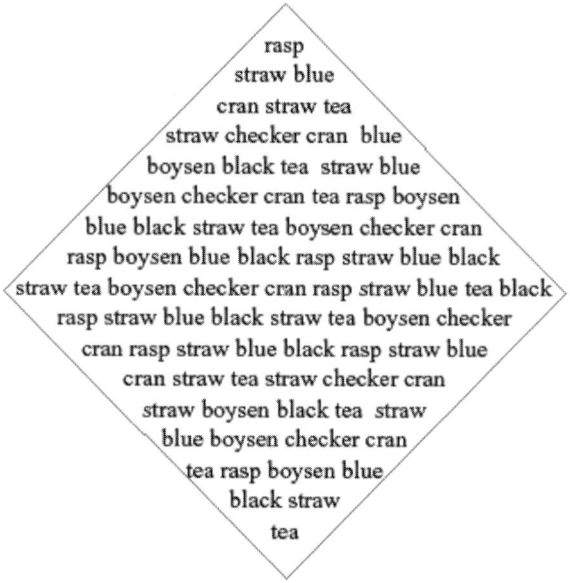

```
                        rasp
                     straw blue
                   cran straw tea
               straw checker cran  blue
             boysen black tea  straw blue
          boysen checker cran tea rasp boysen
        blue black straw tea boysen checker cran
      rasp boysen blue black rasp straw blue black
    straw tea boysen checker cran rasp straw blue tea black
      rasp straw blue black straw tea boysen checker
        cran rasp straw blue black rasp straw blue
          cran straw tea straw checker cran
             straw boysen black tea  straw
               blue boysen checker cran
                 tea rasp boysen blue
                    black straw
                        tea
```

Using Character and Paragraph Styles

A style is a group of formatting attributes, such as font, font size, color, and tracking, that is applied to text. You use the Character Styles palette to create styles for individual words or characters, such as a footnote, and you use the Paragraph Styles palette to apply a style to a paragraph. Paragraph styles include formatting options such as indents and drop caps. Using styles saves you time, and it keeps your work consistent. If you create styles for an Illustrator document, the styles are saved with the document and are available to be loaded for use in other documents.

Format text in an object

1. Select all of the text in the rotated square.

2. Click the **Align center button** ≡ in the Paragraph palette.

   > TIP When filling an object other than a square or a rectangle with text, centering the text is often the best solution.

3. Click the **Character palette name tab** next to the Paragraph palette name tab, then change the font size to 9 pt.

4. Click the **Leading text box**, type **11**, click the **artboard** to deselect the text, then compare your work to Figure B-12.

   It's OK if the line breaks in your document differ from the text in the figure.

5. Click the **Selection Tool** ▶, then click the **diamond-shaped text**.

   Both the text and the object that contains the text are selected.

6. Copy the text object.

   Both the text and the object are copied.

7. Click **Window** on the menu bar, then click **Berry Symposium** at the bottom of the menu.

   > TIP All open Illustrator documents are listed at the bottom of the Window menu

8. Paste the text object into the Berry Symposium document.

You used the Paragraph and Character palettes to format text in the object. You used the Selection Tool to select the text object, and then you copied and pasted it into the Berry Symposium document.

Make guides and use the Lock command

1. Click **View** on the menu bar, then click **Show Rulers**, if necessary.

2. Using Figure B-13 as a reference, position your pointer in the top horizontal ruler, click and drag the pointer straight down to the 5" mark on the vertical ruler, then release the mouse to create a guide.

   TIP You may need to move the toolbox out of the way to see the vertical ruler.

3. Position a vertical guide at the 5" mark on the horizontal ruler.

   TIP To change the color or style of guides, click Edit (Win) or Illustrator (Mac) on the menu bar, point to Preferences, then click Guides & Grid. The Guides & Grid Preferences dialog box is shown in Figure B-14.

4. Click **View** on the menu bar, point to **Guides**, then verify that Lock Guides is checked.

5. Click the **Selection Tool** , if necessary.

(continued)

FIGURE B-13
Making guides

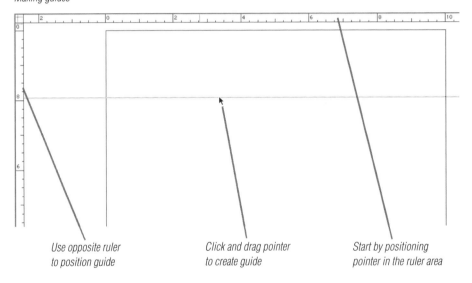

Use opposite ruler
to position guide

Click and drag pointer
to create guide

Start by positioning
pointer in the ruler area

Creating Text and Gradients

FIGURE B-14

Guides & Grid Preferences settings

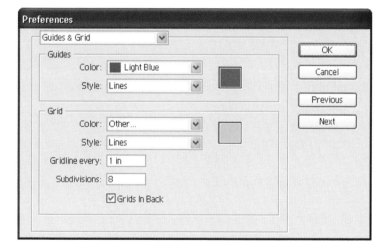

6. Select the text object, then align the center point of the text object with the intersection of the guides.

> TIP Use the arrow keys on your keypad to nudge the selection right, left, up, or down.

7. Click **Object** on the menu bar, point to **Lock**, then click **Selection**.

> TIP Locking objects is standard practice. You can also lock a selection by first selecting an object, then pressing [Ctrl][2] (Win) or ⌘ [2] (Mac). Make it a point to remember the quick key.

8. Save your work.

You created a horizontal and a vertical guide that intersect at the center of the artboard. You then aligned the center of the diamond text object with the intersection of the guides, and locked the diamond text object.

POSITION TEXT ON A PATH

What You'll Do

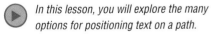

In this lesson, you will explore the many options for positioning text on a path.

Using the Path Type Tools

Using the Type on a Path Tool or the Vertical Type on a Path Tool, you can type along a straight or curved path. This is the most compelling of Illustrator's text effects, and it opens up a world of possibilities for the designer and typographer.

You can move text along a path to position it where you want. You can "flip" the text to make it run in the opposite direction—on the opposite side of the path. You can also change the baseline shift to modify the distance of the text's baseline in relation to the path. A positive value "floats" the text above the path, and a negative value moves the text below the path. You can modify text on a path in the same way you would modify any other text element. Figure B-15 shows an example of text on a path, whereas Figure B-16 shows an example of text flipped across a path.

FIGURE B-16
Text flipped across a path

Text flowed along
a sharply curved
path often presents
kerning challenges

Flow text on a path

1. Click the **Ellipse Tool** ⬭, press **[Alt]** (Win) or **[option]** (Mac), then click the center of the artboard.

   Pressing [Alt] (Win) or [option] (Mac) while you click a shape tool on the artboard ensures that the center of the shape will be drawn from the point that you clicked.

2. Enter **2.9** for the width and the height of the circle in the Ellipse dialog box, then click **OK**.

3. Click the **Type on a Path Tool** ⤻, then click anywhere on the edge of the circle.

   | TIP   The Type on a Path Tool may be hidden beneath the current type tool.

   A flashing cursor appears, and the circle loses its fill color.

4. Type **three rivers** in lowercase, using Times New Roman PS MT for the font.

   | TIP   If you do not have Times New Roman PS MT, substitute a similar font.

5. Click the **Selection Tool** ▸ to select the text by its baseline, then change the font size to 47 pt.

   You will see three brackets—one at the beginning of the path, one at the end of the path, and one at the midpoint between the two brackets. These brackets allow you to move text along a path.

   | TIP   Text flowed on a circle will often require kerning, especially when it is set at a large point size.

6. Compare your screen to Figure B-17.

You created a 2.9" circle from its center, then typed along the circle's path using the Type on a Path Tool. You changed the font and font size using the Character palette.

FIGURE B-17
Text on a circular path

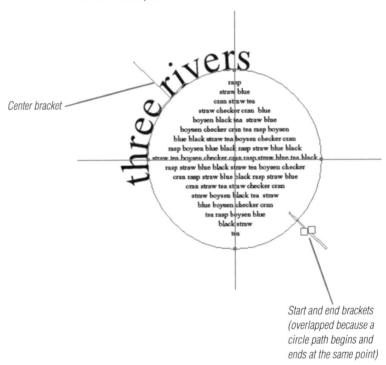

Center bracket

Start and end brackets
(overlapped because a
circle path begins and
ends at the same point)

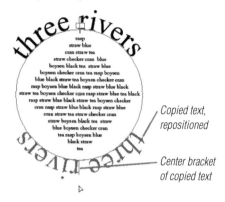

Copied text,
repositioned

Center bracket
of copied text

Baseline shift

Center bracket of copied text

Move text along a path

1. Click **View** on the menu bar, point to **Guides**, then click **Hide Guides**.

2. Using the Selection Tool ![k], drag the **center bracket** until the text is centered at the top of the circle.

3. Click **Edit** on the menu bar, click **Copy**, click **Edit** on the menu bar, then click **Paste in Front**.

4. Drag the **center bracket** of the copied text clockwise to move the copied text to the position shown in Figure B-18.

5. Drag the **center bracket** of the copied text straight up to flip the text across the path, as shown in Figure B-19.

   TIP Enlarge your view of the artboard if you have trouble dragging the bracket.

6. Click the **Baseline text box** in the Character palette, type **-21**, as shown in Figure B-20, then press **[Enter]** (Win) or **[return]** (Mac).

7. Click the **Type Tool** ![T], highlight **three rivers** at the bottom of the circle, then type **symposium**.

8. Click the **Selection Tool** ![k], then drag the **center bracket** to center the text at the bottom of the circle, if necessary.

9. Lock the two text objects, save your work, then compare your image to Figure B-21.

You moved and copied text along a path, flipped its direction, changed the baseline shift, then locked both text objects.

CREATE COLORS AND GRADIENTS

What You'll Do

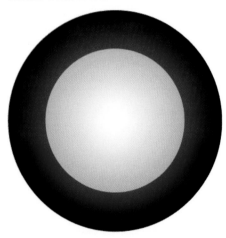

In this lesson, you will use the Color palette, the Gradient palette, and the Swatches palette to create, name, and save colors and gradients.

Using the Gradient Palette

A **gradient** is a graduated blend between colors. The Gradient palette is the command center for creating and adjusting gradients. In the palette, you will see a slider that represents the gradient you are creating or working with. The slider has at least two colors. The leftmost color is the starting color, and the rightmost color is the ending color.

The colors used in a gradient are represented in the Gradient palette by small house-shaped icons called **stops**. The Gradient palette, shown in Figure B-22 shows a two-color gradient.

The point at which two colors meet in equal measure is called the **midpoint** of the gradient. The midpoint is represented by the diamond above the slider. The midpoint does not necessarily need to be positioned evenly between the starting and ending colors. You can change the midpoint by moving the diamond.

The Swatches palette contains standard gradients that come with the software. To create your own original gradients, start by clicking an object filled with an existing gradient. You can then modify that existing gradient in the Gradient palette. You can change either or both the beginning and ending colors. You can change the location of the midpoint. You can also add additional colors into the gradient, or remove existing colors.

QUICKTIP

As you work to perfect a gradient, you can see how your changes will affect the gradient automatically, by filling an object with the gradient that you are working on. As you make changes in the Gradient palette, the changes will be reflected in the object.

You can define a gradient as linear or radial. A linear gradient can be positioned left to right, up and down, or on any angle. You can change the angle of the gradient by entering a new value in the Angle text box in the Gradient palette.

Think of a radial gradient as a series of concentric circles. With a radial gradient, the starting color appears at the center of the gradient. The blend radiates out to the ending color. By definition, a radial gradient has no angle ascribed to it.

Using the Color Palette

The Color palette is where you move sliders to mix new colors for fills, strokes, and gradients. You can also use the palette to adjust the color in a filled object. The palette has five color modes: CMYK, RGB, Grayscale, HSB, and Web Safe RGB. The palette will default to CMYK or RGB, depending on the color mode you choose when creating a new document. Grayscale mode allows you to create shades of gray in

percentages of black. If you select a filled object and choose the HSB mode, you can adjust its basic color (hue), the intensity of the color (saturation), and the range of the color from light to dark (brightness). If you are designing illustrations for the Internet, you might consider using Web Safe RGB mode to create colors that are in accordance with colors defined in HTML.

Rather than use the sliders, you can also type values directly into the text boxes. For example, in CMYK mode, a standard red color is composed of 100% Magenta and 100% Yellow. The notation for this callout would be 100M/100Y. Note that you don't list the zero values for Cyan (C) and Black (K). In RGB mode (0-255), a standard orange color would be noted as 255R/128G.

Adding Colors and Gradients to the Swatches Palette

Once you have defined a color or a gradient to your liking, it's a smart idea to save it by dragging it into the Swatches palette. Once a color or gradient is moved into the Swatches palette, you can name it by double-clicking it, then typing a name in the Swatch Options dialog box. You can't, however, modify it. For example, if you click a saved gradient and adjust it in the Gradient palette, you can apply the new gradient to an object, but the original gradient in the Swatches palette remains unaffected. You can save the new gradient to the Swatches palette for future use.

FIGURE B-22
Gradient palette

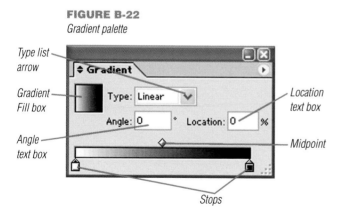

Type list arrow

Gradient Fill box

Angle text box

Location text box

Midpoint

Stops

FIGURE B-23
Color palette

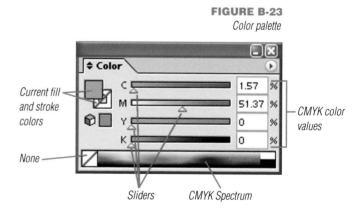

Current fill and stroke colors

None

CMYK color values

Sliders

CMYK Spectrum

Create a gradient and a color

1. Show the guides.

2. Create a 4" circle at the center of the art-board, then apply a yellow fill to the circle.

   The most recently drawn object is automatically placed above the other objects on the artboard.

3. Hide the guides, click **Window** on the menu bar, then click **Gradient** to select it, if necessary.

4. Click **Window** on the menu bar, then click **Color** to select it, if necessary.

5. Click the **Rainbow swatch** in the Swatches palette.

   The yellow fill changes to the Rainbow fill.

6. Click the **Gradient palette list arrow**, then click **Show Options**, if necessary.

7. Click the **yellow stop** on the gradient slider, and drag it off the palette to delete it.

8. Delete the green, aqua, and blue stops.

   | TIP The changes you make to the gradient slider are reflected in the circle.

9. Click the bottom edge of the gradient slider to add a new color stop, then drag the stop along the slider until you see 50% in the Location text box in the Gradient palette as shown in Figure B-24.

10. Verify that the new stop is selected, press and hold **[Alt]** (Win) or **[option]** (Mac), click **orange** in the Swatches palette, then compare your circle to Figure B-25.

   (continued)

FIGURE B-24
Adding and deleting stops

FIGURE B-24
Adding and deleting stops

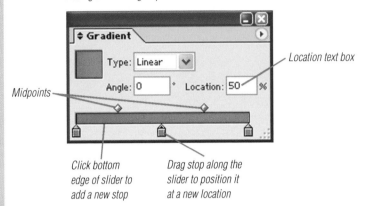

Location text box

Midpoints

Click bottom edge of slider to add a new stop

Drag stop along the slider to position it at a new location

FIGURE B-25
Orange is added to the gradient

Creating Text and Gradients

Black starting and ending colors

Changing the location of the midpoint of two colors

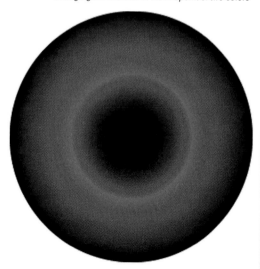

You must select a stop in order to change its color.

> TIP If you don't press [Alt] (Win) or [option] (Mac), as you choose a swatch for your gradient, you will change the selected object's fill to a solid color.

11. Click the **first stop** on the gradient slider, press **[Alt]** (Win) or **[option]** (Mac), then click **black** on the Swatches palette.

12. Repeat Step 11 to apply black to the third stop, then compare your circle to Figure B-26.

13. Click the **orange stop** to select it, then drag each slider in the Color palette until the new CMYK values are 5C/95M/95Y/3K.

> TIP Expand the view of the Color palette, if necessary.

14. Click the **Type list arrow** in the Gradient palette, then click **Radial**.

15. Click the **diamond** at the top of the gradient slider between the first two stops, then drag it to the 87% location on the slider.

16. Compare your circle to Figure B-27.

You applied the Rainbow gradient to the yellow circle. You created a new gradient by deleting the four intermediary stops and adding a new stop to the gradient. You changed the gradient from linear to radial, then adjusted the midpoint of the blend between the starting color and the red intermediate color.

Add gradients and colors to the Swatches palette

1. Double-click the **Scale Tool** 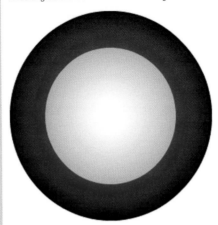, type **65** in the Scale text box, then click **Copy**.

2. Keeping the smaller circle selected, delete the red stop on the gradient slider in the Gradient palette.

3. Change the first stop starting color to white and the ending stop to 0C/40M/50Y/0K.

   | TIP   Press [Alt] (Win) or [option] (Mac).

   When a stop is selected on the gradient slider, the color of that stop appears in the Gradient Stop Color box in the Color palette.

4. Position the midpoint on the gradient slider at 65%.

   Your screen should resemble Figure B-28.

5. Drag the **Gradient Fill box** from the Gradient palette to the Swatches palette, as shown in Figure B-29.

6. Double-click **New Gradient Swatch 1** (the gradient you just added) in the Swatches palette to open the Swatch Options dialog box.

7. Type **Pinky** in the Swatch Name text box, then click **OK**.

8. Click the **last color stop** on the gradient slider.

(continued)

FIGURE B-28

A radial gradient with white as the starting color

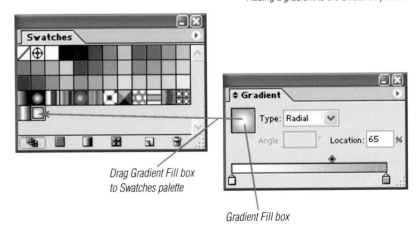

FIGURE B-29

Adding a gradient to the Swatches palette

Drag Gradient Fill box
to Swatches palette

Gradient Fill box

Creating Text and Gradients

FIGURE B-30

Adding a color to the Swatches palette

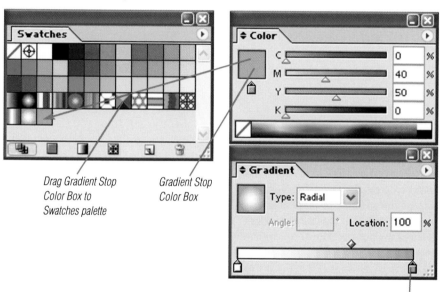

Drag Gradient Stop
Color Box to
Swatches palette

Gradient Stop
Color Box

When a stop is selected,
the color appears in the
Gradient Stop Color Box
in the Color palette

9. Drag the **Gradient Stop Color box** from the Color palette to the Swatches palette to add this color to the Swatches palette, as shown in Figure B-30.

10. Click the **Selection Tool** ▶.

11. Click the **artboard** to deselect the smaller circle.

12. Name the new color swatch **Pinky Ending**, then click **OK**.

13. Click the **large circle**, drag the **Gradient Fill box** in the Gradient palette to the Swatches palette, then name the new gradient **Crimson Gradient**.

14. Save your work.

You used the Gradient palette to create a new gradient. You added the gradient fills from the two circles to the Swatches palette and gave them descriptive names. You added a color named Pinky Ending to the Swatches palette, then created a new gradient called Crimson Gradient.

APPLY COLORS AND GRADIENTS TO TEXT

What You'll Do

In this lesson, you will apply colors to text, convert text into objects, and fill the objects with a gradient.

Applying Fills and Strokes to Text

Regardless of the fill and stroke colors shown in the toolbox, new text is generated by default with a black fill and no stroke. To change the color of text, you must either select the text by highlighting it with a type tool, or switch to a selection tool. When you switch to a selection tool, the text is selected as a single object (a blue baseline and anchor point are revealed). Any color changes you make will affect the text globally. If you want to change the fill or the stroke of an individual character, you must select that character with a type tool.

Converting Text to Outlines

About the only thing you can't do to Illustrator text is fill it with a gradient. To create the effect, you first need to convert the text into objects. You can do this by selecting the text, then using the Create Outlines command on the Type menu. The letterforms, or outlines, become standard Illustrator objects with anchor points and

Working with the stacking order

The stacking order defines how objects will be displayed when they overlap. Illustrator stacks each object, beginning with the first object. Each successive object you create overlaps the previously drawn objects. You can change the stacking order by moving objects forward and backward through the stack, one object at a time. You can also move an object to the very top or the very bottom of the stack with one command. Grouped objects are stacked together behind the top object in the group. If you group two objects that are separated in the stack, the objects in between will be positioned behind the group.

paths able to be modified like any other object—and able to be filled with a gradient. Figure B-31 shows an example of text converted to outlines.

Create Outlines is a powerful feature. Beyond allowing you to fill text with a gradient, it makes it possible to create a document with text and without fonts. This can save you time in document management when sending files to your printer, and will circumvent potential problems with missing fonts or font conflicts.

Once text is converted to outlines, you can no longer change the typeface. Also, the type loses its font information, including sizing "hints" that optimize letter shape at different sizes. Therefore, if you plan to scale type, change its font size in the Character palette before converting to outlines.

FIGURE B-31
Text converted to outlines

Apply color to text

1. Select the two circles, click **Object** on the menu bar, point to **Arrange**, then click **Send to Back**.

   The two circles move behind the locked text objects.

2. Click **Object** on the menu bar, then click **Unlock All**.

   The three text objects you created and locked are now unlocked and selected.

3. Apply the Pinky Ending color as a fill for the three unlocked text objects.

4. Deselect all, then lock the diamond text object.

   Your work should resemble Figure B-32.

You unlocked the three text objects, filled them with the Pinky Ending color, then locked the diamond text object.

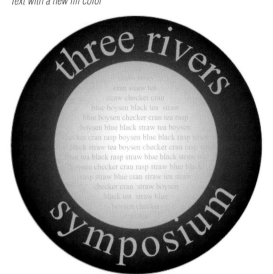

FIGURE B-32
Text with a new fill color

Importing a swatch library

Colors and gradients are saved with the document they were created in, and are not available to be used in other documents. You can, however, import swatches from one document into another. Click Window on the menu bar, point to Swatch Libraries, then click Other Library, which opens the Select a library to open dialog box. Click the document whose swatches you want to import, then click Open. That document's Swatches palette will appear in your current document. When you import a Swatches palette, the palette automatically appears with the name of the document from which it came. The imported Swatches palette is not editable—you cannot add new swatches to it or delete existing ones from it.

FIGURE B-33

Outlines filled with a gradient

Each outline is filled
with the gradient

Create outlines and apply a gradient fill

1. Show the guides.
2. Click **Object** on the menu bar, then click **Show All**.
3. Select the **BERRY** text, click **Object** on the menu bar, point to **Arrange**, then click **Bring to Front**.
4. Click **Type** on the menu bar, then click **Create Outlines**.
5. Apply the Steel gradient in the Swatches palette to fill the text outlines, then deselect the outlines.
6. Using Figure B-33 as a guide, position the BERRY text outlines so that they are centered within the entire illustration, then hide the guides.
7. Save your work.

You showed the BERRY text, moved it to the front, converted it to outlines, then filled the outlines with a gradient.

ADJUST A GRADIENT AND CREATE A DROP SHADOW

What You'll Do

In this lesson, you will use the Gradient Tool to modify how the gradient fills the outlines. You will then explore the effectiveness of a simple drop shadow as a design element.

Using the Gradient Tool

The Gradient Tool is used to manipulate gradient fills that are already applied to objects; it affects only the way a gradient fills an object. To use the tool, you first select an object with a gradient fill. You then drag the Gradient Tool over the object. For both linear and radial gradients, where you begin dragging and where you end dragging determine the length of the blend from starting to ending color. For linear gradients, the angle that you drag in determines the angle at which the blend fills the object. If you apply the same gradient to multiple objects, you can select all the objects and use the Gradient Tool to extend a single gradient across all of them.

If you select and fill multiple objects with a gradient, each object is filled with the entire length of the gradient, from beginning color to ending color.

When you convert text to outlines and apply a gradient fill, the gradient automatically fills each letter independently. In other words, if you fill a five-letter word with a rainbow gradient, each of the five letters will contain the entire spectrum of colors in the gradient. To extend the gradient across all the letters, drag the Gradient Tool from the left edge of the word to the right edge. Figure B-34 shows examples of different angles and lengths of a gradient fill created with the Gradient Tool.

Adding a Drop Shadow

Applying a shadow behind text is an effective design tool to distinguish the text from other objects and add dimension to the illustration. To apply a drop shadow to text, copy the text, then paste the copy behind it. Fill the copy with a darker color, then use the keyboard arrows to move it so that it is offset from the original text. See Figure B-35.

QUICKTIP

When adding subtle design effects to objects, you may want to work without seeing the anchor points and paths on selected items. You can hide them by using the Hide Edges command on the View menu. Hiding edges allows you to work on an object without the distraction of the points and paths.

FIGURE B-34
Using the Gradient Tool

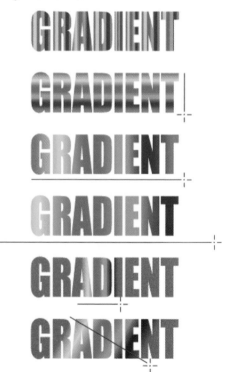

FIGURE B-35
Drop shadow created using the Paste in Back command

Use the Gradient Tool

1. Select the **BERRY text outlines**, if necessary.

2. Click the **Gradient Tool** 🔲, then position the pointer at the top of the B.

3. Drag straight down to the bottom of the B, then release the mouse.

   Your work should resemble Figure B-36.

   > TIP Pressing and holding [Shift] while you drag the Gradient Tool pointer allows you to drag in a perfectly straight line.

4. Switch to the **Selection Tool** ▶, then click the large circle filled with the Crimson Gradient fill behind the text.

5. In the Gradient palette, reposition the red center color stop so that the value in the Location text box reads 82%.

   The red stop in the blend is now positioned behind the three rivers and symposium text, as shown in Figure B-37.

You used the Gradient Tool to flow the gradient from top to bottom in the word BERRY. You adjusted the red stop in the Gradient palette to move the red highlight behind the three rivers and symposium text.

FIGURE B-37
A highlight behind the text

Red stop in a
radial gradient

Creating Text and Gradients

FIGURE B-38
Drop shadow with a 3 pt offset

FIGURE B-39
Drop shadows add dimension

*Drop shadow added
to symposium*

FIGURE B-40
The finished illustration

Add a drop shadow to text

1. Select the word **BERRY**.
2. Apply a 1 pt black stroke to the outlines.
3. Copy the word, then paste in back.
4. Change the fill of the copied object to black.

   | TIP   Even though you can't see the copy of the text in back, it is still selected.

5. Press ↓ three times and ← three times to move the copied text 3 pts down and 3 pts to the left, as shown in Figure B-38.
6. Copy the word symposium, then paste in back.
7. Change the fill of the copied text to black.
8. Using the arrow keys, move the copied text 2 pts down and 2 pts to the left, as shown in Figure B-39.
9. Apply the same drop shadow to the three rivers text.

   | TIP   You might find it easier to select the three rivers text if you first lock the symposium text and the symposium shadow text.

10. Unlock all, select everything on the artboard, then rotate the illustration 15°.
11. Click the **Selection Tool** ⬆, then click the **artboard** to deselect all.

    Your work should resemble Figure B-40.
12. Save your work, then close and save each document.

You applied a black stroke to the display text and then pasted a copy behind. You filled the copy with black, then offset the copy to create a drop shadow effect. You then applied a drop shadow to symposium and three rivers. Finally, you rotated the entire illustration.

Create and format text.

1. Open AI B-3.ai, then save it as **Hole In One**.
2. Using a bold font, type **NOW OPEN** on two lines, using all capital letters. (*Hint*: The font used in Figure B-41 is Impact.)
3. Change the font size to 29 pt and the leading to 25 pt.
4. Change the baseline shift to 0.
5. Change the alignment to center and the horizontal scale to 75%.
6. Position the text in the center of the white circle.
7. Hide the text.
8. Save your work.

Flow text into an object.

1. Copy the tan circle.
2. Paste the copy in front of it.
3. Click the Type Tool, then select all of the green text at the bottom of the artboard, with the Type Tool.
4. Copy the green text.
5. Click the Selection Tool, then click the top tan circle.
6. Click the Area Type Tool, click the edge of the top tan circle, then paste.
7. Center-align the text in the circle.

8. Change the baseline shift to -4 pts.
9. Fill the selected text with the same fill color as the tan circle (50% Orange).
10. In the Color palette, drag the Magenta slider to 40% to darken the text.
11. Hide the text.
12. Save your work.

Position text on a path.

1. Select the black circle.
2. Click the Type on a Path Tool.
3. Using a bold font, type **THE HOLE-IN-ONE** in all capital letters across the top of the circle. (*Hint*: The font in Figure B-41 is Techno Regular.)
4. Change the font size to 34 pt and the fill color to white. (*Hint*: You may need to use a smaller font size, depending on the font you choose.)
5. Click the Selection Tool, click Edit on the menu bar, click Copy, click Edit on the menu bar, click Paste in Front, then move the center bracket clockwise to position the copied text across the bottom of the circle.
6. Highlight the copied text, then type **RESTAURANT & BAR** with the Type Tool.

7. Drag the RESTAURANT & BAR text across the path to flip its direction.
8. Apply a negative baseline shift to move the text below the path. (*Hint*: The baseline shift used in Figure B-41 is -27 pts.)
9. Copy both text objects, then paste them in back.
10. Fill the back copies of the text with black, then move them 2 pts up and 2 pts to the right.
11. Save your work.

Create and apply gradient fills to objects.

1. Apply the Black, White Radial gradient to the small white circle.
2. Change the ending color stop to gray on the Gradient palette. (*Hint*: Press [Alt] (Win) or [option] (Mac) while you select gray.)
3. Save the new gradient in the Swatches palette.
4. Name it **Golf Ball**.
5. Fill the large green circle with the Golf Ball gradient.
6. Change the starting color stop to yellow.
7. Change the ending color stop to a dark green.

8. Move the midpoint of the two colors to the 80% location on the gradient slider.
9. Save the new gradient as **The Rough**.
10. Save your work.

Adjust a gradient and create a drop shadow.

1. Click Object on the menu bar, then click Show All.
2. Deselect all by clicking the artboard.
3. Select NOW OPEN and convert the text to outlines. (*Hint*: Use the Type menu.)
4. Fill the text with the White, Black gradient.
5. Change the starting color stop to black.
6. Create an intermediary white color stop at the 50% mark on the gradient slider.
7. Drag the Gradient Tool starting at the top of the word NOW to the bottom of the word OPEN.
8. Change the middle color stop of the gradient to light gray.
9. Save the new gradient as **Flash**.
10. Deselect the text.
11. Delete the green text from the bottom of the artboard.
12. Convert the remaining text objects into outlines.
13. Select all, then lock all objects.
14. Save your work, compare your illustration to Figure B-41, then close Hole In One.

FIGURE B-41
Completed Skills Review

Creating Text and Gradients

An eccentric California real-estate mogul hires your design firm to "create an identity" for La Mirage, his development of high-tech executive condominiums in Palm Springs. Since he's curious about what you'll come up with on your own, the only creative direction he'll give you is to tell you that the concept is "a desert oasis."

1. Create a new 6" × 6" CMYK Color document, then save it as **La Mirage**.
2. Using a bold font and 80 pt for a font size, type **LA MIRAGE** in all capitals. (*Hint*: The font shown in Figure B-42 is Impact.)
3. Change the horizontal scale to 80%.
4. Change the baseline shift to 0.
5. Apply a -100 kerning value between the two words.
6. Convert the text to outlines, then click the White, Black gradient in the Swatches palette.
7. Using the Color palette, change the first color stop to 66M/100Y/10K. (*Hint*: C value = 0.)
8. Create an intermediary color stop that is 35M/100Y. (*Hint*: C and K values = 0.)
9. Position the intermediary color stop at 60% on the slider.
10. Save the gradient in the Swatches palette, and name it **Desert Sun**.
11. Drag the Gradient Tool from the exact top to the exact bottom of the text.

12. Create a rectangle around the text and fill it with the Desert Sun gradient.
13. Drag the Gradient Tool from the bottom to the top of the rectangle.
14. Send the rectangle to the back of the stack.

FIGURE B-42
Completed Project Builder 1

15. Apply a 1 pt black stroke to LA MIRAGE.
16. Type the tagline: **a desert oasis** in 14 pt lowercase letters.
17. Apply a tracking value of 500 or more to the tagline, then convert it to outlines.
18. Save your work, then close La Mirage.

Your friend owns Loon's Balloons. She stops by your studio with a display ad that she's put together for a local magazine and asks if you can make all the elements work together better. Her only direction is that the balloon must remain pink, the same color as her logo.

1. Open AI B-4.ai, then save it as **Loon's Balloons**.
2. Save the pink fill on the balloon to the Swatches palette, and name it **Pink**.
3. Fill the balloon shape with the Black, White Radial gradient from the Swatches palette.
4. Change the black stop on the gradient slider to Pink.
5. Using the Gradient Tool, change the highlight point on the balloon shape so that it is no longer centered in the balloon shape.
6. Copy the balloon, then paste it in front.
7. Click the Area Type Tool on the block of text that says "specializing in etc."
8. Select all of the text, then cut it.
9. Using the Area Type Tool, fill the top balloon shape with the text.
10. Center the text and apply a -4 baseline shift.
11. Adjust the layout of the text as necessary. (*Hint*: You can force a line of text to the next line by clicking before the first word in the line you want to move, then pressing [Shift][Enter] (Win) or [Shift][return] (Mac).)

12. Move the headline LOON'S BALLOONS so that each word is on a different side of the balloon string.

FIGURE B-43
Completed Project Builder 2

13. Apply a 280 kerning value between the two words.
14. Save your work, compare your screen to Figure B-43, then close Loon's Balloons.

You work in the marketing department of a major movie studio, where you design movie posters and newspaper campaigns. You are respected for your proficiency with typography. Your boss asks you to come up with a "teaser" campaign for the movie *Vanishing Point*, a spy thriller. The campaign will run on billboards in 10 major cities and will feature only the movie title, nothing else.

FIGURE B-44
Completed Design Project

VANISHING POINT

1. Create a new 6" × 6" CMYK Color document, then save it as **Vanishing Point**.
2. Type **VANISHING POINT**, using 100 pt and a bold font. (*Hint*: The font used in Figure B-44 is Impact.)
3. Change the horizontal scale to 50%.
4. Convert the text to outlines.
5. In the Swatches palette, click the White, Black gradient.
6. Drag the Gradient Tool from the exact bottom to the exact top of the letters.
7. Copy the letters, then paste them in front.
8. Fill the copied letters in front with white.
9. Using your arrow keys, move the white letters 2 pts to the left and 12 pts up.
10. Save your work, then compare your text with Figure B-44.
11. Close Vanishing Point.

Firehouse Chili Pepper Company, a local specialty food manufacturer, has hired your team to design a label for its new line of hot sauces. Since this is a new product line, they have no existing materials for your team to start from.

1. Create a new 6" × 6" CMYK Color document, then save it as **Firehouse**.
2. Assign two team members to search the Internet to get design ideas. They should use keywords such as chili, pepper, hot sauce, barbecue, and salsa. What have other designers created to convey these concepts? Is there a broad range of ideas, or are they all pretty much different versions of the same idea? If so, can your group think of something original that works?
3. Assign two other members to go to the grocery store and return with some samples of other products in this niche. Be sure they purchase both products that you've heard of before and products you've never heard of before. Are the known products' design concepts better than the unknown products'? Have the group discuss any correlation between the successful products and better design, if it is evident.
4. Two other team members should be in charge of typographic research and should work closely with the design team. Again, have the group discuss whether it sees a variety of typefaces used in relation with this concept, or whether they are all pretty much the same.
5. While everyone else is researching, the design team should begin brainstorming and sketching out ideas. Although there are no existing materials, the product line's name is very evocative. The team should create design ideas that spring from the concepts of "firehouse" and "chili pepper," as well as from more broad-based concepts such as salsa, Mexico, and fire.

6. Use the skills that you learned in this chapter to create the label. (*Hint*: Fill text outlines with a gradient that conveys "hot." Use reds, oranges, and blacks. Use a bold font for the text so that the gradient will be clearly visible. Position the stops on the slider so that the "hot" colors are prominent in the letterforms.)
7. Save your work, then compare your results with Figure B-45.
8. Close Firehouse.

FIGURE B-45
Completed Group Project

CHAPTER C

DRAWING AND COMPOSING AN ILLUSTRATION

1. Draw straight lines.

2. Draw curved lines.

3. Draw elements of an illustration.

4. Copy attributes between objects.

5. Assemble an illustration.

6. Stroke objects for artistic effect.

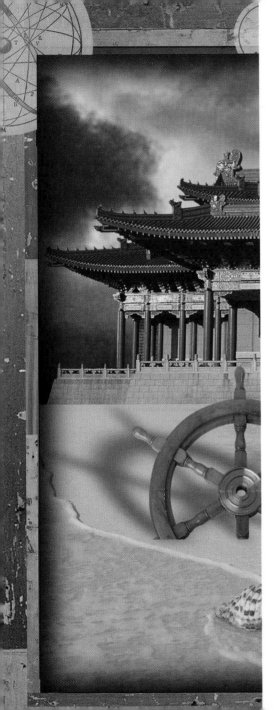

CHAPTER C
DRAWING AND COMPOSING AN ILLUSTRATION

Drawing in Illustrator

You can create any shape using the Pen Tool, which is why it's often called "the drawing tool." More precisely, the pen is a tool for drawing straight lines, curved lines, polygons, and irregularly shaped objects. It is, however, no *more* of a drawing tool than the shape tools—it's just more versatile.

The challenges of the Pen Tool are finite and able to be grasped with no more than 30 minutes' study. As with many aspects of graphic design (and of life!), mastery comes with practice. So make it a point to learn Pen Tool techniques. Don't get frustrated. And use the Pen Tool often, even if it's just to play around making odd shapes.

To master Illustrator, you must master the Pen Tool.

All artists learn techniques for using tools—brushes, chalk, palette knives, etc.

Once learned, those techniques become second nature—subconscious and unique to the artist. Ask yourself, was Van Gogh's mastery of the palette knife a triumph of his hands or of his imagination?

When you draw, you aren't conscious of how you're holding the crayon or how much pressure you're applying to the paper. Much the same goes for Illustrator's Pen Tool. When you are comfortable and confident, you will find yourself effectively translating design ideas from your imagination straight to the artboard—without even thinking about the tool!

When you work with the Pen Tool, you'll want complete control over your artboard. Using the Zoom Tool and the New View feature, you can create custom views of areas of your artboard, making it easy to jump to specific elements of your illustration for editing purposes.

Tools You'll Use

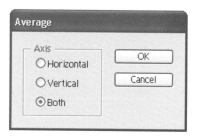

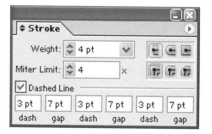

DRAW STRAIGHT LINES

What You'll Do

In this lesson, you will create three new views, then explore basic techniques for using the Pen Tool as you prepare to draw a complex illustration.

Viewing Objects on the Artboard

If you are drawing on paper and you want to see your work up close, you move your nose closer to the paper. Computers offer more effective options. As you have already seen, the Zoom Tool is used to enlarge areas of the artboard for easier viewing. When you are working with the Pen Tool, your view of the board becomes more critical, as anchor points are tiny, and you will often move them in 1 point increments.

Instead of clicking the Zoom Tool to enlarge an area, you can click and drag it over the area you want to zoom in on, creating a **marquee**, a rectangular, dotted line that surrounds the area you drag over. When you release the Zoom Tool, the marquee disappears, and whatever was in the marquee is magnified as much as possible while still fitting in the window.

The New View command allows you to save any view of the artboard. Let's say you zoom in on an object. You can save that view and give it a descriptive name, using the New View command. The name of the view is then listed at the bottom of the View menu, so you can return to it at any time by selecting it. Saving views is an effective way to increase your productivity.

Drawing Straight Segments with the Pen Tool

You can use the Pen Tool to make lines, also known as paths; you can also use it to create a closed shape such as a triangle or a pentagon. When you click the Pen Tool to make anchor points on the artboard, straight segments are automatically placed between the points. When the endpoints of two straight segments are united by a point that point is called a **corner point**. Figure C-1 shows a simple path drawn with five anchor points and four segments.

Perfection is an unnecessary goal when you are using the Pen Tool. Anchor points and segments can be moved and repositioned. New points can be added and deleted. Use the Pen Tool to create the general shape that you have in your mind. Once the object is complete, use the Direct Selection Tool to perfect—or tweak—the points and segments. "Tweaking" a finished object— making small, specific improvements—is always part of the drawing process.

Aligning and Joining Anchor Points

Often, you will want to align anchor points precisely. For example, if you have drawn a diamond-shaped object with the Pen Tool, you may want to align the top and bottom points on the same vertical axis and then align the left and right points on the same horizontal axis to perfect the shape.

The **Average** command is a simple and effective choice for aligning points. With two or more points selected, you can use the Average command to align them on the horizontal axis, on the vertical axis, or on both the horizontal and vertical axes. Two points aligned on both the horizontal and vertical axes are positioned one on top of the other.

Why is the command named Average? The name is appropriate, because when the command moves two points to line them up on a given axis, that axis is positioned at the average distance between the two points. Thus, each moves the same distance.

The **Join** command unites two anchor points. When two points are positioned in different locations on the artboard, the Join command creates a segment between them. When two points are aligned on both the horizontal and vertical axes and are joined, the two points become one.

You will often use the Average and Join commands in tandem. Figure C-2 shows two pairs of points that have each been aligned on the horizontal axis, then joined with the Join command.

FIGURE C-1

Elements of a path composed of straight segments

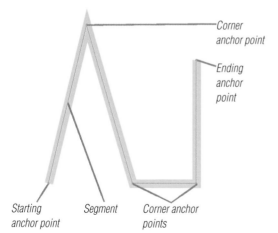

Corner anchor point

Ending anchor point

Starting anchor point   Segment   Corner anchor points

FIGURE C-2

Join command unites open points

Points to be joined

Points to be joined

Two paths created by the Join command

Create new views

1. Open AI C-1.ai, then save it as **Straight Lines**.

2. Click the **Zoom Tool** 🔍, then position it at the upper-left corner of the artboard.

3. Click and drag a **selection box** that encompasses the entire yellow section, as shown in Figure C-3.

   The area within the selection box is now magnified.

4. Click **View** on the menu bar, then click **New View**.

5. Name the new view **yellow**, then click **OK**.

6. Press and hold **[Spacebar]** to access the Hand Tool 🖐, then drag the **artboard** upward until you have a view of the entire pink area.

7. Create a new view of the pink area, and name it **pink**.

   > TIP If you need to adjust your view, you can quickly switch to a view of the entire artboard by pressing [Ctrl][0] (Win) or ⌘[0] (Mac), then create a new selection box with the Zoom Tool.

8. Create a new view of the green area, named **mint**.

9. Click **View** on the menu bar, then click **yellow** at the bottom of the menu.

   The Illustrator window changes to the yellow view.

   > TIP You can change the name of a view by clicking View on the menu bar, then clicking Edit Views.

You used the Zoom Tool to magnify an area of the artboard. You then named and saved the new view of the artboard. You named and saved two other views.

FIGURE C-3

Drag the Zoom Tool to select what will be magnified

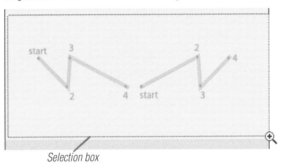

Selection box

FIGURE C-4
Four anchor points and three segments

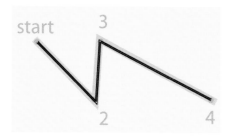

FIGURE C-5
Click the path with the Pen Tool to add a new point

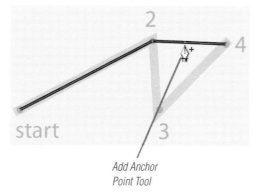

Add Anchor
Point Tool

FIGURE C-6
Move an anchor point with the Direct Selection Tool

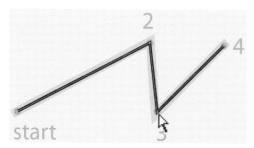

1. Verify that you are still in the yellow view, then click the **Pen Tool** ✒.

2. Set the fill color to [None], the stroke color to black, and the stroke weight to 1 pt.

3. Using Figure C-4 as a reference, click the **Pen Tool** ✒ on position 1 (start).

4. Click **position 2**, then notice the segment that is automatically drawn between the two anchor points.

5. Click **position 3**, then click **position 4**.

   TIP If you become disconnected from the current path you are drawing, undo your last step, then click the last anchor point with the Pen Tool and continue.

6. Press **[Ctrl]** (Win) or ⌘ (Mac) to switch to the Selection Tool ▶, then click the artboard to stop drawing the path and to deselect it.

   You need to deselect one path before you can start drawing a new one.

7. Click **position 1 (start)** on the next path, then click **position 2**.

8. Skip over position 3 and click **position 4**.

9. Using Figure C-5 as a guide, position the Pen Tool anywhere on the segment between points 2 and 4, then click to add a new anchor point.

   TIP When the Pen Tool is positioned over a selected path, the Add Anchor Point Tool appears.

10. Click the **Direct Selection Tool** ▶, then drag the **new anchor point** to position 3, as shown in Figure C-6.

Using the Pen Tool, you created two straight paths.

Close a path and align the anchor points

1. Click **View** on the menu bar, then click **pink**.

2. Click the **Pen Tool** on the start/end position at the top of the polygon, then click **positions 2 through 6**.

3. Position the **Pen Tool** over the first point you created, then click to close the path, as shown in Figure C-7.

4. Switch to the **Direct Selection Tool**, click **point 3**, press and hold **[Shift]**, then click **point 6**.

   TIP Use the [Shift] key to select multiple points.

   Anchor points that are selected appear as solid blue squares; anchor points that are not selected are white or hollow squares.

5. Click **Object** on the menu bar, point to **Path**, then click **Average**.

6. Click the **Horizontal option button** in the Average dialog box, then click **OK**.

   The two selected anchor points align on the horizontal axis, as shown in Figure C-8.

7. Select both the start/end point and point 4.

8. Use the Average command to align the points on the vertical axis.

9. Select both point 2 and point 5, then use the Average command to align the points on both axes, as shown in Figure C-9.

You drew a closed path, then used the Average command to align three sets of points. You aligned the first set on the horizontal axis, the second on the vertical axis. You aligned the third set of points on both axes, which positioned them one on top of the other.

FIGURE C-7
Close a path at its starting point

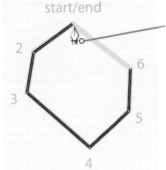

A small circle appears next to the Pen Tool when you position it over the first anchor point

FIGURE C-8
Two points aligned on the horizontal axis

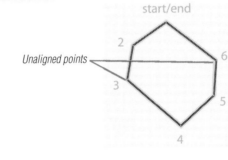
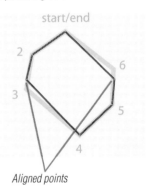

Unaligned points

Aligned points

FIGURE C-9
Averaging two points on both the horizontal and vertical axes

FIGURE C-10

Cutting points also deletes the segments attached to them

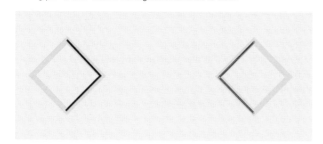

FIGURE C-11

Join command unites two distant points with a straight segment

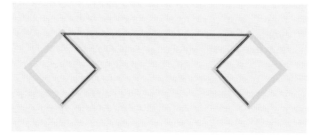

FIGURE C-12

Joining the two open anchor points on an open path closes the path

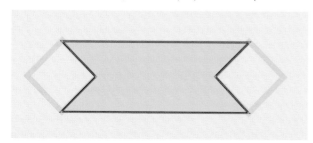

Join anchor points

1. Switch to the mint view of the artboard.

2. Use the Pen Tool 🖋 to trace the two diamond shapes.

   > TIP Remember to deselect the first diamond path with the Selection Tool before you begin tracing the second diamond.

3. Click the **left anchor point** of the first diamond with the Direct Selection Tool 🔍, click **Edit** on the menu bar, then click **Cut**.

   Cutting points also deletes the segments attached to them.

4. Cut the right point on the second diamond.

   Your work should resemble Figure C-10.

5. Select the top point on each path.

6. Click **Object** on the menu bar, point to **Path**, then click **Join**.

   The points are joined by a straight segment, as shown in Figure C-11.

   > TIP The similarity of the quick keys for Average and Join makes them easy to work with in tandem.

7. Join the two bottom points.

8. Apply a yellow fill to the object, then save your work.

   Your work should resemble Figure C-12.

9. Close the Straight Lines document.

You drew two closed paths. You cut a point from each path, which deleted the points and the segments attached to them, creating two open paths. You used the Join command, which drew a new segment between the two top points and the two bottom points on each path. You then applied a yellow fill to the new object.

DRAW CURVED LINES

What You'll Do

In this lesson, you will use the Pen Tool to draw and define curved paths, and learn techniques to draw lines that abruptly change direction.

Defining Properties of Curved Lines

When you click to create anchor points with the Pen Tool, the points are connected by straight segments. You can "draw" a curved path between two anchor points by *clicking and dragging* the Pen Tool to create the points, instead of just clicking. Anchor points created by clicking and dragging the Pen Tool are known as **smooth points**.

When you use the Direct Selection Tool to select a point connected to a curved segment, you will expose the point's **direction lines**, as shown in Figure C-13. The angle and length of the direction lines determine the arc of the curved segment. Direction lines are editable. You can click and drag the **direction points** at the end of the direction lines to reshape the curve. Direction lines function only to define curves and do not appear when you print your document.

A smooth point always has two direction lines that move together as a unit. The two curved segments attached to the smooth point are both defined by the direction lines.

When you manipulate the direction lines on a smooth point, you change the curve of both segments attached to the point, always maintaining a *smooth* transition through the anchor point.

When two paths are joined at a corner point, the two paths can be manipulated independently. A corner point can join

two straight segments, one straight segment and one curved segment, or two curved segments. That corner point would have zero, one, or two direction lines, respectively. Figure C-14 shows examples of smooth points and corner points.

FIGURE C-13

Direction lines define a curve

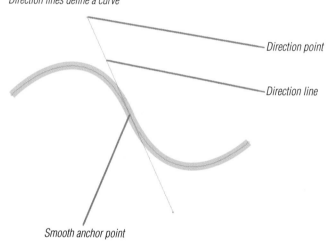

Direction point

Direction line

Smooth anchor point

FIGURE C-14

Smooth points and corner points

A corner point joining
two straight segments

A corner point joining
one straight and one
curved segment

A smooth point

A corner point joining
two curved paths (note
the direction lines)

When a corner point joins one or two curved segments, the direction lines are unrelated and are often referred to as "broken." When you manipulate one, the other doesn't move.

Converting Anchor Points

The Convert Anchor Point Tool changes corner points to smooth points and smooth points to corner points.

To convert a corner point to a smooth point, you click and drag the Convert Anchor Point Tool on the anchor point to *pull out* direction lines. See Figure C-15.

The Convert Anchor Point Tool works two ways to convert a smooth point to a corner point, and both are very useful when drawing.

FIGURE C-15
Converting a corner point to a smooth point

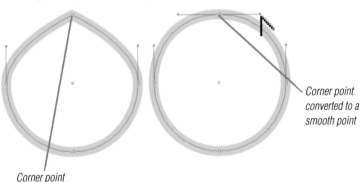

Corner point

Corner point
converted to a
smooth point

When you click directly on a smooth point with the Convert Anchor Point Tool, the direction lines disappear. The two attached segments lose whatever curve defined them and become straight segments, as shown in Figure C-16.

You can also use the Convert Anchor Point Tool on one of the two direction lines of a smooth point. The tool "breaks" the direction lines and allows you to move one independently of the other. The smooth point is converted to a corner point that now joins two unrelated curved segments.

Once the direction lines are broken, they remain broken. You can manipulate them independently with the Direct Selection Tool; you no longer need the Convert Anchor Point Tool to do so.

FIGURE C-16
Converting smooth points to corner points

Smooth point

Smooth point converted to a corner point

Corner point converted to a smooth point

Toggling between the Pen Tool and the selection tools

Drawing points and selecting points go hand in hand, and you will often switch back and forth between the Pen Tool and one of the selection tools. Clicking from one tool to the other in the toolbox is unnecessary and will impede your productivity. To master the Pen Tool, you *must* incorporate the keyboard command for "toggling" between the Pen Tool and the selection tools. With the Pen Tool selected, press [Ctrl] (Win) or ⌘ (Mac), which will switch the Pen Tool to the Selection Tool or the Direct Selection Tool, depending on which tool you used last.

Draw and edit a curved line

1. Open AI C-2.ai, then save it as **Curved Lines 1**.

2. Click the **Pen Tool** , then position it over the first point position on the line.

3. Click and drag upward until the pointer is at the center of the purple star.

4. Position the Pen Tool over the second point position.

5. Click and drag down to the red star.

6. Using the same method, trace the remainder of the blue line, as shown in Figure C-17.

7. Click the **Direct Selection Tool** .

8. Select the second anchor point.

9. Click and drag the **direction handle** of the *top* direction line to the second purple star, as shown in Figure C-18.

   The move changes the shape of *both* segments attached to the anchor point.

10. Select the third anchor point.

11. Drag the **bottom direction handle** to the second red star, as shown in Figure C-19.

12. Manipulate the direction lines to restore the curves to their appearance in Figure C-17.

13. Save your work, then close the Curved Lines 1 document.

You traced a curved line by making smooth points with the Pen Tool. You used the Direct Selection Tool to manipulate the direction lines of the smooth points and adjust the curves. You then used the direction lines to restore the line to its original curves.

FIGURE C-17
Smooth points draw continuous curves

FIGURE C-18
Moving one direction line changes two curves

Click the Direct Selection Tool on any smooth point to expose its direction lines

FIGURE C-19
Round curves are distorted by moving direction lines

FIGURE C-20
Smooth points are converted to corner points

FIGURE C-21
Smooth points restored from corner points

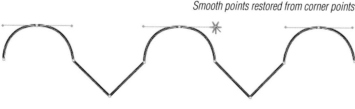

Convert anchor points

1. Open AI C-3.ai, then save it as **Curved Lines 2**.

2. Click **View** on the menu bar, then click **View #1**.

3. Click the **Direct Selection Tool** ↖ any-where on the black line.

    Six anchor points become visible.

4. Click **Object** on the menu bar, point to **Path**, then click **Add Anchor Points**.

    Five anchor points are added that do not change the shape of the line.

5. Click the **Convert Anchor Point Tool** ⌐ , then click each of the five new anchor points.

    | TIP   The Convert Anchor Point Tool is hidden beneath the Pen Tool.

    The smooth points are converted to corner points, as shown in Figure C-20.

6. Click the six original anchor points with the Convert Anchor Point Tool.

7. Starting from the left side of the line, posi-tion the Convert Anchor Point Tool over the sixth anchor point.

8. Click and drag the **anchor point** to the purple star.

    The corner point is converted to a smooth point.

9. Using Figure C-21 as a guide, convert the corner points to the left and right of the new curve.

You added five new anchor points to the line, then used the Convert Anchor Point Tool to convert all 11 points from smooth to corner points. You then used the Convert Anchor Point Tool to convert three corner points to smooth points.

Draw a line with curved and straight segments

1. Click **View** on the menu bar, then click **View #2**.

2. Click the **Pen Tool** ✎, position it over the first point position, then click and drag down to the green star.

3. Position the Pen Tool over the second point position, then click and drag up to the purple star, as shown in the top section of Figure C-22.

4. Click the **second anchor point**.

   The direction line you dragged is deleted, as shown in the lower section of Figure C-22.

5. Click the **third point position** to create the third anchor point.

6. Position the Pen Tool over the third anchor point, then click and drag a direction line up to the green star.

7. Position the Pen Tool over the **fourth point position**, then click and drag down to the purple star.

8. Click the **fourth anchor point**.

9. Position the Pen Tool over the fifth position, then click.

10. While the Pen Tool is still positioned over the fifth anchor point, click and drag a direction line down to the green star.

11. Finish tracing the line, then deselect the path.

You traced a line that has three curves joined by two straight segments. You used the technique of clicking the previous smooth point to convert it to a corner point, allowing you to change the direction of the path.

FIGURE C-22

Click to convert an open smooth point to a corner point

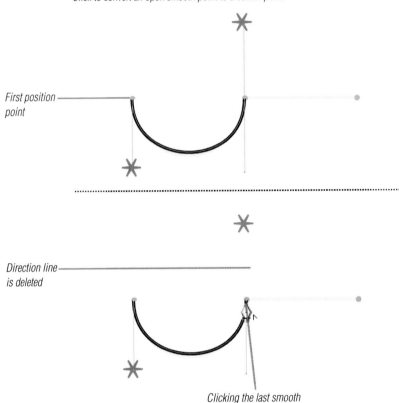

First position point

Direction line is deleted

Clicking the last smooth point you drew converts it to a corner point

FIGURE C-23

Use the Convert Anchor Point Tool to "break" the direction lines and redirect the path

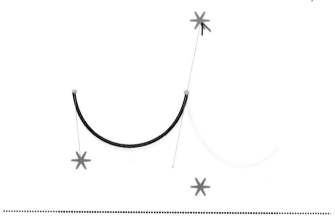

1. Click **View** on the menu bar, then click **View #3**.

2. Position the Pen Tool over the first point position, then click and drag down to the purple star.

3. Position the Pen Tool over the second point position, then click and drag up to the red star, as shown in the top section of Figure C-23.

4. Press and hold **[Alt]** (Win) or **[option]** (Mac) to switch to the Convert Anchor Point Tool, then click and drag the **direction handle** on the red star down to the second purple star, as shown in the lower section of Figure C-23.

   TIP Press [Alt] (Win) or [option] (Mac) to toggle between the Pen and the Convert Anchor Point Tools.

5. Release [Alt] (Win) or [option] (Mac), then continue to trace the line using the same method.

   TIP If you switch between the PenTool and the Convert Anchor Point Tool using the toolbox, instead of using [Alt] (Win) or [option] (Mac), you will disconnect from the current path.

6. Save your work, then close the Curved Lines 2 document.

You used the Convert Anchor Point Tool to "break" the direction lines of a smooth point, converting it to a corner point in the process. You used the redirected direction line to define the next curve in the sequence.

DRAW ELEMENTS OF AN ILLUSTRATION

What You'll Do

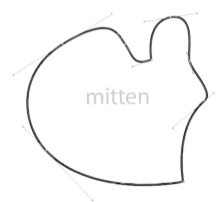

mitten

▶ *In this lesson, you will draw 14 elements of an illustration. By tracing previously drawn elements, you will develop a sense of where to place anchor points when drawing a real-world illustration.*

Starting an Illustration

Getting started with drawing an illustration is often the hardest part. Sometimes the illustration will be an image of a well-known object or a supplied sketch or a picture. At other times, the illustration to be created will exist only in your imagination. In either case, the challenge is the same: How do you translate the concept from its source to the Illustrator artboard?

Drawing from Scratch

Drawing from scratch means that you start with a new Illustrator document and create the illustration, using only the Illustrator tools. This approach is common, especially when the goal is to draw familiar items such as a daisy, a fish, or the sun, for example.

Illustrator's shape tools (such as the Ellipse Tool) combined with the transform tools (such as the Rotate Tool) make the program very powerful for creating geometric designs from scratch. The Undo and Redo commands allow you to experiment, and

you will often find yourself surprised by the design you end up with!

Typographic illustrations—even complex ones—are often created from scratch.

Many talented illustrators and designers are able to create complex graphics off the cuff. It can be an astounding experience to watch an illustrator start with a blank artboard and, with no reference material, produce sophisticated graphics—graphics with attitude and expression and emotion, with unexpected shapes and subtle relationships between objects.

Tracing a Scanned Image

Using the Place command, it is easy to import a scanned image into Illustrator. For complex illustrations—especially those of people or objects with delicate relationships, such as maps or blueprints—many designers find it easier to scan a sketch or a photo and import it into Illustrator as a guide or a point of reference.

Tracing a scanned image is not "cheating." An original drawing is an original drawing, whether it is first created on a computer or on a piece of paper. Rather than being a negative, the ability to use a computer to render a sketch is a fine example of the revolutionary techniques that illustration software has brought to the art of drawing. Figure C-24 shows an illustration created from scratch in Illustrator, and Figure C-25 shows a scanned sketch that will be the basis for the illustration you will create throughout this chapter.

FIGURE C-24
An illustration created from scratch

FIGURE C-25
Place a scanned sketch in Illustrator, and you can trace it or use it as a visual reference

Draw a closed path using smooth points

1. Open AI C-4.ai, then save it as **Snowball Parts**.

2. Click **View** on the menu bar, then click **Arm**.

3. Verify that the fill color is set to [None] and the stroke color is set to black.

4. Click the **Pen Tool** 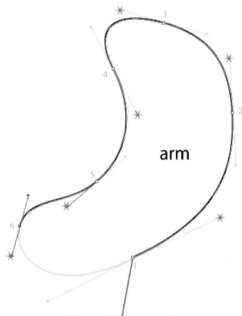, position it over point 1, then click and drag a **direction line** to the green star on the right side of the 1.

5. Go to position 2, then click and drag a **direction line** to the next green star.

   > TIP   Watch the blue preview of the new segment fall into place as you drag the Pen Tool. This will help you understand when to stop dragging the direction line.

6. Using the same method, continue to draw points 3 through 6, then compare your screen to Figure C-26.

7. Position the Pen Tool over point 1.

8. Press and hold **[Alt]** (Win) or **[option]** (Mac), then click and drag to position the ending segment and close the path.

You drew a curved path. To close the path, you used a corner point, which allowed you to position the ending segment without affecting the starting segment.

FIGURE C-26
Points 1 through 6 are smooth points

arm

When closing a path, pressing [Alt] (Win) or [option] (Mac) converts the end/start anchor point to a corner point

FIGURE C-27
Point 5 is a corner point

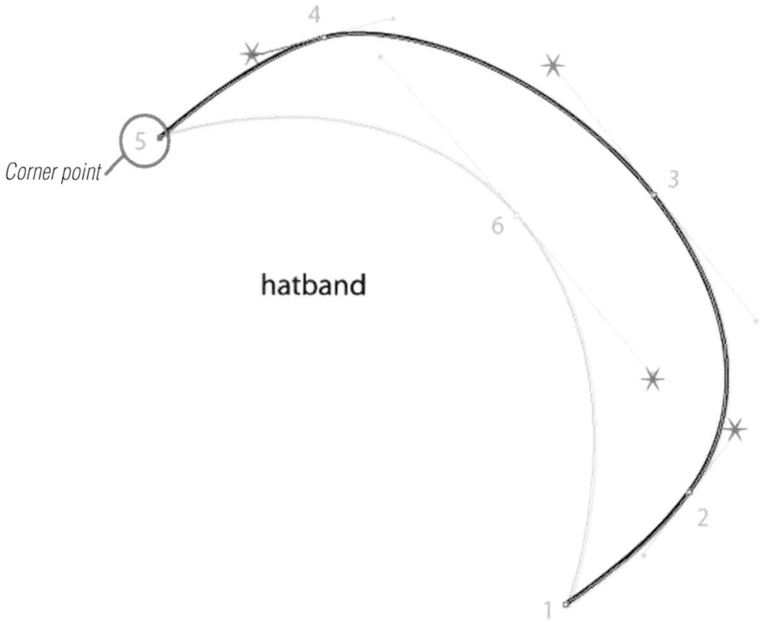

Corner point

hatband

Begin and end a path with a corner point

1. Click **View** on the menu bar, then click **Hatband**.

2. Verify that the fill color is set to [None] and the stroke color is set to black.

3. Click the **Pen Tool** ✎., then click **position 1** to create a corner point.

4. Draw the next two curved segments for positions 2 and 3, using the green stars as guides.

5. Position the Pen Tool over position 4, then click and drag to the green star.

6. Click **position 5** to create a corner point, as shown in Figure C-27.

7. Position the Pen Tool over position 6, then click and drag to the green star.

8. Click **position 1** to close the path with a corner point.

9. Click the **Selection Tool** ▸, then deselect the path.

You began a path with a corner point. When it was time to close the path, you simply clicked the starting point. Since the point was created without direction lines, there were no direction lines to contend with when closing the path.

Redirect a path while drawing

1. Click **View** on the menu bar, then click **Nose**.

   The Nose view includes the nose, mouth, eyebrow, and teeth.

2. Click the **Pen Tool** , then click **point 1** on the nose to start the path with a corner point.

3. Create smooth points at positions 2 and 3.

   The direction of the nose that you are tracing abruptly changes at point 3.

4. Press and hold **[Alt]** (Win) or **[option]** (Mac) to switch to the Convert Anchor Point Tool , then move the top direction handle of point 3 down to the red star, as shown in Figure C-28.

5. Release [Alt] (Win) or [option] (Mac) to switch back to the Pen Tool, click and drag **position 4** to finish drawing the path, click the Selection Tool , then deselect the path.

   The nose element, as shown in Figure C-29, is an open path.

Tracing the nose, you encountered an abrupt change in direction, followed by a curve. You used the Convert Anchor Point Tool to redirect the direction lines on point 3, simultaneously converting point 3 from smooth to corner and defining the shape of the curved segment that follows.

FIGURE C-28
Use the Convert Anchor Point Tool to redirect the path

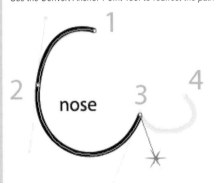

FIGURE C-29
Nose element is an open path

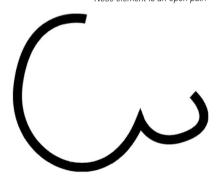

Drawing and Composing an Illustration

FIGURE C-30

Use a scanned sketch as a reference or for tracing

Place a scanned image

1. Click **View** on the menu bar, then click **Fit in Window**.

2. Click **File** on the menu bar, then click **Place**.

3. Navigate to the drive and folder where your Data Files are stored.

4. Click **Snowball Sketch.tif**, then click **Place**.

    A scan of the Snowball Sketch illustration is placed in a bounding box at the center of the artboard.

5. Use the Scale Tool ⬚ to scale the placed file 115%.

    | TIP   You can apply all of the transform tools to placed files.

6. Click the **Selection Tool** ⬚ , move the placed file into the scratch area, then lock it.

7. Draw the remaining elements of the illustration, referring to the sketch in the scratch area or to Figure C-30 for help.

    | TIP   The mouth, eyebrow, and teeth are located in the Nose view.

8. Save your work after you complete each element.

You placed a file of a scanned sketch to use as a reference guide. You scaled the object, dragged it to the scratch area, locked it, then drew the remaining elements of the illustration.

COPY ATTRIBUTES BETWEEN OBJECTS

What You'll Do

▶ You will create four new colors in the Color palette and apply each to one of the illustration elements. Using the Eyedropper and the Paint Bucket Tools, you will paint the remaining items quickly and easily.

Using the Eyedropper and Paint Bucket Tools

Illustrator uses the word **attributes** to refer to that which has been applied to an object that affects its appearance. Typographic attributes, for example, would include font, leading, horizontal scale, etc. Artistic attributes include the fill color, stroke color, and stroke weight.

The Eyedropper and Paint Bucket Tools are handy for applying *all* of an object's attributes to another object. Their icons are particularly apt: The Eyedropper Tool "picks up" an object's attributes, such as fill color, stroke color, and stroke weight, and the Paint Bucket Tool dumps them onto another object.

Adding a Fill to an Open Path

You can think of the letter O as an example of a closed path and the letter U as an example of an open path. Although it seems a bit strange, you are able to add a fill to an open path just as you would to a closed path. The program draws an imaginary straight line between the endpoints of an open path to define where the fill ends. Figure C-31 shows an open path in the shape of a U with a red fill. Note where the fill ends.

FIGURE C-31
A fill color applied to an open path

Apply new attributes to open and closed paths

1. Verify that nothing is selected on the artboard.

2. Create a royal blue color in the Color palette.

3. Fill the arm with the royal blue color, then change its stroke weight to 6 pt.

   > TIP Use the views at the bottom of the View menu to see and select each element you need to work with. The mouth, eyebrow, and teeth are located in the Nose view.

4. Deselect the arm, then create a deep red color in the Color palette.

5. Fill the hatband with the deep red color, then change its stroke weight to 3 pt.

6. Deselect the hatband, then create a flesh-toned color in the Color palette that is 20% magenta and 56% yellow.

7. Fill the head with the flesh tone; don't change the stroke weight.

8. Fill the pompom with white; don't change the stroke weight.

9. Fill the mouth with black; don't change the stroke weight.

10. Compare your work with Figure C-32.

You applied new attributes to five closed paths by creating three new colors, using them as fills, then changing the stroke weight on two of the objects.

FIGURE C-32
New attributes applied to five elements

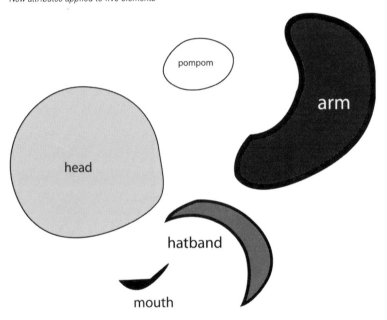

Drawing and Composing an Illustration

FIGURE C-33

Use the Eyedropper Tool to apply the attributes of one object to another . . . with one click!

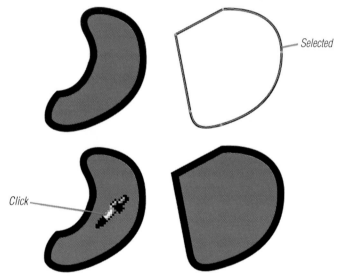

Selected

Click

Copy attributes with the Eyedropper Tool

1. Select the torso.

2. Click the **Eyedropper Tool** , then click the **blue arm**.

   As shown in Figure C-33, the torso takes on the same fill and stroke attributes as the arm.

3. Switch to the Selection Tool , select the hat, then click the **Eyedropper Tool** on the hatband.

4. Select all the unfilled objects, except for the pompom and the eyebrow.

5. Click the **Eyedropper Tool** , then click the **blue arm**.

   The attributes of the arm are applied to all of the selected objects.

You applied the same attributes from one object to another by first selecting the object you wanted to apply the attributes to, then clicking the object with the desired attributes, using the Eyedropper Tool.

Apply attributes with the Paint Bucket Tool

1. Deselect all.

2. Click the **Eyedropper Tool** 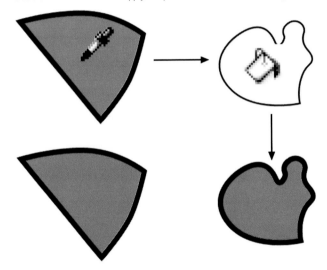, if necessary, then click the **red hat**.

3. Click the **Paint Bucket Tool** in the toolbox.

   | TIP The Paint Bucket Tool is hidden beneath the Eyedropper Tool.

4. Click the **mitten**, as shown in Figure C-34.

   | TIP The Paint Bucket Tool applies the sampled attributes to *unselected* items.

5. Press **[Alt]** (Win) or **[option]** (Mac) to switch to the Eyedropper Tool, then click the **head**.

6. Switch to the Paint Bucket Tool, then click the **nose**.

7. Switch to the Eyedropper Tool, click the **pompom**, switch to the Paint Bucket Tool, then click the **eye**, the **snowball**, and the **teeth**.

8. Switch to the Eyedropper Tool, then click the **mouth**.

(continued)

FIGURE C-34

Use the Paint Bucket Tool to apply sampled attributes to unselected objects

FIGURE C-35

All elements ready to be assembled

9. Switch to the Paint Bucket Tool , then click the **iris** in the middle of the eye.

> TIP You can press [Caps Lock] to use a precise cursor rather than the Paint Bucket icon.

10. Save your work, then compare your screen to Figure C-35.

You used the Eyedropper Tool to sample a filled object. You then clicked the Paint Bucket Tool on another object, which took on the attributes of the sampled object. You used this method to apply color to the remaining objects in the document.

ASSEMBLE AN ILLUSTRATION

What You'll Do

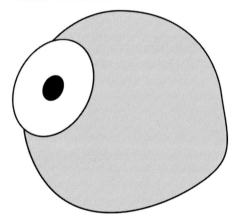

In this lesson, you will arrange the elements that you drew in Lesson 4 to create a composed illustration.

Assembling an Illustration

Illustrator's basic stacking order design is sophisticated enough to compose any illustration. Assembling an illustration with multiple objects will test your fluency with the stacking order commands: Bring to Front, Send to Back, Bring Forward, Send Backward, Paste in Front, Paste in Back, Group, Lock, Unlock All, Hide, and Show All. The sequence in which you draw the elements determines the stacking order (newer elements are in front of older ones), so you'll almost certainly need to adjust the stacking order when assembling the elements. Locking and hiding placed elements will help you to protect the elements when they are positioned correctly.

FIGURE C-36
Eye positioned on the head

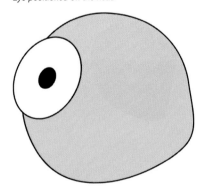

FIGURE C-37
Second eye is a copy of the first

FIGURE C-38

Nose pasted in front of the left eye

*The nose behind
the left eye*

*The nose in front
of the left eye*

FIGURE C-39

Eyebrow positioned over the right eye

FIGURE C-40

All elements in position

Assemble the illustration

1. Select and copy all the elements on the artboard.

2. Create a new CMYK Color document that is 9" × 9", then save it as **Snowball Assembled**.

3. Paste the copied elements into the Snowball Assembled document.

4. Deselect all objects, select the head, click **Object** on the menu bar, point to **Arrange**, then click **Send to Back**.

5. Group the eye and the iris, then position the eye on the head as shown in Figure C-36.

6. Click the **eye**, press **[Alt]** (Win) or **[option]** (Mac), then drag to create a copy of it, as shown in Figure C-37.

7. Position the nose on the face, cut the nose, select the left eye, then paste in front.

   The nose is pasted in the same position, but now it is in front of the eye, as shown in Figure C-38.

8. Select the teeth, then bring them to the front.

9. Position the teeth over the mouth, then group them.

10. Position the mouth and the teeth on the head, and the eyebrow over the right eye, as shown in Figure C-39.

11. Finish assembling the illustration, using Figure C-40 as a guide, then save your work.

   TIP Use the Object menu and the Arrange menu command to change the stacking order of objects, as necessary.

You assembled the illustration, utilizing various commands to change the stacking order of the individual elements.

STROKE OBJECTS FOR ARTISTIC EFFECT

What You'll Do

In this lesson, you will experiment with strokes of varying weight and attributes, using options in the Stroke palette. You will then apply pseudo-strokes to all of the objects to create dramatic stroke effects.

Defining Joins and Caps

In addition to applying a stroke weight, you use the Stroke palette to define other stroke attributes, including joins and caps, and whether a stroke is solid or dashed. Figure C-41 shows the Dashed Line utility in the Stroke palette.

Caps are applied to the ends of stroked paths. The Stroke palette offers three choices: Butt Cap, Round Cap, and Projecting Cap. Choose Butt Cap for squared ends and Round Cap for rounded ends. Generally, round caps are more appealing to the eye.

The projecting cap applies a squared edge that extends the anchor point at a distance that is one-half the weight of the stroke. With a projecting cap, the weight of the stroke is equal in all directions around the line. The projecting cap is useful when you align two anchor points at a right angle, as shown in Figure C-42.

FIGURE C-41
The Stroke palette

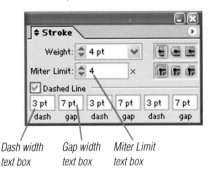

Dash width
text box

Gap width
text box

Miter Limit
text box

FIGURE C-42
Projecting caps are useful when segments meet at right angles

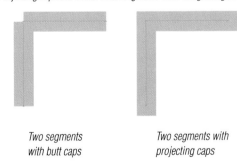

Two segments
with butt caps

Two segments with
projecting caps

Drawing and Composing an Illustration

When two stroked paths form a corner point, **joins** define the appearance of the corner. The default is a miter join, which produces stroked lines with pointed corners. The round join produces stroked lines with rounded corners, and the bevel join produces stroked lines with squared corners. The greater the weight of the stroke, the more apparent the join will be, as shown in Figure C-43.

Defining the Miter Limit

The miter limit determines when a miter join will be squared off to a beveled edge. The miter is the length of the point, from the inside to the outside. The length of the miter is not the same as the stroke weight. When two stroked paths are at an acute angle, the length of the miter will greatly exceed the weight of the stroke, which results in an extreme point that can be very distracting.

The default miter limit is 4, which means that when the length of the miter reaches 4 times the stroke weight, the program will automatically square it off to a beveled edge. Generally, you will find the default miter limit satisfactory, but remain conscious of it when you draw objects with acute angles, such as stars and triangles. Figure C-44 shows the impact of a miter limit on a stroked star with acute angles.

FIGURE C-43
Three types of joins

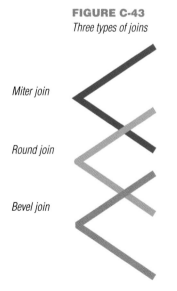

Miter join

Round join

Bevel join

FIGURE C-44
Miter limit affects the length of stroked corner points

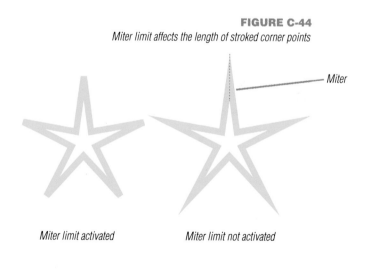

— Miter

Miter limit activated   *Miter limit not activated*

Creating a Dashed Stroke

A dashed stroke is like any other stroked path in Illustrator, except that its stroke has been broken up into a sequence of dashes separated by gaps. The Stroke palette offers you the freedom to customize dashed or dotted lines; enter the lengths of the dashes and the gaps between them in the six dash and gap text boxes. You can create a maximum of three different sizes of dashes separated by three different sizes of gaps. The pattern you establish will be repeated across the length of the stroke.

When creating dashed strokes, remain conscious of the cap choice in the Stroke palette. Butt caps create familiar square dashes, and round caps create rounded dashes. Creating a dotted line requires round caps. Figure C-45 shows two dashed lines using the same pattern but with different caps applied.

Creating Pseudo-Stroke Effects

Strokes around objects—especially black strokes—often contribute much to an illustration in terms of contrast, dimension, and dramatic effect. To that end, you may find the Stroke palette to be limited.

Sometimes, the most effective stroke is no stroke at all. A classic technique that designers have used since the early versions of Illustrator is the "pseudo-stroke," or false stroke. Basically, you place a black-filled copy behind an illustration element, then distort the black element with the Direct Selection Tool so that it "peeks" out from behind the element in varying degrees.

This technique, as shown in Figure C-46, is relatively simple to execute and can be used for dramatic effect in an illustration.

FIGURE C-45

Caps are an important factor in determining the appearance of a dashed line

Round caps

Butt caps

FIGURE C-46

The "pseudo-stroke" effect

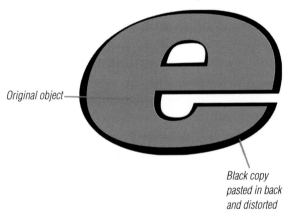

Original object

Black copy pasted in back and distorted

FIGURE C-47
Bevel joins applied to paths

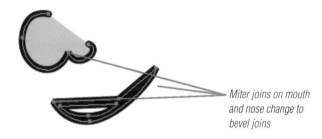

Miter joins on mouth and nose change to bevel joins

FIGURE C-48
Round joins applied to paths

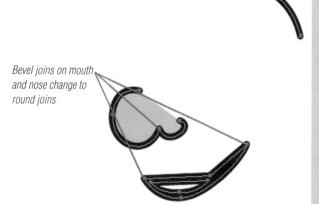

Bevel joins on mouth and nose change to round joins

1. Select the eyebrow, the nose, and the mouth.

2. Click **Select** on the menu bar, then click **Inverse**.

   The selected items are now deselected, and the deselected items are selected.

3. Hide the selected items.

4. Select all, then change the stroke weight to 3 pt.

5. Click the **Stroke palette list arrow**, click **Show Options** if necessary, then click the **Round Cap button** ⊑.

   The caps on open paths are rounded.

6. Click the **Bevel Join button** ⊏.

   The miter joins on the mouth and nose change to a bevel join, as shown in Figure C-47.

7. Click the **Round Join button** ⊏.

   The bevel joins on the mouth and nose change to a round join. See Figure C-48.

8. Remove the stroke from the teeth.

   TIP Use the Direct Selection Tool to select the teeth, since they are grouped to the mouth.

You hid elements so you could focus on the eyebrow, nose, and mouth. You applied round caps to the open paths and round joins to the corner points.

Create a dashed stroke

1. Show all objects, then select all.
2. Deselect the snowball, then hide the selected items.

   The snowball should be the only element showing.
3. Select the snowball, then change the stroke weight to 4 pt.
4. Click the **Dashed Line check box** in the Stroke palette.
5. Experiment with different dash and gap sizes.
6. Toggle between butt and round caps.

   The dashes change from rectangles to ovals.
7. Enter 1 pt dashes and 4 pt gaps.
8. Click the **Round Cap button** 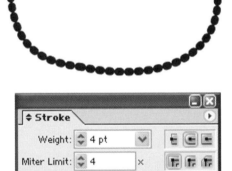, compare your snowball to the one shown in Figure C-49, then show all of the objects that are currently hidden.

You applied a dashed stroke to the snowball object and noted how a change in caps affected the dashes.

FIGURE C-49
Creating a dashed stroke using the Stroke palette

FIGURE C-50

A black copy peeking out beneath the front object

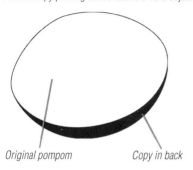

Original pompom   Copy in back

FIGURE C-51

Pompom with the pseudo-stroke effect

FIGURE C-52

Completed illustration

Create pseudo-strokes

1. Copy the pompom, then paste in back.

2. Apply a black fill to the copy.

   > TIP The copy is still selected behind the original white pompom, making it easy to apply the black fill.

3. Click the **white pompom**, then remove the stroke.

4. Lock the white pompom.

5. Using the Direct Selection Tool ▸, select the bottom anchor point on the black copy.

6. Use the arrow keys to move the anchor point 5 pts down, away from the white pompom, using Figure C-50 as a reference.

   The black copy is increasingly revealed as its size is increased beneath the locked white pompom.

7. Move the left anchor point 4 pts to the left.

8. Move the top anchor point 2 pts up, then deselect.

   Your work should resemble Figure C-51.

9. Using the same methods, and Figure C-52 as a reference, create distorted black copies behind all the remaining elements except the torso, the mouth, and the eyebrow.

10. Save your work, then close Snowball Assembled.

You created black copies behind each element, then distorted them, using the Direct Selection Tool and the arrow keys, to create the illusion of uneven black strokes around the object.

Draw straight lines.

1. Create a new 6" × 6" CMYK Color document, then save it as **Montag**.
2. Place the Montag Sketch.tif from the drive and folder where your Data Files are stored into the Montag document.
3. Position the sketch in the center of the artboard, then lock it.
4. Set the fill color to [None] and the stroke to 1 pt black.
5. Use the Pen Tool to create a four-sided polygon for the neck. (*Hint*: Refer to Figure C-53 as a guide.)
6. Draw six whiskers.
7. Save your work.

Draw curved lines.

1. Using the Pen Tool, draw an oval for the eye.
2. Draw a crescent moon shape for the eyelid.
3. Draw an oval for the iris.
4. Save your work.

Draw elements of an illustration.

1. Trace the left ear.
2. Trace the hat.
3. Trace the nose.
4. Trace the left jowl.
5. Trace the right jowl.
6. Trace the tongue.
7. Trace the right ear.
8. Trace the head.
9. Save your work.

Copy attributes between objects.

1. Unlock the placed sketch and hide it.
2. Fill the hat with red.
3. Fill the right ear with 9C/18M/62Y.
4. Fill the nose with black.
5. Fill the eye with white.
6. Select the tongue.
7. Click the Eyedropper Tool, then click the hat.
8. Select the iris.
9. Click the Eyedropper Tool, then click the nose.
10. Deselect all.
11. Click the Eyedropper Tool, then click the right ear.
12. Click the Paint Bucket Tool, then click the neck, the head, the eyelid, the two jowls, and the left ear.
13. Save your work.

Assemble an illustration.

1. Send the neck to the back of the stacking order, then lock it.
2. Send the head to the back, then lock it.
3. Send the left ear to the back, then lock it.
4. Bring the hat to the front.
5. Bring the right ear to the front.
6. Select the whiskers, group them, then bring them to the front.
7. Select the tongue, then cut it.
8. Select the right jowl, then apply the Paste in Back command.
9. Bring the nose to the front.
10. Select the eye, the eyelid, and the iris, then group them.
11. Drag and drop a copy of the eye group. (*Hint*: Press and hold [Alt] (Win) or [option] (Mac) as you drag the eye group.)
12. Select the right jowl.
13. In the Color palette, add 10% K to darken the jowl.
14. Use the Color palette to change the fills on other objects to your liking.
15. Save your work.

Stroke objects for artistic effect.

1. Make the caps on the whiskers round.
2. Change the whiskers' stroke weight to .5 pt.
3. Change the whiskers to dashed lines with small gaps.
4. Unlock all.
5. Select the neck and change the joins to round.
6. Apply pseudo-strokes to the illustration. (*Hint*: Copy and paste the elements behind themselves, fill them with black, lock the top objects, then use the Direct Selection Tool to select anchor points on the black-filled copies. Use the arrow keys on the keyboard to move the anchor points. The black copies will peek out from behind the elements in front.)
7. Click Object on the menu bar, then click Unlock All.
8. Delete the Montag Sketch file behind your illustration.
9. Save your work, compare your illustration to Figure C-53, then close Montag.

FIGURE C-53
Completed Skills Review

The owner of The Blue Peppermill Restaurant has hired your design firm to take over all of their marketing and advertising, saying they need to expand their efforts. You request all of their existing materials—slides, prints, digital files, brochures, business cards, etc. Upon examination, you realize that they have no vector graphic version of their logo. Deciding that this is an indispensable element for future design and production, you scan in a photo of their signature peppermill and trace it.

1. Create a new 6" × 6" CMYK Color document, then save it as **Peppermill Vector**.
2. Place the Peppermill.tif file into the Peppermill Vector document. (*Hint*: The Peppermill.tif file is in the Chapter C Data Files folder.)
3. Scale the placed image 150%, then lock it.
4. Set your fill color to [None], and your stroke to 2 pt black.
5. Using the Zoom Tool, create a selection box around the round element at the top of the peppermill to zoom in on it.
6. Using the Pen Tool, trace the peppermill, then fill it with white.
7. When you finish tracing, tweak the path if necessary, then save your work.

8. Unlock the placed image and cut it from the document.

FIGURE C-54
Completed Project Builder 1

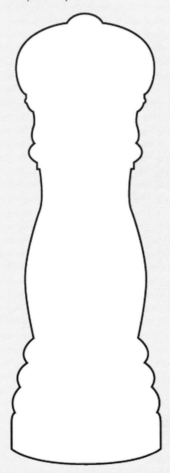

9. Save your work, compare your illustration to Figure C-54, then close Peppermill Vector.

USAchefs.com, your client of three years, contacts you with bad news. They have accidentally deleted their Illustrator "chef logo" from the backup server. They need the vector graphic to produce many of their materials. Their first designer has all the original files, but he has retired to a small island in the Caribbean and cannot be contacted. They want to know if there's anything you can do to recreate the vector graphic.

1. Connect to the Internet, go to *www.course.com*, navigate to the page for this book, click the Online Companion link, then click the link for this chapter.
2. Right-click (Win) or [control] click (Mac) the logo of the chef, click Save Picture As, then save it in your Chapter C Solution Files folder, keeping the same name.
3. Create a new 6" × 6" CMYK Color document, then save it as **USAchefs Logo**.
4. Place the chef logo file into the document and lock it.
5. Zoom in on the chef logo so that you are at a comfortable view for tracing. (*Hint*: Use the Zoom Tool to create a selection box around the logo.)
6. Set your fill color to [None] and your stroke to 1 pt red.
7. Use the Ellipse Tool to trace the head.

8. Use the Pen Tool to trace the hat and the perimeter of the body.
9. Trace the two triangles that define the chef's inner arms.
10. Unlock the placed image and cut it from the document.
11. Fill the head, the hat, and the body with white.

FIGURE C-55
Completed Project Builder 2

12. Fill the triangles with black.
13. Remove the strokes from the objects.
14. Create a black rectangle that encompasses the chef objects.
15. Send the rectangle to the back of the stacking order.
16. Save your work, compare your illustration to Figure C-55, then close USAchefs Logo.

Your design firm is contacted by a company called Stratagem with a request for a proposal. They manufacture molds for plastic products. The terms of the request are as follows: You are to submit a design for the shape of the bottle for a new dishwashing liquid. You are to submit a single image that shows a black line defining the shape. The line art should also include the nozzle. The size of the bottle is immaterial. The design is to be "sophisticated, so as to be in visual harmony with the modern home kitchen." The name of the product is "Sleek."

1. Go to the grocery store and purchase bottles of dishwashing liquid whose shape you find interesting.
2. Use the purchases for ideas and inspiration.
3. Sketch your idea for the bottle's shape on a piece of paper.
4. Scan the sketch and save it as a TIFF file.
5. Create a new Illustrator document, then save it as **Sleek**.
6. Place the scan in the document, then lock it.
7. Trace your sketch, using the Pen Tool.
8. When you are done tracing, delete the sketch from the document.
9. Tweak the line to define the shape to your specifications.
10. Use the Average dialog box to align points to perfect the shape.
11. Save your work, compare your illustration to Figure C-56, then close Sleek.

FIGURE C-56
Completed Design Project

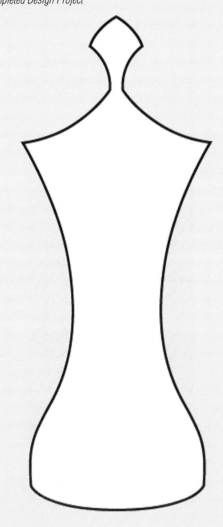

Drawing and Composing an Illustration

You teach a class on digital graphics to junior designers. To stimulate a discussion on shape and design theory, you show the 20-minute "Dawn of Man" sequence of the classic sci-fi movie *2001: A Space Odyssey*.

Note: The central point of this exercise—a group discussion of shapes and their role in the history of mankind—can be had with or without screening *2001: A Space Odyssey*. Should you choose to not show the film, simply omit questions 1 and 2. Rephrase Question 8 so that individuals are instructed to draw any abstract shape from their own imaginations.

The sequence begins millions of years ago with a group of apes, presumably on the African plains. One day, *impossibly*, a tall, black, perfectly rectangular slab appears out of nowhere on the landscape. At first the apes are afraid of it, afraid to touch it. Eventually, they accept its presence.

Later, one ape looks upon a femur bone from a dead animal. With a dawning understanding, he uses the bone as a tool, first to kill for food, and then to kill another ape from an enemy group. Victorious in battle, the ape hurls the bone into the air. The camera follows it up, up, up, and—in one of the most famous cuts in film history—the image switches from the white bone in the sky to the similar shape of a white spaceship floating in space.

1. Have everyone in the group share his or her feelings upon first seeing the "monolith" (the black rectangular slab). What percentage of the group was frightened? Does the group sense that the monolith is good, evil, or neutral?

2. Discuss the sudden appearance of the straight-edged, right-angled monolith against the landscape. What words describe the shapes of the landscape in contrast to the monolith?

3. Have the group debate a central question: Do perfect shapes exist in nature, or are they created entirely out of the imagination of human beings?

4. If perfect shapes exist—if they are *real*—can you name one example? If they are not real, how is it that humankind has proven so many concepts in mathematics that are based on shapes, such as the Pythagorean theorem?

5. What advancements and achievements of humankind have their basis in peoples' ability to conceive of abstract shapes?

6. Can it be said legitimately that the ability to conceive abstract shapes is an essential factor that distinguishes humankind from all the other species on the planet?

7. Create a new document, then save it as **Shape**.

8. Give the members of the group 10 minutes to draw, in Adobe Illustrator, any shape that they remember from the opening sequence, *except* the monolith. When the group has finished, take a count: How many rendered a shape based on the bone?

9. Save your work, compare your results to Figure C-57, then close Shape.

FIGURE C-57
Completed Group Project

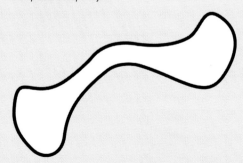

CHAPTER D

TRANSFORMING AND DISTORTING OBJECTS

1. Transform objects.

2. Offset and outline paths.

3. Create compound paths.

4. Work with the Pathfinder palette.

5. Create clipping masks.

CHAPTER D

TRANSFORMING AND DISTORTING OBJECTS

Putting It All Together

Think about a conventional toolbox. You've got a hammer, nails, a few different types of screwdrivers, screws, nuts, bolts, a wrench, and probably some type of measuring device. That set of tools could be used to build anything from a birdhouse to a dollhouse to a townhouse to the White House.

A carpenter uses tools in conjunction with one another to create something, and that something is defined far less by the tools than by the imagination of the carpenter. But even the most ambitious imagination is tempered by the demands of knowing which tool to use, and when.

Illustrator offers a number of sophisticated transform "tools" in the "toolbox," and the metaphor is apt. Each "tool" provides a basic function: a rotation, a scale, a precise move, a precise offset, or a reflection. It is you, the designer, who uses those tools in combination with each other, with menu commands, and with other features, to realize your vision. And like the carpenter's, your imagination will be tempered by your ability to choose the right tool at the right time.

This is one of the most exciting aspects of working in Illustrator. After you learn the basics, there's no map, no blueprint for building an illustration. It's your skills, your experience, your smarts, and your ingenuity that lead you toward your goal. No other designer will use Illustrator's tools quite the same way you do. People who appreciate digital imagery understand this salient point: Although the tools are the same for everyone, the result is *personal*. It's *original*.

Tools You'll Use

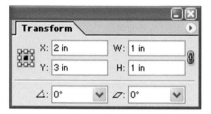

Shear Tool

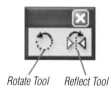

Rotate Tool   Reflect Tool

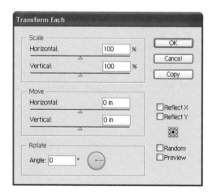

TRANSFORM OBJECTS

What You'll Do

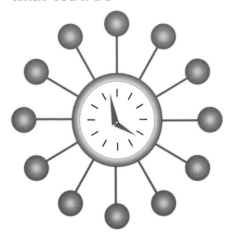

▶ *In this lesson, you will explore options for transforming objects with the transform tools.*

Defining the Transform Tools

When you change an object's size, shape, or position on the artboard, Illustrator defines that operation as a transformation. Transforming objects is a fundamental operation in Illustrator, one you will perform countless times.

Because transformations are so essential, Illustrator provides a number of methods for doing them. As you gain experience, you will naturally adopt the method that you find most comfortable or logical.

The toolbox contains five transform tools: the Rotate, Scale, Reflect, Shear, and Free Transform Tools. The essential functions of the Rotate and Scale Tools are self-explanatory. The Reflect Tool "flips" an object across an imagined axis, usually the horizontal or the vertical axis. However, you can define any diagonal as the axis for a reflection. In Figure D-1, the illustration has been flipped to create the illusion of a reflection in a mirror.

The Shear Tool slants—or skews—an object on an axis that you specify. By definition, the Shear Tool distorts an object. Of the five transform tools, you will probably use the Shear Tool the least, although it is useful for creating a cast shadow or for creating the illusion of depth.

Finally, the Free Transform Tool offers you the ability to perform quick transformations and distort objects in perspective.

Defining the Point of Origin

All transformations are executed in relation to a fixed point; in Illustrator, that point is called the **point of origin**. For each transform tool, the default point of origin is the selected object's center point. However, that point can easily be changed to another point on the object, or to a point elsewhere on the artboard. For example, when a majorette twirls a baton, that baton is essentially rotating on its own center. By contrast, the petals of a daisy rotate around a central point that is not positioned on any of the petals themselves, as shown in Figure D-2.

There are four basic methodologies for making transformations with the transform tools. First, select an object, then do one of the following:

- Click a transform tool, then click and drag anywhere on the artboard. The object will be transformed using its center point as the point of origin.
- Double-click the transform tool, which opens the tool's dialog box. Enter the values by which you want to execute the transformation, then click OK to execute the transformation, or click Copy to create a transformed copy of the selected object. The point of origin for the transformation will be the center point of the selected object.
- Click a transform tool, then click the artboard. Where you click the artboard defines the point of origin for the transformation. Click and drag anywhere on the artboard, and the selected object will be transformed from the point of origin that you clicked.
- Click a transform tool, Press [Alt] (Win) or [option] (Mac), then click the artboard. The tool's dialog box opens, allowing you to enter precise values for the transformation. When you click OK or Copy, the selected object will be transformed from the point of origin that you clicked.

FIGURE D-1

The Reflect Tool flips an image horizontally or vertically

FIGURE D-2

All transformations are executed from a point of origin

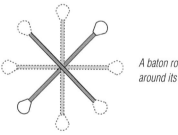

A baton rotating around its own center

Petals of a daisy rotate around a central point

Working with the Transform Again Command

An essential command related to transformations is Transform Again. Whenever you execute a transformation, such as scale or rotate, you can repeat the transformation quickly by using the Transform Again command. This is also true for moving an object. Using the Transform Again command will move an object the same distance and angle entered in the last step. The quickest way to use the Transform Again command is to press [Ctrl][D] (Win) or ⌘[D] (Mac). To remember this quick key command, think D for *duplicate*.

A fine example of the usefulness of the Transform Again command is its ability to make transforming in small increments easy. For example, let's say you have created an object to be used in an illustration, but you haven't decided how large the object should be. Simply scale the object by a small percentage—say 5%—then repeatedly press the quick key for Transform Again. The object gradually gets bigger, and you can choose the size that pleases your eye. If you transform again too many times, and the object gets too big, simply undo repeatedly to decrease the object's size in the same small increments.

Using the Transform Each Command

The Transform Each command allows you to transform multiple objects individually, as shown in Figure D-3. The Transform Each dialog box offers options to move, scale, rotate, or reflect an object, among others. All of them will affect an object independent of the other selected objects.

Without the Transform Each command, applying a transformation to multiple objects simultaneously will often yield an undesired effect. This happens because the selected objects are transformed as a group—in relation to a single point of origin—and are repositioned on the artboard.

FIGURE D-3
Multiple objects rotated individually

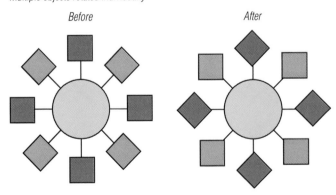

The eight squares are rotated on their own center points

Using the Free Transform Tool

The Free Transform Tool applies an eight-handled bounding box to a selected image. You can move those handles to scale and shear the object. You can click and drag outside the object to rotate the object.

With the Free Transform Tool, transformations always use the selected object's center point as the point of origin. In general, the role of the Free Transform Tool is to make quick, inexact transformations. However, the tool has a powerful, hidden ability. Moving the handles in conjunction with certain keyboard commands allows you to distort the object or distort the object in perspective, as shown in Figure D-4. Press and hold [Shift][Ctrl] (Win) or [Shift]⌘ (Mac) to distort the image. Press and hold [Shift][Alt][Ctrl] (Win) while dragging to distort in perspective. On a Macintosh, press and hold [Shift][option]⌘ to execute the same transformation.

Using the Transform Palette

The Transform palette displays information about the size, orientation, and location of one or more selected objects. You can type new values directly into the Transform palette to modify selected objects. All values in the palette refer to the bounding boxes of the objects, whether the bounding box is visible or not. You can also identify—in the Transform palette—the reference point on the bounding box from which the object will be transformed. To reflect an object vertically or horizontally using the Transform palette, click the Transform palette list arrow, then choose the appropriate menu item, as shown in Figure D-5.

FIGURE D-4
Use the Free Transform Tool to distort objects in perspective

FIGURE D-5
The Transform palette

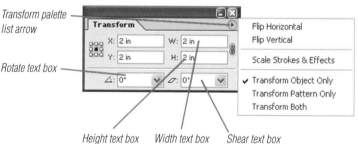

Transform palette list arrow

Rotate text box

Height text box   Width text box   Shear text box

Rotate an object around a defined point

1. Open AI D-1.ai, then save it as **Mod Clock**.

2. Click the **Selection Tool** ⭡, click the **brown line**, then click the **Rotate Tool** ↻.

3. Press and hold **[Alt]** (Win) or **[option]** (Mac), then click the **bottom anchor point** of the line to set the point of origin for the rotation.

   With a transform tool selected, pressing [Alt] (Win) or [option] (Mac) and clicking the artboard defines the point of origin and opens the tool's dialog box.

4. Enter **30** in the Angle text box, then click **Copy**.

5. Press **[Ctrl][D]** (Win) or ⌘ **[D]** (Mac) ten times so that your screen resembles Figure D-6.

   [Ctrl][D] (Win) or ⌘[D] (Mac) is the quick key for the Transform Again command.

6. Select all twelve lines, group them, send them to the back, then hide them.

7. Select the small orange circle, click **View** on the menu bar, then click **Outline**.

(continued)

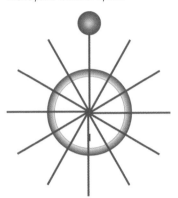

X and Y coordinates

The X and Y coordinates of an object indicate the object's horizontal (X) and vertical (Y) locations on the artboard. These numbers, which appear in the Transform palette, represent the horizontal and vertical distance from the bottom-left corner of the artboard. The current X and Y coordinates also depend on the specified reference point. Nine reference points are listed to the left of the X and Y text boxes in the Transform palette. Reference points are those points of a selected object that represent the four corners of the object's bounding box, the horizontal and vertical centers of the bounding box, and the center point of the bounding box. (You do not need to have the bounding box option turned on to view any of the reference point coordinates.)

FIGURE D-7

Twelve circles rotated around a central point of origin

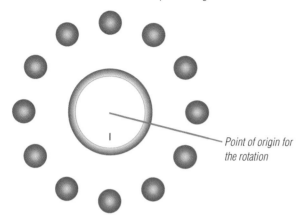

Point of origin for
the rotation

FIGURE D-8

Completed illustration

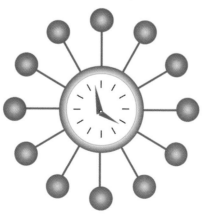

8. Click the **Rotate Tool** ↻ , press and hold **[Alt]** (Win) or **[option]** (Mac), then click the **center point** of the larger circle to set the point of origin for the next rotation.

   The small circle will rotate around the center point of the larger circle.

   > TIP   Outline mode is especially useful for rotations; center points are visible and easy to target as points of origin.

9. Enter **30** if necessary, click **Copy**, apply the Transform Again command ten times, then switch to Preview mode.

   Your screen should resemble Figure D-7.

10. Select the small black vertical dash, then transform again eleven times.

    The dash is also rotated around the center point of the larger circle, since a new point of origin has not been set.

11. Unlock the hands in the scratch area, then move them onto the clock face.

12. Show all, then deselect all to reveal the twelve segments, as shown in Figure D-8.

13. Save your work, then close the Mod Clock.

You selected a point on the brown line, then rotated eleven copies of the object around that point. Second, you defined the point of origin for a rotation by clicking the center point of the larger circle, then rotated eleven copies of the smaller circle and the dash around that point.

Use the Shear Tool

1. Open AI D-2.ai, then save it as **Shear**.

2. Select all, copy, paste in front, then fill the copy with 60% Black.

3. Click the **Shear Tool** ⊡.

   | TIP The Shear Tool is hidden behind the Scale Tool.

4. Press and hold **[Alt]** (Win) or **[option]** (Mac), then click the **bottom-right anchor point** of the letter R to set the origin point of the shear and open the Shear dialog box.

5. Enter **45** in the Shear Angle text box, verify that the Horizontal option button is checked, then click **OK**.

   Your screen should resemble Figure D-9.

6. Click the **Scale Tool** ⊡.

7. Press **[Alt]** (Win) or **[option]** (Mac), then click any bottom anchor point or segment on the sheared objects to set the point of origin for the scale and open the Scale dialog box.

8. Click the **Non-Uniform option button**, enter **100** in the Horizontal text box, enter **50** in the Vertical text box, then click **OK**.

9. Send the sheared objects to the back.

10. Apply a 1 pt black stroke to the orange letters, deselect, then compare your screen to Figure D-10.

11. Save your work, then close the Shear document.

You created a shadow effect using the Shear Tool.

The objects are sheared on a 45° angle in relation to a horizontal axis

The shadow is "cast" from the letters in the foreground

FIGURE D-11

Use the Reflect Tool for illustrations that demand exact symmetry

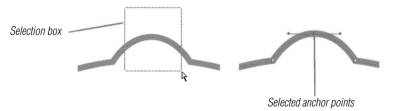

FIGURE D-12

Selecting two anchor points with the Direct Selection Tool

Selection box

Selected anchor points

1. Open AI D-3.ai, then save it as **Reflect**.

2. Select all, then zoom in on the top anchor point.

3. Click the **Reflect Tool** .

   The Reflect Tool is hidden behind the Rotate Tool.

4. Press **[Alt]** (Win) or **[option]** (Mac), then click the **top anchor point** to set the point of origin for the reflection.

5. Click the **Vertical option button**, then click **Copy**.

   A copy is positioned, reflected across the axis that you defined, as shown in Figure D-11.

6. Deselect all, then click the **Direct Selection Tool** .

7. Using Figure D-12 as a guide, drag a selection box around the top two anchor points to select them.

8. Click **Object** on the menu bar, point to **Path**, click **Average**, click the **Both option button**, then click **OK**.

9. Click **Object** on the menu bar, point to **Path**, click **Join**, click the **Smooth option button**, then click **OK**.

10. Select the bottom two anchor points, average them on both axes, then join them in a smooth point to close the path.

11. Save your work, then close the Reflect document.

You created a reflected copy of a path, then averaged and joined two pairs of open points.

OFFSET AND OUTLINE PATHS

What You'll Do

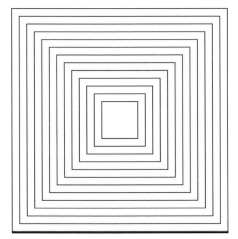

 In this lesson, you will use the Offset Path command to create concentric squares and the Outline Stroke command to convert a stroked path into a closed path.

Using the Offset Path Command

Simply put, the Offset Path command creates a copy of a selected path set off by a specified distance. The Offset Path command is useful when working with closed paths—making concentric shapes or making many copies of a path at a regular distance from the original.

Figure D-13 shows two sets of concentric circles. By definition, the word **concentric** refers to objects that share the same centerpoint, as the circles in both sets do. The set on the left was made with the

Scale Tool, applying an 85% scale and copy to the outer circle, then repeating the transformation ten times. Note that with each successive copy, the distance from the copy to the previous circle decreases. The set on the right was made by offsetting the outside circle -.125", then applying the same offset to each successive copy. Note the different effect.

When you offset a closed path, a positive value creates a larger copy outside the original; a negative value creates a smaller copy inside the original.

Using the Outline Stroke Command

The Outline Stroke command converts a stroked path into a closed path that is the same width as the original stroked path.

This operation is useful if you want to apply a gradient to a stroke. It is also a useful design tool, allowing you to modify the outline of an object more than if it were just a stroke. Also, it is often easier to create an object with a single heavy stroke—for example the letter S—and then convert it to a closed path than it would be to try to draw a closed path directly, as shown in Figure D-14.

FIGURE D-13
Two sets of concentric circles

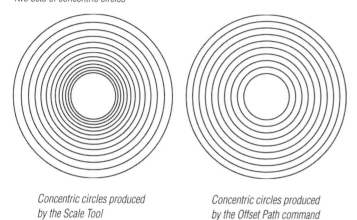

Concentric circles produced by the Scale Tool

Concentric circles produced by the Offset Path command

FIGURE D-14
The Outline Stroke command converts a stroked path to a closed object

Offset a path

1. Open AI D-4.ai, then save it as **Squares**.

2. Select the square.

3. Click **Object** on the menu bar, point to **Path**, then click **Offset Path**.

4. Enter **-.125** in the Offset text box, then click **OK**.

   | TIP   Be sure that your General Units Preference is set to inches.

   A negative value reduces the area of a closed path; a positive value increases the area.

5. Apply the Offset Path command four more times, using the same value.

   | TIP   The Transform Again command does not apply to the Offset Path command because it is not one of the transform tools.

6. Deselect all, save your work, compare your screen to Figure D-15, then close the Squares document.

You used the Offset Path command to create concentric squares.

Concentric squares created with the Offset Path command

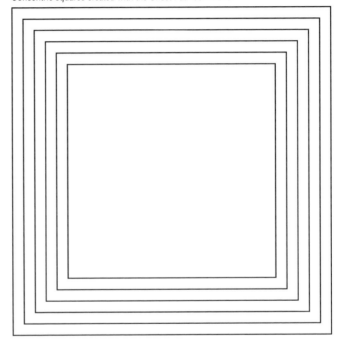

Transforming and Distorting Objects

FIGURE D-16

The Outline Stroke command converts any stroked path into a closed path

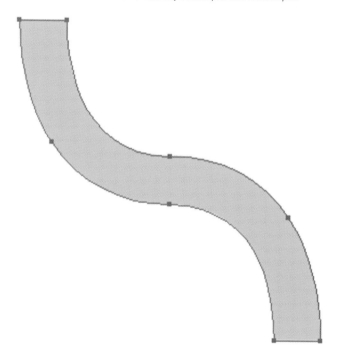

Convert a stroked path to a closed path

1. Open AI D-5.ai, then save it as **Outlined Stroke**.

2. Select the path, then change the weight to 36 pt.

3. Click **Object** on the menu bar, point to **Path**, then click **Outline Stroke**.

   The full weight of the stroke is converted to a closed path, as shown in Figure D-16.

4. Save your work, then close the Outlined Stroke document.

You applied a heavy weight to a stroked path, then converted the stroke to a closed path, using the Outline Stroke command.

CREATE COMPOUND PATHS

What You'll Do

 In this lesson, you will explore the role of compound paths for practical use and for artistic effects.

Defining a Compound Path

Practically speaking, you make a compound path to create a "hole" or "holes" in an object. As shown in Figure D-17, if you were drawing the letter "D," you would need to create a hole in the outlined shape, through which you could see the background. To do so, select the object in back (in this case, the black outline that defines the letter) and the object in front (the yellow object that defines the hole) and apply the Make Compound Path command. When compounded, a "hole" appears where the two objects overlap.

The overlapping object still exists, however. It is simply *functioning* as a transparent hole in conjunction with the object behind it. If you move the front object independently, as shown in Figure D-18, it yields an interesting result. Designers have seized upon this effect and have run with it, creating complex and eye-catching graphics, which Illustrator calls compound shapes.

It is important to understand that when two or more objects are compounded, Illustrator defines them as *one* object. This sounds strange at first, but the concept is as familiar to you as the letter D. You identify the letter D as one object. Although it is drawn with two paths—one defining the outside edge, the other defining the inside edge—it is nevertheless a single object.

Compound paths function as groups. You can select and manipulate an individual element with the Direct Selection Tool, but you cannot change its appearance attributes independently. Compound paths can

be released and returned to their original component objects by applying the Release Compound Path command.

FIGURE D-17
The letter D is an example of a compound path

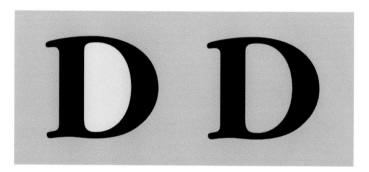

FIGURE D-18
Manipulating compound paths can yield interesting effects

Create compound paths

1. Open AI D-6.ai, then save it as **Simple Compound**.

2. Cut the red circle in the middle of the illustration, then undo the cut.

   The red circle creates the illusion that there's a hole in the life-preserver ring.

3. Select the red background object, then change its fill to the Ocean Blue gradient in the Swatches palette.

   The illusion is lost; the red circle no longer appears as a hole in the life preserver.

4. Select both the white "life preserver" circle and the red circle in the center.

5. Click **Object** on the menu bar, point to **Compound Path**, then click **Make**.

   As shown in Figure D-19, the two circles are compounded, with the top circle functioning as a "hole" in the larger circle behind it.

6. Move the background object left and right, and up and down behind the circles.

   The repositioned background remains visible through the compounded circles.

7. Deselect all, save your work, then close the Simple Compound document.

You selected two concentric circles and made them into one compound path, which allowed you to see through to the gradient behind the circles.

FIGURE D-19

A compound path creates the effect of a hole where two or more objects overlap

Transforming and Distorting Objects

Create special effects with compound paths

1. Open AI D-7.ai, then save it as **Compound Path Effects**.

2. Select all.

   The light blue square is locked and does not become part of the selection.

3. Click **Object** on the menu bar, point to **Compound Path**, then click **Make**.

4. Deselect, click the **Direct Selection Tool** ▸., then click the **edge** of the large blue circle.

5. Click the **center point** of the circle, then scale the circle 50% so that your work resembles Figure D-20.

6. Click **Select** on the menu bar, then click **Inverse**.

7. Click **Object** on the menu bar, point to **Transform**, then click **Transform Each**.

8. Enter **225** in the Horizontal and Vertical text boxes in the Scale section of the Transform Each dialog box, click **OK,** then deselect all.

   Your work should resemble Figure D-21.

9. Using the Direct Selection Tool ▸., click the edge of the center circle, click its center point to select the entire circle, then scale the circle 120%.

10. Apply the Transform Again command twice, then compare your screen to Figure D-22.

11. Deselect all, save your work, then close Compound Path Effects.

You made a compound path out of five small circles and one large circle. You then manipulated the size and location of the individual circles to create interesting designs.

FIGURE D-22

Simple compound paths can yield stunning visual effects

Each of the five small circles is scaled, using its own center point as the point of origin

WORK WITH THE PATHFINDER PALETTE

What You'll Do

▶ *In this lesson, you will use pathfinders to create compound shapes from simple shapes.*

Defining a Compound Shape

Like a compound path, a **compound shape** is two or more paths that are combined in such a way that "holes" appear wherever paths overlap.

The term compound shape is used to distinguish a complex compound path from a simple one. Compound shapes generally assume an artistic rather than a practical role. To achieve the effect, compound shapes tend to be composed of multiple objects. You can think of a compound shape as an illustration composed of multiple compound paths.

Understanding Essential Pathfinder Filters

The **pathfinders** are a group of preset operations that help you combine paths in a variety of ways. Pathfinders are very useful operations for creating complex or irregular shapes from basic shapes. In some cases, the pathfinders will be a means to an end in creating an object; in others, the operation they provide will be the end result you want to achieve.

Illustrator offers ten pathfinders. Pathfinders can be applied to overlapping objects using the Effect menu or the Pathfinder palette. For the purposes of drawing and creating new objects, the following five pathfinders are essential; compare each with Figure D-23.

- **Add to shape area:** Converts two or more overlapping objects into a single, merged object.
- **Subtract from shape area:** Where objects overlap, deletes the frontmost object(s) from the backmost object in a selection of overlapped objects.
- **Intersect shape areas:** Creates a single, merged object from the area where two or more objects overlap.

- **Minus Back:** The opposite of Subtract; deletes the backmost object(s) from the frontmost object in a selection of over-lapped objects.
- **Divide:** Divides an object into its component filled faces. Illustrator defines a "face" as an area undivided by a line segment.

FIGURE D-23

Five essential pathfinders

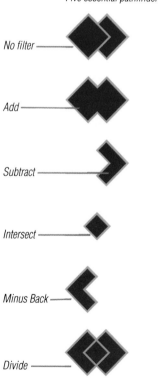

No filter

Add

Subtract

Intersect

Minus Back

Divide

Using the Pathfinder Palette

The Pathfinder palette contains ten buttons for applying pathfinders and for creating compound shapes, as shown in Figure D-24. As you learned earlier, a compound shape is a complex compound path. You can create a compound shape by overlapping two or more objects, then clicking one of the four shape mode buttons in the top row of the Pathfinder palette, or clicking the Pathfinder palette list arrow, then clicking Make Compound Shape. The four shape mode buttons share the *same* buttons as four essential pathfinders: Add to shape area (Add), Subtract from shape area (Subtract), Intersect shape areas (Intersect), and Exclude overlapping shape areas (Exclude). To apply one of these four pathfinders, you must press and hold [Alt] (Win) or [option] (Mac), then click the desired pathfinder button.

FIGURE D-24
The Pathfinder palette

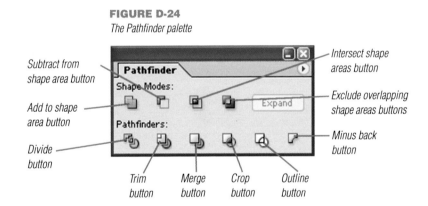

Subtract from shape area button

Add to shape area button

Divide button

Trim button

Merge button

Crop button

Outline button

Intersect shape areas button

Exclude overlapping shape areas buttons

Minus back button

Applying Shape Modes and Pathfinders

Figure D-25 shows a square overlapped by a circle. If you apply the Subtract pathfinder, the overlapped area is deleted from the square. The circle, too, is deleted, as shown in Figure D-26. The result is a simple reshaped object.

With the same starting image, if you apply the Subtract shape mode, the same visual effect is achieved. However, the resulting object is a compound shape, as shown in Figure D-27. This time, the circle is not deleted; it is functioning as a hole or a "knockout" wherever it overlaps the square. The relationship is dynamic: You can move the circle independently at any time to change its effect on the square and the resulting visual effect.

That dynamic relationship is the essential factor that distinguishes applying a pathfinder from applying a shape mode.

When pathfinders are applied to objects, the result is final. When shape modes are applied to objects, the resulting compound shape can be manipulated endlessly.

Figure D-28 shows a group of objects converted into a compound shape using the Make Compound Shape command in the Pathfinder palette.

FIGURE D-25
Two overlapping objects

FIGURE D-26
The effect of applying the Subtract pathfinder

FIGURE D-27
The effect of applying the Subtract shape mode

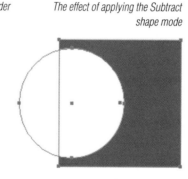

FIGURE D-28
A compound shape

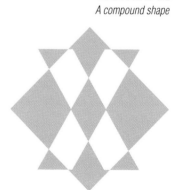

Apply the Add to shape area pathfinder

1. Open AI D-8.ai, then save it as **Heart Parts**.

2. Click **Window** on the menu bar, then click **Pathfinder**, if necessary.

3. Select both circles, press and hold **[Alt]** (Win) or **[option]** (Mac), then click the **Add to shape area button** in the Pathfinder palette.

   The two objects are united. For brevity's sake, Add to shape area will be referred to as Add.

4. Move the diamond shape up so that it overlaps the united circles, as shown in Figure D-29.

5. Click the **Delete Anchor Point Tool**, then delete the top anchor point of the diamond.

6. Select all, press and hold **[Alt]** (Win) or **[option]** (Mac), then click the **Add button** so that your screen resembles Figure D-30.

7. Remove the black stroke, then apply a red fill to the new object.

8. Draw a rectangle that covers the "hole" in the heart, then fill it with black, as shown in Figure D-31.

9. Select all, press **[Alt]** (Win) or **[option]** (Mac), then click the **Add button**.

10. Double-click the **Scale Tool**, then apply a non-uniform scale of 90% on the horizontal axis and 100% on the vertical axis.

You created a single heart-shaped object from two circles and a diamond shape using the Add to shape area pathfinder.

FIGURE D-29
A diamond shape in position for the Add pathfinder

FIGURE D-30
The diamond shape and the object behind it are united with the Add pathfinder

FIGURE D-31
A heart shape created by applying the Add pathfinder to three objects

FIGURE D-32

Circle overlaps the square

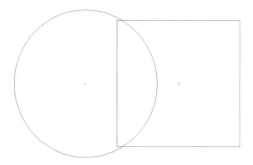

FIGURE D-33

Right circle is a reflected copy of the left one

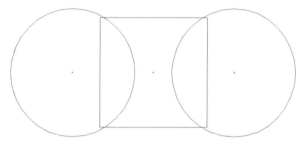

FIGURE D-34

The final shape, with all elements united by the Add pathfinder

Apply the Subtract from shape area pathfinder

1. Rotate the black heart shape 180°, then hide it.

2. Create a square that is 1.5" × 1.5" without a fill color and with a 1 pt black stroke.

3. Create a circle that is 1.75" in width and height.

4. Switch to Outline mode.

5. Move the circle so that it overlaps the square, as shown in Figure D-32.

6. Verify that the circle is still selected, click the **Reflect Tool** , press **[Alt]** (Win) or **[option]** (Mac), then click the **center point** of the square.

7. Click the **Vertical option button**, then click **Copy** so that your work resembles Figure D-33.

8. Select all, press **[Alt]** (Win) or **[option]** (Mac), then click the **Subtract from shape area button** in the Pathfinder palette.

9. Switch to Preview mode, then apply a black fill to the new object.

10. Show all, then overlap the new shape with the black heart shape to make a spade shape.

11. Select all, apply the Add pathfinder, then deselect.

   Your work should resemble Figure D-34.

You overlapped a square with two circles, then applied the Subtract from shape area pathfinder to delete the overlapped areas from the square. You used the Add to shape area pathfinder to unite the new shape with a heart-shaped object to create a spade shape.

Apply the Intersect shape areas pathfinder

1. Click the **Star Tool** ☆ , then click the **artboard**.

2. Enter **1** in the Radius 1 text box, **3** in the Radius 2 text box, and **8** in the Points text box, then click **OK**.

3. Apply a yellow fill to the star and remove any stroke, if necessary.

4. Use the Align palette to align the center points of the two objects, so that they resemble Figure D-35.

5. Copy the black spade, then paste in front.

   Two black spades are now behind the yellow star; the top one is selected.

6. Press and hold **[Shift]**, then click to add the star to the selection.

7. Click the **Intersect shape areas button** 🔲 in the Pathfinder palette.

   The intersection of the star and the copied spade is now a single closed path. Your work should resemble Figure D-36.

8. Save your work, then close Heart Parts.

You created a star and then created a copy of the black spade-shaped object. You used the Intersect shape areas pathfinder to capture the intersection of the two objects as a new object.

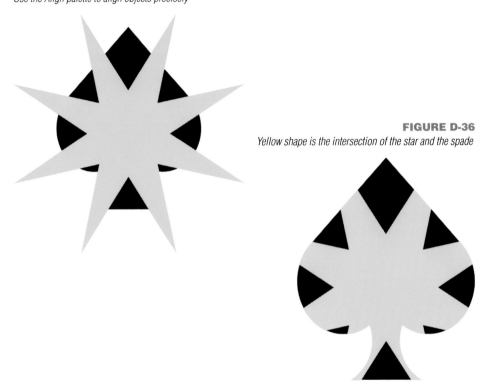

FIGURE D-35
Use the Align palette to align objects precisely

FIGURE D-36
Yellow shape is the intersection of the star and the spade

Working with the Align palette

The Align palette offers a quick and simple solution for aligning selected objects along the axis you specify. Along the vertical axis, you can align selected objects by their rightmost point, leftmost point, or center point. On the horizontal axis, you can align objects by their topmost point, center point, or bottommost point. You can also use the palette to distribute objects evenly along a horizontal or vertical axis. In contrasting the Align palette with the Average command, think of the Average command as a method for aligning anchor points and the Align palette as a method for aligning entire objects.

Blue star is divided into twelve objects by the Divide pathfinder

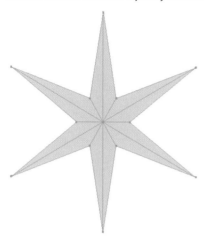

Divide pathfinder is useful for adding dimension

Apply the Divide pathfinder

1. Open AI D-9.ai, then save it as **Divide**.
2. Select the red line, then double-click the **Rotate Tool** ⟳.
3. Enter **30** in the Angle text box, then click **Copy**.
4. Repeat the transformation four times.
5. Select all, then click the **Divide button** 🔲 in the Pathfinder palette.

   The blue star is divided into twelve separate objects, as defined by the red lines, which have been deleted. See Figure D-37.
6. Deselect, click the **Direct Selection Tool** ▸, select the left half of the top point, press **[Shift]**, then select every other object, for a total of six objects.
7. Apply an orange fill to the selected objects.
8. Select the inverse, then apply a yellow fill so that your work resembles Figure D-38.
9. Save your work, then close the Divide document.

You used six lines to define a score pattern, then used those lines and the Divide pathfinder to break the star into twelve separate objects.

Create compound shapes using the Pathfinder palette

1. Open AI D-10.ai, then save it as **Compound Shapes**.

2. Click **View** on the menu bar, then click **Yellow**.

3. Select the two yellow circles, then click the **Exclude overlapping shape areas button** in the Pathfinder palette.

   The area that the top object overlaps becomes transparent.

4. Deselect, click the **Direct Selection Tool**, then move either circle to change the shape and size of the filled areas.

   Figure D-39 shows one effect that can be achieved.

5. Select **Green** from the View menu, select the two green circles, then click the **Intersect shape areas button** in the Pathfinder palette.

   The area not overlapped by the top circle becomes transparent.

6. Deselect, then use the Direct Selection Tool to move either circle to change the shape and size of the filled area.

   Figure D-40 shows one effect that can be achieved.

7. Save your work, then close the Compound Shapes document.

You applied shape modes to two pairs of circles, then moved the circles to create different shapes and effects.

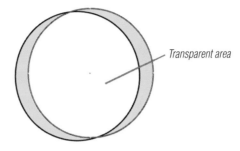

Transparent area

Transparent area

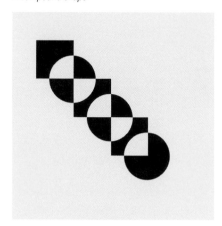

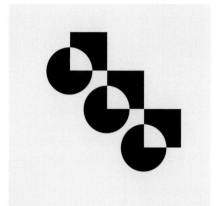

Create special effects with compound shapes

1. Open AI D-11.ai, then save it as **Compound Shape Effects**.

2. Select all, then click the **Exclude overlapping shape areas button** 🔲 in the Pathfinder palette.

   Your work should resemble Figure D-41.

3. Deselect all, click the **Direct Selection Tool** ▶, select the three squares, then move them to the right, as shown in Figure D-42.

4. Drag and drop a copy of the three squares, as shown in Figure D-43.

5. Scale each circle 150% using the Transform Each command.

6. Scale the center circle 200%, then bring it to the front of the stacking order.

7. Click the **Intersect shape areas button** 🔲 in the Pathfinder palette.

   Figure D-44 shows the results of the inter-section. Your final illustration may vary slightly.

   TIP The topmost object affects all the objects behind it in a compound shape.

8. Save your work, then close Compound Shape Effects.

You made three squares and three circles into a compound shape by excluding overlapping shape areas. You then manipulated the size and location of individual elements to create different effects. Finally, you enlarged a circle, brought it to the front, then changed its mode to Intersect. Only the objects that were overlapped by the circle remained visible.

CREATE CLIPPING MASKS

What You'll Do

 In this lesson, you will explore the role of clipping masks for practical use and for artistic effects.

Defining a Clipping Mask

As with compound paths, clipping masks are used to yield a practical result. And as with compound paths, that practical result can be manipulated to create interesting graphic effects.

Practically speaking, you use a clipping mask as a "window" through which you view some or all of the objects behind the mask in the stacking order. When you select any two or more objects and apply the Make Clipping Mask command, the *top object* becomes the mask and the object behind it becomes "masked." You will be able to see only the parts of the masked object that are visible *through* the mask, as shown in Figure D-45. The mask crops the object behind it.

Using Multiple Objects as a Clipping Mask

When multiple objects are selected and the Make Clipping Mask command is applied, the top object becomes the mask. Since every object has its own position in the stacking order, it stands to reason that there can be only one top object.

If you want to use multiple objects as a mask, you can do so by first making them into a compound path. Illustrator regards compound paths as a single object. Therefore, a compound path containing multiple objects can be used as a single mask.

Creating Masked Effects

Special effects with clipping masks are, quite simply, fun! You can position as many objects as you like behind the mask, and position them in such a way that the mask crops them in visually interesting (and eye-popping!) ways. See Figure D-46 for an example.

FIGURE D-45
Clipping mask crops the object behind it

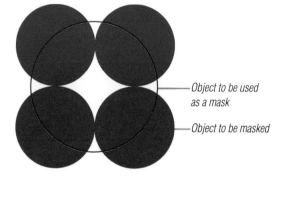

— *Object to be used as a mask*

— *Object to be masked*

— *The result after applying the Make Clipping Mask command*

FIGURE D-46
Masks can be used for stunning visual effects

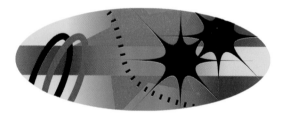

Create a clipping mask

1. Open AI D-12.ai, then save it as **Simple Masks**.

2. Click **View** on the menu bar, then click **Mask 1**.

3. Move the rectangle so that it overlaps the gold spheres, as shown in Figure D-47.

4. Apply the Bring to Front command to verify that the rectangle is in front of all the spheres.

5. Select the seven spheres and the rectangle.

6. Click **Object** on the menu bar, point to **Clipping Mask**, then click **Make**.

7. Deselect, then compare your screen to Figure D-48.

8. Click **View** on the menu bar, then click **Mask 2**.

9. Select the three circles, then move them over the "gumballs."

   The three circles are a compound path.

10. Select the group of gumballs and the three circles, then apply the Make Clipping Path command.

11. Deselect, click **Select** on the menu bar, point to **Object**, then click **Clipping Masks**.

12. Apply a 1 pt black stroke to the masks.

   Your work should resemble Figure D-49.

13. Save your work, then close the Simple Masks document.

You used a rectangle as a clipping mask. Then, you used three circles to mask a group of small spheres, and applied a black stroke to the mask.

FIGURE D-47
Masking objects must be in front of objects to be masked

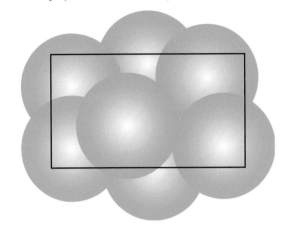

FIGURE D-48
The rectangle masks the gold spheres

FIGURE D-49
A compound path used as a mask

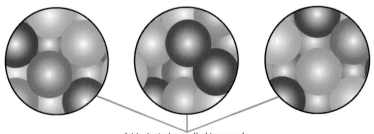

A black stroke applied to a mask

FIGURE D-50
Lining up the letter g

FIGURE D-51
Positioning the magnifying glass

The two objects that make up the magnifying glass are not grouped

FIGURE D-52
A fill and stroke are applied to a mask

The mask

By default, a fill is positioned behind the masked elements, and the stroke is in front of the mask

FIGURE D-53
Large text is masked by the magnifying glass

When a fill is applied to a mask, the fill is positioned behind all the objects that are masked

As the mask moves, different areas of the large text become visible, creating the illusion of a magnifying glass moving over a word

---

Apply a fill to a clipping mask

1. Open AI D-13.ai, then save it as **Magnify**.
2. Move the large outlined text over the small outlined text so that the *g*s align as shown in Figure D-50.
3. Select the smaller text, then hide it.
4. Select the magnifying glass and the handle, then drag them over the letter *g*, as shown in Figure D-51.
5. Deselect all, select only the circle and the text, click **Object** on the menu bar, point to **Clipping Mask**, then click **Make**.

   The circle is the masking object.
6. Deselect, click **Select** on the menu bar, point to **Object**, then click **Clipping Masks**.
7. Use the Swatches palette to apply a light blue fill and a gray stroke to the mask.
8. Change the weight of the stroke to 8 pt, so that your work resembles Figure D-52.
9. Show all, deselect, then compare your screen to Figure D-53.
10. Select the mask only, press and hold **[Shift]**, then click the **magnifying glass handle**.
11. Press the **arrow keys** to move the magnifying glass.
12. Save your work, then close the Magnify document.

You used the circle in the illustration as a clipping mask in combination with the large text. You added a fill and a stroke to the mask, creating the illusion that the small text is magnified in the magnifying glass.

Lesson 5   Create Clipping Masks

Use text as a clipping mask

1. Open AI D-14.ai, then save it as **Mask Effects**.
2. Select the four letters that make the word MASK.

   The word MASK was converted to outlines and ungrouped.
3. Make the four letters into a compound path.
4. Select the compound path and the rectangle behind it.
5. Apply the Make Clipping Mask command, then deselect.
6. Save your work, then compare your text to Figure D-54.

You converted outlines to a compound path, then used the compound path as a mask.

Transforming and Distorting Objects

FIGURE D-55

Curvy object in position to be masked by the letters

FIGURE D-56

Object behind the mask is selected

The rectangle behind
the mask is selected

FIGURE D-57

Curvy object is masked by the letters

MASK

FIGURE D-58

Pasting multiple objects behind a mask yields interesting effects

Use a clipping mask for special effects

1. Position the curvy object with the gradient fill over the mask, as shown in Figure D-55.

2. Cut the curvy object.

3. Use the **Direct Selection Tool** to select the original rectangle behind the mask.

   TIP Click slightly above the mask until you see the rectangle selected, as shown in Figure D-56.

4. Paste in front, then deselect so that your screen resembles Figure D-57.

   The object is pasted in front of the masked rectangle and behind the mask.

5. Click the **Selection Tool**, select the purple dotted line, position it over the letter K, then cut the purple dotted line.

6. Select the mask (rectangle) with the Direct Selection Tool, click **Edit** on the menu bar, then click **Paste in Front**.

7. Using the same technique, mask the other objects on the artboard in any way that you choose.

   When finished, your mask should contain all of the objects, as shown in Figure D-58.

   | TIP Add a stroke to the mask if desired.

8. Save and close Mask Effects.

You created visual effects by pasting objects behind a mask.

Transform objects.

1. Open AI D-15.ai, then save it as **Transformations**.
2. Select "DIVIDE."
3. Scale the text objects non-uniformly: Horizontal = 110% and Vertical = 120%.
4. Rotate the text objects 5°.
5. Shear the text objects 15° on the horizontal axis.
6. Save your work.

Offset and outline paths.

1. Ungroup the text outlines.
2. Using the Offset Path command, offset each letter -.05".
3. Save your work.

Apply Pathfinder filters.

1. Select all.
2. Apply the Divide pathfinder.

3. Fill the divided elements with different colors, using the Direct Selection Tool.
4. Select all, then apply a 1-point stroke. Figure D-59 is an example of the effect. (*Hint*: Enlarge the view of your document window, if necessary.)
5. Save your work, compare your image to Figure D-59, then close the Transformations document.

FIGURE D-59
Completed Skills Review, Part 1

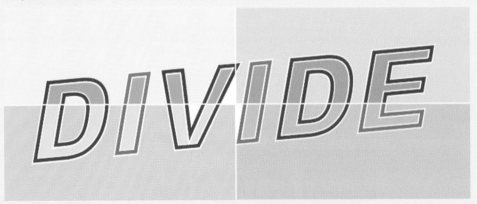

Create compound paths.

1. Open AI D-16.ai, then save it as **Compound Paths**.
2. Select all, then click the Exclude shape mode button.
3. Create a 150% copy of the small square, then transform again two times.
4. Save your work, compare your image to Figure D-60, then close the Compound Paths document.

FIGURE D-60
Completed Skills Review, Part 2

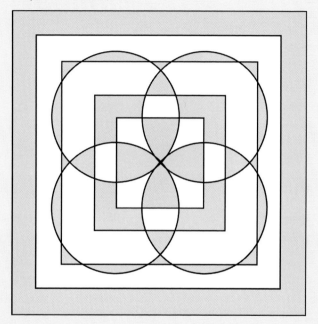

You are entering a contest to design a new stamp. You have decided to use a picture of Mona Lisa, which you have placed in an Illustrator document. You have positioned text over the image. Now, to complete the effect, you want to mimic the perforated edges of a stamp.

1. Open AI D-17.ai, then save it as **Mona Lisa Stamp**.
2. Select all the circles, then make them into a compound path.
3. Add the rectangle to the selection.
4. Apply the Subtract from shape area pathfinder, then deselect all.
5. Save your work, compare your image to Figure D-61, then close Mona Lisa Stamp.

FIGURE D-61
Completed Project Builder 1

Transforming and Distorting Objects

You're contracted to design the logo for Wired Gifts, an online gift site. Your concept is of a geometric red bow. You feel that your idea will simultaneously convey the concepts of gifts and technology.

1. Open AI D-18.ai, then save it as **Wired Gifts**.
2. Switch to Outline mode.
3. Select the small square, click the Rotate Tool, press and hold [Alt] (Win) or [option] (Mac), then click the center of the large square.
4. Enter **18** in the Angle text box, then click Copy.
5. Repeat the transformation 18 times.
6. Delete the large square at the center.
7. Switch to Preview mode.
8. Select all, then fill all the squares with blue.
9. Apply the Divide pathfinder to the selection.
10. Fill the objects with the Red Bow gradient.
11. Delete the object in the center of the bow. (*Hint:* Use the Direct Selection Tool to select the object.)
12. Select all, then remove the black stroke from the objects.
13. Save your work, compare your illustration with Figure D-62, then close Wired Gifts.

FIGURE D-62
Completed Project Builder 2

Transforming and Distorting Objects

You are a fabric designer for a line of men's clothing. The line is known for its conservative patterns and styles. You are asked to supervise a team that will design new patterns for men's ties. You will present your recommended new patterns using Illustrator.

1. Create a new CMYK Color document and name it **Ties**.
2. Create a square, rotate it 45°, then reshape it using the Direct Selection Tool by dragging the top anchor point straight up to create the shape of a tie.
3. Use a square and the Subtract from shape area pathfinder to square off the top of the diamond.
4. Draw a second polygon to represent the tie's knot.
5. Lock the two polygons.
6. Create a small circle, then copy it using the Move dialog box to create a polka dot pattern that exceeds the perimeter of both polygons.
7. Unlock the polygons, then bring them to the front.
8. Create a compound path out of the two polygons.
9. Select all, then use the polygons to mask the polka-dot pattern.
10. Apply a fill to the mask, save your work, compare your image to Figure D-63, then close Ties.

FIGURE D-63
Completed Design Project

Transforming and Distorting Objects

You are the design department manager for a toy company, and your team's next project will be to design a dartboard that will be part of a package of "Safe Games" for kids. The target market is boys and girls ages six to adult. Your team will design only the board, not the darts.

1. Create a new CMYK Color document and name it **Dartboard**.
2. Have part of the group search the Internet for pictures of dartboards.
3. Have two members research the sport of throwing darts. What are the official dimensions of a dartboard? Is there an official design? Are there official colors?
4. The other team members should discuss which colors should be used for the board, keeping in mind that the sales department plans to position it as a toy for both girls and boys.
5. The team should also discuss whether they will use alternate colors even if the research team learns the official colors for a dartboard.
6. Using the skills you learned in this chapter, work together to design a dartboard, using Figure D-64 as a guide.
7. Save your work, compare your image to Figure D-64, then close Dartboard.

FIGURE D-64
Completed Group Project

CHAPTER

WORKING WITH LAYERS

1. Create and modify layers.

2. Manipulate layered artwork.

3. Work with layered artwork.

4. Create a clipping set.

CHAPTER 5
WORKING WITH LAYERS

Designing with Layers

When you're creating complex artwork, keeping track of all the items on the artboard can become quite a challenge. Small items hide behind larger items, and it becomes difficult to find them, select them, and work with them. The Layers palette solves this problem. Using the Layers palette, you organize your work by placing objects or groups of objects on separate layers. Artwork on layers can be manipulated and modified independently from artwork on other layers. The Layers palette also provides effective options to select, hide, lock, and change the appearance of your work. In addition, layers are an effective solution for storing multiple versions of your work in one file.

Tools You'll Use

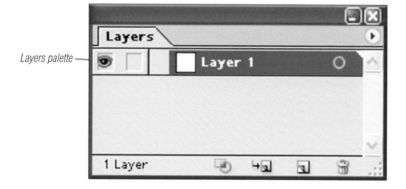

Layers palette —

CREATE AND MODIFY LAYERS

What You'll Do

In this lesson, you will create new layers and explore options in the Layers palette for viewing, locking, hiding, and selecting layers and layered artwork.

Creating Layers and Sublayers

Layers are a smart solution for organizing and managing a complex illustration. For example, if you were drawing a map of your home state, you might put all the interstate freeways on one layer, the local freeways on a second layer, secondary roads on a third layer, and all the text elements on a fourth layer.

As the name suggests, the Layers palette consists of a series of layers. The number of layers that a document can have is limited only by your computer's memory. By default, every Illustrator document is created with one layer, called Layer 1. As you work, you can create new layers and move objects into them, thereby segregating and organizing your work. The first object that is placed on Layer 1 is placed on a sublayer called <Path>. Each additional object placed on the same layer is placed on a separate <Path> sublayer.

Importing an Adobe Photoshop file with layers

When you use the Open command to import a layered Photoshop file into Illustrator CS, you have the option to open that file with its layers intact. In the Photoshop Import dialog box that appears, select *Convert Photoshop layers to objects and make text editable where possible.* When you see the Photoshop file on the Illustrator artboard, open the Illustrator Layers palette and you will see that Illustrator has preserved as much of the Photoshop layer structure as possible.

Each layer has a thumbnail, or miniature picture of the objects on that layer, to the left of the layer name. Thumbnails display the artwork that is positioned on all of the sublayers in the layer. You can change the size of the rows in the Layers palette using the Layers Palette Options dialog box on the Layers palette menu. Layers and sublayers can also be given descriptive names to help identify their contents.

The stacking order of objects on the artboard corresponds to the hierarchy of layers in the Layers palette. Artwork in the top layer is at the front of the stacking order, while artwork in the bottom layer is in the back. The hierarchy of sublayers corresponds to the stacking order of the objects within a single layer.

Illustrator offers two basic ways to create new layers and sublayers. You can click the New Layer or New Sublayer command in the Layers palette menu, or you can click the Create New Layer or Create New Sublayer button in the Layers palette. Figure E-1 shows a simple illustration and its corresponding layers in the Layers palette.

Duplicating Layers

In addition to creating new layers, you can duplicate existing layers by clicking the Duplicate command in the Layers menu, or by dragging a layer or sublayer onto the Create New Layer button in the Layers palette. When you duplicate a layer, all of the artwork on the layer is duplicated as well. Note the difference between this and copying and pasting artwork. When you copy and paste artwork, the copied artwork is pasted on the same layer.

FIGURE E-1
Layers palette

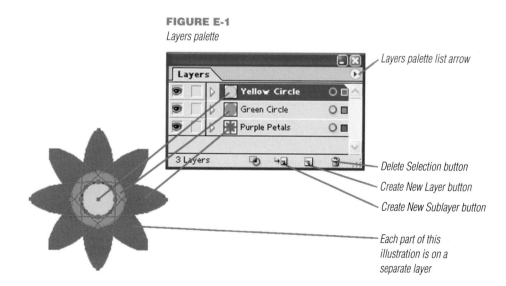

Layers palette list arrow

Delete Selection button

Create New Layer button

Create New Sublayer button

Each part of this illustration is on a separate layer

Setting Layer Options

The Layer Options dialog box offers a wealth of options for working with layered artwork, many of which are not available to you unless you are working with layers. You can name a layer, and you can also set a color for the layer. When an object is selected, its selection marks will be the same color as specified for the layer, making it easy to differentiate layers of artwork on the artboard.

Also in the Layer Options dialog box are options for locking, unlocking, showing, and hiding artwork on the layer. When you lock a layer, all the objects on the layer are locked and protected. When the Show check box is checked, all the artwork that is contained in the layer is displayed on the artboard. When the Show check box is not checked, the artwork is hidden.

Buttons in the Layers palette represent ways to lock, unlock, hide, and show artwork on each layer, making it unnecessary to use the Layer Options dialog box to activate these functions. The Toggles Visibility button (the eye) lets you hide and show layers, and the Toggles Lock button (the padlock) lets you lock and unlock layers.

The Preview option displays all the artwork on a layer in Preview mode. When the Preview option is not activated, the artwork is displayed in Outline mode. Thus, with layers, some elements on the artboard can be in Preview mode, while others are in Outline mode.

The Print option allows you to choose whether or not to print a layer. This feature is useful for printing different versions of the same illustration. The Dim Images to option reduces the intensity of bitmap images that are placed on the artboard. Dimming a bitmap often makes it easier to trace an image.

Use the Template option when you want to use the artwork on a layer as the basis for a new illustration—for example, if you want to trace the artwork. By default, a template layer is locked and cannot be printed.

Selecting Artwork on Layers and Sublayers

When you select an object on the artboard, its layer is selected (highlighted) in the Layers palette, and the Indicates Selected Art button appears, as shown in Figure E-2. Selecting a layer or sublayer in the Layers palette does not select the artwork on that layer.

Changes that you make to layers in the Layers palette affect the artwork on those layers. For example, if you delete a layer, the artwork on the layer will be deleted. The artwork on a layer will be duplicated if the layer is duplicated. Changing a layer's position in the layers hierarchy will move the artwork forward or backward in the stacking order.

Duplicating the artwork on the artboard does not duplicate the layer that the artwork is on. If you delete all the artwork on a layer, you are left with an empty layer. *A layer is never automatically created, copied, or deleted, regardless of what you do to the artwork on the layer.*

The same is *not* true for sublayers. If you delete or copy artwork that is on a sublayer, the *sublayer* is deleted or copied, respectively.

Selecting All Artwork on a Layer

The Select All command makes it easy to select every object on the artboard in one step. At times, however, you will want to select every object on a layer or sublayer, not every object on the artboard. To select all the artwork on a single layer or sublayer, click the far-right side of a layer to activate the Indicates Selected Art button. This is the same button that appears when you click an object on the artboard to show on which layer or sublayer the object is placed.

FIGURE E-2

The chair on the artboard and in the Layers palette

Selection marks for chair are red, the Chair layer's assigned color

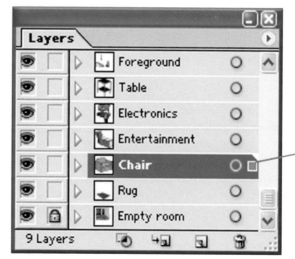

Indicates Selected Art button for Chair layer

Create a new layer

1. Open AI E-1.ai, then save it as **Living Room**.

2. Open AI E-2.ai, then save it as **Showroom**.

   You will work with two documents during this lesson.

3. Click the **Selection Tool** ▸, select the chair, then copy it.

4. Click **Window** on the menu bar, then click **Living Room**.

   ┃ TIP Using the Window menu is an easy way to switch between open documents.

5. Click **Window** on the menu bar, then click **Layers** to select it, if necessary.

   The Layers palette opens, showing two layers. The Empty room layer contains the artwork you see on the artboard. The objects on the Foreground layer are hidden.

6. Click the **Create New Layer button** ▧ in the Layers palette.

   A new layer named Layer 3 appears above the Foreground layer.

7. Click **Edit** on the menu bar, then click **Paste**.

   The chair artwork is pasted into Layer 3.

8. Position the chair on the artboard as shown in Figure E-3.

You created a new layer using the Create New Layer button in the Layers palette, then pasted an object into that new layer.

Chair positioned on its own layer

Thumbnail of chair artwork on Layer 3

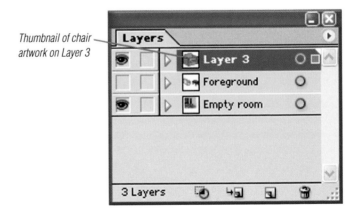

FIGURE E-4
Layer Options dialog box

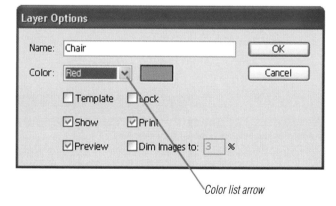

Color list arrow

1. Double-click **Layer 3**.
2. Name the layer **Chair**, then click **OK**.

   The Layers palette reflects the name change.
3. Double-click the **Chair layer**.
4. Click the **Color list arrow**, click **Red**, as shown in Figure E-4, then click **OK**.

   Note that the selection marks on the chair are now red, reflecting the new selection color for the Chair layer.
5. Deselect the chair.

You used the Layer Options dialog box to rename Layer 3 and assign it a color.

Select items on a layer and lock a layer

1. Click the **chair** with the Selection Tool ▶.

   Note that the Indicates Selected Art button appears when the chair is selected, as shown in Figure E-5.

   > TIP The Indicates Selected Art button is the same color as its layer.

2. Deselect the chair.

   The Indicates Selected Art button disappears.

3. Click the right side of the Chair layer where you saw the Indicates Selected Art button.

   The Indicate Selected Art button appears, and the chair artwork is selected.

4. Click either of the two mauve walls in the illustration.

   When an object is selected on the artboard, the layer on which the selected object is placed is highlighted in the Layers palette.

5. Double-click the **Empty room layer**, click the **Lock check box**, then click **OK**.

   The Toggles Lock button 🔒 appears on the Empty room layer, indicating that all the objects on the Empty room layer are locked. See Figure E-6.

You noted the relationship between a selected item and its corresponding layer in the Layers palette. You activated the Indicates Selected Art button and selected the artwork on the Chair layer. You then locked the Foreground layer.

Indicates Selected Art button identifies the layer of a selected object

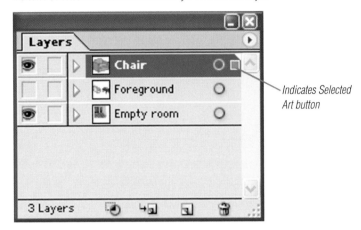

Indicates Selected Art button

FIGURE E-6
Toggles Lock button identifies a locked layer

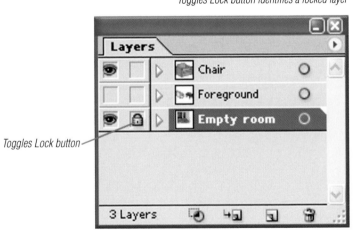

Toggles Lock button

Show and hide layers

1. Double-click the **Foreground layer**.

2. Click the **Show check box**, then click **OK**.

   The objects on the Foreground layer become visible, and the Toggles Visibility button 👁 appears on the Foreground layer.

3. Click the **Toggles Visibility button** 👁 on the Foreground layer to hide the objects.

4. Click the **Toggles Visibility button** (in its off state) ☐ on the Foreground layer to show the objects.

   > TIP The Toggles Visibility and Toggles Lock buttons appear as empty gray squares in their off state.

5. Click the **Toggles Lock button** (in its off state) ☐ on the Foreground layer.

   The **Toggles Lock button** 🔒 appears.

6. Click the **Toggles Visibility button** 👁 on the Foreground layer to hide the objects.

   Your Layers palette should resemble Figure E-7.

7. Save your work.

You used the Toggles Visibility button in the Layers palette to toggle between showing and hiding the artwork on two layers. You also locked the Foreground layer.

FIGURE E-7
Foreground layer is locked and hidden

The absence of the Toggles Visibility button indicates that this layer is hidden

The Toggles Lock button indicates that this layer is locked

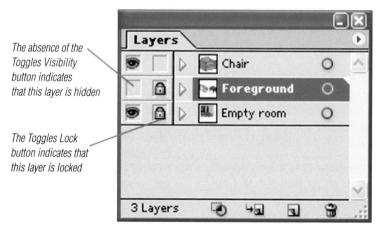

MANIPULATE LAYERED ARTWORK

What You'll Do

In this lesson, you will learn methods for manipulating layers to change the display of layered artwork. You will change the order of layers in the palette, merge layers, work with sublayers, and move objects between layers.

Changing the Order of Layers and Sublayers

The hierarchy of the layers in the Layers palette determines how objects on the artboard overlap. All the objects on a given layer are behind the objects on the layer above it and in front of the objects on the layer beneath it. Multiple objects within a given layer overlap according to their stacking order and can be repositioned with the standard stacking order commands.

To change the position of a layer or sublayer in the hierarchy, simply drag it up or down in the palette. Small black triangles and a heavy horizontal line identify where the layer will be repositioned, as shown in Figure E-8. When you reposition a layer, its sublayers move with it.

Merging Layers

When you have positioned artwork to your liking using multiple layers and sublayers, you will often want to consolidate those layers to simplify the palette. First, you must select the layers that you want to merge. Press [Ctrl] (Win) or $\mathcal{H}$ (Mac) to select multiple layers. Once you have selected the layers that you want to merge, apply the Merge Selected command in the Layers palette menu. When you merge layers, all the artwork from one or more layers moves onto the layer that was last selected before the merge.

Be careful not to confuse merging layers with condensing layers. Condensing layers is simply the process of dragging one layer into another. The repositioned layer becomes a sublayer of the layer it was dragged into.

Defining Sublayers

Whenever you have one or more objects on a layer, you by definition have **sublayers**. For example, if you draw a circle and a square on Layer 1, it will automatically have two sublayers—one for the square, one for the circle. The layer is the sum total of its sublayers.

As soon as the first object is placed on a layer, a triangle appears to the left of the layer name, indicating that the layer contains sublayers. Click the triangle to expand the layer and see the sublayers, then click it again to collapse the layer and hide the sublayers.

Working with Sublayers

When you place grouped artwork into a layer, a sublayer is automatically created with the name <Group>. A triangle appears on the <Group> sublayer, which, when clicked, exposes the sublayers—one for every object in the group, as shown in Figure E-9.

Dragging Objects Between Layers

Sublayers are the easiest objects to move between layers: You can simply drag and drop a sublayer from one layer to another.

You can drag artwork from one layer to another by dragging the Indicates Selected Art button. Select the artwork on the artboard that you want to move; the layer is selected, and the Indicates Selected Art button appears. Drag the button to the destination layer or sublayer, as shown in Figure E-10. If you drag the Indicates Selected Art button to a layer, the artwork becomes the top sublayer in the layer. If you drag the Indicates Selected Art button to a

sublayer, the artwork is grouped with the object already on the sublayer.

If you don't feel comfortable dragging artwork between layers, you have two other options for moving objects between layers. You can simply cut and paste artwork from one layer to another by selecting the object that you want to move, cutting it from the artboard, selecting the layer you wish to place it on, then pasting. You can also use the Send to Current Layer command. Select the artwork you want to move, click the name of the destination layer to make it the active layer, click Object on the menu bar, point to Arrange, then click Send to Current Layer.

FIGURE E-8
Changing the order of layers

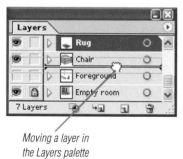

Moving a layer in the Layers palette

FIGURE E-9
A <Group> sublayer

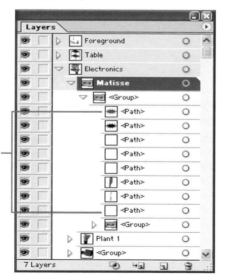

Each object in a group is placed on its own sublayer

FIGURE E-10
Dragging a sublayer to another layer

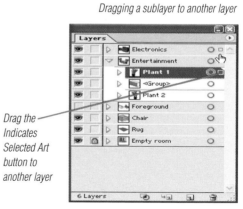

Drag the Indicates Selected Art button to another layer

Change the hierarchy of layers

1. Use the Window menu to switch to the Showroom document, copy the rug, then return to the Living Room document.

2. Press **[Ctrl]** (Win) or ⌘ (Mac), then click the **Create New Layer button** 🔲 in the Layers palette.

   Pressing [Ctrl] (Win) or ⌘ (Mac) creates a new layer at the top of the layer list.

3. Click **Edit** on the menu bar, then click **Paste**.

   The rug is pasted into the new layer because it is the active—or "targeted"—layer.

4. Name the new layer **Rug**, then position the rug artwork with a corner of it hanging slightly off the artboard, as shown in Figure E-11.

5. Click and drag the **Rug layer** and position it below the Chair layer until you see a double black line with small triangles beneath the Chair layer, as shown in Figure E-12, then release the mouse.

   The rug artwork is now positioned below the chair artwork.

You created a new layer at the top of the Layers palette. You pasted artwork into that layer, then moved the layer below another layer in the hierarchy so that the artwork on the two layers overlapped properly on the artboard.

FIGURE E-11
The Rug layer is at the top of the layers hierarchy

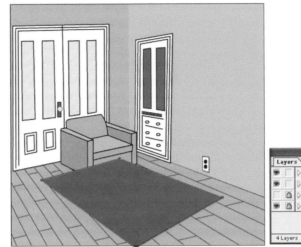

FIGURE E-12
Changing the hierarchy of layers

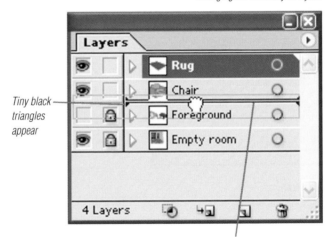

Tiny black triangles appear

Double black line appears beneath the Chair layer

FIGURE E-13

Sculpture artwork positioned on top of the end table

FIGURE E-14

Foreground and Sculpture layers merged

Merged layer

1. Switch to the Showroom document, copy the sculpture, then return to the Living Room document.

2. Press **[Ctrl]** (Win) or ⌘ (Mac), then click the **Create New Layer button** ⬜.

3. Paste the sculpture into the new layer, then name the layer **Sculpture**.

4. Show the Foreground layer, then position the sculpture artwork on the brown end table, as shown in Figure E-13.

5. Deselect the sculpture, then drag the **Foreground layer** above the Sculpture layer in the Layers palette.

6. Unlock the Foreground layer.

7. Click the **Sculpture layer** to select it, press **[Ctrl]** (Win) or ⌘ (Mac), then click the **Foreground layer**.

   When merging layers, the last layer selected becomes the merged layer.

8. Click the **Layers palette list arrow**, then click **Merge Selected**.

   The objects from both layers are merged into the Foreground layer; the Sculpture layer is deleted.

   TIP Layers must be showing and unlocked in order to be merged.

9. Compare your screen to Figure E-14.

   Don't worry that your sculpture is temporarily behind the table.

You merged the Sculpture and the Foreground layers.

Work with sublayers

1. Expand the Foreground layer by clicking the **triangle** ▷ to the left of the layer.

   Three sublayers, all named <Group>, are revealed.

2. Expand the sofa <Group> sublayer by clicking the **triangle** ▷ to the left of it.

   The five paths that compose the sofa are revealed.

3. Select the sofa artwork on the artboard.

   The Indicates Selected Art buttons appear for each of the selected paths, as shown in Figure E-15.

4. Click the **triangle** ▽ to the left of the sofa <Group> sublayer to collapse it, then deselect the sofa.

5. Double-click the **sofa <Group> sublayer**, name it **Sofa**, then click **OK**.

6. Name the sculpture sublayer **Sculpture**, then name the end table sublayer **End Table**.

7. Move the Sculpture sublayer above the End Table sublayer so that your Layers palette resembles Figure E-16.

   Notice that the sculpture artwork is on top of the end table.

8. Click the **triangle** ▽ to the left of the Foreground layer to hide the three sublayers, then hide the Foreground layer.

You viewed sublayers in the Foreground layer. You then renamed the three sublayers in the Foreground layer and rearranged the order of the Sculpture and the End Table sublayers.

Each path in the sofa <Group> sublayer is selected

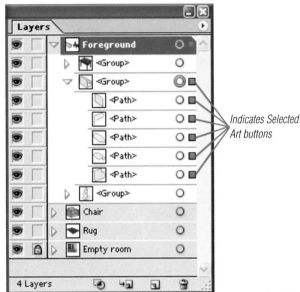

Indicates Selected
Art buttons

FIGURE E-16
Sculpture layer moved above the End Table sublayer

FIGURE E-17
Cabinet and plant are on the same layer

FIGURE E-18
Moving the Plant 2 sublayer

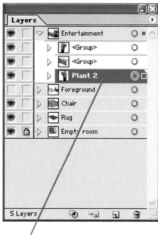

Plant 2 sublayer

FIGURE E-19
The reflected copy of the plant in position

The new plant is positioned behind the cabinet

FIGURE E-20
The reflected copy of the plant, scaled and pruned

Create new sublayers

1. Switch to the Showroom document, copy the cabinet, then return to the Living Room document.
2. Press **[Ctrl]** (Win) or ⌘ (Mac), then click the **Create New Layer button** 🗗 .
3. Name the new layer **Entertainment**, select Violet as the layer color, then click **OK**.
4. Paste the cabinet artwork into the new layer.
5. Copy the plant from the Showroom document, then paste the plant artwork into the Entertainment layer.
6. Position the cabinet artwork and the plant artwork as shown in Figure E-17.
7. Deselect all, expand the Entertainment layer, then select the plant artwork on the artboard.
8. Double-click the **Reflect Tool** 🔁 , click the **Vertical option button**, then click **Copy**.

   The reflected copy of the plant is placed on a new sublayer above the original plant sublayer.
9. Rename the new sublayer **Plant 2**.
10. Move the Plant 2 sublayer to the bottom of the Entertainment sublayer hierarchy, as shown in Figure E-18.
11. Click the **Selection Tool** ▶ , then move the new plant artwork into the position shown in Figure E-19.
12. Scale the new plant artwork 85%, delete or move some leaves on it so that it's not an obvious copy of the original plant, then compare your screen to Figure E-20.

You created and moved new sublayers.

Move objects between layers

1. Switch to the Showroom document, copy the electronics images, then return to the Living Room document.

2. Create a new layer at the top of the hierarchy, name it **Electronics**, choose Magenta as its color, then click **OK**.

3. Paste the electronics on the Electronics layer, then position the electronics artwork on the cabinet.

   The plant on the right needs to be positioned in front of the electronics for the visual to be realistic.

4. Name the top sublayer in the Entertainment layer **Plant 1**, then select the Plant 1 artwork on the artboard.

   The Indicates Selected Art button appears in the Plant 1 sublayer.

5. Drag the **Indicates Selected Art button** from the Plant 1 sublayer to the Electronics layer, as shown in Figure E-21.

   The Plant 1 sublayer moves into the Electronics layer. The Plant 1 sublayer automatically becomes the top sublayer in the Electronics layer.

6. Switch to the Showroom document, copy the Matisse, return to the Living Room document, then create a new layer at the top of the hierarchy, named **Matisse**.

7. Paste the Matisse artwork into the new layer, then position it as shown in Figure E-22.

(continued)

FIGURE E-21
Moving a sublayer from one layer to another

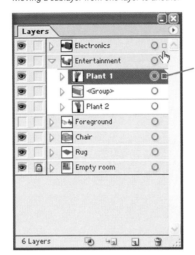

Drag the Indicates Selected Art button to the Electronics layer

FIGURE E-22
The Matisse in position on its own layer

Working with Layers

Moving the Matisse layer into the Electronics layer

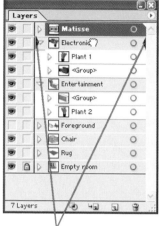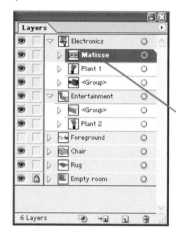

The Matisse layer becomes a sublayer of the Electronics layer

Large black triangles

FIGURE E-24

The lamp and table in position

New Table and Lamp layers

8. Drag the Matisse layer on top of the Electronics layer.

   Two large, black triangles appear on the Electronics layer when the Matisse layer is on top of it, as shown in Figure E-23. The Matisse layer is moved into the Electronics layer as the topmost sublayer.

9. Create new layers for the lamp and the table, copy and paste the lamp and table artwork from the Showroom document to the new layers, then position the artwork so that your illustration resembles Figure E-24.

10. Save your work.

You created a new layer named Electronics, dragged the Plant 1 sublayer into the Electronics layer by dragging its Indicates Selected Art button to the Electronics layer. You then moved the Matisse layer into the Electronics layer by dragging it on top of the Electronics layer.

WORK WITH LAYERED ARTWORK

What You'll Do

 In this lesson, you will explore options for managing your work using the Layers palette.

Using the View Buttons in the Layers Palette

The view options available in the Layers palette make working with layers a smart choice for complex illustrations. The options are targeted: You can apply specific viewing options to each layer in the document. Without layers, your options for viewing your work are limited to the Hide and Show All commands on the Object menu.

The Toggles Visibility button makes it easy to quickly change what can be seen on the artboard. Clicking this button once hides all the artwork on a layer, and the button disappears. Clicking the empty gray square

where the button was shows all of the artwork on the layer, and the button reappears. Pressing [Alt] (Win) or [option] (Mac) and clicking the button once shows all layers; clicking a second time hides all layers except for the layer you clicked.

Pressing [Ctrl] (Win) or ⌘ (Mac) and clicking the button toggles between Outline and Preview modes; all the artwork on the layer will switch between outlined and filled objects. Pressing [Alt][Ctrl] (Win) or [option] ⌘ (Mac) and clicking the button switches all other layers between Outline and Preview modes.

Locating an Object in the Layers Palette

With complex illustrations, layers and sublayers tend to multiply—so much so that you will often find it easiest to work with collapsed layers, those in which you hide the sublayers. Sometimes it can be difficult to identify an object's layer or sublayer, especially if there are multiple copies of the object in the illustration. The Locate Object command offers a simple solution. Select an object on the artboard, click the Layers palette list arrow, then click Locate Object. The layers expand, revealing their sublayers, and the selected object's layer or sublayer is selected.

Reversing the Order of Layers

Another option that the Layers palette offers for managing your artwork is the ability to reverse the order of layers. Select the layers whose order you want to reverse. Press [Shift] to select multiple contiguous (those next to each other in the palette) layers. Press [Ctrl] (Win) or [⌘] (Mac) to select multiple noncontiguous layers. Click the Layers palette list arrow, then click Reverse Order.

Making Layers Nonprintable

The ability to choose whether or not the artwork on a specific layer will print is a useful function, especially during the middle stages of producing an illustration. For example, you could print just the text elements and give them to a copy editor for proofing. You could print just the elements of the illustration that are ready to be shown to the client, holding back the elements that still need work.

Another value of the print option is the ability to print different versions of a document. Let's say you're working on the design of a poster for a client, and you've finalized the artwork but you're still undecided about the typeface for the headline, after narrowing down the choices to five typefaces. You could create five layers, one for the headline formatted in each typeface. Then you would print the illustration five times, each time printing only one of the five different headline layers. This is a smart and simple way to produce comps quickly.

QUICKTIP

You can export Illustrator layers to Photoshop by clicking File on the menu bar, clicking Export, clicking the Save as type list arrow (Win) or the Format list arrow (Mac), clicking Photoshop (∗.PSD) (Win) or Photoshop (psd) (Mac), then clicking Save (Win) or Export (Mac). The Photoshop Export Options dialog box opens. Verify that the Write Layers option button is selected. Click OK to export the layers to a Photoshop document.

Explore view options in the Layers palette

1. Collapse the Electronics and Entertainment layers, then hide them.

2. Press and hold **[Alt]** (Win) or **[option]** (Mac), then click the **Toggles Visibility button**  on the Chair layer.

   All of the layers are displayed.

3. Using the same keyboard commands, click the **Toggles Visibility button** on the Chair layer again.

   All layers, except for the Chair layer, are hidden.

4. Using the same keyboard commands, click the **Toggles Visibility button** on the Chair layer again so that all of the layers are displayed.

5. Move the Foreground layer to the top of the hierarchy.

6. Press **[Ctrl]** (Win) or ⌘ (Mac), then click the **Toggles Visibility button** on the Chair layer.

   The artwork on the Chair layer switches to Outline mode.

7. Using the same keyboard commands, click the **Toggles Visibility button** on the Chair layer again.

8. Press **[Alt][Ctrl]** (Win) or **[option]** ⌘ (Mac), then click the same **Toggles Visibility button**.

   The artwork on every layer, except for the Chair layer, switches to Outline mode, as shown in Figure E-25.

9. Using the same keyboard commands, click the **Toggles Visibility button** again.

You learned keyboard commands to explore view options in the Layers palette.

FIGURE E-25
The Chair layer shown in Preview mode and all other layers shown in Outline mode

FIGURE E-26
Duplicating the Lamp layer

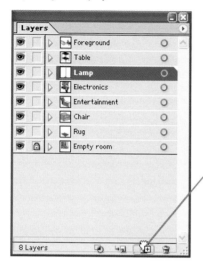

To duplicate a layer and its
contents, drag it on top of the
Create New Layer button

FIGURE E-27
Positioning the second lamp

Locate, duplicate, and delete layers

1. Select the Plant 2 artwork on the artboard.

2. Click the **Layers palette list arrow**, then click **Locate Object**.

   The Entertainment layer expands, as does the Plant 2 sublayer.

   TIP The Locate Object command is useful when you are working with collapsed layers or with many layers and sublayers.

3. Collapse the Entertainment layer.

4. Select the Lamp layer, then drag it on top of the Create New Layer button ⬓ , as shown in Figure E-26.

   The Lamp layer and its contents are duplicated.

5. Position the duplicated lamp artwork on the artboard, as shown in Figure E-27.

   TIP The copy of the lamp is directly on top of the original lamp.

6. Drag the **Lamp copy layer** to the Delete Selection button 🗑 in the Layers palette.

You used the Locate Object command to identify a selected object's position in the Layers palette. You duplicated a layer, then deleted it.

Dim placed images

1. Hide all layers, then create a new layer at the top of the hierarchy, named **Photo**.

2. Click **File** on the menu bar, then click **Place**.

3. Navigate to the drive and folder where your Data Files are stored, click **Living Room Original.tif**, then click **Place**.

   The source for the illustration is placed on its own layer, as shown in Figure E-28.

4. Align the photo with the top-left corner of the artboard, if necessary.

5. Double-click the **Photo layer**, click the **Dim Images to check box**, type **50** in the Dim Images to text box, then click **OK**.

   The placed image is less vivid.

   | TIP   Dimming a placed image is useful for tracing.

You created a new layer, placed a photo on the new layer, then used the Layer Options dialog box to dim the photo 50%.

FIGURE E-28
The source of the illustration, placed on its own layer

FIGURE E-29

Using a layer for a message to the printer

Printer: Use photo for reference if necessary. Thank you!
Call me at 555-1234 if any problems.

1. Create a new layer at the top of the hierarchy, named **Message**.

2. Using any font you like, type a message for the printer, as shown in Figure E-29.

3. Convert the message text to outlines. Double-click the **Message layer**, remove the check mark from the Print check box, then click **OK**.

   The Message layer will not print to any output device.

   > TIP When a layer is set to not print, its name is italicized in the Layers palette.

4. Make the Photo layer nonprintable.

5. Hide the Message and Photo layers.

6. Make all the other layers visible.

7. Save your work.

You created a new layer called Message, typed a message for the printer, then designated the Message and Photo layers as nonprintable. You then displayed all of the layers except for the Message and Photo layers.

CREATE A CLIPPING SET

What You'll Do

In this lesson, you will create a clipping mask on a sublayer that will mask the other sublayers in the layer.

Working with Clipping Sets

Adobe uses the terms "clipping mask" and "clipping path" interchangeably. The term **clipping set** is used to distinguish clipping paths used in layers from clipping paths used to mask nonlayered artwork. There's no difference; it's just terminology. Essentially, the term "clipping set" refers to the clipping mask *and* the masked sublayers as a unit.

The following rules apply to clipping sets:
- The clipping mask and the objects to be masked must be in the same layer.
- You cannot use a sublayer as a clipping mask, unless it is a <Group> sublayer. However, the top sublayer in a layer becomes the clipping mask if you first select the layer that the sublayer is in, then create the clipping mask.

- The top object in the clipping set becomes the mask for every object below it in the layer.
- A <Group> sublayer can be a clipping set. The top object in the group will function as the mask.
- Dotted lines between sublayers indicate that they are included in a clipping set.

Flattening Artwork

When you apply the Flatten Artwork command, all visible objects in the artwork are consolidated in a single layer. Before applying the command, select the layer into which you want to consolidate the artwork. If you have a layer that is hidden, you will be asked whether to make the artwork visible so that it can be flattened into the layer, or whether to delete the layer and the artwork on it.

FIGURE E-30

The new <Path> sublayer

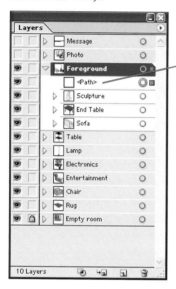

The rectangle is placed on a new sublayer called <Path>, on top of the other sublayers in the Foreground layer

FIGURE E-31

Clipping path masks only the objects on its own layer

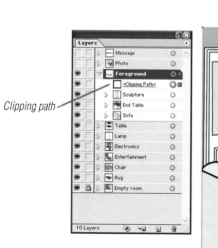

Clipping path

1. Select the Foreground layer, click the **Rectangle Tool** , then create a rectangle that is 6.5" × 6".

2. Position the rectangle so that it aligns exactly with the edges of the artboard.

3. Apply a black stroke to the rectangle and no fill color.

4. Expand the Foreground layer.

   The rectangle, identified as <Path>, is at the top of the sublayers, as shown in Figure E-30.

5. Click the **Make/Release Clipping Mask button** in the Layers palette.

   Any path on the Foreground layer that is positioned off the artboard is masked. The part of the rug that extends beyond the artboard is not masked, because it is not in the same layer as the clipping path. The lamp, too, extends beyond the artboard and is not masked, as shown in Figure E-31.

You created a rectangle, then used it as a clipping path to mask the sublayers below it in its layer.

Copy a clipping mask and flatten artwork

1. Click the **<Clipping Path> layer** to select it.

2. Click **Edit** on the menu bar, click **Copy**, click **Edit** on the menu bar again, then click **Paste in Front**.

   A new sublayer named <Path> is created. The rectangle on the <Clipping Path> sublayer is duplicated on the new <Path> sublayer and can be used to mask other layers.

3. Drag the **Indicates Selected Art button** on the <Path> sublayer down to the Rug layer, as shown in Figure E-32.

4. Expand the Rug layer to see the new <Path> sublayer, select the Rug layer, then click the **Make/Release Clipping Mask button** .

   Compare your Layers palette to Figure E-33. The <Path> sublayer becomes the <Clipping Path> sublayer, and the rectangle on the <Clipping Path> sublayer is used to mask the rug on the artboard.

   (continued)

Moving the copy of the rectangle to the Rug layer

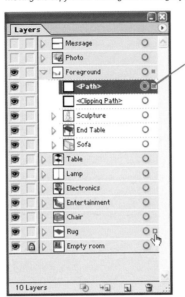

Drag the Indicates Selected Art button to the Rug layer

FIGURE E-33
Using the duplicate rectangle to mask the rug

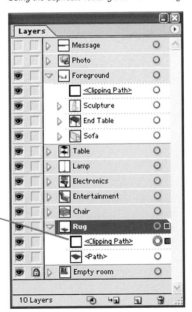

The <Path> sublayer becomes the <Clipping Path> sublayer, and the rectangle on the <Clipping Path> sublayer is used to mask the rug on the artboard

FIGURE E-34
Completed illustration

5. Select the lamp artwork on the artboard, drag the **Indicates Selected Art button** on the Lamp layer to the Sculpture sublayer of the Foreground layer, then deselect all.

   The lamp artwork moves to the Sculpture sublayer and is therefore masked. Your illustration should resemble Figure E-34.

   > TIP   When you drag the Indicates Selected Art button from one layer to another, the selected artwork moves to the new layer, but the layer does not move.

6. Select the empty Lamp layer, then click the **Delete Selection button** 🗑 in the Layers palette.

7. Select the Foreground layer, click the **Layers palette list arrow**, click **Flatten Artwork**, then click **Yes** when you are asked whether or not you want to discard the hidden art on the hidden layers.

8. Click **File** on the menu bar, click **Save As**, then save the file as **Living Room Flat**.

You made a copy of the rectangle, moved the copied rectangle to the Rug layer, then made it into a clipping path to mask the rug artwork. You then moved the lamp artwork into the Sculpture sublayer, which masked the lamp. You deleted the empty Lamp layer and flattened all of the artwork on the Foreground layer.

Create and modify layers.

1. Open AI E-3.ai, then save it as **Gary Garlic**.
2. Create a new layer at the top of the layer hierarchy, named **Text**.
3. Create a new layer at the top of the hierarchy, named **Garlic**.
4. Rename Layer 2 **Pieces**.
5. Save your work.

Manipulate layered artwork.

1. Move the garlic artwork into the Garlic layer.
2. Move the three text groups into the Text layer.
3. Merge the Background layer with the Box Shapes layer so that the Box Shapes layer is the name of the resulting merged layer. (*Hint*: Click the Background layer, press [Ctrl] (Win) or ⌘ (Mac), click the Box Shapes layer, click the Layers palette list arrow, then click Merge Selected.)
4. Move the Pieces layer to the top of the layer hierarchy.
5. Save your work.

Work with layered artwork.

1. View each layer separately to identify the artwork on each.
2. Using Figure E-35 as a guide, assemble Gary Garlic.
3. Merge the Garlic and Pieces layers so that the resulting merged layer will be named Pieces.
4. Select all the artwork on the Pieces layer, then group the artwork.
5. Save your work.

Create a clipping set.

1. Select the Box Shapes layer.
2. Create a rectangle that is 5" wide by 8" deep.
3. Position the rectangle so that it is centered on the artboard.
4. Apply the Make Clipping Mask command.
5. Reposition the masked elements (text and box parts) so that your illustration resembles Figure E-35.
6. Save your work, then close Gary Garlic.

FIGURE E-35
Completed Skills Review

Working with Layers

You are designing an outdoor sign for Xanadu Haircutters, a salon that recently opened in your town. You are pleased with your concept of using scissors to represent the X in Xanadu, and decide to design the logo with different typefaces so that the client will feel she has some input into the final design.

1. Open AI E-4.ai, then save it as **Xanadu**.
2. Create a new layer, then move the ANADU headline into that layer.
3. Make four duplicates of the new layer.
4. Change the typeface on four of the layers, for a total of five versions of the logo.
5. Rename each type layer, using the name of the typeface you chose.
6. Rename Layer 1 Xanadu Sign.
7. View the Xanadu layer five times, each time showing one of the five typeface layers.
8. Save your work, compare your illustration with Figure E-36, then close Xanadu.

FIGURE E-36
Completed Project Builder 1

You are the Creative Director for a Los Angeles design firm that specializes in identity packages for television networks. One of your most important projects this week is delivering the first round of comps for a new cable channel, Milty TV. Your art directors have come up with two concepts—one dark, one light. You decide to bring each to the client with two options for typography, for a total of four comps.

1. Open AI E-5.ai, then save it as **Milty TV**.
2. Select the four pieces of artwork at the top of the artboard, then group them.
3. Group the four pieces of artwork at the bottom of the artboard, then cut them.
4. Create a new layer, name it **Orange Trebuchet**, then paste the artwork.
5. Position the Orange Trebuchet artwork exactly above the blue artwork on the artboard.
6. Rename Layer 1 **Blue Trebuchet**, then duplicate the layer and name it **Blue Comic**.
7. Duplicate the Orange Trebuchet layer, then name it **Orange Comic**.
8. Deselect all, use the Direct Selection Tool to select the large M, change its typeface to Comic Sans MS Regular, then hide the two Orange layers. (*Hint*: If you do not have Comic Sans MS as a typeface, choose another one.)

9. Select the Blue Comic layer, change the M to Comic Sans MS Regular, then hide it.
10. View each of the four layers separately.
11. Save your work, compare your illustration to Figure E-37, then close Milty TV.

FIGURE E-37
Completed Project Builder 2

You are a freelance designer, working out of your house. The owner of the town's largest plumbing company, Straight Flush, has hired you to redesign his logo. He gives you an Illustrator file with a design created by his son. You study the logo, then decide that it lacks cohesion and focus.

1. Open **AI E-6.ai**, then save it as **Straight Flush**.
2. Group the elements of each playing card together.
3. Create four new layers.
4. Move each card to the layer with the corresponding number in the layer name.
5. Select all the layers, click the Layers palette list arrow, then click Reverse Order.
6. Reposition the cards on each layer so that they are in order, directly behind the ace.
7. Adjust the layout of the cards to your liking to create a new layout for the logo.
8. Save your work, compare your illustration with Figure E-38, then close Straight Flush.

FIGURE E-38
Completed Design Project

You are a fabric designer for a line of men's clothing. You are asked to supervise a team that will design new patterns for men's ties. Now that you have studied working with layers, how would you approach building a file that shows three patterns for a tie?

1. Open AI E-7.ai, then save it as **Ties**.
2. Have one group member select objects in the document while the group watches.
3. Have the group discuss how each tie illustration has been created.
4. Have the group discuss how the document would be more practical if built with layers. How many masks would be required to show the three patterns?
   How many layers would be required?
5. Have the group redesign the document with layers so that the three patterns are all in one clipping set with one tie shape functioning as the mask.
6. Save your work, compare your Layers palette with Figure E-39, then close Ties.

FIGURE E-39
Completed Group Project

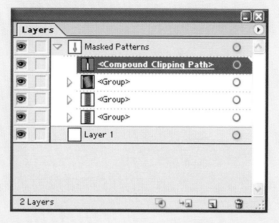

CHAPTER F

WORKING WITH PATTERNS AND BRUSHES

1. Use the Move command.

2. Create a pattern.

3. Design a repeating pattern.

4. Work with the Brushes palette.

5. Work with scatter brushes.

CHAPTER F
WORKING WITH PATTERNS AND BRUSHES

Working with Patterns and Brushes

When you create artwork in Illustrator, that artwork is, of course, an end in and of itself—the result of your efforts in conceiving an image and rendering it, using your skills and talents. As you become more familiar with Illustrator, you will learn to use completed artwork as a component of new illustrations.

Using patterns and brushes is a fine example of this working method. You can design artwork and then use it as a pattern to fill and stroke new artwork. This would be very useful if you were drawing a field

of flowers, or stars in the night sky, or trees on a mountainside.

The powerful options in Illustrator's Brushes palette extend this concept even further. Using brushes, you can extend the role of completed artwork as a stroke, a pattern, or a freestanding illustration of greater complexity. For example, you could create a custom brush stroke, such as a leaf, and then use the Paintbrush Tool to paint with the leaf brush stroke. Instead of being limited to filling or stroking an object with leaves, you could paint leaves wherever you wanted on the artboard.

Tools You'll Use

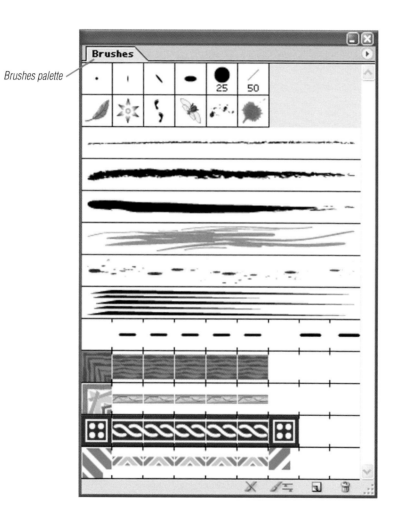

Brushes palette

USE THE MOVE COMMAND

What You'll Do

 In this lesson, you will use the Move command to copy an object at precise offsets and create a simple pattern.

Using the Move Command

The word **offset** comes up when you explore the Move command. Quite simply, the term refers to the distance that an object is moved or copied from a starting location to an ending location. In a simple drop shadow, for example, you can describe the effect by saying, "The black copy behind the original has been offset three points to the left and three points down."

The Move command provides the most effective method for moving an object—or a copy of an object—at precise offsets. In the Move dialog box, you enter the horizontal distance and the vertical distance that you want a selected object to move. A positive value moves the object horizontally to the right, and a negative value moves it to the left. A positive value moves the object vertically up, and a negative value moves it down.

An alternate (and seldom used) method for using the Move dialog box is to enter a value for the distance you want the object to move and a value for the angle it should move on. Entering a distance and an angle is the same as specifying the move in horizontal and vertical values. When you enter values in the Distance and Angle text boxes, the Horizontal and Vertical text boxes update to reflect the move.

Conversely, when you enter values in the Horizontal and Vertical text boxes, the Distance and Angle text boxes update to reflect the move. The Move dialog box is shown in Figure F-1.

FIGURE F-1
Move dialog box

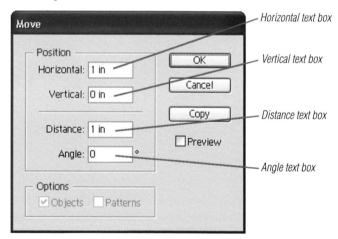

Horizontal text box
Vertical text box
Distance text box
Angle text box

Copy and move objects using the Move dialog box

1. Create a new 4" × 4" CMYK Color document, then save it as **Checkerboard**.

2. Click **Edit** (Win) or **Illustrator** (Mac) on the menu bar, point to **Preferences**, then click **Units & Display Performance**.

3. Verify that the General units of measure are Inches, then click **OK**.

4. Create a ½" square, apply a red fill and no stroke, then position it at the upper-left corner of the artboard.

5. Click **Object** on the menu bar, point to **Transform**, then click **Move**.

6. Enter **.5** in the Horizontal text box, press **[Tab]**, enter **0** in the Vertical text box, then press **[Tab]** again.

   TIP Values in the Distance and Angle text boxes automatically appear, based on the values entered in the Horizontal and Vertical text boxes.

7. Click **Copy**.

   A copy of the square is positioned immediately to the right of the original.

8. Change the fill on the second square to black, select both squares, click **Object** on the menu bar, point to **Transform**, then click **Move**.

9. Enter **1** in the Horizontal text box, then click **Copy**.

10. Click **Object** on the menu bar, point to **Transform**, click **Transform Again**, then repeat this step.

    Your work should resemble Figure F-2.

(continued)

A simple pattern created using the Move command

Working with Patterns and Brushes

FIGURE F-3

A checkerboard created with a single starting square and the Move dialog box

11. Select all, open the Move dialog box, enter **0** in the Horizontal text box, enter **-.5** in the Vertical text box, then click **Copy**.

    | TIP   Apply a negative value to move an object down.

12. Double-click the **Rotate Tool** ↻, enter **180** in the Angle text box, then click **OK**.

13. Select all, open the Move dialog box, enter **-1** in the Vertical text box, then click **Copy**.

14. Apply the Transform Again command twice, then save your work.

    Your screen should resemble Figure F-3.

15. Close the Checkerboard Document.

Starting with a single square, you used the Move command to make multiple copies at precise distances, to create a checkerboard pattern.

CREATE A PATTERN

What You'll Do

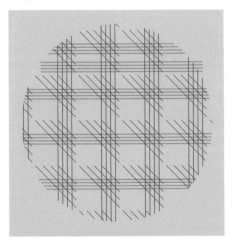

 In this lesson, you will create a pattern from a simple illustration, add it to the Swatches palette, name it, and then fill an object with it.

Creating Patterns

In Illustrator you can design patterns that can be used to fill objects or that can be applied as outlines for objects. You can design patterns that are simple or complex, abstract or specific, and you can save them for future use and applications. The Swatches palette comes pre-loaded with six patterns—Mediterranean Tiles, Pyramids, Honeycomb, Azure Rings, Camouflage, and Jungle Stripes—which you can modify to create your own versions.

To create a pattern, you first create artwork for the pattern, then drag that artwork into the Swatches palette, where it is automatically defined as a pattern swatch. You can use paths, compound paths, or

text in patterns. The following cannot be used as artwork for a pattern: gradients, blends, brush strokes, meshes, bitmap images, graphs, masks, or other patterns.

Designing a Pattern

Patterns repeat. A pattern fills an object by repeating the original pattern, a process called **tiling**. The word is used intentionally as a reference to floor tiles. Illustrator creates pattern fills in much the same way that you would use multiple tiles to cover a floor. Think of the pattern as the floor tile and the object to be filled as the floor.

You design fill patterns by designing one tile. For efficiency with previewing and printing, a pattern tile should be a ½" to 1" square. When saved as a pattern and applied as a fill, the tile will repeat as many times as necessary to fill the object, as shown in Figure F-4.

Many times, you will create a pattern that contains no rectangular objects, such as a polka dot pattern, or a pattern of lines. In these cases, you create a **bounding box** to define the perimeter of the pattern tile. Position an unfilled, unstroked rectangular object at the back of the stacking order of the pattern tile. Illustrator will regard this as the bounding box. All of the objects within the bounding box will be repeated as part of the pattern.

The pattern in Figure F-5 is composed of lines only. The square is used as a bounding box. It defines the perimeter of the tile, and the pattern is created by repeating only the elements that fall within the bounding box. Again, a bounding box must have no fill and no stroke, it must be a rectangle or a square, and it must be the backmost object of the pattern tile.

Controlling How a Pattern Fills an Object

The way a pattern fills an object is tricky to understand. The pattern begins from the origin of the ruler, which is by default at the bottom-left corner of the artboard. In other words, by default, the pattern begins at the bottom-left of the artboard, not the bottom-left corner of the object.

When an object is filled with a pattern, if you move the object, the pattern changes within the object. If you understand the concept of a clipping mask, the pattern fill is easier to understand. Think of it this way: The pattern covers the *entire* artboard; the object that is filled with the pattern functions like a clipping mask—you can see the pattern only through the object.

FIGURE F-4
The tile repeats to fill the object

FIGURE F-5
Bounding box determines the perimeter of the pattern tile

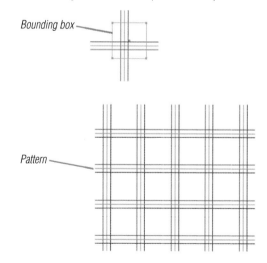

Bounding box

Pattern

The best method for controlling how a pattern appears within an object is to align the ruler origin with the bottom-left corner of the object. To do this, display the rulers, then position your cursor at the top-left corner of the window, where the two rulers meet. The cross hairs are the ruler origin. Drag the cross hairs to the bottom-left corner of the filled object, as shown in Figure F-6. Because the ruler origin and the bottom-left corner of the square are the same point, the first tile is positioned evenly in the corner. The pattern fills the object left to right, bottom to top.

Transforming Patterns

When an object is filled with a pattern, you can choose to transform only the object, only the pattern, or both the object and the pattern. For example, the Scale Tool dialog box, shown in Figure F-7, contains options for determining whether or not the transformation will affect a pattern fill.

QUICKTIP

The options that you choose in one transform tool dialog box will be applied to all transform tool dialog boxes.

When you transform a pattern, all subsequent objects that you create will be filled with the transformed pattern. To return a pattern fill to its nontransformed appearance, fill an object with a different swatch, then reapply the pattern swatch.

FIGURE F-6
Aligning the ruler origin with the bottom-left corner of the filled object

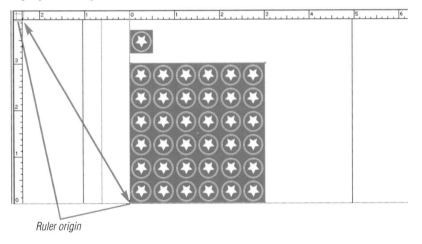

Ruler origin

FIGURE F-7
Options for patterns in the Scale dialog box

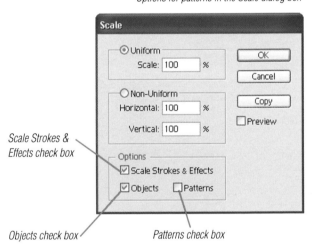

Scale Strokes & Effects check box

Objects check box

Patterns check box

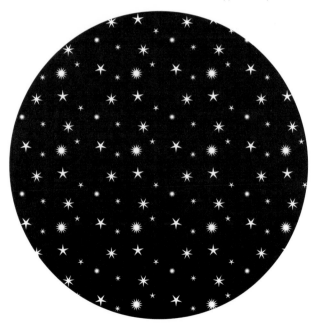

Create a pattern swatch

1. Open AI F-1.ai, then save it as **Starry Night**.

2. Position the ten stars randomly over the black box.

   | TIP   Enlarge your view of the artboard.

3. Change the fill color of the stars to white. Compare your screen to Figure F-8.

4. Group the white stars.

5. Select all, then drag the **artwork** into the Swatches palette.

   The Swatches palette automatically identifies and defines the new swatch as a pattern swatch.

6. Double-click the **new swatch** called New Pattern Swatch 1, name it **Starry Night** in the Swatch Options dialog box, then click **OK**.

7. Delete all the artwork on the artboard.

8. Create a circle that is 4" in diameter.

9. Apply the Starry Night swatch to fill the circle.

   Your screen should resemble Figure F-9.

You created a 1"× 1" collection of objects, selected all of them, then dragged them into the Swatches palette. You named the new pattern swatch, then applied it as a fill for a circle.

Transform pattern-filled objects

1. Select the circle, then double-click the **Scale Tool** 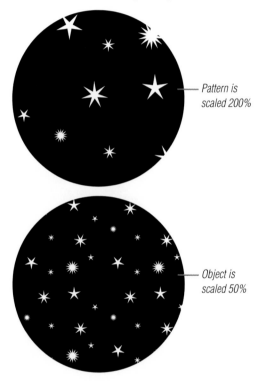.

2. Type **50** in the Scale text box, verify that only the Objects check box is checked in the Options section of the dialog box, then click **OK**.

   The object is scaled 50%; the pattern is not scaled.

3. Drag and drop a copy above the original circle.

4. Double-click the **Scale Tool** .

5. Type **200** in the Scale text box, verify that only the Patterns check box is checked, then click **OK**.

   The pattern is scaled 200%; the object is not scaled. Your screen should resemble Figure F-10.

6. Save your work, then close the Starry Night document.

You experimented with options for scaling a pattern fill and an object independently using the Scale dialog box.

FIGURE F-10
Patterns can be transformed independently of the objects that they fill

Pattern is scaled 200%

Object is scaled 50%

Position a bounding box to define a pattern

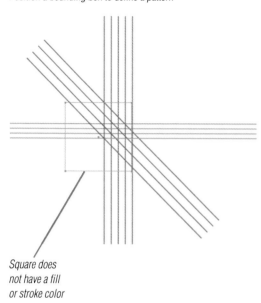

*Square does
not have a fill
or stroke color*

FIGURE F-12

A yellow square behind a line pattern

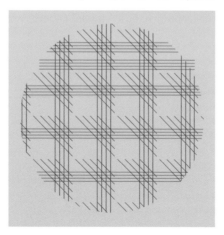

Create a pattern using open paths

1. Open AI F-2.ai, then save it as **Line Pattern**.

2. Create a 1" square.

3. Position the square over the lines, then remove both the fill and the stroke colors, as shown in Figure F-11.

   Note that the rightmost purple line is not within the perimeter of the square.

4. Send the square to the back.

   > TIP If you deselect the square, switch to Outline mode so that you can see the outline of the square to select it, then switch back to Preview mode.

5. Select all, then drag the **objects** into the Swatches palette.

6. Hide the objects on the artboard.

7. Create a 4" circle, then fill it with the new pattern.

8. Create a 5" square, fill it with yellow, remove the stroke color if necessary, send it to the back, then position it behind the circle, as shown in Figure F-12.

   The yellow square is visible behind the pattern because the pattern is composed of lines only.

9. Save your work, then close the Line Pattern document.

You placed a 1" square with no fill or stroke behind a group of straight paths. You used all the objects to create a pattern swatch, with the square defining the perimeter of the pattern tile. You filled a circle with the pattern, then positioned a yellow square behind the circle, creating the effect of a circle pattern within a square.

DESIGN A REPEATING PATTERN

What You'll Do

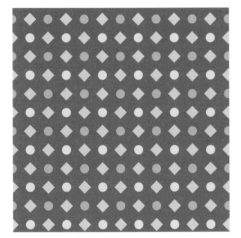

 In this lesson, you will design a visually repetitive pattern. You will then explore options for modifying the pattern after it has been applied as a fill.

Designing Patterns

Simple patterns can be tricky to design. Understanding how patterns tile is important for achieving a desired effect. You will often be surprised to find that the tile you design does not create the pattern that you had in mind.

In Figure F-13, it at first seems logical that the tile on the left could produce the pattern below. However, it requires the more complex tile on the right to produce what appears to be a "simple" pattern.

Another consideration when designing patterns is whether or not you want the pattern to be apparent. If you were designing a plaid pattern, you would by definition want the pattern to be noticed. However, if you were designing artwork for a field of flowers, you might want the pattern to be subtle, if not invisible. An invisible pattern is difficult to create, especially when it's based on a 1" tile!

In every case, precision is important when creating a pattern. If two objects are meant to align, be certain that they do align; don't rely on just your eye. Use dialog boxes to move and transform objects; don't try to do it by hand.

Modifying Patterns

You modify a pattern by editing the artwork in the pattern tile, then replacing the old pattern in the Swatches palette with the new pattern. When you replace the old pattern, any existing objects on the artboard that were filled with the old pattern will automatically update with the new pattern. Of course, you can always leave the original pattern as is and save the edited pattern as a new swatch. This is often a wise move, because you may want to use that original pattern again sometime.

FIGURE F-13
Only the top-right tile could create the pattern

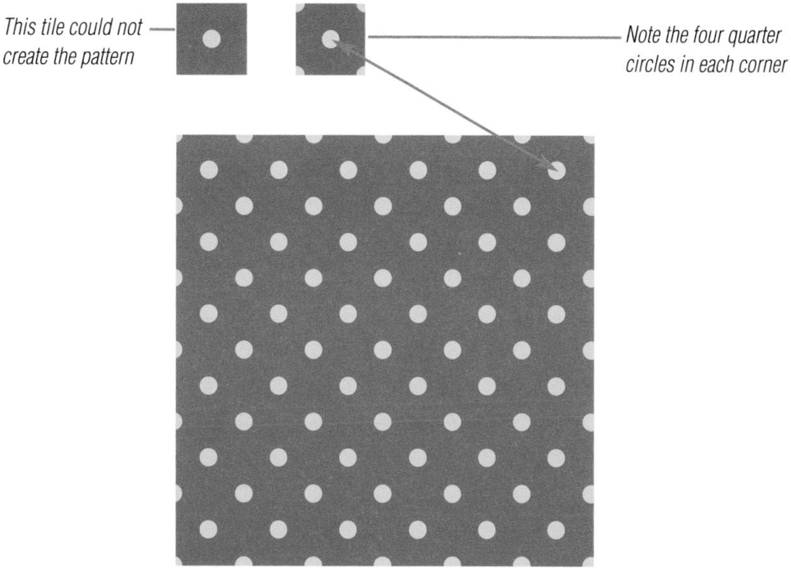

This tile could not create the pattern

Note the four quarter circles in each corner

Create a repeating pattern with precision

1. Open AI F-3.ai, then save it as **Repeating Pattern**.

2. Select the purple circle, click **Object** on the menu bar, point to **Transform**, then click **Move**.

3. Enter **1** in the Horizontal text box, enter **0** in the Vertical text box, then click **Copy**.

   A copy of the purple circle is created at the upper-right corner of the square.

4. Select both purple circles, open the Move dialog box, enter **0** in the Horizontal text box and **-1** in the Vertical text box, then click **Copy**.

   Your screen should resemble Figure F-14.

5. Select the blue diamond, then apply the Transform Again command.

   A copy of the blue diamond is created at the bottom edge of the square.

6. Select both blue diamonds, double-click the **Rotate Tool** ⟳, enter **90** in the Angle text box, then click **Copy**.

   Your work should resemble Figure F-15.

(continued)

Work precisely when designing pattern tiles

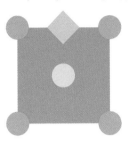

Use dialog boxes to make transformations when designing pattern tiles

Working with Patterns and Brushes

7. Select all, then click the **Divide button** in the Pathfinder palette.

8. Deselect, click the **Direct Selection Tool** , click the **artboard**, then delete the areas of the diamonds and circles that are outside the perimeter of the square, so that your design resembles Figure F-16.

9. Click the **Selection Tool** , select all, drag the **artwork** into the Swatches palette, then name the new pattern **Alpha Shapes**.

10. Delete the artwork on the artboard.

11. Create a 6" × 6" square, fill it with the Alpha Shapes pattern, then center it on the artboard.

12. Compare your screen to Figure F-17.

You used the Move command to position multiple objects in a symmetrical pattern over a 1" square. You then used the Divide pathfinder, which allowed you to select and then delete the areas of objects that were positioned outside the square. You dragged the pattern into the Swatches palette. You named the pattern, then created a square with the pattern as its fill.

FIGURE F-17
A "simple" pattern

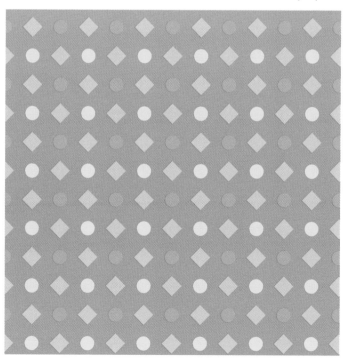

Modify a pattern

1. Drag the **Alpha Shapes pattern** from the Swatches palette to the scratch area at the upper-right corner of the artboard.

2. Click the **Direct Selection Tool**, click the **artboard** to deselect the pattern, then click the **pink section** on the pattern.

3. Change the pink fill to a red fill.

4. Switch to the **Selection Tool**, then select the entire pattern.

5. Press and hold [**Alt**] (Win) or [**option**] (Mac), then drag the **modified pattern** on top of the Alpha Shapes pattern in the Swatches palette.

   The Alpha Shapes pattern is replaced in the Swatches palette, and the fill of the square is updated, as shown in Figure F-18.

   (continued)

FIGURE F-18
Changing the background color of the pattern

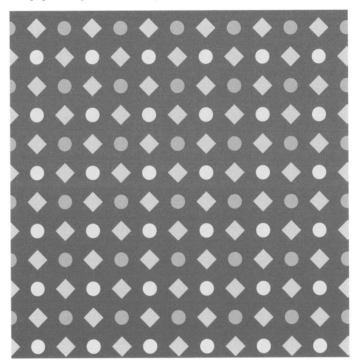

Working with Patterns and Brushes

FIGURE F-19

Updated pattern without the red background

6. Using the Direct Selection Tool ▶., select all of the pattern pieces in the scratch area, except for the red section.

7. Press and hold [**Alt**] (Win) or [**option**] (Mac), then drag the **selected objects** on top of the Alpha Shapes swatch in the Swatches palette.

   Your screen should resemble Figure F-19.

8. Save and close the Repeating Pattern file.

You dragged the Alpha Shapes pattern swatch out of the Swatches palette and onto the scratch area in order to modify it. You changed a color in the pattern, then replaced the old pattern swatch with the new pattern. The object filled with the original pattern was updated to reflect the changes to the pattern. You modified the pattern again by dragging only parts of it to the Swatches palette.

WORK WITH THE BRUSHES PALETTE

What You'll Do

In this lesson, you will create a calligraphic brush, a scatter brush, an art brush, and a pattern brush.

Working with the Brushes Palette

The Brushes palette offers four types of brushes that you can use to add artwork to paths or that you can paint with, using the Paintbrush Tool. Figure F-20 shows the four types of brushes that you can work with in Illustrator. You can work with the brushes that have been pre-loaded, you can modify them, or you can create new brushes.

Calligraphic brushes apply strokes that resemble those drawn with a calligraphic pen. Figure F-21 is an example.

Scatter brushes disperse copies of an object along a path, as shown in Figure F-22.

You can apply artwork—such as an arrow or a feather—to a path with an art brush. **Art brushes** stretch an object along the length of a path, as shown in Figure F-23.

FIGURE F-20
Brushes palette

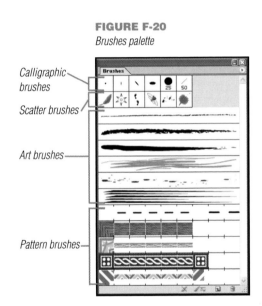

Calligraphic brushes

Scatter brushes

Art brushes

Pattern brushes

Pattern brushes repeat a pattern along a path. Pattern brushes are made with tiles that you create. You can define up to five tiles as components of the pattern: one tile for the side, one for the inner corner, one for the outer corner, and one each for the beginning and ending of the path. Figure F-24 shows five tiles and a pattern that was created with them.

You can create any of the four types of brushes. Artwork for brushes must be composed of simple paths—no gradients, blends, mesh objects, bitmap images, masks, or other brush strokes can be used. Art and pattern brushes cannot include text. You must convert text to outlines before it can be used as artwork for these types of brushes.

FIGURE F-21
A calligraphic brush applied to a path

FIGURE F-22
A scatter brush applied to a path

FIGURE F-23
An art brush applied to a path

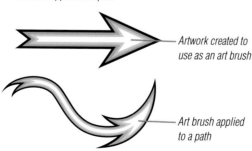

Artwork created to use as an art brush

Art brush applied to a path

FIGURE F-24
Five tiles used for a pattern brush

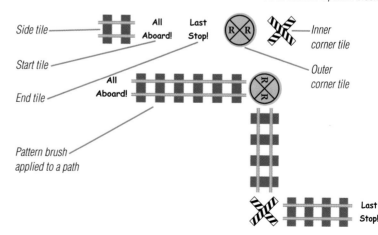

Side tile

Start tile

End tile

Pattern brush applied to a path

Inner corner tile

Outer corner tile

Create a calligraphic brush

1. Open AI F-4.ai, then save it as **Four Brushes**.

2. Click **Window** on the menu bar, then click **Brushes**.

3. Click the **Brushes palette list arrow**, then click **New Brush**.

4. Click the **New Calligraphic Brush option button** in the New Brush dialog box, then click **OK**.

5. Type **Twelve Points** in the Name text box, **45** in the Angle text box, and **12** in the Diameter text box, as shown in Figure F-25, then click **OK**.

   The Twelve Points brush is added to the calligraphy brush section and is selected in the Brushes palette.

6. Click the **Selection Tool** , select the first curved line on the artboard, then click the **Twelve Points brush** in the Brushes palette.

   (continued)

FIGURE F-25
Calligraphic Brush Options dialog box

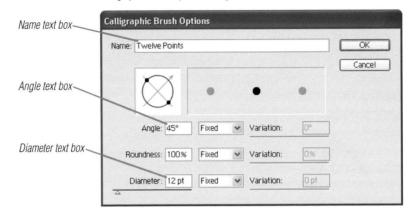

Name text box

Angle text box

Diameter text box

Using the Paintbrush Tool

You can apply any brush in the Brushes palette to any path simply by selecting the path then clicking the brush swatch. Many designers draw a shape with the Pen Tool, then apply their brush of choice. Other designers, however, prefer a more "freehand" approach and use the Paintbrush Tool. The Paintbrush Tool creates paths that are painted with a brush that you preselect in the Brushes palette. In addition to drawing freehand with the tool, you can set options in the tool's dialog box that determine the smoothness of the stroke or the curve and how far the artwork can stray or scatter from the path you draw.

Working with Patterns and Brushes

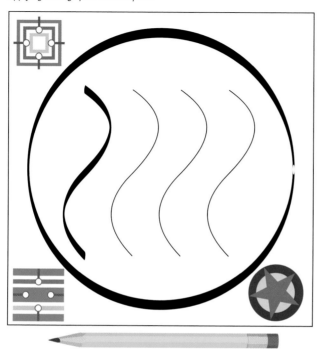

7. Double-click the **Twelve Points brush** in the Brushes palette.

8. Click the **Preview check box** in the Calligraphic Brush Options dialog box, change the Roundness to **20%**, then click **OK**.

9. Click **Apply to Strokes** in the Brush Change Alert dialog box.

   The curved line updates to reflect the changes.

10. Apply the Twelve Points brush to the circle, then deselect all.

    Your screen should resemble Figure F-26.

You created and set the parameters for a new calligraphic brush, which you applied to a curved path and to a circle.

The Pencil, Smooth, and Erase Tools

The Pencil, Smooth, and Erase Tools are grouped together in the toolbox. You can draw freehand paths with the Pencil Tool and then manipulate them using the Direct Selection Tool, the Smooth Tool, and the Erase Tool. The Smooth Tool is used to smooth over line segments that are too bumpy or too sharp. The Erase Tool looks and acts just like an eraser found at the end of a traditional pencil; dragging it over a line segment erases that part of the segment from the artboard.

Create a scatter brush

1. Select the star target in the lower-right corner of the artboard, click the **Brushes palette list arrow**, click **New Brush**, click the **New Scatter Brush option button**, then click **OK**.

2. Name the brush **Star Target**, type **20** in the Size text box, type **60** in the Spacing text box, then click **OK**.

   The Star Target brush is selected in the Brushes palette.

3. Hide the star target artwork on the artboard.

4. Apply the Star Target brush to the second curved line, then apply it to the circle.

   > TIP To remove a brush stroke from a path, select the path, then click the Remove Brush Stroke button ✕ in the Brushes palette.

5. Double-click the **Star Target brush**, change the spacing to **20%**, click **OK**, then click **Apply to Strokes** in the Brush Change Alert dialog box.

6. Save your work, then compare your screen to Figure F-27.

You used a group of simple objects as the artwork for a scatter brush, which you applied to a curved path and to a circle.

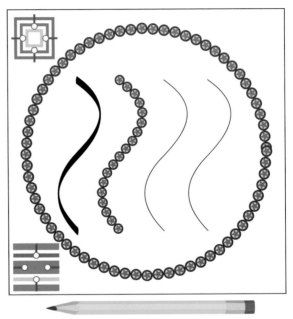

FIGURE F-27
Applying a scatter brush to paths

FIGURE F-28
Applying an art brush to paths

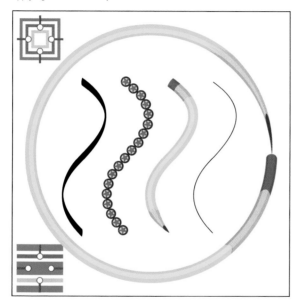

Create an art brush

1. Select the pencil artwork, click the **Brushes palette list arrow**, click **New Brush**, click the **New Art Brush option button**, then click **OK**.

2. Click the **Stroke From Right To Left arrow** ← in the Art Brush Options dialog box.

   The direction arrow in the preview window updates and points in the same direction as the point of the pencil.

3. Enter **75** in the Width text box, then click **OK**.

   The pencil brush is selected in the Brushes palette.

4. Hide the pencil artwork on the artboard.

5. Apply the pencil brush to the third curved line, then apply it to the circle.

6. Save your work, then compare your screen to Figure F-28.

You used an illustration of a pencil as the art for an art brush. You defined the parameters of the art brush—its direction and its size—then applied the brush to a curved path and to a circle.

Create a pattern brush

1. Verify that your Swatches palette is visible.

2. Select the artwork in the lower-left corner of the artboard, drag it into the Swatches palette, then name it **Green Side**.

3. Hide the artwork used for the Green Side swatch on the artboard.

4. Select the artwork in the top-left corner, drag it into the Swatches palette, then name it **Green Corner**.

5. Hide the artwork used for the Green Corner swatch on the artboard.

6. Click the **Brushes palette list arrow**, click **New Brush**, click the **New Pattern Brush option button**, then click **OK**.

7. Name the new brush **Tomato Worm**.

8. Click the **Side Tile box**, then click **Green Side** in the list of patterns.

9. Click the **Outer Corner Tile box**, then click **Green Corner** in the list of patterns, as shown in Figure F-29.

10. Type **40** in the Scale text box, then click **OK**.

The Tomato Worm brush is selected in the Brushes palette.

You dragged the two pieces of artwork into the Swatches palette and named them. You then created a new pattern brush and, in the dialog box, defined the first piece of artwork as the side tile of the brush, and the second as a corner tile.

Pattern Brush Options dialog box

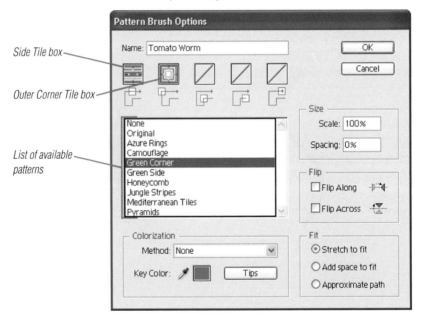

Side Tile box

Outer Corner Tile box

List of available patterns

Working with Patterns and Brushes

FIGURE F-30
Applying the pattern brush to paths

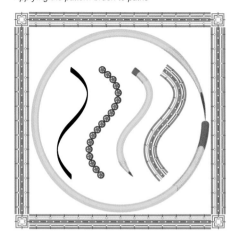

Modify a pattern brush

1. Apply the Tomato Worm brush to the fourth curved line, then apply it to the square.

   Your screen should resemble Figure F-30.

2. Double-click the **Tomato Worm brush** in the Brushes palette.

3. Click the **Start Tile box**, then click **Green Corner** in the list of patterns.

4. Click the **End Tile box**, click **Green Corner** in the list of patterns, click **OK**, then click **Apply to Strokes** in the Brush Change Alert dialog box.

   The curved line now begins and ends with the corner artwork, as shown in Figure F-31.

5. Save your work.

6. Close the Four Brushes document.

You applied the pattern brush to a curved path and to a square. You then modified the brush, adding artwork for a start tile and an end tile.

FIGURE F-31
Modifying the pattern brush

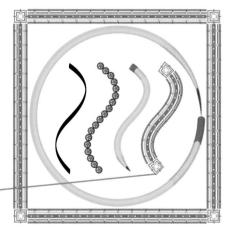

The curved line now begins and ends with the corner artwork

Lesson 4   Work with the Brushes Palette

WORK WITH SCATTER BRUSHES

What You'll Do

bar

▶ In this lesson, you will work with scatter brushes, enter fixed and random values in the Scatter Brush Options dialog box, and view how those values affect your artwork.

Working with Scatter Brushes

The role of brushes in creating artwork is easy to underestimate. Many designers identify them as a method for creating really cool strokes and leave it at that. What they are missing is that brushes can themselves be the best option for creating an illustration.

Of the four types of brushes, the scatter brush best illustrates this point. For example, if you were drawing a pearl necklace, a scatter brush would be your smartest choice for creating the illustration, as opposed to dragging and dropping copies of a single pearl illustration along a path, or creating a blend between two pearls.

Why? The reason is that with the scatter brush, you can manipulate the path endlessly, with precise control of the size, spacing, and rotation of the elements along the path. In addition, you can input a scatter value, which determines how far the objects can be positioned from the path, an option that blending does not offer.

The scatter brush is even more powerful for creating the effect of "randomness." One of the default scatter brushes, Flying Beetle, is a fine example of this effect. In the Scatter Brush Options dialog box, you can apply a random range for size, spacing, scatter, and rotation and create the effect of a three-dimensional swarm of beetles flying in different directions—some of them closer to you and larger, some of them farther away and smaller. See Figure F-32 for an example of this effect.

For each setting in the Brush Options dialog box, you can choose fixed or random values. When you apply random settings to a scatter brush, the positioning of the objects on the path will be different every time you apply the brush.

FIGURE F-32
A swarm of beetles created with the Flying Beetle scatter brush

Modify a scatter brush

1. Open AI F-5.ai, then save it as **Random Flies**.

2. Select the circle, then apply the Flying Beetle scatter brush.

3. Double-click the **Flying Beetle brush** in the Brushes palette, click the **Preview check box** to add a check mark (if necessary), then move the Scatter Brush Options dialog box so that you can see as much of the artboard as possible.

4. Click the **Size list arrow**, then click **Fixed**.

   The beetles become the same size.

   > TIP Press [Tab] to see changes made to the artwork after you change a value in the dialog box.

5. Type **50** In the Size text box.

   The beetles are 50% the size of the original flying beetle artwork.

6. Click the **Scatter list arrow**, click **Fixed**, then type **0** in the Scatter text box.

   The beetles are positioned on the path.

7. Click the **Spacing list arrow**, click **Fixed**, then type **50** in the Spacing text box.

   The beetles are evenly spaced along the path.

8. Click the **Rotation list arrow**, click **Fixed**, then type **0** in the Rotation text box, as shown in Figure F-33.

   The beetles rotate 360° as they move from the beginning to the end of the path.

   (continued)

FIGURE F-33
Scatter Brush Options dialog box

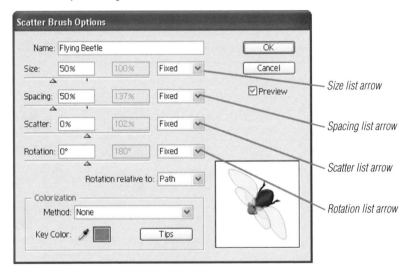

Size list arrow

Spacing list arrow

Scatter list arrow

Rotation list arrow

FIGURE F-34

The Flying Beetle scatter brush, using fixed values

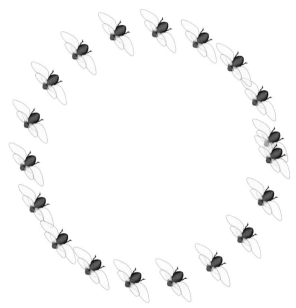

9. Click the **Rotation relative to list arrow**, then click **Page**.

   The beetles no longer rotate along the path.

10. Click the **eyedropper button** 🖋 in the Scatter Brush Options dialog box, then click the **black leg** of the beetle artwork in the preview window of the dialog box.

    The Key Color box turns black.

11. Click the **Method list arrow**, then click **Tints**.

    The beetles are tinted with the new key color. Your work should resemble Figure F-34.

12. Click **OK**, then click **Apply to Strokes** in the Brush Change Alert dialog box.

You explored the parameters that define a scatter brush. You started with scatter brush artwork that was random in size, spacing, scatter, and rotation. By removing the parameters that defined the randomness of the artwork, you gained an understanding of how those parameters created the random effects in the original artwork.

Manipulate random values in a scatter brush

1. Double-click the **Flying Beetle brush** in the Brushes palette.

2. Click the **Size list arrow**, click **Random**, then type **20** in the first Size text box and **100** in the second.

   The beetles will be randomly assigned a size anywhere between 20% and 100% of the original artwork.

3. Click the **Spacing list arrow**, click **Random**, then type **50** in the first Spacing text box and **200** in the second, as shown in Figure F-35.

   The beetles are spaced randomly along the path within the set range of values.

4. Click the **Scatter list arrow**, click **Random**, then type **-100** in the first Scatter text box and **100** in the second.

   These values define the distance from each side of the path that the artwork can be positioned. In the case of a circular path, the first value determines how far into the circle the artwork can be positioned, and the second value determines how far outside the circle.

   (continued)

FIGURE F-35
Scatter Brush Options dialog box

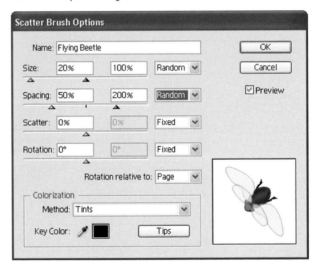

FIGURE F-36

Scatter artwork using random values

5. Click the **Rotation list arrow**, click **Random**, then type **-180** in the first Rotation text box and **180** in the second.

   The artwork can be rotated to any position within a full 360°.

6. Click the **Method list arrow**, click **None**, click **OK**, then click **Apply to Strokes**.

   Figure F-36 is an example of this brush setting.

7. Click the **Remove Brush Stroke button** ⊠ on the Brushes palette, then reapply the Flying Beetle brush.

   The artwork will be different each time you reapply the brush, because the values are determined randomly with each application.

8. Save and close the Random Flies document.

Starting with symmetrical, evenly spaced scatter brush artwork, you manipulated parameters to create artwork that was random in size, spacing, scatter, and rotation values.

Use the Move command.

1. Create a new 6" × 6" CMYK Color document, then save it as **Polka Dot Pattern**.
2. Create a 2" square, then fill it with green, and remove any stroke if necessary.
3. Create a .25" circle, then fill it with white.
4. Align the circle and the square by their center points. (*Hint*: Select both the circle and the square, then click the Horizontal Align Center button and the Vertical Align Center button in the Align palette.)
5. Deselect all, select the white circle, click Object on the menu bar, point to Transform, then click Move.
6. Type -.5 in the Horizontal text box, type .5 in the Vertical text box, then click Copy.
7. Keeping the new circle selected, click Object on the menu bar, point to Transform, then click Move.
8. Type **1** in the Horizontal text box, type **0** in the Vertical text box, then click Copy.

9. Select the two new circles, then move a copy of them 1 inch below by typing **0** in the Horizontal text box, **-1** in the Vertical text box, then clicking Copy.
10. Fill the center circle with light blue.
11. Save your work.

Create a pattern.

1. Select all the artwork, then drag it into the Swatches palette.
2. Name the new swatch **Green Polka**.
3. Delete the artwork on the artboard.
4. Create a 4" square, then fill it with the Green Polka pattern.
5. Double-click the Scale Tool, then scale only the pattern 25%.
6. Save your work.

Design a repeating pattern.

1. Hide the 4" square.
2. Drag the Green Polka pattern swatch from the Swatches palette onto the artboard.

3. Deselect the pattern swatch, draw a diagonal 1 point black line from the bottom-left corner to the top-right corner of the green square.
4. Deselect, select the line with the Selection Tool, then rotate a copy of the line 90°. (*Hint*: Be sure to click the Objects check box in the Rotate dialog box.)
5. Click the Direct Selection Tool, select the five circles, then cut them.
6. Click the Selection Tool, select the two black lines, then paste in front.
7. Select the green square, click Object on the menu bar, point to Path, click Offset Path, type -.5 in the Offset text box, then click OK.
8. Cut the new green square, then paste it in back of the blue circle.
9. Select all the artwork, press and hold [Alt] (Win) or [option] (Mac), then drag the artwork on top of the Green Polka swatch to replace the old pattern with the new one.
10. Delete the artwork from the artboard.

Working with Patterns and Brushes

11. Show all, then save your work. Your square should resemble Figure F-37.

Work with the Brushes palette.

1. Open AI F-6.ai, then save it as **Brushes Review**.
2. Select the snowflake artwork on the artboard, click the Brushes palette list arrow, then click New Brush.
3. Click the New Scatter Brush option button, then click OK.
4. Name the new brush **Snowflake**.
5. Set the size to 20%.
6. Set the spacing to 20%, then click OK.
7. Hide the snowflake artwork on the artboard.
8. Create a circle that is 4" in diameter, then apply the Snowflake scatter brush to the circle.
9. Save your work.

Work with scatter brushes.

1. Double-click the Snowflake scatter brush in the Brushes palette.
2. Set all the Fixed options to Random.
3. Set the size range between 10% and 30%.
4. Set the spacing range between 10% and 40%.
5. Set the scatter range between -30% and 50%.
6. Set the rotation range between 45° and 25°.
7. Click OK, then click Apply to Strokes.
8. Save your work, compare your screen with Figure F-38, then close the Brushes Review document.

FIGURE F-37
Completed Skills Review, Part 1

FIGURE F-38
Completed Skills Review, Part 2

Working with Patterns and Brushes

You work in the textile industry as a pattern designer. Your boss asks you to design a pattern for a new line of shower curtains. Her only direction is that the pattern must feature triangles and at least eight colors.

1. Create a new 6" × 6" CMYK Color document, then save it as **Shower Curtain**.
2. Create a 1" square with a blue fill and no stroke.
3. Copy the square, paste in front, then fill the new square with green.
4. Click Object on the menu bar, point to Path, click Add Anchor Points, then click the Delete Anchor Point Tool. (*Hint*: The Delete Anchor Point Tool is hidden beneath the Pen Tool.)
5. Delete the top-left corner, top-right corner, left side, and right side anchor points, so that the square is converted to a triangle.
6. Use the Move command to create a copy of the two shapes to the right, then two copies below, so that, together, the area of the four tiles is 2" × 2".
7. Change the colors in each tile.
8. Scale the four tiles 15%.
9. Make a new pattern swatch out of the four tiles, then apply the pattern to a 4" square.
10. Save your work, then compare your pattern to Figure F-39.

FIGURE F-39
Completed Project Builder 1

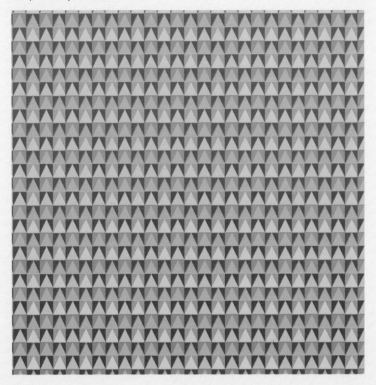

You are a jewelry designer, and you've been hired to create the original design for a new line of necklaces that will be targeted to teenage girls. The necklaces will be made with flat, tinted metals, and you are asked to use bright colors. One catch: Your client tells you that he's "unsure" of what he's looking for and hints that he may make many changes to your design before he's satisfied.

1. Open AI F-7.ai, then save it as **Teen Jewelry**.
2. Create a new scatter brush with the artwork provided.
3. Name the new brush **Smile**.
4. Set the size to 25%.
5. Set the spacing to 30%.
6. Set the rotation to Random.
7. Set the rotation range from -92° to 92°, make it relative to the page, then click OK.
8. Hide the original artwork.
9. Draw a path resembling the arc of a necklace, then apply the Smile scatter brush to the path.
10. Save your work, then compare your pattern to Figure F-40.

FIGURE F-40
Completed Project Builder 2

You own a gallery in Key West called Funky Frames. You are known for designing unusual and festive frames of various sizes. The process of designing the frames is complex, as you use many different kinds of materials. However, they all begin with a brush pattern that you create in Illustrator.

1. Open AI F-8.ai, then save it as **Funky Frames**.
2. Select the left tile, drag it into the Swatches palette, then name it **Side Tile**.
3. Select the right tile, drag it into the Swatches palette, then name it **Corner Tile**.
4. Hide the artwork on the artboard.
5. Create a new pattern brush.
6. Name the new brush **Funky Frame**.
7. Apply the Side Tile swatch as the side tile and the Corner Tile swatch as the outer corner tile.
8. Set the scale value to 50%, then click OK.
9. Apply the Funky Frame pattern brush to a 5" square.
10. Save your work, then compare your pattern to Figure F-41.

FIGURE F-41
Completed Design Project

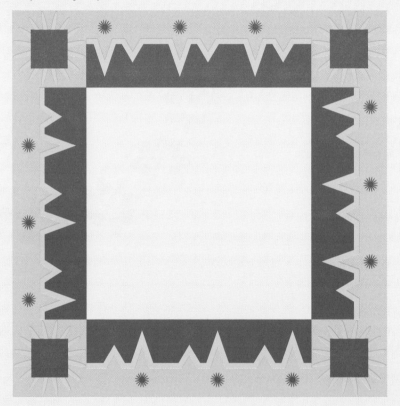

Working with Patterns and Brushes

Your team of graphic designers has been commissioned to design an original plaid pattern, which will be used to produce kilts for the wedding of a famous singer and her Scottish groom. Your only direction is that it must be an original pattern, and it must have at least three colors.

1. Create a new CMYK Color document, then save it as **Original Plaid**.
2. Assign two team members to research the history of plaid patterns and their association with specific groups, families, and organizations.
3. Assign two team members to search the Internet for plaid patterns.
4. Assign two other team members to research the Burberry pattern, one of the most famous patterns ever created.
5. Assign half of the remaining team members to create swatches to compare colors, and the other half to design the pattern.
6. Fill a 6" × 6" square with the new pattern.
7. Save your work, then compare your pattern to Figure F-42.

FIGURE F-42
Completed Group Project

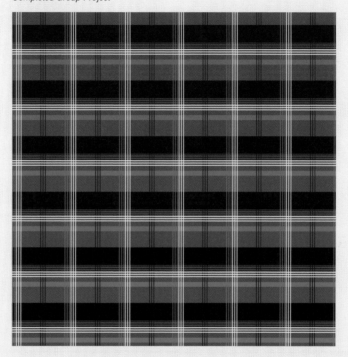

WORKING WITH FILTERS
GRADIENT MESHES, ENVELOPES, AND BLENDS

1. Work with filters.

2. Work with gradient meshes.

3. Work with envelopes.

4. Create blends.

CHAPTER G
WORKING WITH FILTERS
GRADIENT MESHES, ENVELOPES, AND BLENDS

Illustrator software comes programmed with built-in operations—mathematical algorithms—that create specific effects when applied to objects. These include filters, gradient meshes, envelopes, and blends. A variety of color filters are available that affect the color of objects and create color blends between objects. Distort filters twist, pucker, and bloat objects, among other operations. The Create Gradient Mesh command produces a multicolored object on which colors can transition smoothly and flow in different directions. Envelopes are objects that you use to distort other objects. Blends create a series of intermediate objects and colors between two or more selected objects.

When you are working with filters, meshes, envelopes, and blends, you are working at the intermediate level in Illustrator. All are challenging—less in learning how to use them than in activating your imagination for ideas of how to *best* use them. Of the four, meshes and blends are the broadest in scope, offering powerful options for adding color, shape, depth, and perspective to an illustration.

Tools You'll Use

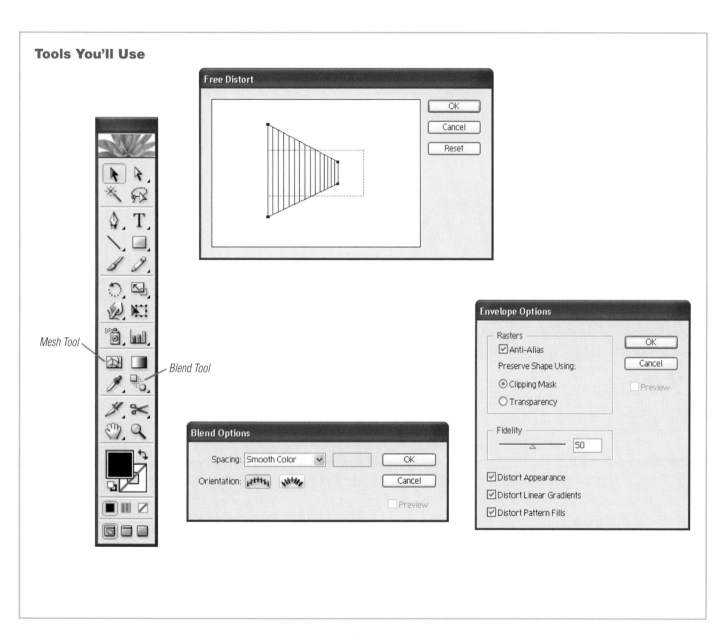

Mesh Tool

Blend Tool

WORK WITH FILTERS

What You'll Do

In this lesson, you will explore options for manipulating colors and basic shapes with filters.

Modifying Shapes with Filters

Illustrator provides a number of filters that you can use to alter the shape of an object. These filters provide simple operations that you can use as a final effect or that you can tweak to create a unique effect. Of the many filters that affect shapes, some are essential operations that you will want to have in your skill set.

The Free Distort filter functions much like the Free Transform Tool. A bounding box is applied to a selected object or objects in a preview window. You can alter any of the four handles on the bounding box to distort the selection. The Free Distort filter is very useful for distorting perspective.

The Pucker & Bloat filter adjusts the segments between an object's anchor points.

FIGURE G-1
Pucker filter applied

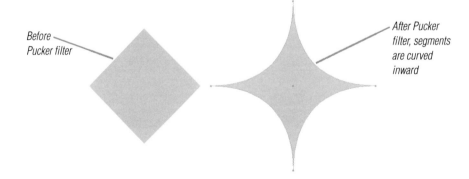

Before Pucker filter

After Pucker filter, segments are curved inward

With a pucker effect, the segments are moved inward, toward the center of the object, while the anchor points are moved outward, as shown in Figure G-1. The bloat effect is achieved by moving the segments outward and the anchor points inward, as shown in Figure G-2.

The Twist filter rotates an object more sharply in the center than it does at the edges, creating a whirlpool effect, as shown in Figure G-3.

Modifying Color with Color Filters

Illustrator offers a number of filters that alter the color of selected objects. You can use color filters to saturate an illustration, which makes its colors more intense. Conversely, you can reduce the saturation of an image, making its colors duller, with a washed-out appearance. Use the Convert to Grayscale filter to completely desaturate an illustration and create the effect of a black-and-white image.

You can also use color filters to make color blends between objects. The Blend Front to Back filter creates a color blend through all the objects in the stacking order, using the frontmost object as the starting color and the backmost object as the ending color. This filter can be very useful for adding the effect of color depth to an illustration.

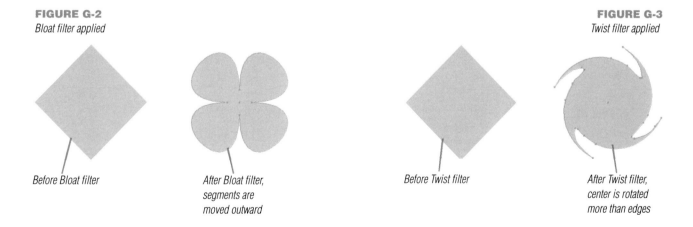

FIGURE G-2
Bloat filter applied

FIGURE G-3
Twist filter applied

Before Bloat filter

After Bloat filter, segments are moved outward

Before Twist filter

After Twist filter, center is rotated more than edges

Use the Free Distort filter

1. Open AI G-1.ai, then save it as **Free Distort**.

2. Select all, click **Filter** on the menu bar, point to **Distort** at the top of the Filter menu, then click **Free Distort**.

   A preview of the selected objects appears in the Free Distort dialog box with a bounding box around them.

3. Using Figure G-4 as a guide, drag the **four bounding box handles** to the locations shown in the figure to distort the lines in perspective, click **OK**, then deselect.

4. Select all, click **Filter** on the menu bar, point to **Distort**, then click **Free Distort**.

5. Click **Reset**, drag the **bounding box handles** to the locations shown in Figure G-5, click **OK**, then deselect.

   Your work should resemble Figure G-6.

   You used the Free Distort filter twice to distort a series of paths in perspective.

FIGURE G-4
Free Distort dialog box

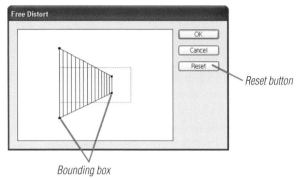

Reset button

Bounding box handles

FIGURE G-5
Move handles independently in the Free Distort dialog box

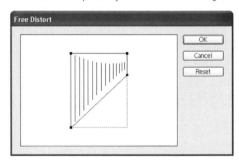

FIGURE G-6
A perspective effect, created with the Free Distort filter

FIGURE G-7

Blending the colors from dark to light enhances the perspective effect

Create a blend with the Colors filter

1. Select all.

2. Click **Object** on the menu bar, point to **Path**, then click **Outline Stroke**.

   The strokes are converted to closed paths.

3. Deselect, then fill the smallest object with yellow.

4. Select all, click **Filter** on the menu bar, point to **Colors**, then click **Blend Front to Back**.

   A color blend is created from the frontmost to the backmost object in the stacking order. Your work should resemble Figure G-7.

   | TIP   The Blend Front to Back filter does not work on open paths.

5. Save your work, then close the Free Distort document.

You converted the stroked paths to outlines, and then used the Blend Front to Back filter to create the effect that the objects lighten as they recede into the distance.

Saturate and desaturate an illustration

1. Open AI G-2.ai, then save it as **Saturation**.

2. Select all, click **View** on the menu bar, then click **Hide Edges**.

3. Click **Filter** on the menu bar, point to **Colors**, then click **Saturate**.

4. Click the **Preview check box**, drag the **Intensity slider** all the way to the right, then click **OK**.

   Your work should resemble Figure G-8.

5. Click **Filter** on the menu bar, point to **Colors**, then click **Convert to Grayscale**.

   Every object is filled with a shade of gray, as shown in Figure G-9.

6. Click **View** on the menu bar, then click **Show Edges**.

7. Deselect all by clicking the artboard.

8. Save your work, then close the Saturation document.

You used the Saturate filter to intensify the color of an image. You then used the Convert to Grayscale filter to remove all chromatic color from the illustration, thereby creating the effect of a black-and-white image.

FIGURE G-8
Illustration with saturated colors

FIGURE G-9
Illustration with the Convert to Grayscale filter applied

Working with Filters, Gradient Meshes, Envelopes, and Blends

The orange shape is bloated, the gray is puckered

The blue circle with added anchor points and the Bloat and Twist filters applied

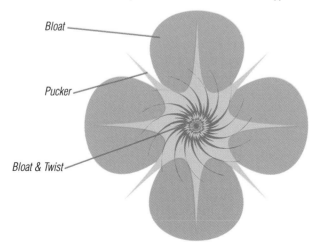

Bloat

Pucker

Bloat & Twist

Apply the Pucker & Bloat and Twist filters

1. Open AI G-3.ai, then save it as **Pucker and Bloat**.

2. Select the large orange square, click **Filter** on the menu bar, point to the **first Distort menu**, then click **Pucker & Bloat**.

3. Type **85** in the text box, then click **OK**.

   > TIP   A positive value produces a bloat effect; a negative value produces a pucker effect.

4. Select the gray circle, click **Object** on the menu bar, point to **Path**, then click **Add Anchor Points**.

5. Click **Filter** on the menu bar, then click **Pucker & Bloat** at the top of the Filter menu.

   The Pucker & Bloat dialog box opens with the settings last used.

6. Type **-75**, then click **OK**.

   Your work should resemble Figure G-10.

7. Select the blue circle, then apply the Add Anchor Points command twice.

8. Open the Pucker & Bloat dialog box, type **180** in the text box, then click **OK**.

9. Click **Filter** on the menu bar, point to the **first Distort menu**, then click **Twist**.

10. Type **90** in the Angle text box, then click **OK**.

    Your work should resemble Figure G-11.

11. Save your work, then close the Pucker and Bloat document.

You applied the Pucker & Bloat filter in varying degrees to each object, producing three distinctly different effects. You also applied the Twist filter.

WORK WITH GRADIENT MESHES

What You'll Do

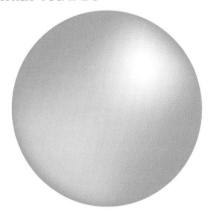

In this lesson, you will create and manipulate a gradient mesh to add dimension to basic shapes.

Working with a Mesh Object

The Mesh Tool and the Create Gradient Mesh command can be used to transform a basic object into a mesh object. A **mesh object** is a single, multicolored object in which colors can flow in different directions, and colors transition gradually from point to point. Meshes exceed the ability of simple radial and linear gradients for applying color blends to objects and are very effective for adding contrast and dimension.

When you create a mesh object, multiple **mesh lines** crisscross the object, joined at their intersections by mesh points. **Mesh points** are diamond-shaped and work just like anchor points, with the added functionality of being able to be assigned a color. When you assign a color to a mesh point, the color gradates outward from the point.

The area between four mesh points is a **mesh patch.** You can apply color to all four mesh points simultaneously by applying

the color to the patch. Work with this method to apply broad color changes to the object.

Mesh points can be added, deleted, and moved along the mesh line without altering the shape of the mesh.

Anchor points are also part of the mesh, and they function as they do on simple paths. Just as with simple paths, you can manipulate the anchor points' direction lines to alter the shape of the mesh. Figure G-12 shows an example of a mesh object.

Creating a Mesh Object

You can create a mesh object from any path. You cannot create a mesh object from compound paths or text objects. You can create a mesh object with the Mesh Tool or by applying the Create Gradient Mesh command.

Generally, you'll be happiest using the Create Gradient Mesh command, which creates a mesh object with regularly spaced mesh lines and mesh points. The Create Gradient Mesh dialog box is shown in Figure G-13. The Mesh Tool adds a mesh point and its intersecting mesh lines where you click. The tool is most effective when you want to add a particular mesh point (say, for a highlight) to an existing mesh.

The Create Gradient Mesh command is always the best choice when converting complex objects.

Once a mesh object has been created, it cannot be converted back into a simple path.

Complex mesh objects are a memory drain and may affect your computer's performance. When creating mesh objects, keep in mind that it's better to create a few simple mesh objects than a single complex one.

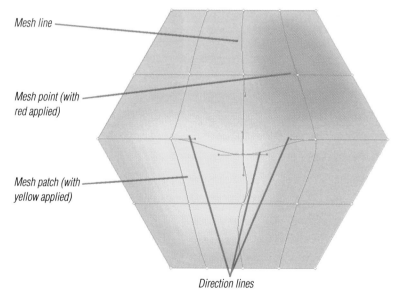

Mesh line

Mesh point (with red applied)

Mesh patch (with yellow applied)

Direction lines

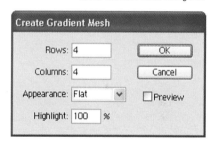

Create a gradient mesh

1. Open AI G-4.ai, then save it as **Circle Mesh**.
2. Select the circle, click **Object** on the menu bar, then click **Create Gradient Mesh**.
3. Type **2** in the Rows text box and **2** in the Columns text box, then click **OK**.
4. Deselect, then click the **edge of the circle** with the Direct Selection Tool �.
5. Select the center mesh point, then change its color to yellow.
6. Move the center mesh point to the green X, as shown in Figure G-14.
7. Move the direction lines at the top, bottom, left, and right of the circle's edge, as shown in Figure G-15.

(continued)

Mesh points can be moved, just like anchor points

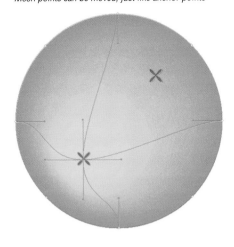

FIGURE G-15
The shape of the mesh is manipulated by direction lines

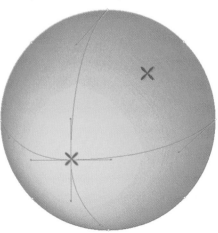

Working with Filters, Gradient Meshes, Envelopes, and Blends

Gradient meshes add dimension to an object

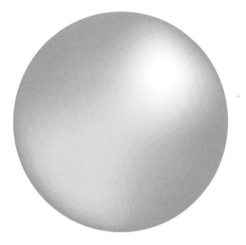

8. Click the **Mesh Tool** ⊞ , then click the **blue X**.

   TIP Press [Shift] while you click the Mesh Tool to add a mesh point without changing to the current fill color.

9. Click the **white swatch** in the Swatches palette to change the color of the mesh point to white.

10. Click the **Selection Tool** ▶, deselect, then hide Layer 2.

    Your work should resemble Figure G-16.

11. Save your work, then close the Circle Mesh document.

You applied a gradient mesh to a circle with the Create Gradient Mesh command, changed the color of a mesh point, then moved the mesh point. You then used the Mesh Tool to expand the mesh. You changed the color of the new mesh point to white to add a highlight to the sphere.

Manipulate a gradient mesh

1. Open AI G-5.ai, then save it as **Heart Mesh**.

2. Select the heart, click **Object** on the menu bar, then click **Create Gradient Mesh**.

3. Type **4** in the Rows text box and **4** in the Columns text box, then click **OK**.

4. Deselect, then click the **edge of the heart** with the Direct Selection Tool .

5. Click the **upper-left mesh point**, as shown in Figure G-17, then change the mesh point color to 10% black, using the Color palette.

   The new color gradates out from the mesh point.

6. Click the **Mesh Tool** .

7. Press and hold **[Shift]**, then drag the **mesh point** along the mesh path to the left, as shown in Figure G-18.

   (continued)

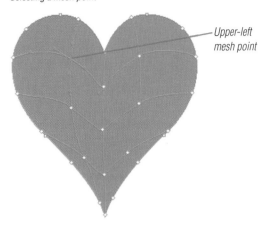

FIGURE G-17
Selecting a mesh point

Upper-left mesh point

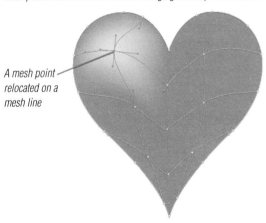

FIGURE G-18
Mesh points can be moved without changing the shape of the mesh

A mesh point relocated on a mesh line

Working with Filters, Gradient Meshes, Envelopes, and Blends

FIGURE G-19

The mesh, reconfigured on both sides of the object

FIGURE G-20

Selecting mesh points

Mesh points at the
edge of the object
are filled with black

FIGURE G-21

Mesh points are like anchor points, with the added functionality of accepting color assignments

Three interior
mesh points,
darkened

FIGURE G-22

Meshes offer the ability to manipulate gradients precisely

8. Repeat Steps 5-7 for the upper-right mesh point, so that your work resembles Figure G-19.

9. Click the **Direct Selection Tool** ⟨ ⟩, press and hold **[Shift]**, then select the 20 mesh points and anchor points along the edge of the heart.

   | TIP   Mesh points appear as diamonds and have the same properties as anchor points, with the added capability of accepting color.

10. Apply a black fill to the selected mesh points.

   The selected anchor points are unaffected. Your work should resemble Figure G-20.

11. Deselect, then select the three mesh points at the lower third of the heart, then apply a 60% black fill so that your work resembles Figure G-21.

12. Select the mesh point at the center of the heart (between the two 10% black highlights).

13. Apply a 60% black fill, deselect, then compare your work to Figure G-22.

14. Save your work, then close the Heart Mesh document.

You applied a gradient mesh to a heart shape, then created highlights by changing the color of two mesh points. Next, you relocated the highlight mesh points without changing the shape of the mesh lines. You then darkened the color of other mesh points to add contrast and dimension to the artwork.

WORK WITH ENVELOPES

What You'll Do

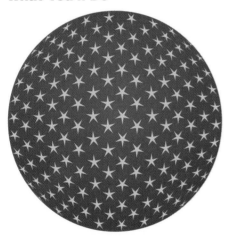

▶ *In this lesson, you will create envelope distortions in three ways: using a top object, using a mesh, and using a warp.*

Defining Envelopes

Envelopes are objects that are used to distort other selected objects; the distorted objects take on the shape of the envelope object.

Imagine that you have purchased a basketball as a gift, and you want to wrap it with paper that has a polka-dot pattern. If these were objects in Illustrator, the basketball would be the envelope object, and the sheet of wrapping paper would be the object to be distorted. Figure G-23 is a good example of what an envelope distortion looks like.

You can make envelopes with objects that you create, or you can use a preset warp shape or a mesh object as an envelope. You can use envelopes with compound paths, text objects, meshes, and blends. Powerful effects can be achieved by applying envelopes to linear gradient fills or pattern fills.

FIGURE G-23
An envelope created using a top object

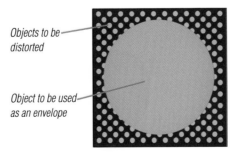

Objects to be distorted

Object to be used as an envelope

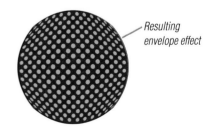

Resulting envelope effect

Creating Envelopes with Top Objects, Meshes, and Warps

You create an envelope by using the Envelope Distort command on the Object menu. The Envelope Distort command offers you three options for creating an envelope: Make with Warp, Make with Mesh, and Make with Top Object. The top object is the topmost selected object. Warps are simply 15 premade shapes to choose from, to use as your top object. Warps are especially useful when you don't want to draw your own top object. The envelope in Figure G-24 was created using the Flag warp. Meshes are the same as gradient meshes made with the Mesh Tool. Creating an envelope with a mesh allows you to apply a mesh to multiple objects, which is not the case when you create a mesh using the Create Gradient Mesh command or the Mesh Tool. The envelope in Figure G-25 was created using a mesh.

Applying Envelopes to Gradient and Pattern Fills

Envelopes can be used to distort objects that have linear gradient fills or pattern fills, but you must first activate the option to do so. In the Envelope Options dialog box, you can check the Distort Linear Gradients or Distort Pattern Fills check box to apply an envelope to either of the fills. Figure G-26 shows the options in the Envelope Options dialog box.

FIGURE G-24
An envelope created using a warp

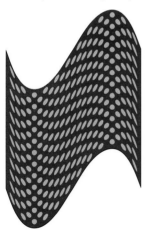

FIGURE G-25
An envelope created using a mesh

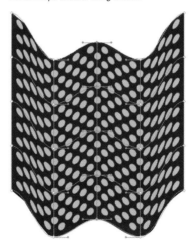

FIGURE G-26
Envelope Options dialog box

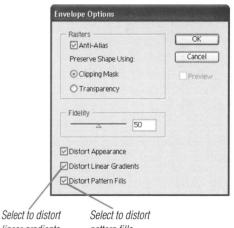

Select to distort linear gradients

Select to distort pattern fills

Create an envelope distortion with a top object

1. Open AI G-6.ai, then save it as **Envelope Top Object**.

2. Copy the yellow circle, paste in front, then hide the copy.

3. Select all, click **Object** on the menu bar, point to **Envelope Distort**, then click **Make with Top Object**.

   Your work should resemble Figure G-27.

4. Show all, then fill the yellow circle with the Purple Berry gradient in the Swatches palette.

5. Send the circle to the back, so that your work resembles Figure G-28.

6. Save your work, then close the Envelope Top Object document.

You used a circle as the top object in an envelope distortion. Because you cannot apply a fill to the circle after it's been used to make the envelope, you filled a copy of the circle with a gradient, then positioned it behind the distorted objects to achieve the effect.

FIGURE G-27
A round envelope distorting a flat star pattern

FIGURE G-28
A radial blend enhancing the effect of an envelope distortion

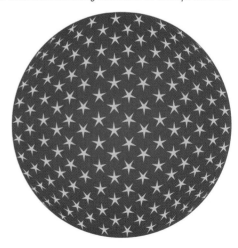

Working with Filters, Gradient Meshes, Envelopes, and Blends

Two columns of mesh points, selected

Select all of the
mesh points in
the second and
fourth columns

FIGURE G-30
An envelope distortion created using a mesh

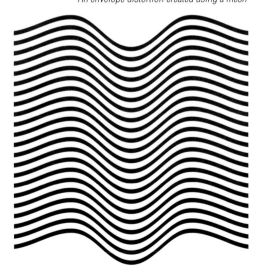

Create an envelope distortion with a mesh

1. Open AI G-7.ai, then save it as **Envelope Mesh**.

2. Select all, click **Object** on the menu bar, point to **Envelope Distort**, then click **Make with Mesh**.

3. Type **4** in the Rows text box and **4** in the Columns text box, then click **OK**.

   There are five mesh points on each horizontal line.

4. Deselect, then select the second and fourth column of mesh points, using the Direct Selection Tool ▶, as shown in Figure G-29.

5. Press and hold **[Shift]**, press ↑ two times, then release [Shift].

   Pressing an arrow key in conjunction with [Shift] moves a selected item ten keyboard increments.

   | TIP   The keyboard increment value can be adjusted in the General Preferences dialog box.

6. Select the middle column of mesh points.

7. Press and hold **[Shift]**, press ↓ two times, deselect, then compare your screen to Figure G-30.

8. Save your work, then close the Envelope Mesh document.

You applied an envelope distortion with a mesh to a series of rectangles, then moved the mesh points to create a wave effect.

Create an envelope distortion with a warp effect

1. Open AI G-8.ai, then save it as **Envelope Warp**.

2. Select all, click **Object** on the menu bar, point to **Envelope Distort**, then click **Make with Warp**.

3. Click the **Style list arrow**, click **Fish**, then click **OK**.

   Your screen should resemble Figure G-31.

4. Undo the distort, then make Layer 2 visible.

5. Select all.

(continued)

(continued)

FIGURE G-31
An envelope distortion created using a warp

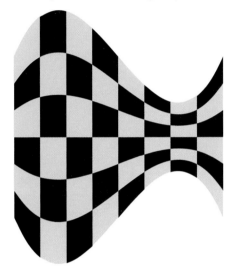

Working with Filters, Gradient Meshes, Envelopes, and Blends

An envelope distortion using a premade shape

6. Click **Object** on the menu bar, point to **Envelope Distort**, then click **Make with Top Object**.

As shown in Figure G-32, you get the same result as you did using the fish-style warp. The reason for this is that using the Envelope Distort feature with a warp is the same as using the feature with a top object—the difference is that warps are pre-made shapes that you can choose, instead of making your own.

7. Save your work, then close the Envelope Warp document.

You applied an envelope distortion with a warp effect—in this case, the Fish warp. You then used an object in the shape of the Fish warp as the top object in a new envelope, with the same result as in the first distortion. Through this comparison, you got a better sense of how Illustrator creates warp effects with envelopes.

Printing color blends and gradient meshes

Print and prepress professionals have long known that some output devices have trouble printing color blends. The most common problem is banding, an effect in which the transitions of the gradient are visibly harsh rather than smooth. This problem was especially common on early PostScript devices. In addition, gradient meshes (which are a newer feature in Illustrator) may print incorrectly, even on PostScript Level 3 printers. If you are having trouble outputting either color blends or meshes, you can print them as bitmaps instead of vectors. To do so, display the Flattener Preview palette, choose Settings in the palette, then save the preset with a descriptive name by clicking the Flattener Preview palette list arrow, then clicking the Save Transparency Flattener Preset. When you are ready to print your document, click File on the menu bar, click Print, click the Advanced category on the left side of the Print dialog box, select the Print as Bitmap check box, choose your named preset from the Preset list arrow, then click Print. Anyone who has experience with printing bitmaps knows that the quality can vary greatly. Use this option only if you are having problems, then decide if the output is acceptable. If not, you may need to go to a professional prepress department to output the file.

CREATE BLENDS

What You'll Do

 In this lesson, you will use blends to manipulate shapes and colors for various effects.

Defining a Blend

A **blend** is a series of intermediate objects and colors between two or more selected objects. If the selected objects differ in color—if they have different fills, for example—the intermediate objects will be filled with intermediate colors. Therefore, in a blend, both shapes and colors are "blended." Figure G-33 is an example of a blend using shapes and colors.

Blends are created with either the Blend Tool or the Make Blend command. You can make blends between two open paths, such as two different lines. You can make blends between two closed paths, such as a square and a star. You can blend between objects filled with gradients. You can even blend between blends, as shown in Figure G-34.

FIGURE G-33
In a blend, both shapes and colors are blended

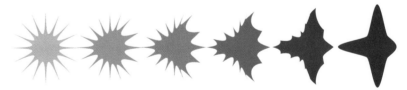

Specifying the Number of Steps in a Blend

The fewer the number of steps in a blend, the more distinct each intermediary object will be. At a greater number of steps, the intermediate objects become indistinguishable from one another, and the blend creates the illusion of being continuous or "smooth."

In the Blend Options dialog box, select from the following options for specifying the number of steps within a blend.

- Specified Steps. Enter a value that determines the number of steps between the start and the end of the blend.
- Specified Distance. Enter a value to determine the distance between the steps in the blend. The distance is measured from the edge of one object to the corresponding edge on the next object.

- Smooth Color. Illustrator determines the number of steps for the blend, calculated to provide the minimum number of steps for a smooth color transition. This is the default option, which poses a bit of a problem in that the minimum number of steps will not always give you the effect you desire, as shown in Figure G-35.

FIGURE G-34
A blend between blends

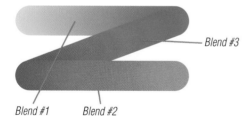

Blend #3

Blend #1   Blend #2

FIGURE G-35
Sometimes, the Smooth Color option doesn't produce the blend effect you desire

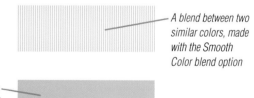

A blend between two similar colors, made with the Smooth Color blend option

A blend between the same two colors, made with 256 specified steps

Manipulating Blends

Once a blend is created, you can change its appearance by making changes to one or more of the original objects. For example, using the Direct Selection Tool, you can select one of the original objects, then change its fill color, stroke color, or stroke weight. Illustrator will automatically update the appearance of the steps to reflect newly added attributes, thus changing the appearance of the entire blend. You can also change a blend by transforming one or more of the original objects, for example by scaling, rotating, or moving them.

You can affect the appearance of a blend by manipulating its spine. When a blend is created, a path is drawn between the starting and ending objects. Illustrator refers to this path as the spine, but it can be manipulated like a path. For example, you can add anchor points to the spine with the Pen Tool, then move them with the Direct Selection Tool. The blend is updated when you alter the spine. Figure G-36 shows how a blend's spine can be manipulated.

One of the most stunning manipulations of a blend happens when you replace its spine. Draw any path with the Pen Tool, then select it along with any blend. Apply the Replace Spine command, and the blend replaces its spine with the new path!

FIGURE G-36

Manipulating the blend's spine changes the blend

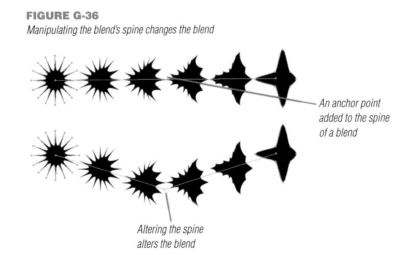

An anchor point added to the spine of a blend

Altering the spine alters the blend

FIGURE G-37

The red and blue objects blended with five steps

Create blends between shapes

1. Open AI G-9.ai, then save it as **Blended Shapes**.

2. Click the **Blend Tool** ⬚, click anywhere on the orange square, then click anywhere on the green square.

   | TIP   You can click the Blend Tool on two
   | or more unselected objects to blend them.

3. Click the **Selection Tool** ▶, select the red and blue squares, then double-click the **Blend Tool** ⬚.

4. Click the **Spacing list arrow**, click **Specified Steps**, type **5** in the Spacing text box, then click **OK**.

5. Click **Object** on the menu bar, point to **Blend**, then click **Make**.

   Five intermediary squares are created, as shown in Figure G-37.

(continued)

6. Switch to the Selection Tool ▶, then deselect the blend.

7. Click the **Blend Tool** ▯, then click the **three purple shapes**.

8. Keeping the purple blend selected, click **Object** on the menu bar, point to **Blend**, then click **Blend Options**.

> TIP You can also access the Blend Options dialog box by double-clicking the Blend Tool.

9. Click the **Spacing list arrow**, click **Specified Steps**, type **2** in the Steps text box, then click **OK**.

The intermediary steps are reduced to two.

10. Deselect the purple blend.

11. Select the Heart view on the View menu.

12. Double-click the **Blend Tool** ▯, change the Specified Steps to 256, then click **OK**.

13. Click the **heart**, click the **small pink circle** in the center of the heart, then deselect.

The 256 intermediary steps blend the heart to the circle in both color and shape. Your screen should resemble Figure G-38.

14. Save your work, then close the Blended Shapes document.

You used the Blend Tool to create a smooth blend and evenly distributed shapes between two sets of squares. You created a blend between differing shapes, then used the Blend Options dialog box to change the number of steps in the blend. You also used a smooth blend to add dimension to the heart.

FIGURE G-38
Blends are very effective for adding dimension to objects

FIGURE G-39

A blend between two open paths

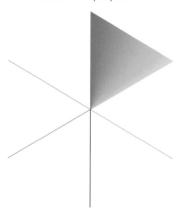

FIGURE G-40

This color effect could not be reproduced with a gradient

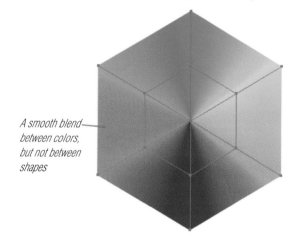

A smooth blend between colors, but not between shapes

FIGURE G-41

The blended paths are masked by a circle

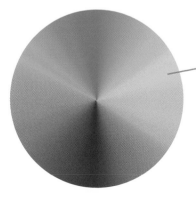

The use of 256 specified steps improves the appearance of the blend

Create a clockwise color blend

1. Open AI G-10.ai, then save it as **Clockwise Blend**.

2. Double-click the **Blend Tool** 🖫., click the **Spacing list arrow**, click **Specified Steps**, type **256** in the Spacing text box, then click **OK**.

3. Click the top of the green line, then click the top of the yellow line to create a blend, as shown in Figure G-39.

   > TIP The Blend Tool pointer turns black when it is successfully positioned over an anchor point.

4. Click the remaining five lines, ending with the green line, to make five more blends, so that your work resembles Figure G-40.

5. Draw a circle over the blend that does not exceed the perimeter of the blend.

6. Select all, click **Object** on the menu bar, point to **Clipping Mask**, then click **Make**.

7. Click the **Selection Tool** ▶, deselect, then compare your image to Figure G-41.

8. Save your work, then close the Clockwise Blend document.

You created blends between six lines. You specified the number of steps between each pair of paths to be 256, which resulted in a visually uninterrupted blend. You then masked the blend with a circle.

Edit blends

1. Open AI G-11.ai, then save it as **Blends on a Path**.

2. Click the **blended objects** with the Selection Tool ▶.

3. Click **Object** on the menu bar, point to **Blend**, then click **Reverse Front to Back**.

   The stacking order of the blended objects is reversed.

4. Click **Object** on the menu bar, point to **Blend**, then click **Reverse Spine**.

   The order of the objects on the path is reversed.

5. Select all.

6. Click **Object** on the menu bar, point to **Blend**, click **Replace Spine**, then deselect.

   The curved path becomes the new spine for the blend, as shown in Figure G-42.

7. Save your work, then close the Blends on a Path document.

You reversed the stacking order of a blend, then reversed its spine. You then replaced the spine with a curved path to create a 3-D effect.

Blends can be applied to paths

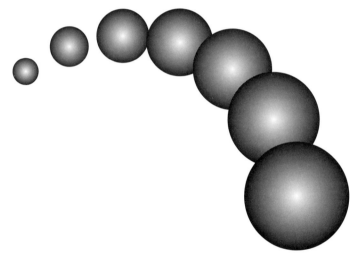

Working with Filters, Gradient Meshes, Envelopes, and Blends

A simple blend between open paths

Chrome letters created with a blend and a mask

Create color effects with blends

1. Open AI G-12.ai, then save it as **Chrome**.
2. Double-click the **Blend Tool** , then change the number of specified steps to **256**, if necessary.
3. Switch to Outline mode, click the **Selection Tool** , then select the five paths at the bottom of the artboard.

   Two of the paths are stroked with white and cannot be seen in Preview mode.
4. Switch to Preview mode, click the **Blend Tool** , then, starting from the bottom of the artboard, create a blend between each pair of paths, so that your work resembles Figure G-43.
5. Position the text over the blend.
6. Keeping the text selected, click **Object** on the menu bar, point to **Compound Path**, then click **Make**.
7. Select all, click **Object** on the menu bar, point to **Clipping Mask**, then click **Make**.
8. Deselect all, click **Select** on the menu bar, point to **Object**, then click **Clipping Masks**.
9. Apply a 2-point black stroke to the mask.
10. Deselect, save your work, compare your screen to Figure G-44, then close the Chrome document.

You created blends between five paths, then masked the blend with text.

Work with filters.

1. Create a new 6" × 6" CMYK Color document, then save it as **Filter Skills**.
2. Create a 4" circle with a red fill and no stroke.
3. Apply the Add Anchor Points command.
4. Apply the Bloat filter at 25%.
5. Apply the Twist filter at 50°.
6. Use the Scale Tool dialog box to make a 75% copy of the object.
7. Apply the Transform Again command four times.
8. Fill the top object with dark purple.
9. Select all, then use the Colors filter to blend the objects from front to back.
10. Save your work, deselect, compare your illustration with Figure G-45, then close the Filter Skills document.

Work with gradient meshes.

1. Open AI G-13.ai, then save it as **Mesh Skills**.
2. Select the yellow hexagon.
3. Apply the Create Gradient Mesh command with 4 rows and 4 columns.

4. Click the Direct Selection Tool, deselect the hexagon, then click the edge of it.
5. Select the top row of mesh points, then click orange in the Swatches palette. (*Hint*: Click and drag the Direct Selection Tool on the artboard to create a selection box that includes the top row of mesh points.)
6. Select the middle row of mesh points, then click red in the Swatches palette.
7. Select the four mesh patches at the bottom of the hexagon, then click Orange in the Swatches palette. (*Hint*: Select each mesh patch one at a time.)
8. Select the five mesh points at the bottom of the hexagon, then click Black in the Swatches palette.
9. Save your work, deselect, then compare your mesh object with Figure G-46.
10. Close the Mesh Skills document.

Work with envelopes.

1. Open AI G-14.ai, then save it as **Envelope Skills**.
2. Click Object on the menu bar, point to Envelope Distort, then click Envelope Options.

3. Verify that there is a check mark in the Distort Pattern Fills check box, then click OK.
4. Position an octogon above the square with the pattern fill. (*Hint*: Click the Polygon Tool, click the artboard, type 8 in the Sides text box, then click OK.)
5. Select all, click Object on the menu bar, point to Envelope Distort, then click Make with Top Object.
6. Enlarge the size of the illustration, if you wish to.
7. Save your work, deselect, compare your illustration to Figure G-47, then close the Envelope Skills document.

Create blends.

1. Open AI G-15.ai, then save it as **Star**.
2. Create a 5% copy of the star.
3. Fill the copy with white.
4. Double-click the Blend Tool, then change the Specified Steps value to 256 if necessary.
5. Blend the two stars.
6. Save your work, deselect, then compare your illustration to Figure G-48.
7. Close the Star document.

FIGURE G-45
Completed Skills Review

FIGURE G-46
Completed Skills Review

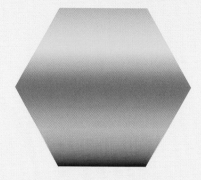

FIGURE G-48
Completed Skills Review

FIGURE G-47
Completed Skills Review

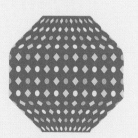

Working with Filters, Gradient Meshes, Envelopes, and Blends

The owner of Tidal Wave Publishing hires your design firm to redesign their logo. She shows you her original logo—a meticulous line drawing of a wave. She explains that the line drawing has been their logo for more than 25 years, and she feels that it's time for something "more contemporary." She cautions you that she doesn't want anything that feels "too artificial" or looks like "cookie-cutter computer graphics."

1. Create a new 6" × 6" document, then save it as **Tidal Wave**.
2. Create an ellipse that is .5" wide and 4.5" tall, then fill it with black and no stroke.
3. Apply the Add Anchor Points command five times.
4. Apply the Twist filter at 45°.
5. Apply the Twist filter six more times using 45° each time. (*Hint*: Click Filter on the menu bar, then click Apply Twist at the top of the menu.)
6. Deselect, save your work, compare your illustration to Figure G-49, then close the Tidal Wave document.

FIGURE G-49
Completed Project Builder 1

Miltie Berger, a famous journalist from Los Angeles, commissions your design firm to create a logo for her new column, which will be titled "Poison Pen." She explains that it will be a gossip column that will "skewer" all the big names in Hollywood. Refer to Figure G-49 as you perform the steps.

1. Open AI G-16.ai, then save it as **Poison Pen**.
2. Double-click the Blend Tool, set the number of specified steps to 40, click OK, then click anywhere on the two white objects on the right side of the artboard to blend them. (*Hint*: They do not need to be selected first.)
3. Deselect, then click the Direct Selection Tool.
4. Select only the bottom object of the blend, then change its fill color to black and its stroke color to white. (*Hint*: Refer to this new object as the "feather" blend.)
5. Click the Selection Tool, select the very narrow white curved stroke at the center of the artboard, copy it, paste in front, then hide the copy.
6. Select the white stroke again, click Object on the menu bar, point to Path, then click Outline Stroke.
7. Deselect all, double-click the Blend Tool, change the number of steps to 256, then blend the white outlined stroke with the pointy black quill shape that is behind it.

8. Lock the new blend, then show all. The hidden white stroke appears and is selected.
9. Click the Selection Tool, press and hold [Shift], then click the "feather" blend to add it to the selection.

FIGURE G-50
Completed Project Builder 2

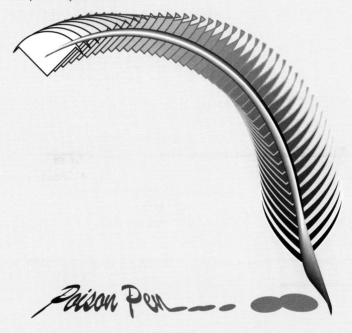

10. Click Object on the menu bar, point to Blend, then click Replace Spine.
11. Save your work, compare your illustration with Figure G-50, then close the Poison Pen document.

Working with Filters, Gradient Meshes, Envelopes, and Blends

You create graphics for a video game company. Your assignment for the morning is to create an illustration for a steel cup that will be used to store magical objects in a game.

1. Open AI G-17.ai, then save it as **Steel Cup**.
2. Select the gray object, then apply the Create Gradient Mesh command using 8 rows and 3 columns.
3. Deselect, then click the edge of the mesh object with the Direct Selection Tool.
4. Press and hold [Shift], then click the four vertical mesh points that make up the center column of the mesh.
5. Click the Color palette list arrow, then click Grayscale, if necessary.
6. Make sure the Fill button is active in the toolbox, then drag the K slider in the Color palette to 20% to lighten the selected mesh points.
7. Select the top right mesh patch and darken it, using the Color palette.
8. Select the mesh points along the left edge and the bottom edge of the "steel cup," then click Black.
9. Continue selecting vertical rows of mesh points and lighten or darken them to create a stainless steel effect. (*Hint*: The mesh points at the bottom edge of the cup should remain black.)
10. Hide the gradient mesh object.

11. Click the edge of the black object with the Direct Selection Tool, then select the five horizontal mesh points in the second row from the top.
12. Fill the row of mesh points with white.

FIGURE G-51
Completed Design Project

13. Deselect, then show all.
14. Save your work, compare your steel cup with Figure G-51, then close the Steel Cup document.

You own a small design firm in the Caribbean, and your group has just been contracted to do a major project for the island of Saint Claw, a new nation in the West Indies. Having recently gained independence, Saint Claw wants you to consult with their new government on the design of their flag. After the first meeting, you begin working on a composite illustration. Your only direction from the government group is that the flag must be composed of abstract shapes—no words, stars, symbols, etc.

1. Create a new 6" × 6" CMYK Color document, then save it as **Saint Claw Flag**.
2. Assign two group members to the job of inventing the history of Saint Claw and its recent struggle for independence.
3. Assign two group members to search the Internet and collect pictures of as many flags from Caribbean nations as they can find.
4. Have your designers experiment with different width-to-height ratios in determining the shape of the banner.
5. Assign two group members to garner fabric samples from local merchants and textile designers.
6. After you've sketched a design, recreate the design in Illustrator with an envelope distort so that the flag appears to be waving.
7. Save your work, compare your illustration to Figure G-52, then close the Saint Claw Flag document.

FIGURE G-52
Completed Group Project

CHAPTER H

WORKING WITH TRANSPARENCY, EFFECTS, AND GRAPHIC STYLES

1. Use the Transparency palette and the Color Picker.

2. Apply effects to objects.

3. Use the Appearance palette.

4. Work with graphic styles.

CHAPTER H

WORKING WITH TRANSPARENCY, EFFECTS, AND GRAPHIC STYLES

Appearance attributes are properties that you apply to an object that affect only the look of the object; its underlying structure is not affected. After you apply an appearance attribute to an object, you can later remove it, leaving the original object—and any other attributes—unaltered.

The Transparency palette allows you to control the **opacity** of an object—the degree to which it is "see through." The Transparency palette also includes a list of **blending modes** to choose from. Blending modes are fun, preset filters that control how colors blend when two objects overlap.

Effects are a type of appearance attribute and are listed on the Effect menu. Many effects have the same name as other Illustrator commands and filters. However, unlike commands and filters, effects can be applied to and removed from objects without changing them.

Many effect dialog boxes include a color box that, when clicked, opens up the Color Picker dialog box, or simply the Color Picker. Of all the ways to choose colors in Illustrator, using the Color Picker is the most sophisticated. In this dialog box, you can specify colors numerically as CMYK, RGB, HSB, or hexadecimal (a numbering system based on 16). You can also access the Color Picker by double-clicking the fill or stroke buttons in the toolbox.

Many effects listed on the Effect menu are available only for documents in the RGB Color mode. If you are working in CMYK Color mode, these effects will be unavailable. If you apply one of these effects, and then convert the document to CMYK Color mode, you will lose the effect. For these reasons, be aware that some effects that you apply in RGB Color mode may be difficult—if not impossible—to print. If you plan to print the illustration, download the file to your printer in RGB Color mode as a test.

Graphic styles are named sets of appearance attributes. In much the same way that you can create a new color and then name it and save it in the Swatches palette, you can name and save a set of appearance attributes in the Graphic Styles palette. As a style, that set of appearance attributes can be easily—and consistently—applied to other objects.

Tools You'll Use

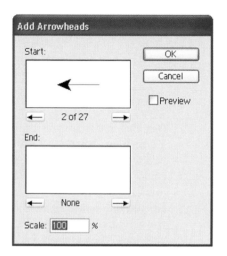

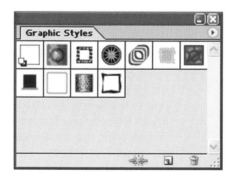

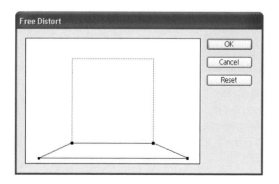

USE THE TRANSPARENCY PALETTE AND THE COLOR PICKER

What You'll Do

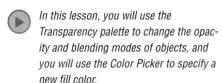

In this lesson, you will use the Transparency palette to change the opacity and blending modes of objects, and you will use the Color Picker to specify a new fill color.

Understanding Opacity

The term **opacity** derives from the word "opaque," which describes an object that is neither transparent nor translucent, that is not "see through." By default, objects in Illustrator are created with 100% opacity—that is, they are opaque. Whenever one object overlaps another on the artboard, the top object hides all or part of the object behind it. If you were drawing a face behind a veil, clouds in a blue sky, or fish in a tinted goldfish bowl, the ability to affect the opacity of objects would be critical to creating the illustration. Figure H-1 shows an example of opacity.

Working with the Transparency Palette

The Transparency palette allows you to control the degree to which an object is transparent. You can change the opacity amount by dragging the Opacity slider in the palette. The Opacity slider works with percentages, with 100% being completely opaque and 0% being completely transparent, or invisible.

Working with Blending Modes

Blending modes are preset filters in the Transparency palette that vary the way that the colors of objects blend with the colors of underlying objects when they overlap them. You cannot determine the amount or intensity of a blending mode; you can simply choose whether or not to apply one. Thus, you will find yourself working with blending modes by trial and error. Blending modes are fun to experiment with. Apply a blending mode—if you like it, keep it. If not, try another.

Of all the blending modes, the most essential is Multiply. The Multiply blending mode makes the top object transparent and blends the colors of the overlapped and overlapping objects in an effect that is similar to overlapping magic markers. Objects that overlap black become black, objects that overlap white retain their original color, and as with magic markers, objects with color darken when they overlap other colors.

Imagine you were drawing a puddle of pink lemonade spilled on a black, white, and yellow tiled floor. You would use the Multiply blending mode on the object you draw to represent the lemonade, as shown in Figure H-2. The color of the lemonade would not change where it overlapped the white tiles, because multiplying a color with white produces no change in the color. The lemonade would appear black where it overlapped the black tiles, because any color multiplied with black produces a black result. Where the pink lemonade overlapped the yellow tiles, the area would appear as a dark orange.

Because the Multiply blending mode reproduces real-world color situations, it is important for you to identify it as an essential component of your skills set. Don't forget that it's there!

Reducing opacity causes objects to appear translucent

Multiply blending mode mimics the effect of overlapping transparent ink, like a magic marker

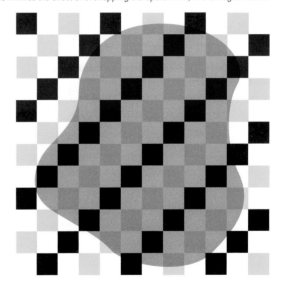

Working with the Color Picker

You use the Color Picker to specify new colors to be used as fills, strokes, or part of effects, such as drop shadows. The easiest way to access the Color Picker is to double-click the Fill or Stroke button in the toolbox.

In addition to allowing you to choose a new color, the Color Picker offers a valuable opportunity for studying the most fundamental color model, HSB, or Hue, Saturation, and Brightness.

The **hue** is the color itself. Blue, red, orange, and green are all hues. The Color Picker identifies hues based on the concept of a color wheel. Because there are 360 degrees to a circle, the hues on the color wheel are numbered 0–360. This is why you see a small degree symbol beside the H (hue) text box in the Color Picker dialog box. The color wheel is represented in the Color Picker by the vertical color

slider. Move the triangles along the color slider and watch the number in the H (hue) text box change to identify the corresponding hue on the color slider.

Does this mean that only 360 colors can be specified in the Color Picker? No, because each hue is modified by its saturation and brightness value.

Saturation refers to the intensity of the hue. A comparison of the colors of a tomato and a cranberry would be a fine illustration of different saturation values. Both have hues that fall within a "red" range. However, the tomato's red is far more intense, or saturated. In the Color Picker, 100% is the highest degree of saturation. A saturation value of 0% means that there is no hue, only a shade of gray. A black-and-white photo, for example, has no saturation value.

The reds of the tomato and cranberry also differ in brightness. The tricky thing about

understanding the brightness component of a color is that the term "brightness" is so common that it's difficult to know how it applies specifically to colors. A good example is a room with no windows filled with furniture and artwork. If you flood the room with light, all of the colors of the objects in the room will appear at their most vivid. If you have only a single, dim light source (like a flickering candle), the colors will appear less vivid, and many hues will be indistinguishable from others. If there were no light source whatsoever, no colors would appear, because in the absence of light there is no color.

In the Color Picker, 100% is the highest degree of brightness. A brightness of 0% is always black, regardless of the hue or saturation value specified. Thus, 100% saturation and 100% brightness produce a "pure" hue. Any lesser amount of saturation or brightness is a degradation of the hue.

Working with Transparency, Effects, and Graphic Styles

The Color Picker, shown in Figure H-3, is made up of a large color field. The color field represents the current hue and all of its variations of saturation and brightness. By dragging the circle around in the color field, you can sample different saturation and brightness values of the selected hue. Saturation values lie on the horizontal axis; as you move the circle left to right, the saturation of the color increases from 0% to 100%. Note that the colors along the left edge of the color field are only shades of gray. This is because the colors along the left edge have 0% saturation.

Brightness values lie on the vertical axis. All the colors at the bottom of the field are black (0% brightness). The color's brightness increases as you move up. Thus, the pure hue (100% saturation and 100% brightness) is at the top-right corner of the field.

For a hands-on example of these essential color concepts, you can drag the circle cursor around the color field. As the sampled color changes, you'll see that the H (hue) number remains constant while the S (saturation) and B (brightness) numbers change. You can change the hue by dragging the triangles along the color slider.

FIGURE H-3
Color Picker dialog box

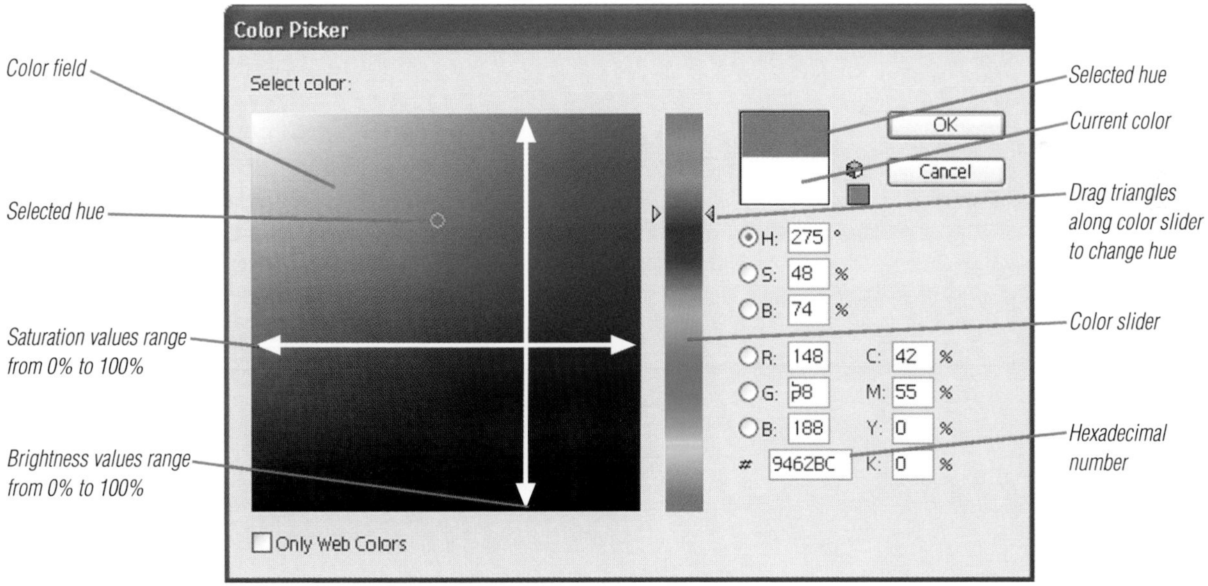

Color field

Selected hue

Saturation values range from 0% to 100%

Brightness values range from 0% to 100%

Selected hue

Current color

Drag triangles along color slider to change hue

Color slider

Hexadecimal number

Change the opacity and blending mode of objects

1. Open AI H-1.ai, then save it as **Transparency**.
2. Click **Window** on the menu bar, then click **Transparency**.
3. Select both the yellow circle and the letter T. The selection appears in the Transparency palette.
4. Click the **Opacity list arrow**, then drag the **Opacity slider** to 50.
5. Select the cyan and magenta circles, click the **Opacity list arrow**, then drag the **Opacity slider** to 20 so that your screen resembles Figure H-4.
6. Select the T and the three circles, then change the opacity to 100%.
7. Click the **Blending Mode list arrow**, click **Multiply**, then deselect all so that your screen resembles Figure H-5.
8. Save your work, then close the Transparency document.

You explored the results of changing the opacity of objects and the color effects achieved when you applied the Multiply blending mode to overlapping objects.

The three circles and the T at reduced opacity

Effect of the Multiply blending mode on overlapping objects

FIGURE H-6

Small circle indicates the saturation and brightness values of the selected hue

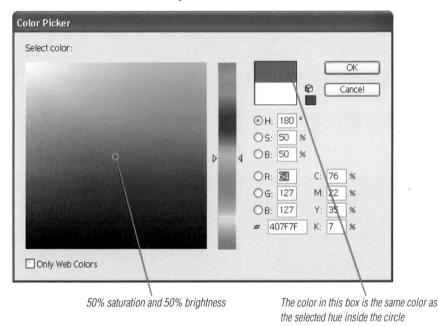

50% saturation and 50% brightness

The color in this box is the same color as the selected hue inside the circle

1. Open AI H-2.ai, then save it as **Limeade**.

2. Double-click the **Fill button** in the toolbox.

3. Type **240** in the H (hue) text box, type **100** in the S (saturation) text box, then type **100** in the B (brightness) text box.

   The triangles jump to the blue section of the color slider, and the circle in the color field moves to the top-right corner of the field.

4. Drag the triangles along the color slider down until the H (hue) value is 180.

   Note that the values change in the CMYK and RGB text boxes.

5. Type **50** in the S text box, then press [**Tab**].

   The circle in the color field moves left to 50% of the width of the color field, and the values in the CMYK and RGB text boxes are updated to reflect the change.

6. Type **50** in the B text box, then press [**Tab**].

   The color circle moves down to 50% of the height of the color field, as shown in Figure H-6.

7. Type **40** in the R text box, type **255** in the G text box, type **0** in the B text box, then click **OK**.

8. Add the new color to the Swatches palette, name it **Lime Green**, then save your work.

You used the Color Picker to select a new fill color. You sampled different colors, entered specific values for hue, saturation, and brightness, and entered specific values for red, green, and blue. You then added the new color to the Swatches palette.

APPLY EFFECTS TO OBJECTS

What You'll Do

▶ *In this lesson, you will work with a series of useful effects, using the Effect menu.*

Working with Effects

The commands listed on the Effect menu can be applied to objects to alter their appearance without altering the object itself. You can apply effects that distort, transform, outline, and offset a path—among other effects—without changing the original size, anchor points, and shape of the object. The object in Figure H-7 is a simple square with a number of effects applied to it, creating the appearance of a complex illustration.

So what is the point of working with effects? The best answer is that working with effects offers you the ability to change your mind and change your work at any point, because each effect can be easily removed from an object without disturbing other effects that may be applied to it.

When you work with effects, all of your actions are recorded and listed in the Appearance palette. You can, at any time, select an effect in the palette and modify its settings or delete it. When you work without effects—let's say, when you apply the Twist filter—the twist is applied to the object and affects the object. As you continue working, you continue to affect and alter your work. But what happens if, 20 steps later, you decide that you want to decrease the amount of the twist that you applied? You will have to undo everything you've done since applying the twist, then start all over again. If you had applied the Twist effect instead of the Twist filter, you could simply double-click the effect in the Appearance palette, then decrease the amount at which the twist is applied.

The Appearance palette is also a record of what you've done to create an illustration thus far—another benefit of working with effects.

You will note that many of the Effect commands are the same as other commands that you will find on the Filter menu. This can be a bit confusing. Remember that effects are different because they change only the look of the object, not the object itself.

FIGURE H-7
One square with multiple effects applied

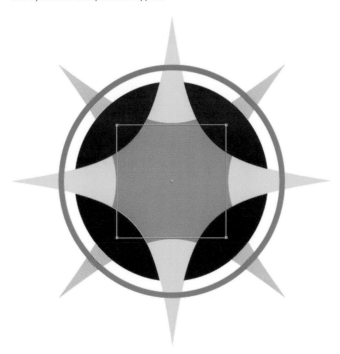

Apply a Bloat effect

1. Click **Window** on the menu bar, then click **Appearance**.

2. Click the **Selection Tool**, then click each letter object in LIMEADE so that they are all selected.

   The Appearance palette displays a new entry called Mixed Objects, meaning that mixed objects are selected. The A and the D are compound paths, while the remaining letters are regular paths.

3. Click **Effect** on the menu bar, point to **Distort & Transform**, then click **Pucker & Bloat**.

4. Type **11** in the text box, then click **OK**.

   The Pucker & Bloat item is listed in the Appearance palette.

5. Compare your image to Figure H-8.

   The selection marks represent those of the letters *before* the Bloat effect was applied, reflecting the fact that the original objects have not been actually changed by the effect.

You applied a Bloat effect to letter objects. You noted that the effect was listed in the Appearance palette and that the selection marks of the object did not change as a result of the applied effect.

Pucker & Bloat effect applied to letter objects

Selection marks show that the original objects have not been changed by the Bloat effect

Inner Glow effect affects the black stroke

Inflate Warp effect

Apply an Inner Glow and a Warp effect

1. Fill the LIMEADE letter objects with Lime Green.

2. Click **Effect** on the menu bar, point to the **first Stylize command**, then click **Inner Glow**.

3. Type **.15** in the Blur text box.

   | TIP If your dialog box does not show inches, type .15 in in the Blur text box.

4. Click the **color box** next to the Mode list arrow to open the Color Picker.

5. Type **10** in the C text box, **0** in the M text box, **100** in the Y text box, and **0** in the K text box, then click **OK**.

6. Click **OK** again to close the Inner Glow dialog box.

7. Apply a 3-pt black stroke to the letters so that your work resembles Figure H-9.

   The stroke does not appear black because the Inner Glow effect is altering its appearance.

8. Click **Effect** on the menu bar, point to **Warp**, then click **Inflate**.

9. Type **30** in the Bend text box.

10. Type **-30** in the Horizontal text box, click **OK**, then deselect.

   Your work should resemble Figure H-10.

You applied the Inner Glow effect to the letter objects, increased the Blur value, then specified the color of the glow, using the Color Picker. You applied a 3-pt black stroke, creating an interesting effect in conjunction with the Inner Glow effect. You then applied the Inflate Warp effect.

Apply a Drop Shadow effect

1. Select all of the LIMEADE letter objects.
2. Click **Effect** on the menu bar, point to **Stylize**, then click **Drop Shadow**.
3. Click the **Mode list arrow**, then click **Normal**.
4. Click the **Opacity list arrow**, then drag the **Opacity slider** to 100.
5. Click the **Color option button**, then click the **color box** to open the Color Picker.
6. Type **240** in the H text box, type **100** in the S and B text boxes, then click **OK**.

   The new color appears in the color box in the Drop Shadow dialog box.
7. Click **OK** to close the Drop Shadow dialog box.

   The Drop Shadow effect is listed in the Appearance palette.
8. Compare your screen to Figure H-11.

You filled the LIMEADE letter objects with Lime Green, then applied the Drop Shadow effect, using the Normal blending mode. You also accessed the Color Picker from within the Drop Shadow dialog box to determine the color of the shadow.

FIGURE H-11
Drop Shadow effect with a Normal blending mode

Normal blending mode produces an opaque drop shadow

Grain effect, isolated on its own layer

FIGURE H-13
Grain effect, multiplied at 25% opacity

Apply a Grain effect

1. Verify that the LIMEADE letter objects are still selected, copy them, then paste in front.

2. Verify that the Layers palette is displayed, create a new layer, then move the selected art to the new layer.

    TIP Move the selected art by dragging the Indicates Selected Art button on Layer 1 to the new layer.

3. Click **Effect** on the menu bar, point to **Texture**, then click **Grain**.

4. Type **71** in the Intensity text box, type **61** in the Contrast text box, then click **OK**.

5. Click the **Toggles Visibility button** 👁 on Layer 1 to hide Layer 1 so that you can see the results of the effect on Layer 2, as shown in Figure H-12, then click the **Toggles Visibility button** again to show the layer.

    Note that the drop shadow areas were included when the Grain effect was applied.

6. Click the **Opacity list arrow** on the Transparency palette, then drag the **Opacity slider** to 25.

    TIP When you change the opacity of a layer, all objects on the layer are affected.

7. Click the **Blending Mode list arrow**, then click **Multiply**.

8. Deselect, save your work, then compare your screen to Figure H-13.

You viewed LIMEADE on a new layer to view the Grain effect independently. You changed the opacity of the copied letters, then changed the blending mode to Multiply, allowing the original letters to be seen through the effect.

USE THE APPEARANCE PALETTE

What You'll Do

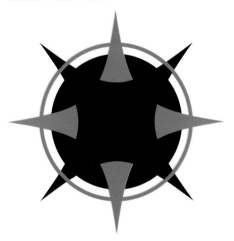

In this lesson, you will explore the role of the Appearance palette in controlling the appearance attributes of objects.

Working with the Appearance Palette

The Appearance palette does far more than simply list appearance attributes. It is the gateway for controlling and manipulating all of the appearance attributes of your artwork. The Appearance palette, as shown in Figure H-14, shows you the fills, strokes, and effects that have been applied to your artwork and offers you the ability to manipulate those attributes.

When you select an object on the artboard, the Appearance palette lists the associated attributes. Fills and strokes are listed according to their stacking order (front to back), and effects are listed in the order in which they are applied. You can double-click an effect in the Appearance palette to open the effect's dialog box, which will show the settings you used to apply the effect. This is an extremely valuable function of the palette. Imagine opening an illustration after six months and trying to remember how you built it! The Appearance palette provides a trail.

When you have applied a set of attributes to an object, and you then draw a new object, the new object will automatically "inherit" the set of attributes. If you want to remove them, simply click the Reduce to Basic Appearance button in the Appearance palette. You can also click the New Art Maintains Appearance button in the Appearance palette. When selected, the button converts to the New Art Has Basic Appearance button, which means that any newly created art will not inherit any attributes.

Duplicating Items in the Appearance Palette

A strange operation that you can execute with the Appearance palette is the application of multiple fills (and strokes) to a single object. Simply select the Fill attribute in the Appearance palette, then click the Duplicate Selected Item button in the palette. You can also duplicate an attribute by clicking the Appearance palette list arrow, then clicking Duplicate Item.

The Appearance palette is the only place where you can duplicate a fill. One would likely ask oneself, "Why would I need two fills anyway?" The answer is that you don't need two fills. The Appearance palette uses the second fill as a means to create a new object as part of the illustration. The second fill can be distorted and transformed and made to appear as an additional object, as shown in Figure H-15. In this figure, the black circle is the original fill, and the yellow and pink objects are duplicate fills. Note that the distortion (Pucker) and transformation (Rotate) of the duplicate fills are *effects* and were not created with a filter or a transform tool. Thus, this is a single object despite its appearance.

Duplicating an effect in the Appearance palette intensifies the effect.

Changing the Order of Appearance Attributes

You can change the order of attributes in the Appearance palette simply by dragging them up or down. The hierarchy of attributes directly affects the appearance of the object. For example, if you dragged the yellow fill attribute in the Appearance palette above the pink fill attribute, the illustration would appear as shown in Figure H-16.

FIGURE H-14
Appearance palette

Appearance thumbnail
An effect

Appearance palette list arrow
Clear Appearance button
Reduce to Basic Appearance button
Duplicate Selected Item button
Delete Selected Item button

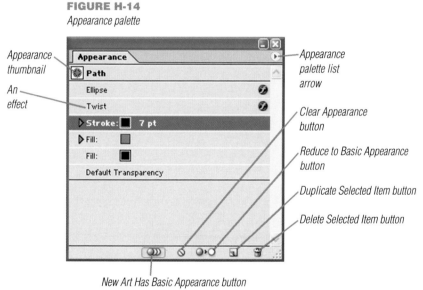

New Art Has Basic Appearance button

FIGURE H-15
Pink and yellow attributes are copies of the black fill

FIGURE H-16
The pink attribute is moved behind the yellow attribute

Modify effects

1. Hide Layer 2.
2. Select the LIMEADE letter objects on Layer 1, then double-click **Drop Shadow** in the Appearance palette.
3. Click the **Mode list arrow**, then click **Multiply**.
4. Type **.15** in the X Offset text box, then click **OK**.

   Your work should resemble Figure H-17.
5. Select Inner Glow in the Appearance palette, click the **Appearance palette list arrow**, then click **Duplicate Item**.

   The Inner Glow effect is intensified.
6. Deselect, then compare your work to Figure H-18.

You double-clicked the Drop Shadow item in the Appearance palette to access the effect's dialog box, which listed the parameters of the effect as you previously applied it. You changed the blending mode of the effect to Multiply, which allowed you to see the lime wallpaper through the blue shadow. You also changed the horizontal offset of the drop shadow. In the Appearance palette, you duplicated the Inner Glow effect.

Drop Shadow effect with a Multiply blending mode

*Multiply blending mode produces
transparent drop shadow*

Inner Glow effect is intensified when duplicated in the Appearance palette

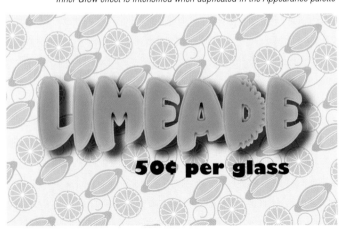

Working with Transparency, Effects, and Graphic Styles

Line inherits the current attributes in the Appearance palette

Add Arrowheads dialog box

Start window

End window

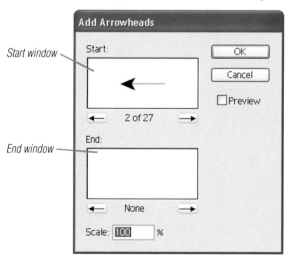

Remove effects from new art

1. Verify that you see the New Art Maintains Appearance button ⬠ in the Appearance palette.

   TIP If you do not see the New Art Maintains Appearance button, click the New Art Has Basic Appearance button to switch to the New Art Maintains Appearance button.

2. Change the fill to [None] and the stroke to black in the toolbox.

3. Click the **Pen Tool** ✎, click to the left of the number 5, press [**Shift**], then click directly below the L so that your work resembles Figure H-19.

   Notice that the line automatically inherits the effects in the Appearance palette.

4. Click the **Reduce to Basic Appearance button** ⬠ in the Appearance palette.

   The effects are removed from the new line.

5. Using the Stroke palette, click the **Round Cap button** ⬒, click the **Dashed Line check box**, type **6** in the first dash text box, then press [**Enter**] (Win) or [**return**] (Mac).

6. Click **Effect** on the menu bar, point to the **first Stylize command**, then click **Add Arrowheads**.

7. Click the **right arrow** below the Start window until you see arrowhead 2 of 27.

8. Click the **left arrow** below the End window until you see None, as shown in Figure H-20, then click **OK**.

   The Add Arrowheads effect is listed in the Appearance palette.

   (continued)

9. Click the **New Art Maintains Appearance
   button**  in the Appearance palette so that
   you see the New Art Has Basic Appearance
   button ⬚.

   When you click the New Art Maintains
   Appearance button, it becomes the New Art
   Has Basic Appearance button. When the New
   Art Has Basic Appearance button is active,
   newly created art will not inherit the current
   attributes.

10. Click the **Rectangle Tool** ⬚, draw a
    rectangle around the lime wallpaper back-
    ground, then remove the dashes so that the
    stroke is solid.

    The rectangle does not inherit the Add
    Arrowheads effect.

11. Show Layer 2, then deselect so that your
    screen resembles Figure H-21.

12. Save your work, then close the Limeade
    document.

*You created a simple line, noting that it automati-
cally inherited the effects in the Appearance
palette, then you removed the effects. You added
the Add Arrowheads effect. You then chose the
New Art Has Basic Appearance button in the
Appearance palette, and, when you drew a rectangle, noted that it did not inherit any effects.*

FIGURE H-21
Black rectangle has a basic appearance

FIGURE H-22
Appearance palette

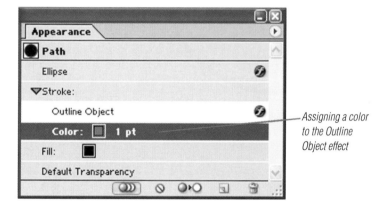

Assigning a color to the Outline Object effect

1. Create a new 6" × 6" CMYK Color document, then save it as **Triple Fill**.

2. Create a 2" square with a black fill and no stroke.

3. Click **Effect** on the menu bar, point to **Convert to Shape**, then click **Ellipse**.

4. Verify that the Relative option button is selected, type **.25** in the Extra Width text box, type **.25** in the Extra Height text box, then click **OK**.

   The square appears as a larger circle.

5. Click the **Stroke item** in the Appearance palette, click **Effect** on the menu bar, point to **Path**, then click **Outline Object**.

   The Outline Object effect is listed under the Stroke item.

6. Click the **Color attribute** under the Stroke item in the Appearance palette, then click **Green** in the Swatches palette.

   Compare your Appearance palette with Figure H-22.

   (continued)

7. In the Stroke palette, change the weight of the stroke to 7 pt.

8. Click **Effect** on the menu bar, point to **Path**, click **Offset Path**, type **.25** in the Offset text box, then click **OK**.

   Your screen should resemble Figure H-23.

9. Click the **triangle** ▽ next to the Stroke item in the Appearance palette to collapse the detail in the Stroke section.

10. Click the **Fill item** in the Appearance palette, then click the **Duplicate Selected Item button** ⬙ in the Appearance palette.

11. Keeping the original Fill item selected, click **Green** in the Swatches palette.

12. Click **Effect** on the menu bar, point to **Distort & Transform**, click **Pucker & Bloat**, type **-65** in the text box, then click **OK**.

   The green fill is distorted above the black fill, as shown in Figure H-24.

   (continued)

Outer circle is created with the Offset Path effect

Duplicated fill effect is distorted

Duplicated effect ——

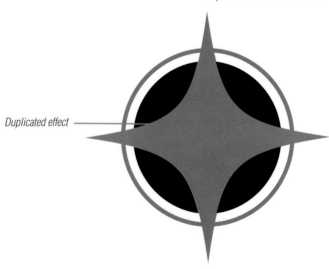

Working with Transparency, Effects, and Graphic Styles

Rotation on the third fill is an effect

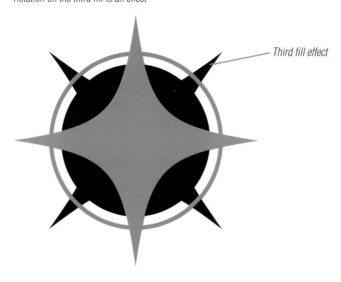

Third fill effect

FIGURE H-26
Changing the order of effects changes appearance

13. Click the **top Fill item** in the Appearance palette, then click the **Duplicate Selected Item button** 🔲 in the Appearance palette.

14. Click the **middle Fill item**, click **Effect** on the menu bar, point to **Distort & Transform**, click **Transform**, type **45** in the Angle text box, then click **OK**.

15. Click the **Color attribute** under the middle Fill item, then change it to black so that your work resembles Figure H-25.

16. Click the **middle Fill item**, drag it above the top Fill item so that your work resembles Figure H-26, then save and close the Triple Fill document.

Note that the illustration is a single object— as such, it can be used as a style.

You applied a number of effects to a simple square, creating the appearance of multiple objects. You also changed the appearance of the illustration by changing the order of the items in the Appearance palette.

WORK WITH GRAPHIC STYLES

What You'll Do

In this lesson, you will create and apply graphic styles.

Creating and Applying Graphic Styles

Graphic styles are named sets of appearance attributes that are accessed in the Graphic Styles palette. To create a new style, select the artwork whose attributes you want to save as a style, then do one of the following:

- Click the New Graphic Style button in the Graphic Styles palette.
- Drag a selected object from the artboard into the Graphic Styles palette.
- Drag a thumbnail from the Appearance palette into the Graphic Styles palette.

A graphic style can include fills, strokes, effects, patterns, opacity settings, blending modes, gradients, and effects. However, a graphic style can be created from a *single* set of attributes only. Only one object needs to be selected in order to create a new graphic style. The Graphic Styles palette is shown in Figure H-27.

Merging graphic styles

You can create new graphic styles by merging two or more graphic styles in the Graphic Styles palette. [Ctrl] click (Win) or ⌘ click (Mac) to select all the graphic styles that you want to merge, click the Graphic Styles palette list arrow, then click Merge Graphic Styles. The new graphic style will contain all of the attributes of the selected graphic styles and will be added to the Graphic Styles palette as a new graphic style.

When you apply a graphic style to an object, the new graphic style overrides any graphic style that was previously applied to the object. When you apply a graphic style to a group or a layer, all objects in the group or on the layer take on the graphic style's attributes. Graphic styles are associated with the layers they are applied to. If you remove an object from a layer that has a graphic style applied to it, the object will lose the graphic style attributes.

FIGURE H-27
Graphic Styles palette

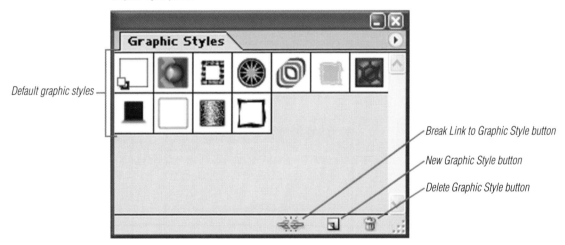

Default graphic styles

Break Link to Graphic Style button

New Graphic Style button

Delete Graphic Style button

Create a new graphic style

1. Open AI H-3.ai, then save it as **Dolphin Blue**.

2. Create a rectangle that is 1" wide and 2" tall.

3. Fill the rectangle with the Blue Radial swatch and remove any stroke.

4. Click the **Gradient Tool** ▣, then drag the **Gradient Tool pointer** from just below the top-left corner to the bottom-right corner of the rectangle.

   Try to make your fill resemble Figure H-28.

5. Click **Effect** on the menu bar, point to **Stylize**, click **Round Corners**, type **.15** in the Radius text box, then click **OK**.

6. Click **Effect** on the menu bar, point to **Stylize**, then click **Outer Glow**.

7. Change the color to black in the Color Picker, click **OK**, type **.1** in the Blur text box, then click **OK**, so that your work resembles Figure H-29.

8. Click **Window** on the menu bar, then click **Graphic Styles**.

9. Select all, then drag the **thumbnail** next to Path: Graphic Style in the Appearance palette to the Graphic Styles palette, as shown in Figure H-30.

10. Double-click the **new swatch** in the Graphic Styles palette, then name it **Dolphin Blue**.

You created an illustration with the Round Corners and Outer Glow effects, then saved the appearance attributes as a new graphic style in the Graphic Styles palette.

FIGURE H-30
Creating a new graphic style

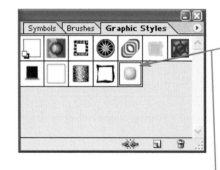
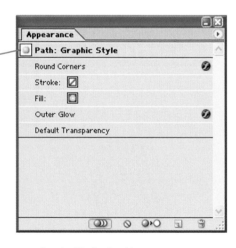

Drag the appearance thumbnail to the Graphic Styles palette to create a new graphic style

Dolphin Blue graphic style applied to an object

Dolphin
blue

1. Cut the rectangle from the artboard.
2. Click **Object** on the menu bar, then click **Show All**.

   A dolphin object and the words Dolphin blue appear.
3. Deselect all, select the dolphin artwork, then click **Dolphin Blue** in the Graphic Styles palette.

   Your work should resemble Figure H-31.

You applied a graphic style to a simple object.

Apply a graphic style to text

1. Click the **Graphic Styles palette list arrow**; if there is a check mark to the left of Override Character Color, click **Override Character Color** to remove the check mark.

2. Select the text, then click **Dolphin Blue** in the Graphic Styles palette.

   The text takes on all the attributes of the graphic style except the fill color, which remains black.

3. Undo your last step.

4. Click the **Graphic Styles palette list arrow**, click **Override Character Color**, then apply the Dolphin Blue graphic style to the Dolphin blue text.

   Your work should resemble Figure H-32.

5. Undo your last step, click **Type** on the menu bar, then click **Create Outlines** to convert the text to outlines.

6. Ungroup the outlines, then apply the Dolphin Blue graphic style to the objects so that your work resembles Figure H-33.

7. Compare the text fills in Figure H-33 to those in Figure H-32.

You explored three ways of applying a graphic style to text and text outlines for different effects.

FIGURE H-32
Dolphin Blue graphic style applied to text

FIGURE H-33
Dolphin Blue graphic style applied to each object

Working with Transparency, Effects, and Graphic Styles

FIGURE H-34

Artwork modified with a stroke and a second Outer Glow effect

Duplicate outer glow added to dolphin

Modify a graphic style

1. Select all, then apply a 1.5-pt. green stroke to the dolphin and the letters.

2. Deselect, select only rhe dolphin, click the **Outer Glow item** in the Appearance palette, then click the **Duplicate Selected Item** button .

3. Double-click the **duplicate Outer Glow item** in the Appearance palette, then change the opacity to 17% in the Outer Glow dialog box.

4. Click the **color box** in the Outer Glow dialog box to open the Color Picker.

5. Type **32** in the H (hue) text box, **100** in the S (saturation) text box, and **100** in the B (brightness) text box, then click **OK**.

6. Click **OK** again to close the Outer Glow dialog box, then deselect all.

    Your work should resemble Figure H-34.

7. Press and hold [**Alt**] (Win) or [**option**] (Mac), then drag the **thumbnail** from the Appearance palette directly on top of the Dolphin Blue graphic style in the Graphic Styles palette.

    The Dolphin Blue graphic style is updated to include the green stroke and the orange outer glow.

8. Save your work, then close Dolphin Blue.

You modified the Dolphin Blue graphic style by changing the settings in the Appearance palette, then replacing the old graphic style with the new appearance attributes.

Use the Transparency palette and the Color Picker.

1. Open AI H-4.ai, then save it as **Channel Z**.
2. Double-click the Fill button in the toolbox to open the Color Picker, create a color using the following values: hue = 59, saturation = 34, and brightness = 74, then drag the new color to the Swatches palette.
3. Select the square on the artboard, show the Gradient palette, if necessary, click the black color stop on the gradient slider, press [Alt] (Win) or [option] (Mac), then click the new color swatch in the Swatches palette. The new color replaces black on the gradient slider.
4. Change the opacity of the square to 60%.
5. Save your work.

Apply effects to objects.

1. In the Appearance palette, duplicate the Fill item.
2. Keep the original Fill item selected, click Effect on the menu bar, point to Texture, click Grain, click the Grain Type list arrow, then click Regular.

3. Type **70** for the Intensity and **60** for the Contrast, then click OK.
4. Click the Stroke item in the Appearance palette, then add a 1-pt. orange stroke.
5. Click Effect on the menu bar, point to Path, click Offset Path, type **.1** in the Offset text box, then click OK.
6. Save your work.

Use the Appearance palette.

1. Select the top Fill item in the Appearance palette.
2. Click Effect on the menu bar, point to the first Stylize command, click Round Corners, type **1** in the Radius text box, then click OK.
3. In the Transparency palette, change the blending mode to Multiply.
4. Select the bottom Fill item, then apply the Grain effect using the same settings that you previously used.
5. Expand the top Fill item, if necessary, double-click Grain to open the Grain dialog box, then change the Intensity to 100.

6. Duplicate the top Fill item, then change the Color attribute of the middle Fill item to the Orange Black gradient in the Swatches palette.
7. Remove the Round Corners effect from the top Fill item.
8. Collapse the three Fill items and the Stroke item.
9. Delete the Opacity: 60% Multiply item from the palette.
10. Save your work.

Work with graphic styles.

1. Show the Graphic Styles palette, if necessary.
2. Drag the thumbnail from the Appearance palette to the Graphic Styles palette.
3. Name the new graphic style **Static**.
4. Cut the artwork from the artboard.
5. Click Object on the menu bar, then click Show All.
6. Verify that Override Character Color is checked in the Graphic Styles palette menu.
7. Apply the Static style to the text.

8. Expand the Stroke item in the Appearance palette, then change its color to black and its weight to 1.5 pt.
9. Double-click the Offset Path item, then change the offset to .15.
10. Update the Static graphic style with the new attributes by pressing [Alt] (Win) or [option] (Mac) as you drag the thumbnail in the Appearance palette on top of the Static style in the Graphic Styles palette.
11. Save your work, compare your screen to Figure H-35, then close Channel Z.

FIGURE H-35
Completed Skills Review

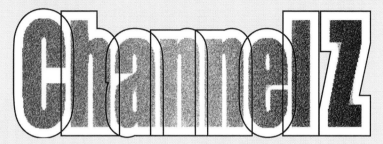

The local VFW has contracted you to design their monthly newsletter. You are happy, because it means a regular monthly payment. However, since their budget is modest, you decide to create templates so that your work is as streamlined as possible. One design element of the newsletter that is used every month is a red, white, and blue frame positioned around pictures. You decide to create this as a style in Illustrator.

1. Open AI H-5.ai, then save it as **Flag Frame**.
2. Show the Brushes palette, then apply the 10-pt Oval brush to the square.
3. Click Effect on the menu bar, point to Stylize, then click Round Corners.
4. Type **.15** in the Radius text box, then click OK.
5. In the Appearance palette, duplicate the stroke, then change the duplicate stroke color to blue.
6. Click the Offset Path command on the Effect menu. (*Hint*: Point to Path.)
7. Type **.18** in the Offset text box, then click OK.
8. Click the Transform command on the Effect menu. (*Hint*: Point to Distort & Transform.)

9. Type **90** in the Angle text box to rotate the blue frame.
10. Save the appearance attributes as a new graphic style in the Graphic Styles palette.

FIGURE H-36
Completed Project Builder 1

11. Name the new graphic style **Red and Blue Frame**.
12. Save your work, compare your screen to Figure H-36, then close Flag Frame.

Northstar Couriers has contracted you to design their logo, which is simply their name, NORTHSTAR. They tell you that your design will be applied to everything from their mail packs to their letterhead to their shipping vans.

1. Open AI H-6.ai, then save it as **Northstar**.
2. Select the square, then duplicate its fill in the Appearance palette.
3. Change the fill color to white, then click the Pucker & Bloat command on the Effect menu. (*Hint*: Point to Distort & Transform.)
4. Type **-77** in the text box, then click OK.
5. Select the top Fill item, then click the Transform command on the Effect menu. (*Hint*: Point to Distort & Transform.)
6. Type **20** in both the Horizontal and Vertical text boxes of the Scale section, then click OK.
7. Double-click Transform in the Appearance palette.
8. Type **-.25** in the Horizontal text box and **.25** in the Vertical text box of the Move section, then click OK.
9. Save the attributes as a new graphic style named Star in the Graphic Styles palette.
10. Cut the artwork from the artboard.

11. Type the word **NORTHSTAR** in 72-pt. Impact, then convert the text to outlines. (*Hint*: Click Type on the menu bar, then click Create Outlines.)
12. Ungroup the outlines.

FIGURE H-37
Completed Project Builder 2

13. Apply the Star graphic style to the text objects.
14. Save your work, compare your illustration to Figure H-37, then close Northstar.

Starlight.com, a local Web site that lists the schedules of the city's nightlife, has hired you to redesign their site. Part of that redesign will require a new masthead. They give you no specific direction on how they want their name displayed, but they do tell you that whatever design you create will be applied to other headlines throughout the site.

1. Open AI H-7.ai, then save it as **Starlight**.
2. Select the black square, then duplicate its fill in the Appearance palette.
3. Click the Free Distort command on the Effect menu. (*Hint*: Point to Distort & Transform.)
4. Move the top two selection handles down and outward, as shown in Figure H-38, then click OK.
5. Select the top Fill item in the Appearance palette, click Effect on the menu bar, point to Stylize, click Feather, type **.05** in the Feather Radius text box, then click OK.
6. Change the color of the top Fill item to 40% Black.
7. Select the bottom Fill item, then click Inner Glow on the Effect menu. (*Hint*: Point to Stylize.)
8. Specify the color for the glow as hue = 56, saturation = 100, and brightness = 84, change the blending mode to Normal and the Blur to .1, then click OK.
9. Save the attributes as a new graphic style named Starlight Glow in the Graphic Styles palette.

10. Cut the artwork from the artboard.
11. Type the word **STARLIGHT** in 72- Impact.
12. Apply the Starlight Glow graphic style to the text.
13. Save your work, compare your screen to Figure H-39, the close Starlight.

FIGURE H-38
Free Distort dialog box

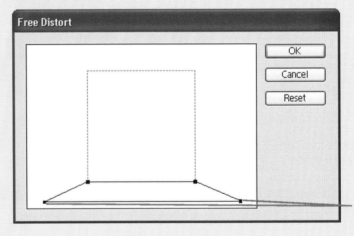

Drag top two points down and outward to these positions

FIGURE H-39
Completed Design Project

Working with Transparency, Effects, and Graphic Styles

This group project is designed to test your understanding of the workings of the Appearance palette and the way effects are applied. The challenge is to look at a piece of finished artwork and determine how and why the final effect was achieved.

Note: This exercise requires that you have already completed Project Builder 2 on page H-33.

1. Open Northstar.ai (the finished file that you created in Project Builder 2), then save it as **Appearance palette test**.
2. Draw a rectangle around the word Northstar, fill the rectangle with red, send it to the back, then deselect so that your image resembles Figure H-40.
3. Note that the white "stars" are more visible against the red background.
4. Poll the group: When you executed the steps from Project Builder 2, how many noticed that the "stars" are letters?
5. Here's the test: Have each member of the group write down an explanation—as long as need be—of how the effects applied in the steps yielded this result. The group member should reiterate steps and explain how each contributed to the final result.

FIGURE H-40
Group Project

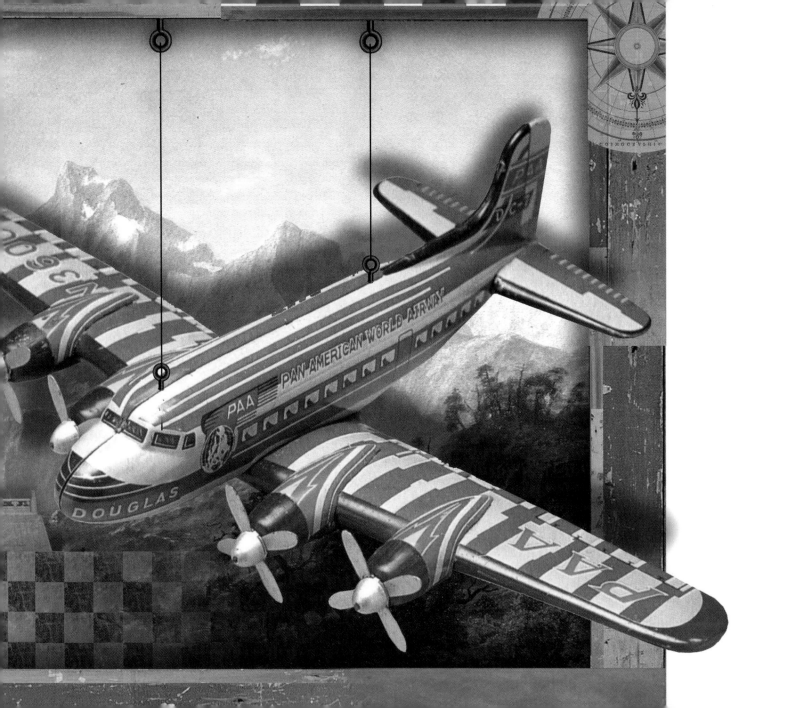

CHAPTER I

CREATING GRAPHS IN ILLUSTRATOR

1. Create a graph.

2. Edit a graph using the Graph Data window.

3 Use the Group Selection Tool.

4. Use the Graph Type dialog box.

5. Create a combination graph.

6. Create a custom graph design.

7. Apply a custom design to a graph.

8. Create and apply a sliding-scale design.

CHAPTER 1
CREATING GRAPHS IN ILLUSTRATOR

When you think of graphs, you probably think of those premade, click-a-button graphs that you can make with any presentation or financial software package. As a designer, you'll be really excited by the graphs that you can create with Illustrator's graph tools. When your project calls for a graph, you can enter the data directly into Illustrator, then have all of Illustrator's design and drawing power behind you when it comes to designing the graph.

For the right project, visually interesting and smartly designed graphs are a very powerful tool for conveying information. Think of using graphs as an opportunity for expressing data artistically. Since people naturally pay more attention to a well-designed graph than to blocks of text, using graphs in a presentation will help you to make your points more persuasively.

Tools You'll Use

*Group
Selection
Tool*

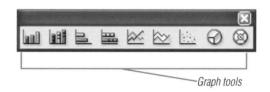

Graph tools

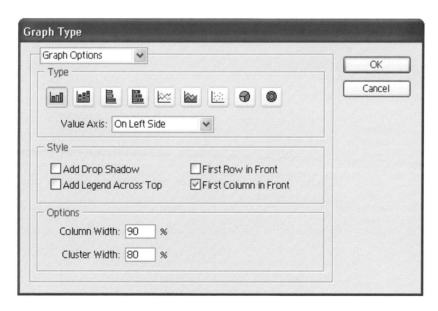

CREATE A GRAPH

What You'll Do

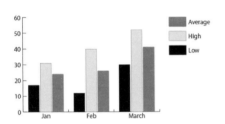

In this lesson, you will enter data and create a column graph.

Defining a Graph

A **graph** is a diagram of data that shows relationships among a set of numbers. A set of data can be represented by a graphic element, such as a bar, line, or point. Different types of graphs are used to emphasize different aspects of a display.

Illustrator offers nine types of graphs:
- Column
- Stacked column
- Bar
- Stacked bar
- Line
- Area
- Scatter
- Pie
- Radar

The right type of graph can help you to simplify complex data and communicate a message more effectively. In Illustrator, you can convert one type of graph into another type and create custom designs that you can then apply to the graph.

Changing the number of decimal points in graph data

Numbers in the Graph Data window are initially displayed with two decimals. For example, if you type the number 86, it appears as 86.00. To modify the number of decimals in any or all cells in the Graph Data window, click the cell(s) that you want to change, then click the Cell style button in the Graph Data window. The Cell Style dialog box opens. Increase or decrease the number in the Number of decimals text box to change the decimal place (set it to 0 if you do not want any decimal place), then click OK. You can also increase or decrease the column width in the Cell Style dialog box by changing the value in the Column width text box.

Creating a Graph

Before you create a graph, it is important to understand how data is plotted in Illustrator's Graph Data window. The first column (vertical axis) of the Graph Data window is reserved for category labels, while the first row (horizontal axis) is reserved for legend labels. See Figure I-1.

Category labels describe non-numeric data, such as the months of the year, the days of the week, or a group of salespersons' names.

Legend labels describe numeric data that may change, such as weekly sales totals, payroll amounts, or daily temperatures; they appear in a box next to the graph, called the legend.

The legend, like a map legend, contains the legend labels and small boxes filled with colors that represent the columns on the graph.

FIGURE I-1

FIGURE I-1
Entering category labels and legend labels

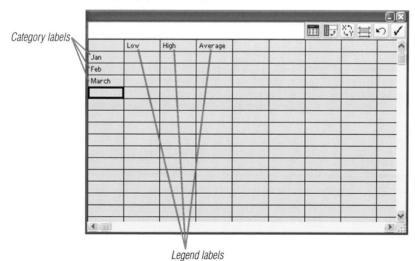

Category labels

Legend labels

Create a column graph

1. Open AI I-1.ai, then save it as **Graph**.

2. Verify that you are using inches as your General unit of measure by checking your Units & Display Performance Preferences.

3. Click the **Column Graph Tool** 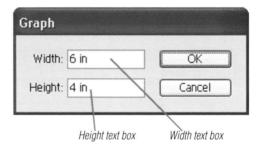, then click the center of the artboard.

4. Type **6** in the Width text box and **4** in the Height text box, as shown in Figure I-2, then click **OK**.

   The Graph Data window appears in front of the graph. The Graph Data window consists of rows and columns. The intersection of a row and a column is called a **cell**. The first cell, which is selected, contains the number 1.00 as sample data to create a temporary structure for the graph. The appearance of the graph will change after you enter your own data.

5. Press [**Delete**] (Win) or [**delete**] (Mac), then press [**Tab**] to eliminate the 1.00 from the first cell and select the next cell in the first row.

   You must always remove the number 1.00 from the first cell before entering new data.

6. Type **Low**, press [**Tab**], type **High**, press [**Tab**], then type **Average**.

   You have entered three legend labels.

   (continued)

FIGURE I-2

Graph dialog box

Height text box   Width text box

FIGURE I-3
Graph Data window

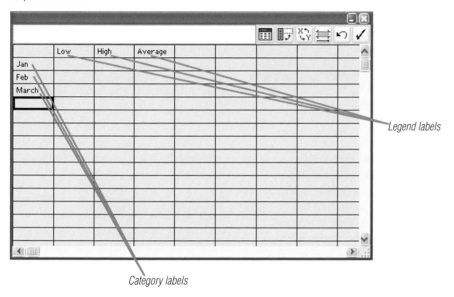

Legend labels

Category labels

FIGURE I-4
Column graph

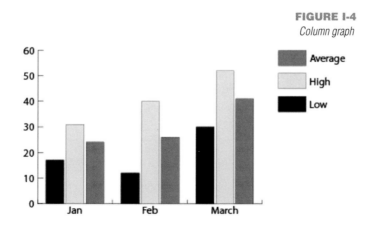

7. Click the **second cell** in the first column, type **Jan**, press [**Enter**] (Win) or [**return**] (Mac), type **Feb**, press [**Enter**] (Win) or [**return**] (Mac), type **March**, then press [**Enter**] (Win) or [**return**] (Mac).

You have entered three category labels. Compare the positions of your labels with those shown in Figure I-3.

> TIP Category labels are listed vertically and legend labels are listed horizontally in the Graph Data window. If you enter your labels incorrectly, you can click the Transpose row/column button in the Graph Data window to switch them.

8. Enter the remaining data shown on the artboard, using [Tab] and [Enter] (Win) or [Tab] and [return] (Mac), and the four arrow keys on your keyboard to move between cells.

> TIP Often you will want to create labels that consist of numbers, such as a ZIP code or the year 2008. Since these labels are meant to describe categories, they must be set in quotes ("2002") so that Illustrator will not mistake them for data that should be plotted.

9. Close the Graph Data window, saving the changes you made, then reposition the graph on the artboard (if necessary).

10. Deselect, save your work, then compare your graph to Figure I-4.

You defined the size of the graph, then entered three legend labels, three category labels, and numbers in the Graph Data window.

EDIT A GRAPH USING THE GRAPH DATA WINDOW

What You'll Do

	Low	High	Average				
Jan	17.00	31.00	24.00				
Feb	12.00	40.00	26.00				
March	30.00	52.00	41.00				

 In this lesson, you will change the data that is the basis of the column graph, then update the graph to reflect the new data.

Editing Data and Graphs

A project that calls for a graph often calls for edits to the graph. Fortunately, it is easy to make changes to the data that defines the graph . . . and just as easy to update the graph. For every graph in Illustrator, the data that was used to plot it is stored in the Graph Data window. The data is editable; when you make changes to the data, simply click the Apply button in the Graph Data window to preview the changes to the graph.

When you create text and data in another program that you want to use in an Illustrator graph, the document must be saved as a text-only file with commas separating each number from the next. If you are importing an Excel worksheet, it must be saved as a text (tab-delimited) file for Illustrator to support it.

Importing data from other software programs

You can import graph data from a text file or a Microsoft Excel worksheet into the Graph Data window in Illustrator. To import data, you must have the Graph Data window open and selected. Click the Import data button. You will then be prompted to open the file you wish to import.

FIGURE I-5

Changing data in the Graph Data window

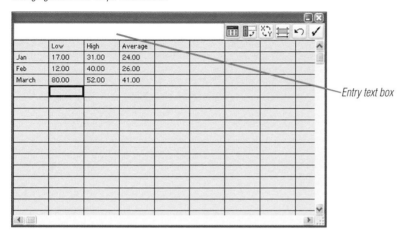

—Entry text box

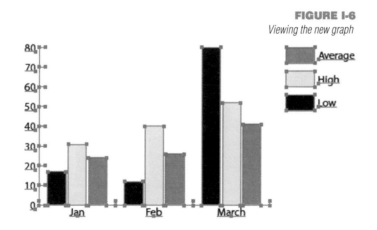

FIGURE I-6

Viewing the new graph

Edit data in a graph

1. Click **View** on the menu bar, then click **Hide Page Tiling**, if necessary.

2. Click the **Selection Tool** , then select and delete the text at the top of the artboard.

3. Click the **graph**, click **Object** on the menu bar, point to **Graph**, then click **Data**.

   TIP The separate objects that make up the graph are automatically grouped when the graph is created.

4. Click the cell that contains the number 30.00, type **80**, press [**Enter**] (Win) or [**return**] (Mac), then compare your screen to Figure I-5.

   When you click a cell, the number in the cell becomes highlighted in the entry text box of the Graph Data window, allowing you to change it to a new number.

5. Click the **Apply button** ✓ in the Graph Data window, then compare your graph to Figure I-6.

6. Change the number 80.00 to 34, click the cell that contains the number 41.00, type **43**, then press [**Enter**](Win) or [**return**](Mac).

7. Close the Graph Data window, then save changes when prompted.

   TIP To remove data from cells in the Graph Data window select the cells from which you want to delete the data, click Edit on the menu bar, then click Clear.

You edited the graph's data in the Graph Data window, then clicked the Apply button to view the changes to the graph.

USE THE GROUP SELECTION TOOL

What You'll Do

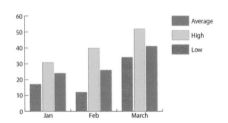

In this lesson, you will use the Group Selection Tool to easily select different areas of the graph for modification.

Using the Group Selection Tool

Graphs are grouped objects, consisting of many individual groups grouped together. Each set of colored columns represents an individual group within the larger group. For example, all of the black columns in Figure I-7 represent the low temperatures for each month. The gray columns are the average-temperature group, and the light gray columns are the high-temperature group.

The Group Selection Tool allows you to select entire groups within the larger group for the purpose of editing them with the Illustrator tools and menu commands.

FIGURE I-7

Individual groups within a graph

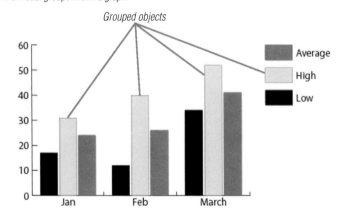

FIGURE I-8

Changing the color of the low-temperature group to red

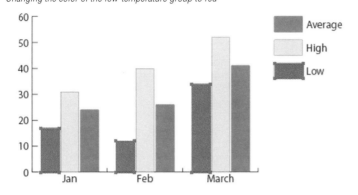

Use the Group Selection Tool

1. Click the artboard to deselect the graph.

2. Click the **Group Selection Tool** ▶⁺ .

   The Group Selection Tool is hidden beneath the Direct Selection Tool.

3. Click the **first black column** above the Jan label, then click again.

   The first click selects the first black column, and the second click selects the two remaining black columns.

4. Click the **first black column** a third time to select the low-temperature legend box.

   If you click too many times, you will eventually select the entire graph instead of an individual group. In that case, deselect and try again.

5. Change the fill color of the selected columns to red, as shown in Figure I-8.

6. Click the **first light gray column** above the Jan label, click it again, click it a third time, then change the fill color of the high-temperature columns and legend box to yellow.

7. Select the gray columns and legend box, change the fill color to green, then deselect all.

   Your graph should resemble Figure I-9.

8. Save your work.

   | TIP   The text labels, value axis labels, and legend labels are also individual groups within the larger graph group. Click twice to select them, then change their font, size, or color as desired.

You used the Group Selection Tool to select groups within the graph quickly and easily, then changed the colors of the columns and the legend boxes.

FIGURE I-9

Column graph with new colors applied

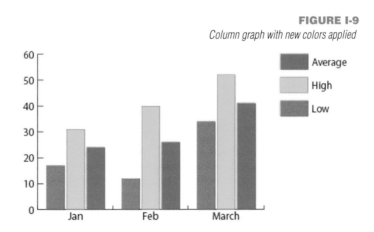

USE THE GRAPH TYPE DIALOG BOX

What You'll Do

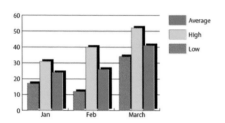

In this lesson, you will modify the graph using the Graph Type dialog box.

Using the Graph Type Dialog Box

The Graph Type dialog box provides a variety of ways to change the look of your graph. For example, you can add a drop shadow behind the columns in a graph or change the appearance of the tick marks.

Tick marks are short lines that extend out from the value axis, which is the vertical line to the left of the graph. Tick marks help viewers interpret the meaning of column height by indicating incremental values on the value axis. You can also move the value axis from the left side of the graph to the right side, or display it on both sides.

Values on the value axis can be changed, and symbols such as $, %, and ° can be added to the numbers for clarification.

Choosing a chart type

Keep in mind the following guidelines when choosing a chart type:
- Pie or column charts are typically used to show quantitative data as a percentage of the whole.
- Line or bar charts are used to compare trends or changes over time.
- Area charts emphasize volume and are used to show a total quantity rather than to emphasize a portion of the data.
- Scatter or radial charts show a correlation between variables.

FIGURE I-10
Graph Type dialog box

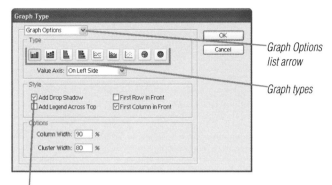

Graph Options
list arrow

Graph types

Add Drop Shadow
check box

FIGURE I-11
Choosing options for the value axis

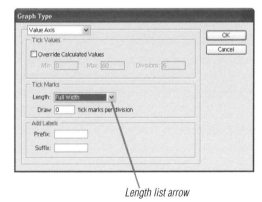

Length list arrow

FIGURE I-12
Graph with full-width tick marks and a drop shadow

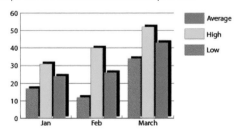

1. Click the **Selection Tool** , then click the **graph**.

    The entire graph must be selected to make changes in the Graph Type dialog box.

2. Click **Object** on the menu bar, point to **Graph**, then click **Type**.

3. Click the **Add Drop Shadow check box**, as shown in Figure I-10.

4. Click the **Graph Options list arrow**, then click **Value Axis**.

    All of the options in this window now refer to the value axis, which is the vertical line located to the left of the columns on the graph.

5. Click the **Length list arrow** in the Tick Marks section of the window, click **Full Width**, compare your Graph Type dialog box to Figure I-11, then click **OK**.

6. Deselect the graph, save your work, then compare your graph to Figure I-12.

    TIP   The Graph Type dialog box does not provide an option for displaying the number or value that each column in the graph represents. For example, it will not display the number 32 on top of a column that represents 32°. If you want to display the actual values of the data on the chart, you must add those labels manually, using the Type Tool.

You used the Graph Type dialog box to add a drop shadow to the graph and to extend the tick marks to run the full width of the graph.

CREATE A COMBINATION GRAPH

What You'll Do

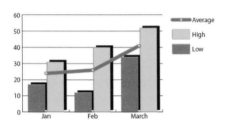

In this lesson, you will create a combination graph to show one set of data as compared to other data.

Defining a Combination Graph

A **combination graph** is a graph that uses two graph styles to plot numeric data. This type of graph is useful if you want to emphasize one set of numbers in comparison to others. For example, if you needed to create a column graph showing how much more paper than glass, plastic, or aluminum is recycled in a major city over a one-year period, you could plot the paper recycling data as a line graph, leaving the other recycling categories as columns. Your audience would be able to compare how much more paper is recycled than the other three products by looking at the line in relationship to the columns on the graph.

FIGURE I-13
Graph Type dialog box

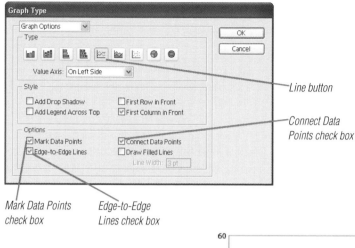

Line button

Connect Data
Points check box

Mark Data Points
check box

Edge-to-Edge
Lines check box

FIGURE I-14
Selecting the line graph

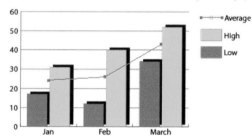

FIGURE I-15
Formatting the line graph

Markers

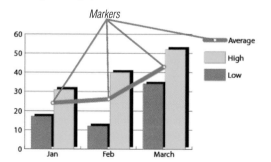

Create a combination graph

1. Click the **Group Selection Tool**, then select all four items of the Average (green) group.

2. Click **Object** on the menu bar, point to **Graph**, then click **Type**.

3. Click the **Line button**, then click the **Add Drop Shadow check box** to remove the check mark.

4. Click the **Edge-to-Edge Lines check box**, make sure that there are check marks in the Mark Data Points and Connect Data Points check boxes, as shown in Figure I-13, then click **OK**.

   The four green columns are replaced by four small square markers.

5. Click the **artboard** to deselect the graph.

6. Click the **Group Selection Tool**, then click the first line segment connecting the markers three times to select the entire line and the corresponding information in the legend, as shown in Figure I-14.

7. Click **Object** on the menu bar, point to **Arrange**, then click **Bring to Front**.

8. Change the stroke weight to 10 pt, the fill color of the line to [None], the stroke color of the line to green, and the cap to a round cap.

9. Deselect, select the four gray markers using the Group Selection Tool, change their fill color to white, then deselect again.

10. Save your work, compare your graph to Figure I-15, then close the Graph document.

You created a combination graph.

CREATE A CUSTOM GRAPH DESIGN

What You'll Do

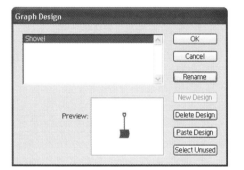

 In this lesson, you will define artwork that will be used for a custom graph.

Creating a Custom Graph Design

A **custom graph design** is simply a picture of something used to replace traditional columns, bars, or markers in Illustrator graphs. For example, when reporting on financial news, newspapers such as *USA Today* often print graphs made with custom designs of coins or dollars instead of columns and bars.

Only vector-based objects can be used for custom graph designs. You cannot use bitmaps, objects created with the Paintbrush Tool, or objects filled with gradients.

Illustrator contains predefined column and marker designs. To use these column or marker designs, start Illustrator, then open Column & Marker Designs1.ai or Column & Marker Designs2.ai, located in the Adobe Illustrator CS\ Sample Files\Graph Designs folder. Start a new document and create a graph. Select the graph, click Object on the menu bar, point to Graph, then click Column. All of the column designs will appear in the Graph Column dialog box.

Using supplied custom graph designs

Illustrator comes with two documents full of custom designs that you can apply to graphs. These designs include flags, cats, hammers, diamonds, dollar signs, stars, and men and women. In addition, three-dimensional objects such as cylinders, hexagons, cubes, arrows, and pyramids are available.

FIGURE I-16

Creating a custom graph design

Part A

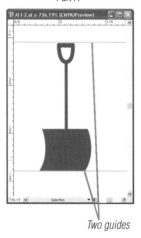

Part B

Two guides

Rectangle is the
same height as the
shovel and sent
behind the shovel

Part C

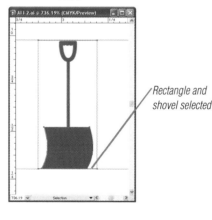

Rectangle and
shovel selected

FIGURE I-17

Graph Design dialog box

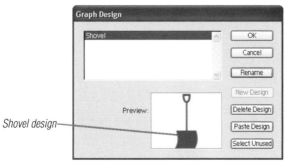

Shovel design

Create a custom graph design

1. Open AI I-2.ai, then save it as **Snow**.

2. Click **View** on the menu bar, then click **Shovel**.

3. Show the rulers (if necessary), then align two guides with the top and bottom of the shovel, as shown in Part A of Figure I-16.

4. Change the fill and stroke colors to [None] in the toolbox.

5. Click the **Rectangle Tool** ▭, then create a rectangle around the shovel that snaps to the top and bottom guides, as shown in Part B of Figure I-16.

   The height of the rectangle should exactly match the height of the custom design, to ensure that data values are represented correctly on the graph.

6. While the rectangle is still selected, click **Object** on the menu bar, point to **Arrange**, then click **Send to Back**.

   The rectangle must be behind the illustration.

7. Select both the rectangle and the shovel, as shown in Part C of Figure I-16, click **Object** on the menu bar, point to **Graph**, then click **Design**.

8. Click **New Design**, click **Rename**, name the design **Shovel**, then click **OK**.

   The shovel design appears in the Graph Design dialog box, as shown in Figure I-17.

9. Click OK to close the Graph Design dialog box, then save your work.

You created a custom design for graphs, using the Graph Design dialog box.

APPLY A CUSTOM DESIGN TO A GRAPH

What You'll Do

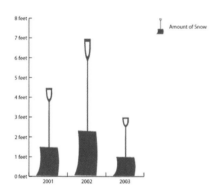

In this lesson, you will apply the shovel custom design to a graph.

Applying a Custom Design to a Graph

Custom designs are typically applied to column graphs and line graphs. Illustrator provides four options for displaying custom designs on a graph: uniformly scaled, vertically scaled, repeating, and sliding.

Uniformly scaled designs are resized vertically and horizontally, whereas vertically scaled designs are resized only vertically. Figure I-18 shows an example of a uniformly scaled design, and Figure I-19 shows an example of a vertically scaled design. Repeating designs assign a value to the custom design and repeat the design as many times as necessary. For example, if the shovel is assigned a value of 1 foot of snow, 3 shovels would represent 3 feet of snow. Sliding-scale designs allow you to define a point on the custom design from which the design will stretch, thereby leaving everything below that point uniform.

FIGURE I-18

A uniformly scaled custom design

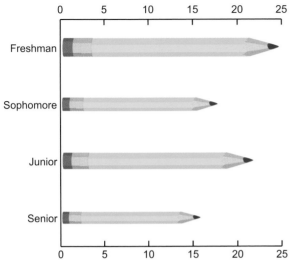

Hours of homework per week

FIGURE I-19

A vertically scaled custom design

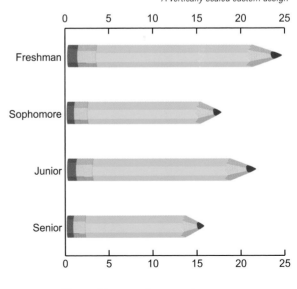

Hours of homework per week

Apply a custom graph design

1. Click **View** on the menu bar, then click **Fit in Window**.

2. Select the **graph** with the **Selection Tool** ⬉.

3. Click **Object** on the menu bar, point to **Graph**, then click **Column**.

   The Graph Column dialog box shows a list of custom designs you can apply to your graph.

4. Click **Shovel**, then verify that Vertically Scaled is selected for the Column Type, and that the Rotate Legend Design check box is not checked, as shown in Figure I-20.

   (continued)

(continued)

FIGURE I-20
Graph Column dialog box

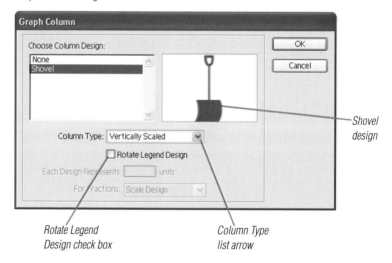

Shovel design

Rotate Legend Design check box

Column Type list arrow

5. Click **OK**.

   The three columns on the graph are replaced with shovels, each a different length, indicating how many feet of snow fell in each year.

6. Click the **artboard to** deselect the graph, so that your work resembles Figure I-21.

7. Save your work.

   TIP   To remove a custom design from a graph, select the graph, then click None in the Graph Column dialog box.

You selected a custom design in the Graph Design dialog box, you selected Vertically Scaled for the column type, and then you applied the custom design to a graph. The artwork is scaled vertically— taller or shorter—to represent the graph data.

FIGURE I-21
Shovel custom design applied to the graph

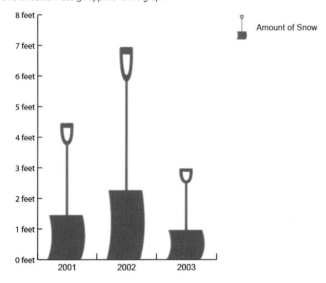

CREATE AND APPLY A SLIDING-SCALE DESIGN

What You'll Do

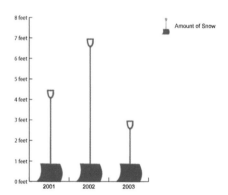

In this lesson, you will define the area on the shovel design that will be affected by a sliding-scale design. Then you will apply a sliding-scale design to the existing graph.

Creating a Sliding-Scale Design and Applying It to a Graph

When you apply a vertically scaled design style to a column graph, the entire design stretches to accommodate the value assigned to it. This expansion may present a problem if the custom design needs to maintain an aspect ratio. For example, a custom logo design might become unreadable if it is stretched too far. For this reason, a vertically scaled design can sometimes be unsatisfactory.

The answer to the problem is the sliding-scale design, which allows you to define a point on the custom design from which the graph will stretch. Thus a portion of the design can be specified to remain at its original size and not stretch. Figure I-22 shows an example of a sliding-scale design.

FIGURE I-22
A sliding-scale design

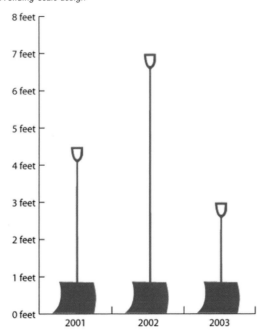

Create and apply a sliding-scale design

1. Return to the Shovel view, click **View** on the menu bar, point to **Guides**, click **Clear Guides**, then set the stroke color to black in the toolbox.

2. Using the **Pen Tool** ✎, draw a black line across the shovel, as shown in Figure I-23.

3. Click the **Selection Tool** ▶, select the entire line, click **View** on the menu bar, point to **Guides**, then click **Make Guides**.

   The black line turns into a guide, as shown in Figure I-23.

4. Click **View** on the menu bar, point to **Guides**, then verify that there is not a check mark to the left of Lock Guides.

5. Select the shovel, the rectangle, and the guide, so that all three objects are selected, as shown in Figure I-23.

   TIP Drag a selection box around the shovel to make sure you select the rectangle too, or switch to Outline view to see the outline of the rectangle. Because the rectangle has no fill or stroke, it is "invisible" in Preview view.

   (continued)

FIGURE I-23
Creating a sliding-scale design

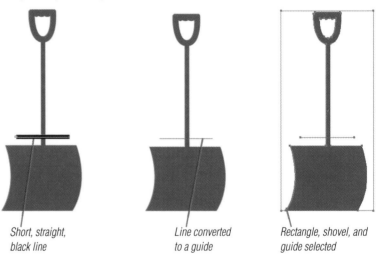

Short, straight,
black line

Line converted
to a guide

Rectangle, shovel, and
guide selected

FIGURE I-24
Graph Column dialog box

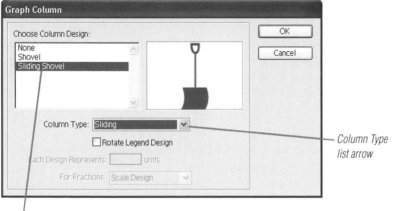

Sliding Shovel design

Column Type
list arrow

6. Click **Object** on the menu bar, point to **Graph**, then click **Design**.

7. Click **New Design**, click **Rename**, name the design **Sliding Shovel**, click **OK**, then click **OK** again to close the Graph Design dialog box.

8. Hide the guides, fit the document in the window, then select the graph.

9. Click **Object** on the menu bar, point to **Graph**, click **Column**, click **Sliding Shovel**, click **Sliding** from the Column Type list, as shown in Figure I-24, then click **OK**.

10. Deselect, then save your work.

Notice that the scoop of the shovel remains equal in all three columns, as shown in Figure I-25.

11. Close the Snow document.

You created a guide on top of the shovel design to identify the area of the artwork that will not be scaled in the graph. You then saved the new artwork as a new sliding-scale design.

FIGURE I-25
Completed graph

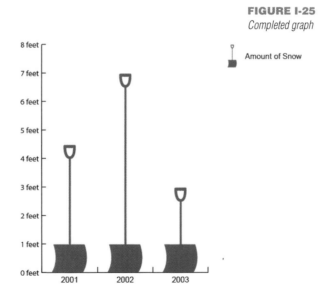

Amount of Snow

Create a graph.

1. Open AI I-3.ai, then save it as **Weather**.
2. Click the Column Graph Tool, then click the artboard.
3. Type **6** in the Width text box, type **4** in the Height text box, then click OK.
4. Delete the number 1.00 from the first cell in the Graph Data window.
5. Press [Tab] to select the next cell in the first row.
6. Type **Rain**, press [Tab], type **Sun**, press [Tab], type **Clouds**, then press [Tab].
7. Click the second cell in the first column, type **August**, press [Enter] (Win) or [return] (Mac), type **September**, press [Enter] (Win) or [return] (Mac), type **October**, then press [Enter] (Win) or [return] (Mac).
8. Enter the rest of the data that is supplied in the upper-left corner of the artboard to fill in the cells underneath Rain, Sun, and Clouds.
9. Close the Graph Data window, saving your changes to it.
10. Move the graph onto the artboard, if necessary.

Edit a graph using the Graph Data window.

1. Hide the page tiling, if necessary.
2. Delete the text at the top of the artboard.
3. Click the graph to select it.
4. Click Object on the menu bar, point to Graph, then click Data.
5. Click the cell that contains the number 7, and change it to 8.
6. Click the cell that contains the number 20, and change it to 19.
7. Drag the Graph Data window down slightly to view the artboard, then click the Apply button in the Graph Data window.
8. Close the Graph Data window.
9. Save your work.

Use the Group Selection Tool.

1. Deselect the graph, then click the Group Selection Tool.
2. Click the first black column above the August label, click a second time, then click a third time to select the Rain group.
3. Change the fill color of the selected columns to green.
4. Change the fill color of the Sun group to yellow.
5. Change the fill color of the Clouds group to violet.
6. Save your work.

Use the Graph Type dialog box.

1. Click the Selection Tool, then click the graph.
2. Click Object on the menu bar, point to Graph, then click Type.
3. Click the Add Drop Shadow check box, if necessary, to add a drop shadow.
4. Click the Graph Options list arrow, then click Value Axis.
5. Click the Length list arrow in the Tick Marks section of the window, then click Full Width.
6. Click OK.
7. Save your work.

Create a combination graph.

1. Deselect the graph, then, using the Group Selection Tool, select the entire Sun group.
2. Click Object on the menu bar, point to Graph, then click Type.
3. Click the Line button.
4. Click the Add Drop Shadow check box to deselect the option.
5. Click the Edge-to-Edge Lines check box.
6. Verify that both the Mark Data Points and Connect Data Points check boxes are checked, then click OK.
7. Click the artboard to deselect the graph.
8. Using the Group Selection Tool, select the line that connects the markers and the small corresponding line in the legend.
9. Change the stroke weight of the line to 10 pt.
10. Remove the fill color from the line, then change the stroke color of the line to yellow.
11. Save your work, compare your graph to Figure I-26, then close the Weather document.

Create a custom graph design.

1. Open AI I-4.ai, then save it as **Flowers**.
2. Click View on the menu bar, then click Flower.
3. Click View on the menu bar, then click Show Rulers, if necessary.
4. Drag two guides from the horizontal ruler; position one at the very top of the flower, and the other at the bottom of the stem.
5. Lock the guides, then set the fill and stroke colors to [None] in the toolbox.

6. Create a rectangle that is slightly wider than the width of the flower, and that snaps to the top and bottom of the guides.
7. Send the rectangle to the back. (*Hint*: If you deselect the rectangle and cannot see it, switch to Outline view, repeat Step 7, then switch back to Preview view.)
8. Select the flower and the rectangle.
9. Click Object on the menu bar, point to Graph, then click Design.
10. Click New Design, click Rename, name the design **Flower**, click OK, then click OK again.

FIGURE I-26
Completed Skills Review, Part 1

Apply a custom design to a graph.

1. Click View on the menu bar, then click Graph.
2. Select the graph with the Selection Tool.
3. Click Object on the menu bar, point to Graph, then click Column.
4. Click Flower, then make sure that Vertically Scaled is chosen for the Column Type.
5. Click the Rotate Legend Design check box to remove the check mark, then click OK.
6. Click the artboard to deselect the graph.
7. Save your work.

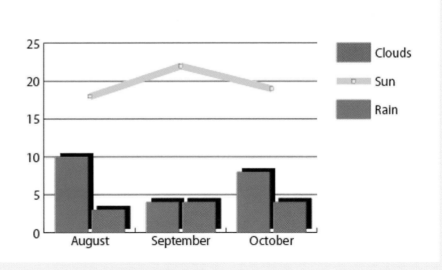

Create and apply a sliding-scale design.

1. Click View on the menu bar, then click Flower.

2. Click View on the menu bar, point to Guides, then click Clear Guides.

3. Set the stroke color to black and the fill color to [None].

4. Click the Pen Tool and create a short horizontal line above the two green leaves.

5. Switch to the Selection Tool, then click the black line. (*Hint*: Before switching to the Selection Tool, only the last anchor point on the line is selected.)

6. Click View on the menu bar, point to Guides, then click Make Guides.

7. Click View on the menu bar, point to Guides, then remove the check mark before Lock Guides, if necessary.

8. Select the flower, rectangle, and guide. (*Hint*: You may need to switch to Outline view to see the rectangle in order to select it, or you can drag a selection box around the items with the Selection Tool.)

9. Click Object on the menu bar, point to Graph, then click Design.

10. Click New Design, click Rename, name the design **Sliding Flower**, then click OK twice to close the Graph Design dialog box.

11. Click View on the menu bar, click Graph, then select the graph.

12. Click Object on the menu bar, point to Graph, then click Column.

13. Click Sliding Flower, click Sliding from the Column Type list arrow, then click OK.

14. Click View on the menu bar, point to Guides, then click Hide Guides.

15. Deselect the graph.

16. Save your work, compare your graph to Figure I-27, then close the Flowers document.

FIGURE I-27
Completed Skills Review, Part 2

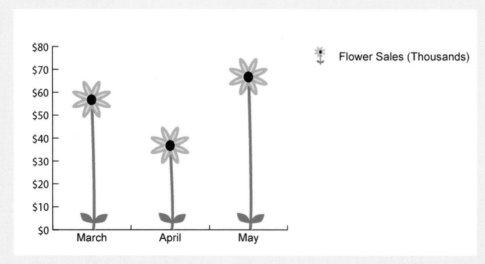

Creating Graphs in Illustrator

You are applying for financial aid to pursue a master's degree in nutrition and have been asked to submit your monthly living expenses. You decide to present the information in a simple column chart.

1. Open AI I-5.ai, then save it as **Expenses**.
2. Create a 6" wide by 4" tall column graph.
3. Delete 1.00 from the first cell, then press [Tab].
4. Type **Monthly Expenses**. (*Hint*: Don't worry if the title is not in full view.)
5. Enter the data as shown in Figure I-28.
6. Close the Graph Data window, saving your changes to the data.
7. Change the fill color of the graph columns and legend box to red.
8. Place a drop shadow behind the columns.
9. Click Object on the menu bar, point to Graph, click Type, click the Graph Options list arrow, click Value Axis, type **$** in the Prefix text box, then click OK.
10. Click Object on the menu bar, point to Graph, click Type, click the Graph Options list arrow, click Value Axis, click the Length list arrow under Tick Marks, click Full Width, then click OK.
11. Compare your graph to Figure I-29, save your work, then close the Expenses document.

FIGURE I-28
Project Builder 1 data

	Monthly ...
Rent	400.00
Car	200.00
Phone	85.00
Elec	25.00
Cable	30.00
Food	130.00
Gas	90.00

FIGURE I-29
Completed Project Builder 1

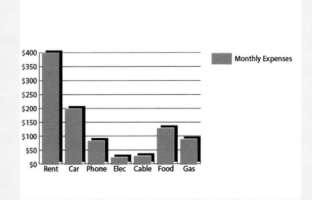

Creating Graphs in Illustrator

ILLUSTRATOR I-29

You own an independent market research consulting business that specializes in the television industry. You have recently conducted a survey of 1000 people who describe their television-watching habits as "regularly watch television." The question they were asked was "What is your favorite TV program?" Your research assistants have tabulated the data and supplied the breakdown to you as a column graph in an Illustrator file. You note that the words under the columns are running into each other, and you decide the graph would work better as a pie chart.

1. Open AI I-6.ai, then save it as **TV Pie**.
2. Create a 6" wide by 4" tall column graph.
3. Delete 1.00 from the first cell, then press [Tab].
4. Type **What is your favorite TV program?**
5. Using the information at the top of the artboard, enter the rest of the data.
6. Close the Graph Data window, saving your changes to the data.
7. Verify that the graph is selected, click Object on the menu bar, point to Graph, then click Type.

8. Click the Pie button, remove the check mark in the Add Drop Shadow check box, if necessary, then click OK.
9. Click Object on the menu bar, point to Graph, then click Data.
10. Click the Transpose row/column button in the Graph Data window. (*Hint*: The Transpose row/column button is the second button in the Graph Data window.)
11. Close the Graph Data window, save changes, then delete the information at the top of the artboard.
12. Save your work, compare your graph to Figure I-30, then close the TV Pie document.

FIGURE I-30
Completed Project Builder 2

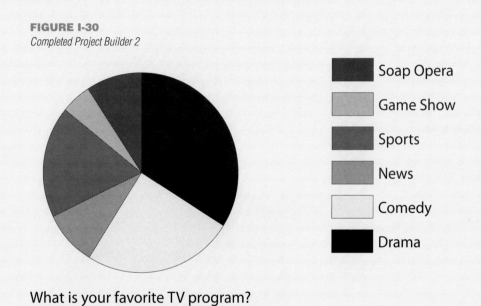

What is your favorite TV program?

You are a freelance designer, and you are hired by a small market research company that specializes in television. They are submitting an annual report to one of their network clients. The report contains a number of pie charts. They want you to design a look that is more "eye catching."

1. Open AI I-7.ai, then save it as **Designer Pie**.
2. Click the Group Selection Tool, then click the largest wedge two times. (*Hint*: The largest wedge and the Drama legend box are selected.)
3. Change the fill of the two objects to red.
4. Moving clockwise, fill the remaining wedges and legend boxes with orange, yellow, green, blue, and violet, respectively.
5. Deselect all, click the Direct Selection Tool, drag a marquee to select the pie chart only, then scale the chart 150%.
6. Deselect, click the Type Tool, type **34%** on top of the red wedge, change the font size to 27 pt, then set the fill color to white.
7. Moving clockwise, type the following percentage values on the remaining wedges: **25**, **9**, **18**, **5**, and **9**. (*Hint*: Change the fill color of the values on top of the yellow and orange wedges to black.)
8. Using the Direct Selection Tool, move each word from the legend over its corresponding wedge. (*Hint*: The words "Game Show"

and "Soap Opera" must be positioned outside of their corresponding wedge because they are too long.)
9. Change the fill color of Sports and Drama to white.
10. Hide the legend boxes, then reposition the What is your favorite TV program? text, and any other objects if necessary.
11. Select only the wedges of the graph, using the Direct Selection Tool.

FIGURE I-31
Completed Design Project

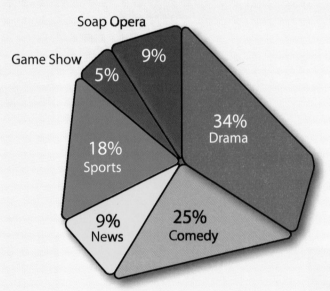

What is your favorite TV program?

12. Click Effect on the menu bar, point to Stylize, click Drop Shadow, choose Normal from the Mode list arrow, then click OK.
13. Click Effect on the menu bar, point to Stylize, click Round Corners, type **.139**, then click OK.
14. Apply a 2-pt black stroke to the pie wedges.
15. Save your work, compare your graph to Figure I-31, then close Designer Pie.

You are the chief designer of an in-house design group in a large department store. The head of the Digital Department has asked you to help with a presentation that shows how computers, scanners, and printers have been selling in comparison to one another over the last four weeks. Specifically, she wants you to create a graph that emphasizes how many more scanners she sells each week than computers or printers.

1. Gather the weekly sales data from each of the three departments, which is as follows:

	Computers	Printers	Scanners
Week One	11	13	55
Week Two	12	15	40
Week Three	14	6	61
Week Four	9	11	35

2. Draw a simple bar graph on the chalkboard, showing the sales relationships among the three products.
3. Have some members of the group discuss what would be the best type of graph to convey the data.
4. Have other members of the group decide the colors and fonts that will be used in the graph.
5. Create a new CMYK Color document, then save it as **Sales**.
6. Create a column graph that is 4" wide by 4" high.

7. Enter the data (from Step 1) in the Graph Data window.
8. Close the Graph Data window, saving changes to it.
9. Select the Scanners group, using the Group Selection Tool, then apply the line graph type to it.

FIGURE I-32
Completed Group Project

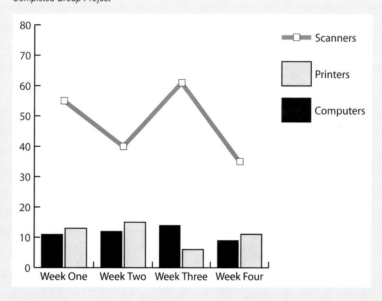

10. Change the color and thickness of the line graph so that it is easy to see.
11. Format the rest of the graph (labels, Printers group, and Computers group) if desired.
12. Save your work, compare your graph to Figure I-32, then close the Sales document.

CHAPTER J
DRAWING WITH SYMBOLS

1. Create symbols.

2. Place symbol instances.

3. Modify symbols and symbol instances.

4. Create symbol instance sets.

5. Modify symbol instance sets.

CHAPTER 1
DRAWING WITH SYMBOLS

In Illustrator, the file size of a document is largely determined by the number and complexity of objects in the document. The greater the number of objects in the document, the greater the file size. A large number of objects with gradients, blends, and effects *greatly* increases the file size. When you are creating graphics for the World Wide Web, file size becomes a serious concern.

Illustrator CS offers symbols as a solution for creating complex files while maintaining a relatively low file size. Symbols are art objects that you create and store in the Symbols palette.

Imagine that you were drawing a field of flowers, and you have drawn a pink, a blue, and a yellow flower. Each flower has a radial gradient in its center and color blends to add dimension to the petals and green leaves. Now imagine that you must drag and drop 200 copies of each to create your field of flowers! Along with a cramp in your hand, you would have an unusually large Illustrator file.

With the three flowers defined as symbols, you can create 200 symbol instances of each flower symbol quickly and easily. The key is: You haven't actually added the complex artwork multiple times, because the instances don't really exist as artwork. They are merely a reference to the original artwork that is the symbol; the instances function only to show the positioning of the symbol artwork on the artboard. Think of it this way: Symbol instances are merely virtual representations of a symbol.

Symbolism tools allow you to edit large numbers of symbol instances quickly and effectively. Whenever you are using the same artwork multiple times in a document, consider using symbols to save time and disk space.

Tools You'll Use

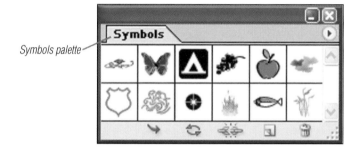

Symbols palette

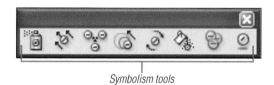

Symbolism tools

CREATE SYMBOLS

What You'll Do

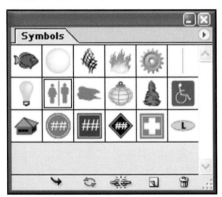

 In this lesson, you will create symbols from Illustrator artwork and save them in the Symbols palette.

Creating Symbols

A **symbol** is artwork that you store in the Symbols palette and reuse in the document. You can create symbols from any Illustrator artwork, including text, compound paths, and grouped paths. Symbols may also include blends, effects, brush strokes, gradients, and even other symbols. The Symbols palette, as shown in Figure J-1, is a great place to store artwork that you plan to use again. When you use symbol artwork, you can modify it on the artboard, while retaining its original appearance in the palette. In this way, you can think of the Symbols palette as a database of your original art.

FIGURE J-1
Symbols palette

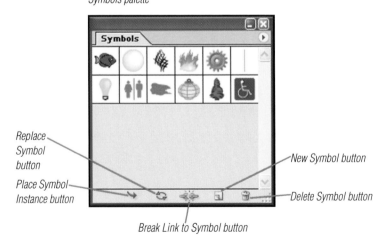

Replace Symbol button

Place Symbol Instance button

New Symbol button

Delete Symbol button

Break Link to Symbol button

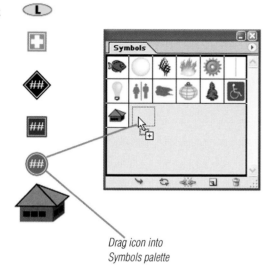

Drag icon into
Symbols palette

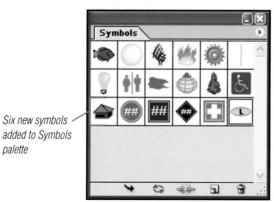

Six new symbols
added to Symbols
palette

Create symbols

1. Open AI J-1.ai, then save it as **Trail Map**.

2. Click **Window** on the menu bar, then click **Symbols**.

3. Select the brown house picture in the scratch area.

4. Click the **Symbols palette list arrow**, then click **New Symbol**.

5. Type **Ski Lodge** in the Name text box of the Symbol Options dialog box, then click **OK**.

   The Ski Lodge symbol becomes a new symbol in the Symbols palette.

6. Select the green circle icon in the scratch area, then drag it into the Symbols palette, as shown in Figure J-2.

7. Double-click the **green circle icon** in the Symbols palette, then name it **Novice**.

8. Add the blue square icon to the Symbols palette, then name it **Intermediate**.

9. Add the black diamond icon to the Symbols palette, then name it **Expert**.

10. Add the red square icon to the Symbols palette, then name it **First Aid**.

11. Add the yellow oval icon to the Symbols palette, then name it **Chairlift**.

    Your Symbols palette should resemble Figure J-3.

12. Delete the Ski Lodge, Novice, Intermediate, Expert, First Aid, and Chairlift icons in the scratch area, then save your work.

You created new symbols by using the Symbols palette menu and by dragging and dropping.

PLACE SYMBOL INSTANCES

What You'll Do

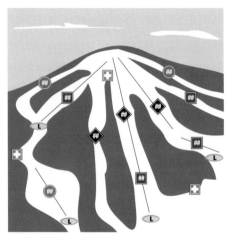

In this lesson, you will place symbol instances on the artboard.

Placing Instances of Symbols

If a symbol is artwork that is stored in the Symbols palette, then the artwork—when put to use in the document—is called a **symbol instance**. You can place a symbol instance on the artboard by first selecting the symbol in the Symbols palette, then dragging it to the artboard, or by selecting it, then clicking the Place Symbol Instance button in the Symbols palette or the Place Symbol Instance command on the Symbols palette menu, as shown in Figure J-4.

Symbol instances are "linked" to their corresponding symbols in the palette. This relationship introduces powerful functionality when you work with symbol instances. For example, you can select all the instances of a symbol by selecting the symbol in the palette and then clicking the Select All Instances command on the palette menu.

FIGURE J-4
Placing a symbol instance

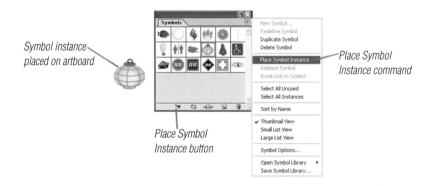

Symbol instance placed on artboard

Place Symbol Instance command

Place Symbol Instance button

FIGURE J-5

Positioning symbol instances

FIGURE J-6

Positioning copies of the Chairlift symbol instance

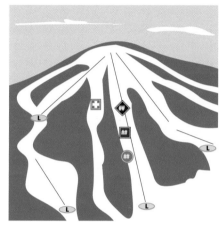

FIGURE J-7

Positioning the Novice, Intermediate, Expert, and First Aid symbol instances

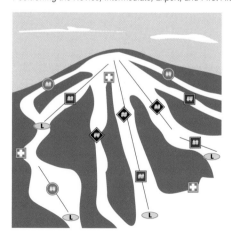

Place instances of a symbol

1. Click the **Novice symbol** in the Symbols palette.

2. Click the **Symbols palette list arrow**, then click **Place Symbol Instance**.

   A single Novice symbol instance appears on the artboard.

3. Drag the **Novice symbol instance** to the location shown in Figure J-5.

4. Click the **Intermediate symbol** in the Symbols palette, then drag it to the artboard above the Novice symbol instance.

5. Drag a **symbol instance** of the Expert, First Aid, and Chairlift symbols onto the artboard, then position them as shown in Figure J-5.

6. Press and hold [**Alt**] (Win) or [**option**] (Mac), drag and drop three copies of the Chairlift symbol instance, then position them as shown in Figure J-6.

7. Copy and reposition the Novice, Intermediate, Expert, and First Aid symbol instances so that your screen resembles Figure J-7.

   Dragging and dropping copies is the easiest way to duplicate the symbol instances.

8. Save your work.

You placed symbol instances of five symbols on the artboard. You then duplicated the symbol instances and positioned them on the artboard.

MODIFY SYMBOLS AND
SYMBOL INSTANCES

What You'll Do

▶ In this lesson, you will modify both symbol instances and the symbols themselves.

Modifying Symbol Instances

When working with symbol instances, approach them as you would any other Illustrator artwork. You can transform symbol instances by using commands on the Object menu or by using any of the transform tools. You can cut, copy, and drag and drop copies of symbol instances. You can perform any operation from the Transparency, Appearance, and Styles palettes. For example, you can reduce the opacity of a symbol instance and you can apply effects, such as a drop shadow or a distortion.

Symbols are most often composed of multiple objects, such as you would expect to find in a drawing of a butterfly or a flower, for example. When you select a symbol instance on the artboard, its selection marks show only a simple bounding box, as shown in Figure J-8; the individual elements of the artwork are not selected.

You can, however, select the individual components of a symbol instance by using the Expand command on the Object menu. The bounding box disappears, and the individual elements of the artwork are available to be selected (and modified), as shown in Figure J-9.

Modifying Symbols

Once you have modified a symbol instance, you can use the modified artwork on the artboard to redefine the associated symbol in the palette. When you do so, all existing symbol instances are updated and reflect the changes to the symbol. If you don't want a particular symbol instance to be updated, you can select the instance and break the link to the symbol. The symbol instance will no longer be associated with the symbol.

You can also modify a symbol instance on the artboard and use it to create a new symbol without affecting the original symbol that it is based on. Thus, the Symbols palette is very useful for storing subtle or dramatic variations of artwork. For example, if you are drawing a landscape that features a wind farm, you can draw a single windmill, save it as a symbol, rotate the blades on the original artwork, then save a new symbol, and so on.

Edit symbol instances

1. Select the green Novice symbol instance in the lower-left corner of the artboard.

   A bounding box identifies the selection. The elements of the artwork cannot be selected individually.

2. Click **Object** on the menu bar, then click **Expand**.

3. In the Expand dialog box, verify that the Object check box is checked and the Fill check box is not checked, then click **OK**.

   The elements of the symbol instance are selected individually.

4. Deselect the symbol instance, click the **Type Tool** T., highlight the two # signs in the symbol instance, then type **1**.

   Your screen should resemble Figure J-10.

5. Using the same method, expand the Novice, Intermediate, and Expert symbol instances, then change their numbers to those shown in Figure J-11.

6. Select all of the symbol instances and each of the blue lines, then hide them.

   > TIP Do not use the Select All command to select the symbol instances and the blue lines.

   Your screen should resemble Figure J-12.

You used the Expand command to allow you to select individual elements of a symbol instance and edit those elements.

FIGURE J-10
Editing a symbol instance

Replace ## with 1

FIGURE J-11
Adding numbers to symbol instances

FIGURE J-12
The artboard with the symbol instances hidden

FIGURE J-13

Positioning four symbol instances of the Ski Lodge symbol

FIGURE J-14

Updated instances of the Ski Lodge symbol

This ski lodge graphic is
not updated because it
is no longer linked to
the Ski Lodge symbol

Edit a symbol

1. Position four symbol instances of the Ski Lodge symbol, as shown in Figure J-13.

2. Select the bottom-right Ski Lodge symbol instance, then click the **Break Link to Symbol button** in the Symbols palette.

3. Select the top Ski Lodge symbol instance, then click the **Break Link to Symbol button**.

4. Scale the top ski lodge artwork 50%.

5. Press and hold [**Alt**] (Win) or [**option**] (Mac), then drag the **scaled artwork** on top of the Ski Lodge symbol in the Symbols palette.

   The three symbol instances of the Ski Lodge symbol are updated, as shown in Figure J-14. The bottom ski lodge artwork does not change.

6. Click the **Sequoia symbol**, then place one instance of the symbol in the scratch area.

7. Click the **Break Link to Symbol button**.

8. Deselect, click the **Direct Selection Tool**, remove the brown "tree trunk" areas from the symbol instance, then reduce the artwork 50%.

9. Press and hold [**Alt**] (Win) or [**option**] (Mac), then drag the **edited tree artwork** on top of the Sequoia symbol in the Symbols palette.

10. Delete the Sequoia symbol instance in the scratch area.

You edited symbols by modifying instances, then replacing the original symbols with the edited artwork. You protected a symbol instance from modification by breaking its link.

Transform symbol instances

1. Select the six green objects within the snow area of the artboard, then change their fill color to the Tree Shadow swatch so that your screen resembles Figure J-15.

2. Click the **Sequoia symbol** in the Symbols palette.

3. Click the **Place Symbol Instance button** ↘ in the Symbols palette, then position the instance on the artboard, as shown in Figure J-16.

4. Drag and drop nine copies of the Sequoia symbol instance on the artboard, so that your screen resembles Figure J-17.

(continued)

FIGURE J-15
Six objects filled with the Tree Shadow color

FIGURE J-16
Positioning the Sequoia symbol instance

FIGURE J-17
Positioning nine copies of the Sequoia symbol instance

FIGURE J-18

Positioning 14 copies of the Sequoia symbol instance

5. Verify that the Sequoia symbol is still selected in the Symbols palette, click the **Symbols palette list arrow**, then click **Select All Instances**.

   All instances of the Sequoia symbol are selected on the artboard.

6. Scale the symbol instances 75%.

7. Drag and drop 14 copies of the newly scaled Sequoia symbol instance to the opposite side of the artboard, as shown in Figure J-18.

   | TIP   Press [Alt](Win) or [option](Mac) while dragging to create copies.

8. Save your work.

You positioned one instance of a symbol on the artboard, then copied it nine times. You used the Select All Instances command to quickly select the ten instances of the symbol, scaled them 75%, then positioned 14 copies of the scaled symbol instance.

CREATE SYMBOL INSTANCE SETS

What You'll Do

In this lesson, you will use the Symbol Sprayer Tool to create sets of symbol instances and mixed symbol instance sets.

Creating a Symbol Instance Set

Instead of creating symbol instances one at a time using the Symbols palette, you can use the Symbol Sprayer Tool to create multiple symbol instances quickly. Imagine that you have a symbol of a star and you want to draw a night sky filled with stars. The Symbol Sprayer Tool would be a good choice for applying the star symbol multiple times.

Symbol instances created with the Symbol Sprayer Tool are called **symbol instance sets.** Incorporate the term "set" into your work with symbols to differentiate the multiple symbol instances created with the Symbol Sprayer Tool from individual instances of a symbol that you create using the Symbols palette.

To create a symbol instance set, click the symbol that you want to use in the Symbols palette, then drag the Symbol Sprayer Tool where you want the symbols to appear on the artboard.

Working with Symbol Instance Sets

When you create a symbol instance set with the Symbol Sprayer Tool, the entire set of symbols is identified within a bounding box, as shown in Figure J-19. If the set is selected and you begin clicking and dragging the Symbol Sprayer Tool again, the new symbol instances will be added to the selected set—even if the new symbol instances are outside of the existing set's bounding box. (The bounding box will expand to encompass the new symbol instances.)

You can also create mixed symbol instance sets. Mixed symbol instance sets include symbol instances based on more than one symbol. To create a mixed symbol instance set, create your first set of symbol instances, click a different symbol in the Symbols palette, then click and drag the Symbol Sprayer Tool where you want the new symbols to appear on the artboard. The new symbol instances will be added to the existing set, as shown in Figure J-20.

Even though a symbol instance set, by definition, appears as multiple objects, it is best to think of it as a single object. A symbol instance set can be modified and transformed (as a whole). Figure J-21 shows a symbol instance set that has been reflected using the Reflect Tool.

FIGURE J-19
A symbol instance set created with the Symbol Sprayer Tool

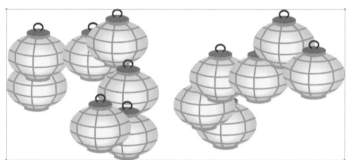

FIGURE J-20
A mixed symbol instance set

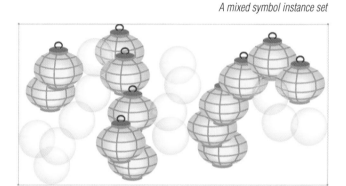

FIGURE J-21
A symbol instance set transformed with the Reflect Tool

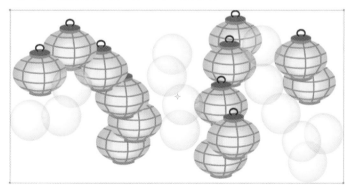

Setting Options for the Symbol Sprayer Tool

The Symbol Sprayer Tool has many options to help you control the dispersion of symbol instances. You can access these options in the Symbolism Tools Options dialog box by double-clicking the Symbol Sprayer Tool in the toolbox.

The Diameter setting determines the brush size of the tool. Use a larger brush size to disperse symbol instances over a greater area of the artboard. Note that the brush size does not determine the size of the symbol instances themselves.

The Intensity setting determines the number of instances of the symbol that will be sprayed. The higher the intensity setting, the greater the number of symbol instances that will be dispersed in a given amount of time.

The Symbol Set Density setting determines how closely the symbol instances will be positioned to each other. The higher the density setting, the more closely packed the instances will appear. Figure J-22 shows a symbol instance set with a high symbol set density, and Figure J-23 shows a symbol instance set with a low symbol set density.

FIGURE J-22

A symbol instance set with a high symbol set density

FIGURE J-23

A symbol instance set with a low symbol set density

Expanding a Symbol Set

Despite the many options available with the Symbol Sprayer Tool, it is often difficult to position multiple symbols exactly where you want them. For this reason alone, it is best to think of the Symbol Sprayer Tool as a means to quickly disperse symbol instances but not as a tool to position symbols precisely.

Once you have created a symbol instance set that contains roughly the number of symbol instances you want to work with and have positioned them roughly where you want them to be on the artboard, you can then apply the Expand command to release the set into individual symbol instances. Figure J-24 shows a symbol instance set expanded into individual symbol instances.

The power of this operation cannot be overstated. Once expanded, all the symbol instances of the set are available to you to be transformed, repositioned, duplicated, or deleted. Expand the individual symbol instances to be able to select their component parts.

FIGURE J-24

A symbol instance set expanded into individual symbol instances

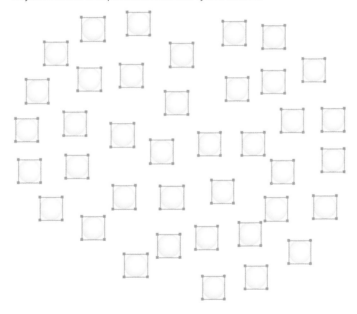

Use the Symbol Sprayer Tool

1. Click the **Sequoia symbol** in the Symbols palette, if necessary.

2. Double-click the **Symbol Sprayer Tool** .

3. Type **.5** in the Diameter text box, type **3** in the Intensity text box, type **5** in the Symbol Set Density text box, then click **OK**.

4. Click and drag the **Symbol Sprayer Tool** to spray instances of the Sequoia symbol over the gray areas so that your artboard resembles Figure J-25.

   TIP Don't try to create all the instances in one move. Click and drag the Symbol Sprayer Tool multiple times in short bursts. Your results will vary from the figure.

5. Press and hold [**Alt**] (Win) or [**option**] (Mac), then click the **Symbol Sprayer Tool** over symbol instances that you do not want to include to remove them, if necessary.

6. Select the symbol set, click **Object** on the menu bar, click **Expand**, verify that only the Object check box is checked, then click **OK**.

7. Using the Direct Selection Tool , move the individual Sequoia symbol instances so that your work resembles Figure J-26.

   You may also copy and/or delete instances, if necessary.

8. Click **Object** on the menu bar, click **Show All**, then while the hidden objects are still selected, bring them to the front, then deselect.

   Your screen should resemble Figure J-27.

9. Save your work, then close Trail Map.

You defined the diameter, the intensity, and the symbol set density for the Symbol Sprayer Tool. You then used the Symbol Sprayer Tool to create a set of Sequoia symbols.

FIGURE J-25

Instances of the Sequoia symbol created with the Symbol Sprayer Tool

FIGURE J-26

Symbol instances removed from the set

FIGURE J-27

The majority of the trail map artwork is created with symbol instances

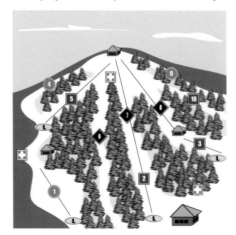

FIGURE J-28

Spraying instances of the Red Stone symbol

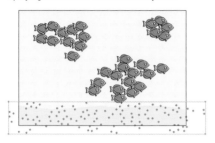

FIGURE J-29

Spraying instances of the Purple Stone symbol

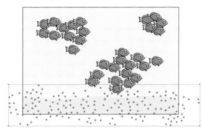

FIGURE J-30

Spraying instances of the Green Stone, Orange Stone, and Tan Stone symbols

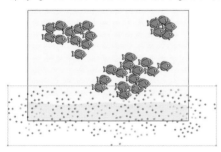

FIGURE J-31

Masking the mixed symbol instance set

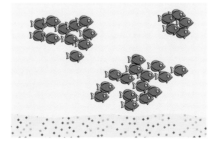

1. Open AI J-2.ai, then save it as **Fish Tank**.

2. Click the **Red Stone symbol** in the Symbols palette.

3. Double-click the **Symbol Sprayer Tool**.

4. Type **1** in the Diameter text box, type **8** in the Intensity text box, type **5** in the Symbol Set Density text box, then click **OK**.

5. Click and drag the **Symbol Sprayer Tool** over the "sand," as shown in Figure J-28.

6. Click the **Purple Stone symbol**, then drag the **Symbol Sprayer Tool** over the "sand," as shown in Figure J-29.

    The Purple Stone symbols are added to the set, creating a mixed symbol instance set.

7. Add the Green Stone, Orange Stone, and Tan Stone symbols to the set, so that your screen resembles Figure J-30.

8. Select the sand object, copy it, paste in front, then bring the copy to the front.

9. Press and hold [**Shift**], then click the **mixed symbol instance set** so that the sand and the set of rocks are selected.

10. Click **Object** on the menu bar, point to **Clipping Mask**, click **Make**, deselect, then save your work.

    The sand acts as a mask to hide the rocks that extend beyond the sand object, as shown in Figure J-31.

You used five different symbols and the Symbol Sprayer Tool to create a mixed set of symbol instances.

MODIFY SYMBOL INSTANCE SETS

What You'll Do

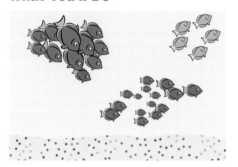

▶ In this lesson, you will use various symbolism tools to modify symbol instance sets.

Using Symbolism Tools

Illustrator offers seven symbolism tools that you can use to modify symbol instances or sets of symbol instances. You will most often use the symbolism tools to affect symbol instances within a set, since individual symbol instances are easy to select and modify directly with transform tools and menu commands. Table J-1 lists each symbolism tool and its function. Figure J-32 shows an illustration of a symbol instance set with each tool applied to the set.

TABLE J-1: Symbolism Tools

symbolism tool	function
Symbol Sprayer Tool	Places symbol instances on the artboard.
Symbol Shifter Tool	Moves symbol instances and/or changes their stacking order in the set
Symbol Scruncher Tool	Pulls symbol instances together or apart
Symbol Sizer Tool	Increases or decreases the size of symbol instances
Symbol Spinner Tool	Rotates symbol instances
Symbol Stainer Tool	Changes the color of symbol instances gradually to the current fill color in the toolbox
Symbol Screener Tool	Increases or decreases the transparency of symbol instances
Symbol Styler Tool	Applies the selected style in the Styles palette to symbol instances

When you apply symbolism tools to mixed symbol instance sets, each corresponding symbol must be selected in the Symbols palette in order for each type of symbol instance to be modified by the tool. For example, imagine you have created a mixed symbol instance set of four types of flowers (daisy, tulip, rose, and lily) and only the daisy symbol is selected in the Symbols palette. If you apply a symbolism tool to the mixed symbol instance set, only the instances of the daisy symbol will be modified.

When working with symbolism tools, it is also important that you set realistic goals. The symbolism tools are particularly useful if you have created a symbol set that is intended to appear random. For example, if you use symbol instances to render multiple stars in the night sky, the symbolism tools will be an excellent choice for modifying their orientation on the artboard. However, if your goal is to position symbol instances precisely in your artwork, you should expand the symbol set and use the selection tools and transform tools to modify each instance directly.

FIGURE J-32
Applying the symbolism tools

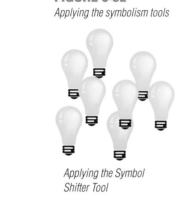

Applying the Symbol Shifter Tool

Applying the Symbol Sizer Tool

Applying the Symbol Spinner Tool

Applying the Symbol Stainer Tool

Applying the Symbol Screener Tool

Applying the Symbol Scruncher Tool

Applying the Soft Cast Shadow style with the Symbol Styler Tool

Use the Symbol Stainer Tool

1. Click **Object** on the menu bar, then click **Unlock All**.

2. Deselect, then select the set of fish symbol instances.

3. Change the fill color in the toolbox to green.

4. Click the **Symbol Stainer Tool** .

   The Symbol Stainer Tool is hidden beneath the Symbol Sprayer Tool.

   | TIP   Press and hold the current Symbol tool until you see all of the Symbol tools, then click the Tearoff tab at the end of the row of tools to create a floating palette of all of the symbolism tools.

5. Click and drag the **Symbol Stainer Tool** over the 11 fish symbol instances in the upper-left region of the artboard so that your work resembles Figure J-33.

   | TIP   Using the Symbol Stainer Tool results in increased file size and may tax your computer's performance.

6. Position the Symbol Stainer Tool over the bottommost fish symbol instance in the same group.

   (continued)

Applying the Symbol Stainer Tool with a green fill

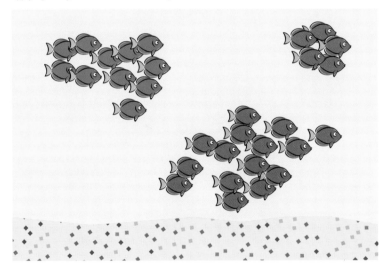

Drawing with Symbols

FIGURE J-34

Applying the Symbol Stainer Tool with a yellow fill

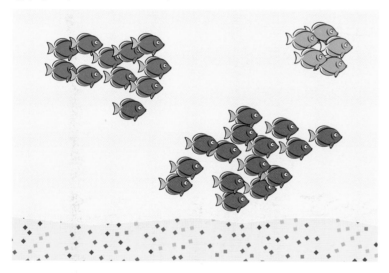

7. Press and hold [**Alt**] (Win) or [**option**] (Mac), then press and hold your mouse button for approximately two seconds.

   Pressing [Alt] (Win) or [option] (Mac) while using the Symbol Stainer Tool gradually removes color applied by the Symbol Stainer Tool. The symbol instance that you clicked returns to its original blue color. The surrounding symbol instances are not affected as directly; their color changes toward the original blue color, but remains somewhat green. Your results may vary.

8. Change the fill color in the toolbox to yellow.

9. Drag the **Symbol Stainer Tool** over the five fish symbol instances in the upper-right region of the artboard, so that your work resembles Figure J-34.

You used the Symbol Stainer Tool to modify the color of symbol instances within a set.

Use the Symbol Shifter Tool

1. Double-click the **Symbol Shifter Tool** to open the Symbolism Tools Options dialog box.

   The Symbol Shifter Tool is hidden beneath the current symbolism tool.

2. Type **.25** in the Diameter text box, then click **OK**.

3. Position the Symbol Shifter Tool over any of the green fish, press and hold [**Shift**], then click the **fish instance**.

   The symbol instance is brought to the front of the set.

   > TIP It's usually a good idea to enter a small diameter setting when you want to affect the stacking order of instances in a set. A larger brush will affect the stacking order of surrounding instances.

4. Press and hold [**Shift**][**Alt**] (Win) or [**Shift**][**option**] (Mac), then click a **green fish**.

   The symbol instance is sent to the back. Figure J-35 shows an example of the green fish instances after the stacking order has been affected by the Symbol Shifter Tool. Compare your choices and results.

5. Change the diameter setting of the Symbol Shifter Tool to 2.5.

6. Click and drag the **Symbol Shifter Tool** over the yellow fish until they no longer touch each other, as shown in Figure J-36.

   Your results may vary.

You used the Symbol Shifter Tool to change the stacking order of instances within the symbol set and to move symbol instances within the set.

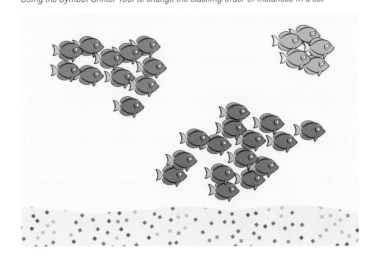

FIGURE J-36
Using the Symbol Shifter Tool to reposition instances within the set

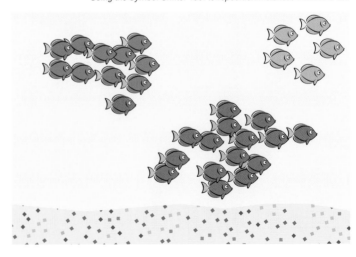

Using the Symbol Spinner Tool on the green fish

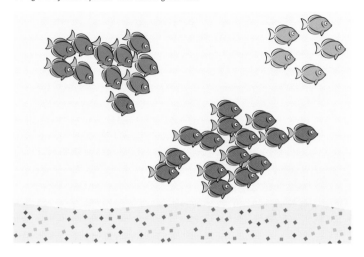

Using the Symbol Spinner Tool on the yellow fish

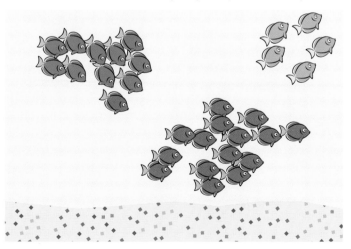

Use the Symbol Spinner Tool

1. Double-click the **Symbol Spinner Tool** .

2. Type **2.6** in the Diameter text box, type **10** in the Intensity text box, then click **OK**.

3. Position the Symbol Spinner Tool over the center of the green fish group.

4. Click and drag slightly to the right, so that the fish rotate, as shown in Figure J-37.

   Your results may vary.

   > TIP The blue arrows that appear when you click and drag the Symbol Spinner Tool are not always reliable predictors of the final rotation of the symbol instances. The diameter and intensity settings and the location of the tool in regard to the instances all affect the impact of the rotation.

5. Position the Symbol Spinner Tool over the center of the yellow fish group.

6. Click and drag slightly to the upper-left so that the yellow fish rotate, as shown in Figure J-38.

   Your results may vary.

You used the Symbol Spinner Tool to rotate symbol instances within the set.

Use the Symbol Sizer Tool

1. Double-click the **Symbol Sizer Tool** 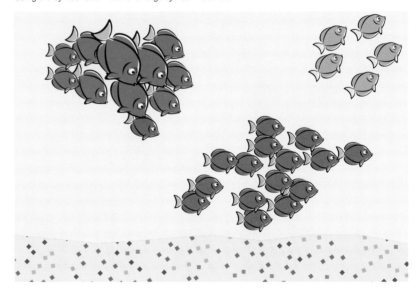.

2. Type **2** in the Diameter text box, type **8** in the Intensity text box, then click **OK**.

3. Position the Symbol Sizer Tool over the center of the green fish group.

4. Press and hold the mouse button for approximately two seconds so that your work resembles Figure J-39.

   Your results may vary.

5. Position the Symbol Sizer Tool over the center of the blue fish group.

(continued)

FIGURE J-39
Using the Symbol Sizer Tool to enlarge symbol instances

Drawing with Symbols

6. Press and hold [**Alt**] (Win) or [**option**] (Mac), then press and hold the mouse button for approximately three seconds.

7. Deselect all, then save your work.

   Your screen should resemble Figure J-40. Your results may vary.

8. Close the Fish Tank document.

You used the Symbol Sizer Tool to change the size of symbol instances within the set.

FIGURE J-40
Using the Symbol Sizer Tool to reduce symbol instances

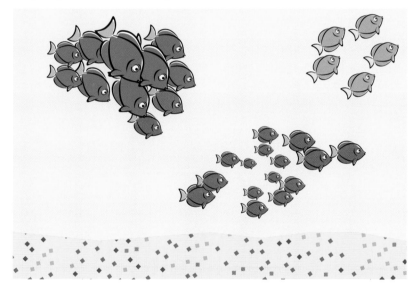

Create symbols.

1. Open AI J-3.ai, then save it as **Winter Ball**.
2. Show the Brushes palette, then drag the Radiant Star brush onto the artboard.
3. Verify that the Symbols palette is displayed, then drag the Radiant Star artwork into the Symbols palette.
4. Name the new symbol **Snowflake**.
5. Delete the Radiant Star artwork from the artboard.

Place symbol instances.

1. Click the Snowflake symbol in the Symbols palette.
2. Click the Place Symbol Instance button on the Symbols palette.
3. Position the symbol instance between the words ball and December.

Modify symbols and symbol instances.

1. Scale the Snowflake symbol instance 40%, then reposition the Snowflake symbol instance, if necessary.
2. Click Effect on the menu bar, point to Distort & Transform, click Pucker & Bloat, type **40** in the text box, then click OK.
3. Change the opacity of the symbol instance to 60%.

4. Click the Break Link to Symbol button.
5. Press [Alt] (Win) or [option] (Mac), then drag the modified snowflake artwork directly on top of the Snowflake symbol in the Symbols palette.

Create symbol instance sets.

1. Double-click the Symbol Sprayer Tool.
2. Type **1** for the Diameter, **1** for the Intensity, and **1** for the Symbol Set Density in the Symbolism Tools Options dialog box.
3. Spray approximately 25 symbol instances of the Snowflake symbol evenly over the artboard.

Modify symbol instance sets.

1. Use the Symbol Sizer Tool to enlarge and reduce symbol instances.
2. Expand the symbol set.
3. Move or delete symbols to your liking.
4. Save your work, then compare your illustration to Figure J-41. (*Hint*: Your results will vary from the figure.)
5. Close Winter Ball.

FIGURE J-41
Completed Skills Review

You work in the design department of a major Internet portal site. As part of the promotion of this year's Hooray for Hollywood Awards, your site will link to the Awards' site. You are asked to create a banner that says "click here to meet the stars" against a starry sky.

1. Open AI J-4.ai, then save it as **Hollywood**.
2. Double-click the Symbol Sprayer Tool.
3. Type **2** for the Diameter, **1** for the Intensity, and **10** for the Symbol Set Density.

4. Click the 5 Point Star symbol in the Symbols palette, then drag the Symbol Sprayer Tool across the gradient-filled rectangle.
5. Repeat Step 4, using the 8 Point Star symbol and the 4 Point Star symbol in the Symbols palette.
6. Expand the symbol set.
7. Use the Symbol Shifter Tool to move or delete symbol instances that overlap each other.

8. Use the Symbol Sizer Tool to enlarge and reduce symbol instances to add depth and variety.
9. Show all to reveal the semitransparent text.
10. Save your work, compare your illustration to Figure J-42, then close the Hollywood document.

FIGURE J-42
Completed Project Builder 1

You work at a busy design firm. Your boss e-mails you an Illustrator file. He tells you that the file contains a symbol of the American flag that he saved some months ago. He wants you to update the existing symbol in the Symbols palette so that the flag is scaled 25% and the opacity of the flag is 40%. He also wants the new symbol to show the flag waving.

1. Open AI J-5.ai, then save it as **Flag Symbol**.
2. Show the Symbols palette, if necessary, then place an instance of the American Flag symbol on the artboard.
3. Break the link between the symbol instance and the symbol.
4. Click Object on the menu bar, point to Envelope Distort, then click Make with Warp.
5. Click the Style list arrow, then click Flag.
6. Type **-30** for the Bend value, then click OK.
7. Scale the artwork 25%.
8. Show the Transparency palette, if necessary, then change the opacity of the artwork to 40%.
9. Replace the original American Flag symbol with the modified artwork, then remove the flag artwork from the artboard.
10. Save your work, then compare your Symbols palette with Figure J-43.
11. Close the Flag Symbol document.

FIGURE J-43
Completed Project Builder 2

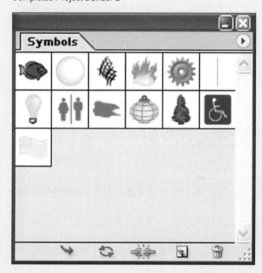

The nice lady who works at your town's Chamber of Commerce has created a poster for this year's Memorial Day parade and asks you if you could jazz it up. Since your firm is very busy, your improvements must be quick and simple. You e-mail a file containing a symbol of the American flag to an employee with instructions for updating the symbol. He e-mails the file back to you with the updated symbol, and you paste the parade text into the file.

1. Open AI J-6.ai, then save it as **Memorial Day**.
2. Fill the black rectangle with orange, then hide it.
3. Select all the elements on the artboard, then hide them.
4. Place an instance of the American Flag symbol in the lower-left corner of the artboard.
5. Create a pattern out of the American Flag symbol instances that covers the entire artboard. (*Hint*: Refer to Figure J-44 for ideas.)
6. Select all the symbol instances, group them, then send them to the back.
7. Show all, then deselect all.
8. Select the orange rectangle and the symbol instances, then make a clipping mask.
9. Apply a 10% cyan fill and a 3 point black stroke to the clipping mask.
10. Save your work, compare your screen to Figure J-44, then close Memorial Day.

FIGURE J-44
Completed Design Project

Drawing with Symbols

You own a design firm in Silicon Valley that specializes in solutions for Web sites. You are approached by a representative of Black Swan Technologies, a global company noted for engineering breakthrough devices in the medical field. The representative tells you that he wants you to redesign the splash page of their Web site to convey the fact that they work with all sectors of the medical industry. The company's motto is "We Are Everywhere."

1. Open Al J-7.ai, then save it as **Black Swan Technologies**.
2. Assemble your design team to discuss the Black Swan Technologies logo.
3. Does anybody think that parts of the logo suggest a bat more than a bird?
4. How does the group think that the concept "We Are Everywhere" can be incorporated visually into the splash page?
5. Discuss how reproducing the logo as a symbol presents possibilities for a splash page design based on the phrase "We Are Everywhere."
6. Create a new symbol using the swan artwork. (*Hint*: Modify the artwork using any Illustrator tools or features that you want before adding the new symbol to the Symbols palette.)

7. Use the swan symbol and the symbolism tools to create a new splash page for Black Swan Technologies.

FIGURE J-45
Completed Group Project

8. Save your work, then compare your results with Figure J-45.
9. Close Black Swan Technologies.

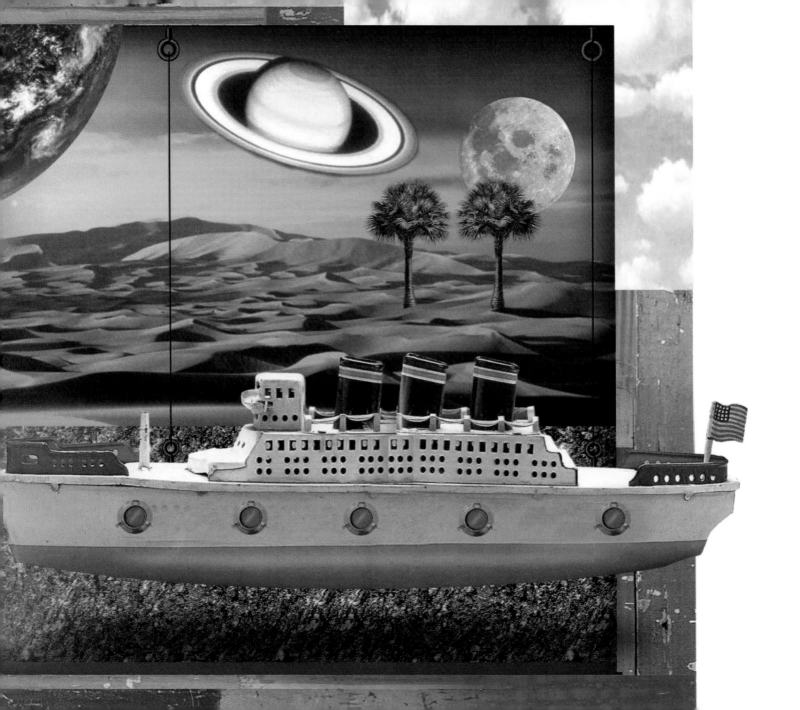

CHAPTER K

CREATING 3D OBJECTS

1. Extrude objects.

2. Revolve objects.

3. Manipulate surface shading and lighting.

4. Map artwork to 3D objects.

CHAPTER K
CREATING 3D OBJECTS

Of all the new features in Illustrator CS, the 3D effect is the most exciting. With unprecedented ease, you can transform a simple two-dimensional (2D) object into an eye-popping three-dimensional (3D) graphic. You can extrude 2D objects to give them depth, and you can add interesting details by applying a bevel edge. You can revolve 2D objects around an axis to create stunning 3D graphics, complete with surface shading and highlights. You have a number of options for manipulating that surface shading. Apply diffuse shading for subtle highlights, or apply plastic shading to make the object reflect light as though its surface were shiny. You can even add and delete light sources to dramatically change the way a 3D graphic is lit. If that's not enough, once you've designed the 3D object, you can "map" 2D graphics, making them appear to "wrap around" the 3D object. Very cool! So get ready for an entire chapter devoted to this fun new feature in Illustrator CS!

Tools You'll Use

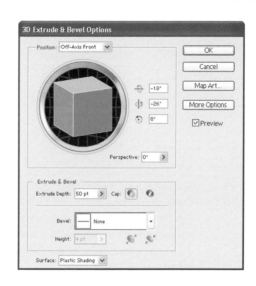

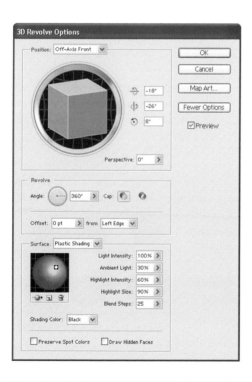

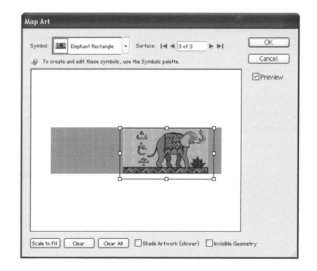

EXTRUDE OBJECTS

What You'll Do

In this lesson, you will use the 3D Extrude & Bevel effect to extrude objects.

Extruding Objects

Illustrator's **Extrude & Bevel** effect applies a three-dimensional effect to two-dimensional objects. A two-dimensional object has two axes: an X axis representing the width and a Y axis representing the height. When you **extrude** an object you add depth to an object by extending it on its Z axis, as shown in Figure K-1. An object's Z axis is always perpendicular to the object's front surface.

Figure K-2 shows four 2D objects before and after being extruded. Note the changes to each object's fill color on the front surface and the light and dark shadings on the other surfaces. These shadings create the 3D effect and are applied automatically when the Extrude & Bevel effect is applied.

QUICKTIP

3D effects may produce fills with flaws. These are usually screen aberrations—an issue with your monitor—and don't show when you print the document.

FIGURE K-1
Identifying the Z-axis on an extruded object

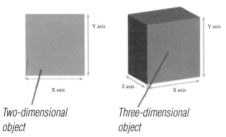

Two-dimensional object

Three-dimensional object

FIGURE K-2
Four objects before and after being extruded

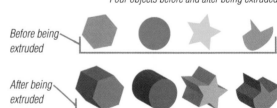

Before being extruded

After being extruded

You determine the degree of extrusion by changing the Extrude Depth value in the 3D Extrude & Bevel Options dialog box, shown in Figure K-3. Extrusion depth is measured in points. The greater the value, the more the object is extended on its Z axis, as shown in Figure K-4.

Use the Cap buttons in the 3D Extrude & Bevel Options dialog box to make extruded objects appear solid or hollow. The Turn cap on for solid appearance button is the default setting. It produces an object in which the front and back faces (surfaces) are solid, as shown in Figure K-5. The Turn cap off for

FIGURE K-3
3D Extrude & Bevel Options dialog box

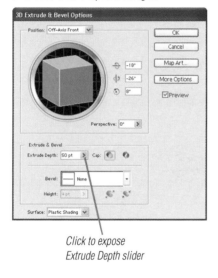

Click to expose
Extrude Depth slider

FIGURE K-4
Two objects extruded to different depths

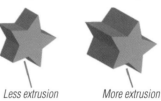

Less extrusion   *More extrusion*

FIGURE K-5
Activating the "solid cap" button

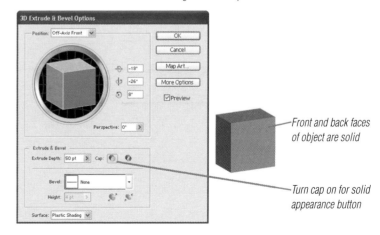

Front and back faces
of object are solid

Turn cap on for solid
appearance button

hollow appearance button makes the front and back faces invisible, producing an object that appears hollow, as shown in Figure K-6.

Rotating 3D Objects

The 3D Extrude & Bevel Options dialog box offers controls for rotating extruded objects.

You can rotate the object manually by dragging the rotation cube, shown in Figure K-7. The three text boxes to the right of the cube represent the selected object's X, Y, and Z axes. When you rotate the cube, the values in these text boxes update to reflect the changes you make. You may also enter

values in these text boxes to rotate the selected object at specific angles.

Once an object has been extruded, you can use the rotation cube to view any surface of the object—front, back, left, right, etc. The surface shading will update whenever you rotate an object.

FIGURE K-6
Activating the "hollow cap" button

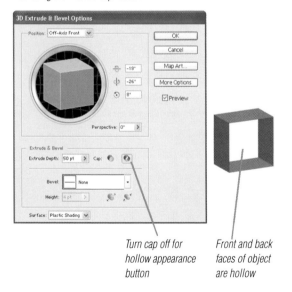

Turn cap off for hollow appearance button

Front and back faces of object are hollow

FIGURE K-7
Options for rotating 3D objects

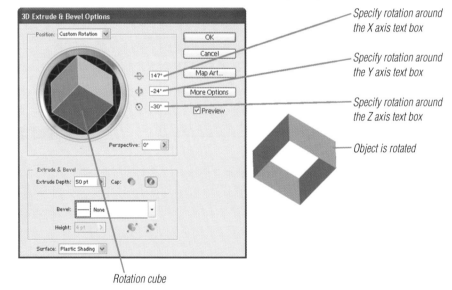

Specify rotation around the X axis text box

Specify rotation around the Y axis text box

Specify rotation around the Z axis text box

Object is rotated

Rotation cube

Extruding Compound Paths

Applying the Extrude & Bevel effect to a compound path can yield results that are visually very interesting. Figure K-8 shows a simple compound path—a circle with a square "knocked out" from its center—positioned in front of a light blue square. Figure K-9 shows the same object after being extruded.

Generally speaking, the more surfaces that an object has, the more interesting the 3D effect will be. Figure K-10 shows a complex compound path, and Figure K-11 shows the results when the Extrude & Bevel effect is applied.

FIGURE K-8
Simple compound path

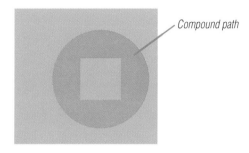

Compound path

FIGURE K-10
Complex compound path

FIGURE K-9
Simple compound path, extruded

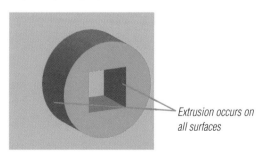

Extrusion occurs on all surfaces

FIGURE K-11
Complex compound path, extruded

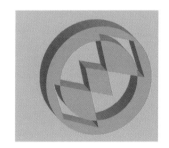

Applying a Bevel Edge to an Extruded Object

The dictionary defines the term **bevel** as the angle that one surface makes with another when they are not at right angles.

Figure K-12 shows an example of a graphic with a bevel edge.

The Bevel menu, shown in Figure K-13, offers ten pre-defined bevel shapes that you can apply to the edges of extruded objects.

The width of the bevel edge is controlled by the Height slider. Figure K-14 shows six objects, each with a different bevel shape applied to its edge. Each bevel has a width of 4 points.

FIGURE K-12

Identifying a bevel edge

FIGURE K-13

Viewing the Bevel menu

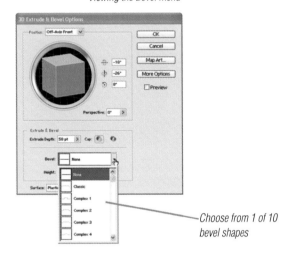

Choose from 1 of 10 bevel shapes

FIGURE K-14

Six objects with bevel shapes applied to edges

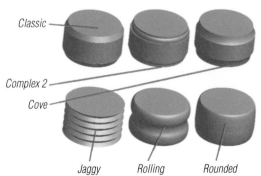

Classic

Complex 2

Cove

Jaggy   Rolling   Rounded

As shown in Figure K-15, text can be extruded without first having to convert it to outlines. Once extruded, you can add a bevel edge to text. Figure K-16 shows the same text with the Rounded bevel shape.

Because many letters are complex shapes, applying a bevel to extruded text often causes problems. Simply put, the shapes are too intricate to be rendered with a bevel edge. In Figure K-16, the two Ts and the E handle the

bevel edge quite well, but you can see that the X is becoming disfigured. In Figure K-17, the Classic bevel shape has been applied. The X isn't rendered properly with the Classic bevel shape applied to its edge.

The "X" is becoming disfigured

FIGURE K-17
Identifying problems with a bevel edge

The "X" isn't rendered properly

Whenever Illustrator is having difficulty rendering an object with a bevel edge, a warning appears in the 3D Extrude & Bevel Options dialog box, shown in Figure K-18. When problems do occur, sometimes there is no solution. Your best bet, however, is to reduce the width of the bevel. Figure K-19 shows the same text with the same Classic bevel shape shown in Figure K-17, but in this figure, the bevel width has been reduced from four points to three points. The dialog box continues to warn that there may be problems with the bevel edge. Though that may be the case, the problems are less obvious.

FIGURE K-18
Warning regarding a bevel edge

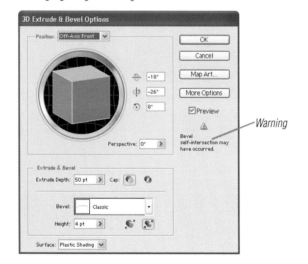

Warning

FIGURE K-19
Reducing the width of a bevel edge

The "X" is rendered fairly well

When you apply a bevel shape to an object's edge, you can decide how the bevel will be applied to the object using the Bevel Extent In and Bevel Extent Out buttons in the 3D Extrude & Bevel Options dialog box. The Bevel Extent In button produces a bevel edge that carves away from the edge of the existing object. The Bevel Extent Out button adds the bevel edge to the object. Figure K-20 shows the Bevel Extent Out and Bevel Extent In buttons. Generally speaking, the Bevel Extent In option is the better choice, because it stays within the already-established boundaries of the object.

FIGURE K-20
Bevel Extent Out and Bevel Extent In buttons

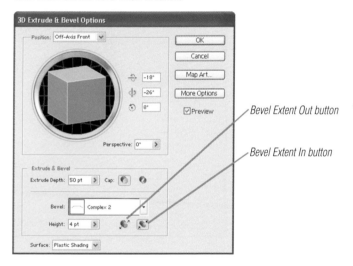

Bevel Extent Out button

Bevel Extent In button

Extrude an object

1. Open AI K-1.ai, then save it as **Extrude Objects**.
2. Click **View** on the menu bar, then click **Blue Square**.
3. Click the **Selection Tool** ▶, select the **blue square**, click **View** on the menu bar, then click **Hide Edges**.
4. Click **Effect** on the menu bar, point to **3D**, then click **Extrude & Bevel**.
5. Position the 3D Extrude & Bevel Options dialog box so that you can see the blue square, then click the **Preview check box**.

   As shown in Figure K-21, the blue square is extruded 50 points on the Z axis.
6. Click the **Extrude Depth list arrow**, drag the **slider** to 96 pt, then click **OK**.

   (continued)

FIGURE K-21

Applying the 3D Extrude & Bevel effect

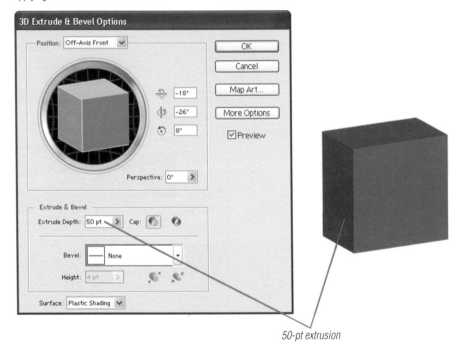

50-pt extrusion

Creating 3D Objects

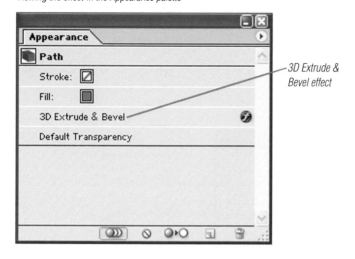

*3D Extrude &
Bevel effect*

7. Click **Window** on the menu bar, then click
   Appearance.

   As shown in Figure K-22, the Appearance
   palette lists the 3D Extrude & Bevel effect
   applied to the object.

8. Double-click **3D Extrude & Bevel** in the
   Appearance palette to open the dialog box,
   then click **Preview**.

9. Click the **Turn cap off for hollow appearance
   button** ⊙.

   The object's front and back "capping faces"
   become transparent, making the object
   appear hollow.

10. Click **OK**, then compare your work to
    Figure K-23.

*You applied the 3D Extrude & Bevel effect to a
selected object, increased the depth of the extrusion,
then changed the cap so that the 3D object would
appear hollow.*

FIGURE K-23
Viewing the extrusion with hollow caps

Extrude and rotate an object

1. Click **View** on the menu bar, then click **Orange Star**.

2. Select the star, click **Effect** on the menu bar, point to **3D**, then click **Extrude & Bevel**.

3. Click the **Preview check box**, then change the Extrude Depth value to 60 pt.

4. Position your cursor over the top-front edge of the rotation cube so that a rotate cursor appears, as shown in Figure K-24.

5. Click and drag to rotate the cube, noting that the value in the Specify rotation around the X axis text box is the only value that changes as you drag.

(continued)

FIGURE K-24
Manipulating the rotation cube manually

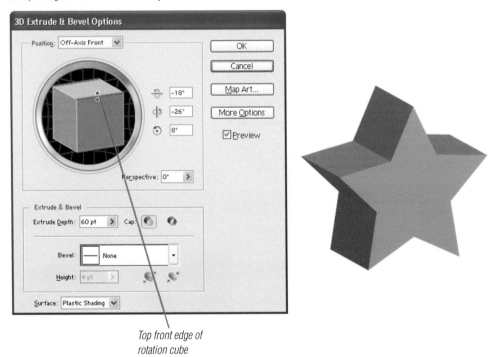

Top front edge of
rotation cube

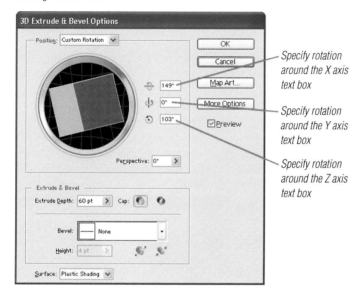

Specify rotation around the X axis text box

Specify rotation around the Y axis text box

Specify rotation around the Z axis text box

6. Experiment with different rotations by dragging the rotation cube from all sides, and note the changes to the orange star object on the page.

7. Double-click the **Specify rotation around the X axis text box** to select its contents, type **149**, then press **[Tab]**.

   > TIP   Include the negative sign when you select the contents in the Specify rotation around the X axis text box.

8. Type **0** in the Specify rotation around the Y axis text box, press **[Tab]**, type **103** in the Specify rotation around the Z axis text box, press **[Tab]**, then compare your dialog box to Figure K-25.

9. Click **OK**, then compare your work to Figure K-26.

You applied the 3D Extrude & Bevel effect to a star-shaped object, then manipulated the rotation cube to rotate the object.

FIGURE K-26
Viewing the rotated star

Extrude a compound path

1. Click **View** on the menu bar, then click **Target**.

2. Select all three circles, click **Object** on the menu bar, point to **Compound Path**, then click **Make**.

3. Click **Effect** on the menu bar, point to **3D**, then click **Extrude & Bevel**.

4. Click the **Preview check box**, then change the Extrude Depth value to 100 pt.

5. Experiment with different rotations by dragging the rotation cube from all sides.

6. Double-click the **Specify rotation around the X axis text box**, type **28**, then press **[Tab]**.

   TIP If the negative sign is not selected when you double-click the value in the Specify rotation around the X axis text box, make sure you select it before you type 28.

7. Type **-26** in the Specify rotation around the Y axis text box, press **[Tab]**, type **8** in the Specify rotation around the Z axis text box, then press **[Tab]**.

8. Click **OK**, then compare your work to Figure K-27.

You created a compound path, applied the 3D Extrude & Bevel effect, then rotated the graphic, all the time noting the visual effect created by applying the effect to a compound path.

Viewing the 3D Extrude & Bevel effect applied to a compound path

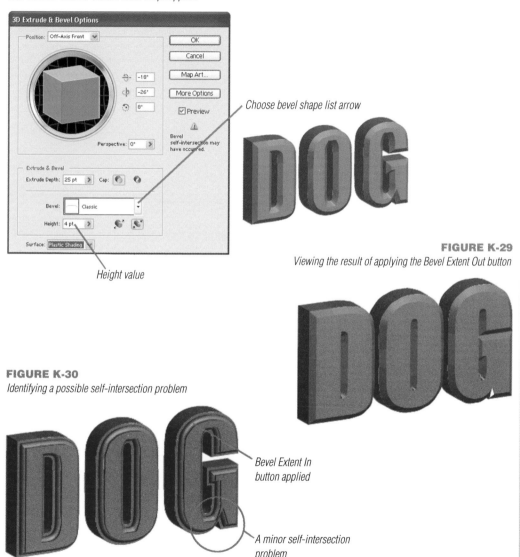

FIGURE K-28
Text outlines with the Classic bevel shape applied

Choose bevel shape list arrow

Height value

FIGURE K-29
Viewing the result of applying the Bevel Extent Out button

FIGURE K-30
Identifying a possible self-intersection problem

Bevel Extent In
button applied

A minor self-intersection
problem

1. Click **View** on the menu bar, then click **DOG**.

   The text has been converted to outlines and made into a compound path.

2. Click the **Selection Tool** ▸, click any letter of the text, click **Effect** on the menu bar, point to **3D**, then click **Extrude & Bevel**.

3. Click the **Preview check box**, then change the Extrude Depth value to 25 pt.

4. Click the **Choose bevel shape list arrow**, click **Classic**, verify that the Height value is set to 4 pt, then compare your screen to Figure K-28.

5. Note that the Bevel Extent In button is pressed, click the **Bevel Extent Out button** ◌, then note the change to the graphic, as shown in Figure K-29.

6. Click the **Bevel Extent In button** ◌, click the **Choose bevel shape list arrow**, then click **Complex 2**.

7. Note the warning in the dialog box that says Bevel self-intersection may have occurred, then compare your graphic to Figure K-30.

8. Click **OK**, save your work, then close Extrude Objects.

You applied two bevel shapes to extruded text outlines. You also experimented with the Bevel Extent In and Bevel Extent Out buttons.

REVOLVE OBJECTS

What You'll Do

In this lesson, you will use the 3D effect to revolve objects.

Revolving Objects

In addition to extruding, **revolving** is another method that Illustrator CS provides for applying a 3D effect to a 2D object. Imagine taking a large, hard cover book and opening it so much that its front and back covers touch. The pages would fan out from one cover to the other, all of them with their inside edges adhering to the spine of the book. This example is similar to what happens when the Revolve effect is applied to an object.

Revolving an object "sweeps" a path in a circular direction around the Y axis. Figure K-31 shows a familiar shape—the letter E—before and after the Revolve effect is applied. The blue selection

FIGURE K-31
The letter E before and after being revolved

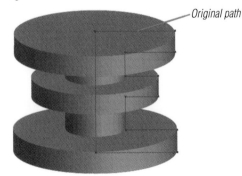

Original path

marks show the original path, and the left edge of that path is the Y axis around which the path was revolved. The surface shading is applied automatically with the effect.

By default, an object is revolved around a vertical axis that represents its leftmost point. An example of this is shown in Figure K-32. The 3D Revolve Options dialog box, shown in Figure K-33, also offers the option to revolve the object from its right edge. Revolving the object from its right edge yields an entirely different result, shown in Figure K-34.

FIGURE K-32
Revolving an object around its left edge

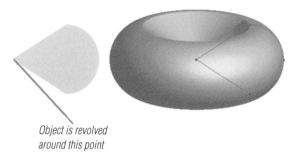

Object is revolved around this point

FIGURE K-33
Choosing the edge for the revolution

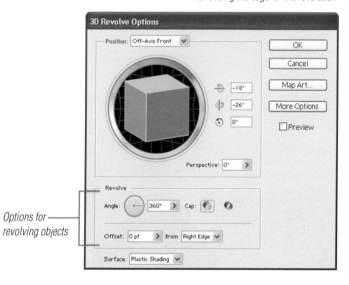

Options for revolving objects

FIGURE K-34
Revolving an object around its right edge

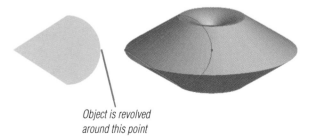

Object is revolved around this point

Because a revolution occurs around a vertical axis, in most cases, the starting path will depict half of the object you want to revolve. This is more easily explained with examples. Figure K-35 shows the original path and the result of applying the Revolve effect to that path. Note how the original path is a two-dimensional half of the revolved three-dimensional object.

Once revolved, an object can be rotated by manipulating the rotation cube in the 3D Revolve Options dialog box. This feature is extremely powerful with a revolved graphic. You can use the rotation cube to present all surfaces of the graphic. Figure K-36 shows four sides of the bottle graphic, all of them created by manipulating the rotation cube.

Revolving Multiple Objects

You can apply the Revolve effect to multiple paths simultaneously. Paths to be revolved

Identifying the path used to produce the revolved 3D graphic

A revolved graphic rotated four ways

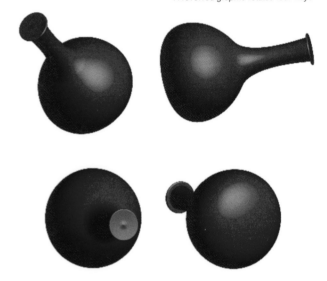

can be open or closed paths. As shown in Figure K-37, when multiple paths are selected and the Revolve effect is applied, each path is revolved around its own axis. For this reason, it is often best to align the left edges of multiple paths on the same Y axis, as shown in Figure K-38.

As the figure shows, aligning separate paths on the same Y axis can be useful when revolving. However, unwanted results can occur when rotating those paths, even when they are aligned on the same Y axis. Figure K-39 shows the same two paths being rotated. Note that because they are separate paths, they rotate separately—each on its own axis. This problem can be resolved by grouping the paths.

FIGURE K-37

Multiple paths revolved on their own axis

Two separate objects

Two separate objects—each revolved around its own axis

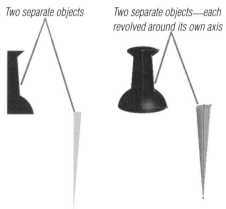

FIGURE K-39

Multiple paths rotated on their own axis

Separate, ungrouped paths rotate separately

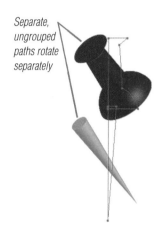

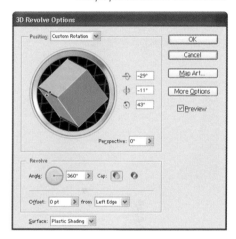

FIGURE K-38

Multiple paths aligned on the same axis then revolved

Two separate objects aligned on their left edges

Two separate objects—each revolved around its own axis

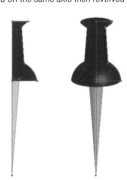

Revolving Grouped Objects

When grouped, multiple paths are revolved around a single axis. This can yield unexpected results. In Figure K-40, the two paths (left) are grouped, but they don't share the same Y axis. When revolved, both paths revolve around the leftmost axis.

When multiple paths are grouped and revolved, they will also rotate together. Figure K-41 shows four versions of two grouped and revolved paths after they have been rotated in the Revolve Options dialog box. In every case, the two paths rotate together because they are grouped. Compare this to Figure K-39, in which the

two ungrouped paths rotated separately, each on its own axis.

Applying an Offset to a Revolved Object

By default, an object is revolved around a vertical axis that represents its leftmost point. Figure K-42 illustrates this point.

FIGURE K-40

Two grouped paths revolved around a single Y-axis

Two paths, grouped   *Grouped paths revolved around the leftmost axis*

Leftmost axis

FIGURE K-41

Four grouped paths after being revolved and rotated

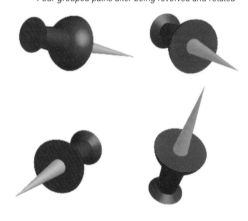

FIGURE K-42

Object revolved around its leftmost point

Leftmost point   *Leftmost point*

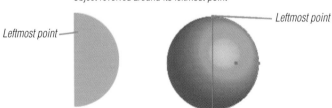

Increasing the Offset value in the Revolve Options dialog box, shown in Figure K-43, increases how far from the Y axis the object is revolved. Figure K-44 shows the same revolved object from K-42 with a 90-point offset value. The path revolves around the same Y axis, but it does so at a distance of 90 points. Figure K-45, in which the object has been rotated, shows the offset more clearly. Try to visualize that the object is a series of half circles rotated around a single vertical axis—90 points from that vertical axis.

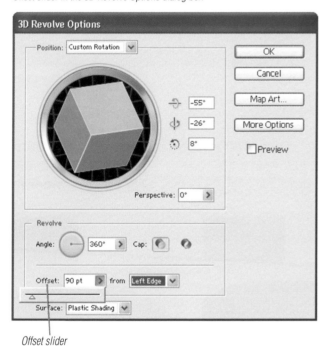

Offset slider

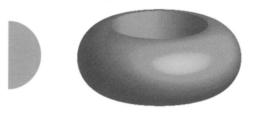

Revolve an object

1. Open AI K-2.ai, then save it as **Green Bottle**.

2. Click the **Selection Tool**, click the **green object**, click **View** on the menu bar, then click **Hide Edges** (if necessary).

3. Click **Effect** on the menu bar, point to **3D**, click **Revolve**, then click the **Preview check box**.

   As shown in Figure K-46, the object is revolved on its axis and appears as a bottle. Highlights and shadows are applied automatically.

4. Click **OK**, save your work, then close Green Bottle.

You revolved a simple object to produce a three-dimensional graphic.

Revolve multiple objects

1. Open AI K-3.ai, then save it as **Revolve Objects**.

2. Select the second row of blue objects, click **Effect** on the menu bar, point to **3D**, then click **Revolve**.

3. Click the **Preview check box**.

   Each object is revolved on its own axis.

4. Click **OK**, then compare your work to Figure K-47.

   The graphic on the left has a hard edge because the original object was a rectangle. The round edge of the original object on the right produced a 3D graphic that also has a round edge.

(continued)

Highlights and shadows applied automatically

Creating 3D Objects

5. Select the **second row of red objects**, click **Effect** on the menu bar, point to **3D**, then click **Revolve**.

6. Click **OK**, deselect all, then compare your work to Figure K-48.

   The first two graphics produced spheres when revolved, but only the middle graphic is a perfect sphere. The two crescent shapes, because they face in opposite directions, produce two drastically different results when revolved.

7. Deselect all, select the **rightmost red object**, double-click **3D Revolve** in the Appearance palette, manipulate the rotation cube to rotate the graphic any way that you like, then click **OK**.

   Figure K-49 shows one possible result.

8. Save your work, then close Revolve Objects.

   You selected multiple objects, applied the 3D Revolve effect, then noted that each object was revolved on its own axis. You compared the results with the original objects, then rotated one of the revolved objects.

FIGURE K-49
Rotating a revolved object

Revolve grouped objects

1. Open AI K-4.ai, then save it as **Push Pins**.

2. Click **View** on the menu bar, click **Green Pin**, then select the two objects in the Green Pin view.

   | TIP The two objects in Green Pin view are not grouped.

3. Click **Effect** on the menu bar, point to **3D**, then click **Revolve**.

4. Click the **Preview check box**, then note the effect on the objects on the page.

5. Manipulate the rotation cube in any direction.

   As shown in Figure K-50, the two objects are each rotated on their own axis and the illustration is no longer realistic.

   | TIP Because your rotation will differ, your results will differ from the figure.

6. Click **OK**, click **View** on the menu bar, click **Red Pin**, click one of the objects in the Red Pin view.

   | TIP The two objects are grouped.

7. Click **Effect** on the menu bar, point to **3D**, click **Revolve**, then click the **Preview check box**.

   As shown in Figure K-51, because the two objects are grouped, they are both revolved around the same axis.

(continued)

Rotating revolved objects that are not grouped

FIGURE K-51
Two grouped objects revolved around the same axis

Two grouped objects revolved around the same axis

8. Click **OK**, click **View** on the menu bar, click **Blue Pin**, select the two objects, click **Object** on the menu bar, then click **Group**.

9. Click **Effect** on the menu bar, point to **3D**, click **Revolve**, then click the **Preview check box**.

   As shown in Figure K-52, the two grouped objects are revolved around the same axis. Because they both share the same axis (their left edge) the illustration is realistic.

   TIP   The selection edges are showing in the figure so that you can see the left edge that both graphics share.

10. Manipulate the rotation cube in any direction that you like.

    Figure K-53 shows one possible result.

11. Click **OK**, save your work, then close Push Pins.

You explored the results of revolving grouped and ungrouped objects. With the green pin, you noted that ungrouped objects cannot be rotated together. With the red pin, you noted that grouped objects are revolved around the same axis. With the blue pin, you noted that grouped objects can be rotated together.

FIGURE K-53
Rotating revolved objects that are grouped

Offset a revolved object

1. Open AI K-5.ai, then save it as **Desk Lamp**.

2. Select the silver object, click **Effect** on the menu bar, point to **3D**, click **Revolve**, then click **OK**.

3. Select the gold diagonal line, click **Effect** on the menu bar, point to **3D**, click **Revolve**, then click the **Preview check box**.

   As shown in Figure K-54, the object's left-most point is the axis around which it is revolved.

(continued)

FIGURE K-54

Revolving an object around its leftmost point

Leftmost point of
original object

4. Double-click the **Offset text box**, type **50**, press **[Tab]**, then compare your work to Figure K-55.

   The object is revolved at a radius that is 50 points from its axis.

5. Click **OK**, save your work, then close Desk Lamp.

You used an increased offset value to manipulate how an object is revolved in relation to its axis.

FIGURE K-55
Revolving an object with a 50-pt offset from its axis

50-pt offset from
leftmost point

MANIPULATE SURFACE SHADING AND LIGHTING

What You'll Do

In this lesson, you will familiarize yourself with the controls that allow you to manipulate the highlight effects of a 3D object.

Applying Surface Shading

When the Extrude & Bevel effect or the Revolve effect is applied to an object, surface shading and lighting are applied automatically. However, you can manipulate these effects.

Surface shading controls how the object's surface appears. When an object is revolved, four surface shadings are available: Wireframe, No Shading, Diffuse Shading, and Plastic Shading. Examples of all four are shown in Figure K-56.

Plastic shading is the default surface shade. With plastic shading, the object reflects light as though it were made of a shiny plastic material. Distinct highlight areas appear on the surface of an object.

Diffuse shading offers a surface that reflects light in a soft, diffuse pattern. With Diffuse Shading, no distinct highlights appear on the surface of the object.

The Wireframe option makes all surfaces transparent and shows the object's geometry. The No Shading option, as its name suggests, applies no new shading to the object. Its surface is identical to that of the 2D object.

Manipulating Lighting Controls

When you choose Diffuse Shading or Plastic Shading, a number of lighting controls are available for you to manipulate the lighting effects that are applied to the object automatically.

- Lighting Intensity controls the strength of the light on the object. The range for lighting intensity is 0-100, with 100 being the default.
- Ambient Light is a very useful control. It determines how the object is lit globally. The range for Ambient Light is 0-100. Any changes that you make with the Ambient Light slider affect the brightness of the object uniformly, though the effect is much more pronounced in the shadow areas than in the highlights. Decreasing the ambient light noticeably makes the shadow areas darker, which increases the overall contrast of the object, from shadow to

FIGURE K-56
Four surface shading choices

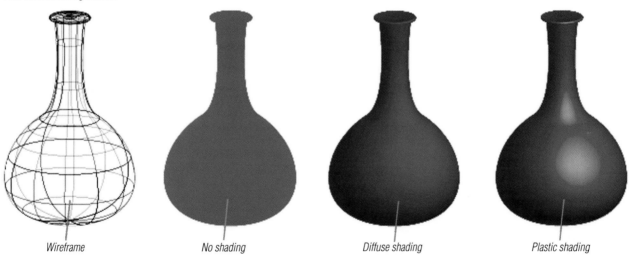

Wireframe   No shading   Diffuse shading   Plastic shading

highlight. Figure K-57 shows two objects, one with 60% ambient light and one with 20% ambient light.

- As its name implies, **Highlight Intensity** controls how intense a highlight appears. The more intense the highlight, the more white it appears. Figure K-58 shows two objects, one with 100% highlight intensity and one with 60%

highlight intensity. Note that at 100%, the highlight is too white and "glaring." At 60%, the highlight is a good mixture of white and the object's color.

- Highlight Size controls how large the highlights appear on the object.
- Blend Steps controls how smoothly the shading appears on the object's surface and is most visible in the transition

from the highlight areas to the diffusely lit areas. The range for blend steps is 1-256, with higher numbers producing more paths and therefore smoother transitions. If your computer can handle it, use 256 blend steps, but be aware that the higher the number, the more computer memory will be required to render the object.

FIGURE K-57
Comparing ambient lighting

FIGURE K-58
Comparing highlight intensity

60% ambient lighting   *20% ambient lighting*

100% highlight intensity   *60% highlight intensity*

Manipulating Light Sources

In addition to manipulating lighting controls, you can manipulate the light itself. When Diffuse Shading or Plastic Shading is chosen as the surface shading, a default light source, shown in Figure K-59, is applied. You can drag the light source to a new location to light the object from a different angle, as shown in Figure K-60. This can be very effective for manipulating the overall lighting of the object.

In addition to relocating the default light source, you can add additional light sources by clicking the New Light button. By default, the new light source appears at the center of the lighting key, but it too can

FIGURE K-59
Viewing default light source settings

FIGURE K-60
Relocating a light source

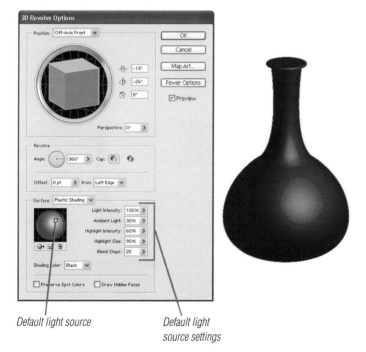

Default light source

Default light source settings

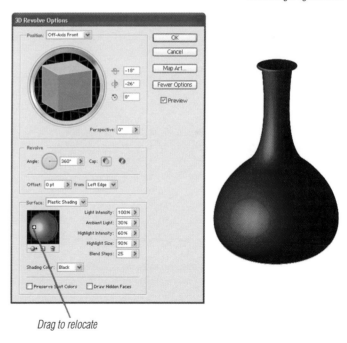

Drag to relocate

be relocated, as shown in Figure K-61. You can apply different light intensity values to individual light sources. It is often a good idea for one light source to be more dominant than the other(s).

You delete a light source by selecting it and then clicking the Delete Light button. The Move selected light to back of object button moves the light source to the back of the object. This is often most effective when

there's a background object that allows the back light to be more apparent. In Figure K-62, the second light has been moved behind the object; the highlights on the right side of the object are from the back light.

FIGURE K-61
Relocating a second light source

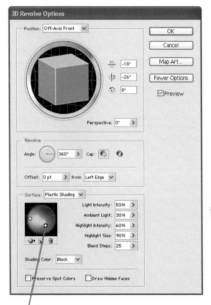

Second light source

FIGURE K-62
Using a light source as a back light

Back light source

Move selected
light to back of
object button

Highlight from back light source

Creating 3D Objects

Viewing the object with the Plastic Shading surface applied

1. Open AI K-6.ai, then save it as **Surface Lighting**.
2. Click the **object** to select it, then double-click **3D Revolve** in the Appearance palette.
3. Click the **Preview check box**, then note the subtle lighting effects on the object.

   The Diffuse Shading surface type is applied to the object.
4. Click the **Surface list arrow**, then click **No Shading**.
5. Click the **Surface list arrow**, then click **Wireframe**.
6. Click the **Surface list arrow**, click **Plastic Shading**, then compare your artwork to Figure K-63.

You examined four types of surface shadings as applied to a revolved object.

Manipulate lighting controls

1. Click **More Options** in the dialog box.

2. Click the **Ambient Light list arrow**, then drag the **slider** to 20.

3. Click the **Highlight Intensity list arrow**, then drag the **slider** to 75.

4. Click the **Highlight Size list arrow**, then drag the **slider** to 75.

5. Click the **Light Intensity list arrow**, drag the **slider** to 50, note the change in the object, then drag the **slider** to 100.

6. Click the **Blend Steps list arrow**, then drag the **slider** to 128.

7. Click **OK**, then compare your artwork to Figure K-64.

You manipulated five surface shading controls, noting their effect on a 3D object.

Manipulate light sources

1. Verify that the green object is selected, double-click **3D Revolve** in the Appearance palette, then click the **Preview check box**.

2. Drag the **light** to the top center of the sphere, as shown in Figure K-65.

(continued)

Manipulating surface shading on a 3D object

Relocating a light

Relocated light source

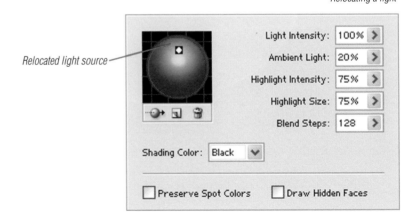

Creating 3D Objects

FIGURE K-66

Relocating the new light

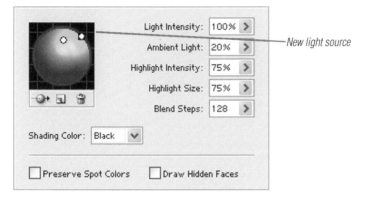

New light source

3. Click the **New Light button** ⊡ to add a second light.

> TIP By default, a new light is positioned at the center of the sphere.

4. Drag the **new light** to the top-right corner of the sphere, as shown in Figure K-66.

5. Click the **New Light button** ⊡ to add a third light, then move it to the location shown in Figure K-67.

6. Click **OK**, compare your work to Figure K-68, then compare Figure K-68 to Figure K-64 to see the results of adding the two lights.

7. Save your work, then close Surface Lighting.

You added and positioned lights to modify the lighting effects applied to the 3D object.

FIGURE K-67

Relocating the third light

Third light source

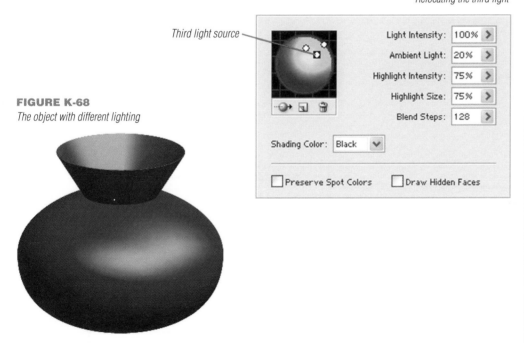

FIGURE K-68

The object with different lighting

MAP ARTWORK TO 3D OBJECTS

What You'll Do

In this lesson, you will map 2D artwork to a 3D object.

Mapping Artwork

Once you have created a three-dimensional object, you can "map" two-dimensional artwork to the three-dimensional object. A good example of this concept is a soup can and a soup label. The two dimensional soup label is designed and printed. It is then wrapped around the three-dimensional soup can.

The process of mapping a 2D object to a 3D object first includes converting the 2D object to a symbol. Figure K-69 shows a revolved 3D object and 2D artwork that will be mapped to it.

To map the artwork, you first select the 3D object, then click Map Art in the 3D Revolve Options dialog box. In the Map Art

FIGURE K-69
Viewing 3D artwork and 2D artwork to be mapped

2D Illustrator artwork —

3D object —

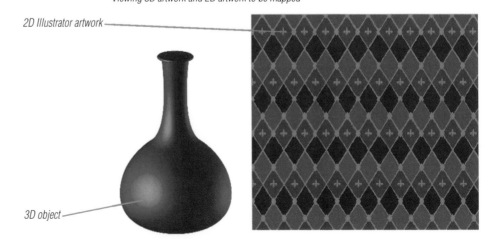

dialog box, shown in Figure K-70, you must first choose which surface you intend to map the art to. When you click the surface buttons, the active surface is shown in red wireframe on the 3D object. In this example, we are mapping the wrapping paper to surface 1 of 4, which is shown in Figure K-71.

The grid pattern represents the *complete* surface of surface 1 of 4. Understand that this means not only the surface that you see—the front surface—but the entire surface, all the way around. For this exercise, we're interested in mapping the wrapping paper to the surface that we can see—the front surface. That area is defined by the curved lines, identified in Figure K-71.

FIGURE K-70
Map Art dialog box

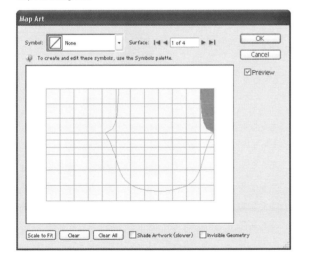

FIGURE K-71
Identifying the surface to be mapped

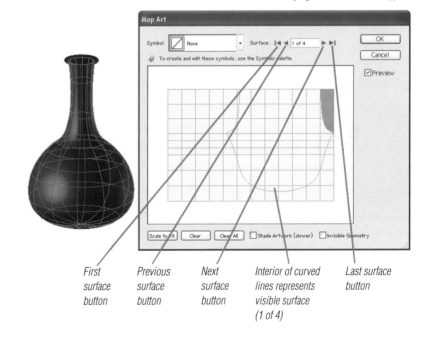

First surface button

Previous surface button

Next surface button

Interior of curved lines represents visible surface (1 of 4)

Last surface button

Once you have chosen the surface, you then choose the symbol to be mapped by clicking the Symbol list arrow and selecting the appropriate symbol. When you do so, the symbol artwork is centered on the grid. In this example, the symbol is named Wrapping Paper. For this exercise, we drag the artwork so that it completely covers the curved lines that represent the front face, as shown in Figure K-72.

Once the artwork is mapped, it reshapes itself to the three-dimensional object, as shown Figure K-73.

FIGURE K-72

Positioning the symbol artwork

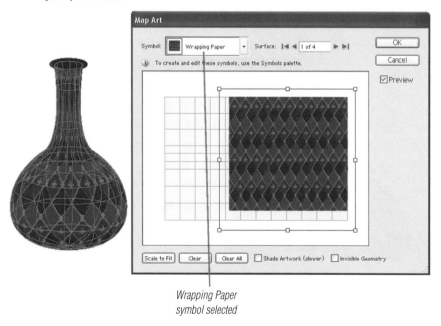

Wrapping Paper symbol selected

FIGURE K-73

Viewing the mapped art

FIGURE K-74

Creating the "tea can" and "lid"

1. Open AI K-7.ai, then save it as **Tea Can**.

2. Select all, click **Effect** on the menu bar, point to **3D**, click **Revolve**, then click **OK**.

   Your artwork should resemble Figure K-74.

3. Open AI K-8.ai, select all, click **Edit** on the menu bar, click **Copy**, close the document, then return to Tea Can.ai.

4. Click **Window** on the menu bar, click **Symbols**, click **Edit** on the menu bar, click **Paste**, then drag the pasted artwork into the Symbols palette to create a new symbol.

5. Delete the pasted artwork from the artboard.

6. Double-click the **new symbol** in the Symbols palette, type **Elephant Rectangle** in the Symbol Options dialog box, then click **OK**.

7. Open AI K-9.ai, select all, copy the artwork, close the document, return to Tea Can.ai, then paste the artwork.

8. Drag the pasted artwork into the Symbols palette to create a new symbol, then delete the pasted artwork from the artboard.

9. Name the new symbol **Elephant Circle**.

You used the 3D Revolve effect to create the artwork to which the 2D artwork will be mapped. You then created two symbols, one for each part of the 2D artwork.

Map rectangular artwork

1. Click the **Selection Tool** ↖, click the **silver object**, then press ↑ eight times so that the silver artwork is fully "under" the purple lid.

2. Double-click **3D Revolve** in the Appearance palette to open the 3D Revolve Options dialog box, click the **Preview check box**, then click **Map Art**.

3. Note that the Surface text box reads 1 of 3 and that a red line indicates that surface on the object, as shown in Figure K-75.

4. Click the **Next Surface button** ▶ two times, so that the Surface text box reads 3 of 3.

   The light gray areas of the layout grid represent the visible area of the silver object at this viewing angle.

5. Click the **Symbol list arrow**, then click **Elephant Rectangle**.

6. Drag the **top-left and bottom-right resizing handles** on the symbol's bounding box so that the artwork fits into the light gray areas of the layout grid, as shown in Figure K-76.

   (continued)

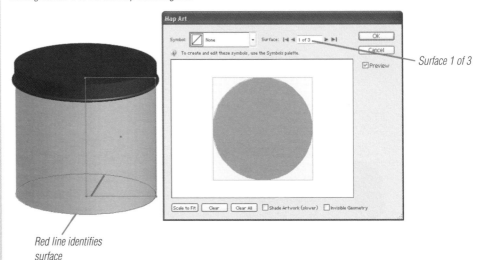

Surface 1 of 3

Red line identifies surface

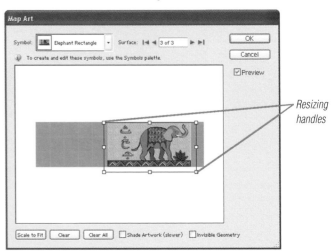

Resizing handles

Creating 3D Objects

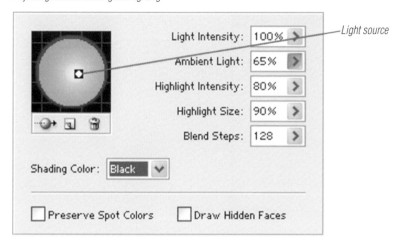

Light source

7. Drag the **bottom-middle resizing handle** up slightly so that the silver "can" will show beneath the "elephant label."

8. Click the **Shade Artwork (slower) check box**.

9. Click **OK**, change the ambient light setting to 65%, change the highlight intensity setting to 80%, change the number of blend steps to 128, then move the light to the location shown in Figure K-77.

10. Click **OK**, deselect all, then compare your work to Figure K-78.

In the Map Art dialog box, you selected the symbol that you wanted to map and the surface that you wanted to map it to. You resized the symbol artwork so that it fit onto the surface properly, then you activated the shading option to make the artwork appear more realistic as a label. You modified surface shading settings and lighting to improve the appearance of the artwork.

FIGURE K-78

Viewing the mapped art

Map round artwork

1. Click the **purple "cover" object**, double-click **3D Revolve** in the Appearance palette, click the **Preview check box**, then click **Map Art**.

2. Click the **Next Surface button** ▶ once, so that the Surface text box reads 2 of 5.

3. Click the **Symbol list arrow**, then click **Elephant Circle**.

4. Point to the **upper-right resizing handle** until a rotate cursor appears, then drag to rotate the graphic to the position shown in Figure K-79.

5. Click **OK** to close the Map Art dialog box, click **OK** again, deselect all, then compare your artwork to Figure K-80.

You mapped a circular piece of 2D artwork to an oval 3D object.

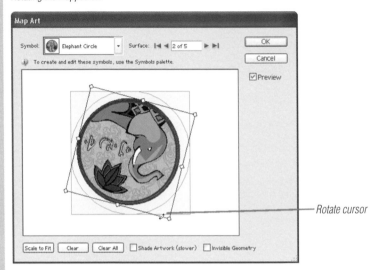

Rotate cursor

FIGURE K-81

Positioning the artwork

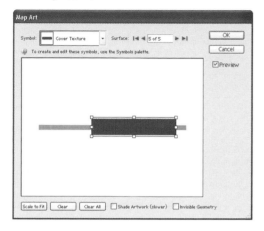

FIGURE K-82

Relocating the light

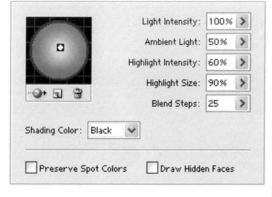

FIGURE K-83

Viewing the finished artwork

1. Open AI K-10.ai, select all, copy the artwork, close the document, then return to Tea Can.ai.

2. Verify that the Symbols palette is visible, click **Edit** on the menu bar, click **Paste**, then drag the pasted artwork into the Symbols palette to create a new symbol.

3. Delete the pasted artwork from the artboard.

4. Double-click the **new symbol** in the Symbols palette, type **Cover Texture**, then click **OK**.

5. Click the **purple "cover" object**, double-click **3D Revolve (Mapped)** in the Appearance palette, click the **Preview check box**, then click **Map Art**.

6. Click the **Next Surface button** ▶ until the Surface text box reads 5 of 5.

7. Click the **Symbol list arrow**, then click **Cover Texture**.

8. Position the symbol artwork so that it covers the entire light gray area, shown in Figure K-81.

9. Click **OK** to close the Map Art window, then drag the light to the location shown in Figure K-82.

10. Click **OK**, deselect all, then compare your work to Figure K-83.

11. Save your work, then close Tea Can.

You mapped artwork to the front face of a 3D object to add texture.

Extrude objects.

1. Open AI K-11.ai, then save it as **Extrude & Bevel Skills**.
2. Click the Selection Tool, select the blue octagon, click View on the menu bar, then click Hide Edges.
3. Click Effect on the menu bar, point to 3D, click Extrude & Bevel, then click the Preview check box.
4. Click the Extrude Depth list arrow, then increase the depth to 75 pt.
5. Click the Turn cap off for hollow appearance button, then click OK.
6. Select the orange letter H, click Effect on the menu bar, point to 3D, then click Extrude & Bevel.
7. Click the Preview check box, then change the Extrude Depth value to 60 pt.
8. Double-click the Specify rotation around the X axis text box to select its contents, type **17**, then press **[Tab]**.
9. Type **-17** in the Specify rotation around the Y axis text box, press [Tab], type **-31** in the Specify rotation around the Z axis text box, then click OK.
10. Select the green octagon and the two objects inside it, click Object on the menu bar, point to Compound Path, then click Make.
11. Click Effect on the menu bar, point to 3D, then click Extrude & Bevel.
12. Click the Preview check box, then experiment with different rotations by clicking and dragging the rotation cube from all sides.

13. Double-click the Specify rotation around the X axis text box, type **26**, then press [Tab].
14. Type **-9** in the Specify rotation around the Y axis text box, press [Tab], then type **3** in the Specify rotation around the Z axis text box.
15. Click OK.
16. Select the hollow blue octagon at the top of the artboard, then double-click 3D Extrude & Bevel in the Appearance palette.

FIGURE K-84
Completed Skills Review, Part 1

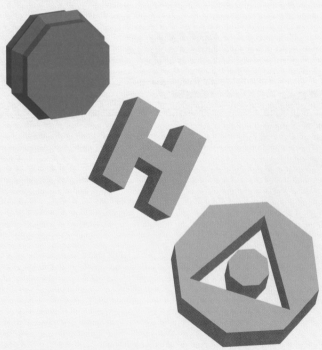

17. Click the Preview check box, then click the Turn cap on for solid appearance button.
18. Click the Bevel list arrow, click Complex 4, then drag the Height slider to 6.
19. Click the Bevel Extent Out button, drag the Height slider to 10, click OK, then compare your work to Figure K-84.
20. Save your work, then close Extrude & Bevel Skills.

Creating 3D Objects

Revolve objects.

1. Open AI K-12.ai, then save it as **Gold Urn**.
2. Click the Selection Tool, select all, click View on the menu bar, then click Hide Edges (if necessary).
3. Click the Horizontal Align Left button in the Align palette.
4. Click Effect on the menu bar, point to 3D, click Revolve, then click the Preview check box.
5. Manipulate the rotation cube in any direction, note that the three objects all rotate on their own axes, then click Cancel.
6. Click Object on the menu bar, then click Group.
7. Click Effect on the menu bar, point to 3D, click Revolve, then click the Preview check box.
8. Manipulate the rotation cube in any direction.
9. Click Cancel.
10. Click Effect on the menu bar, point to 3D, click Revolve, then click the Preview check box.
11. Click the Offset list arrow, change the offset value to 48, then click OK.

Manipulate surface shading and lighting.

1. Double-click 3D Revolve in the Appearance palette.
2. Click the Preview check box, click the Surface list arrow, then click No Shading.
3. Click the Surface list arrow, then click Diffuse Shading.
4. Click the Surface list arrow, then click Plastic Shading.
5. Click More Options, if necessary, click the Ambient Light list arrow, then drag the slider to 35.
6. Drag the light to the top center of the sphere.
7. Click the New Light button to add a second light.
8. Drag the Light Intensity slider to 25.

Map artwork to 3D objects.

1. Drag the Offset slider to 0, then click Map Art.
2. Click the Next Surface button until the Surface text box reads 5 of 13.

3. Click the Symbol list arrow, then click Wrapping Paper.
4. Click OK.
5. Click OK, then compare your work to Figure K-85.
6. Save your work, then close Gold Urn.

FIGURE K-85
Completed Skills Review, Part 2

You are a freelance illustrator, and you have been hired to draw an old-fashioned lava lamp to be part of a montage. To begin work on the illustration, you decide to draw three paths, then use the 3D Revolve effect.

1. Open AI K-13.ai, then save it as **Lava Lamp**.
2. Click the Selection Tool, then drag the three path segments so that they are aligned with the blue guide.
3. Hide the guides.
4. Select all, click Effect on the menu bar, point to 3D, then click Revolve.
5. Click the Preview check box, note the results, then click Cancel.
6. Group the three paths, apply the Revolve effect again, then click the Preview check box.
7. Click More Options, if necessary, apply Plastic Shading as the surface shading, then drag the Ambient Light slider to 35.
8. Click OK, deselect all, then compare your work to Figure K-86.
9. Save your work, then close Lava Lamp.

FIGURE K-86
Completed Project Builder 1

Creating 3D Objects

You are a designer for a game company, and you are designing the packaging for a chess game. You decide to use basic shapes and the 3D Revolve effect to create a graphic for the cover art.

1. Open AI K-14.ai, then save it as **Chess Pawn**.
2. Click the Selection Tool, then align each shape with the black rules.
3. Hide the Assembled layer, then verify that the Pawn Parts layer is targeted.
4. Select all on the Pawn Parts layer, then hide edges.
5. Click Effect on the menu bar, point to 3D, then click Revolve.
6. Click the Preview check box, note the results, then click Cancel.
7. Click the Horizontal Align Left button in the Align palette.
8. Press and hold [Alt] (Win) or [option] (Mac), then click the Add button in the Pathfinder palette.
9. Click Effect on the menu bar, point to 3D, click Revolve, then click the Preview check box.
10. Select the contents of the Specify rotation around the X axis text box, type **-47**, then click OK.
11. Click the White Pawn swatch in the Swatches palette, then compare your work to Figure K-87.
12. Save your work, then close Chess Pawn.

FIGURE K-87
Completed Project Builder 2

You are a designer for a T-shirt company. Presently, your assignment is to develop shirts that feature peoples' names in 3D. To come up with a design, you experiment using your own name.

1. Create a new 8" × 8" document, then save it as **T-Shirt Text**.
2. Type your first name in a bold font at a large point size. (*Hint*: The typeface used in Figure K-88 is 216 pt Antique Olive Bold Condensed.)
3. Change the fill color to something other than black.
4. Click Effect on the menu bar, point to 3D, then click Extrude & Bevel.
5. Click the Preview check box, then change the Extrude Depth value to one of your liking.
6. Choose a bevel shape that you like.
7. Click OK, then compare your work to Figure K-88, which shows one possible result.
8. Save your work, then close T-Shirt Text.

FIGURE K-88
Sample Completed Design Project

This group project is designed to challenge the group's ability to visualize simple paths and how they will appear when the 3D Revolve effect is applied. The group will look at nine graphics, all of which are simple paths to which the 3D Revolve effect has been applied. Each member of the group should take a piece of paper and a pencil and try to draw the simple path that is the basis for each graphic. Note that for each 3D graphic, no rotation or offset has been applied—each is the result of simply applying the 3D Revolve effect to a simple path. Note also that two of the simple paths are open paths, and the other seven are all closed paths.

1. Refer to Figure K-89.
2. Look at Graphic #1, and try to visualize what it would look like if the 3D Revolve filter were removed.
3. Using a pencil and paper, draw the original path that was used to create the graphic.
4. Do the same for the remaining eight graphics.
5. Open AI K-15.ai, then save it as **Mystery Shapes**.
6. Select each graphic, then delete the 3D Revolve effect from the Appearance palette.
7. Compare your pencil drawings to the graphics in the file.
8. Save Mystery Graphics, then close the file.

FIGURE K-89
Reference for Group Project

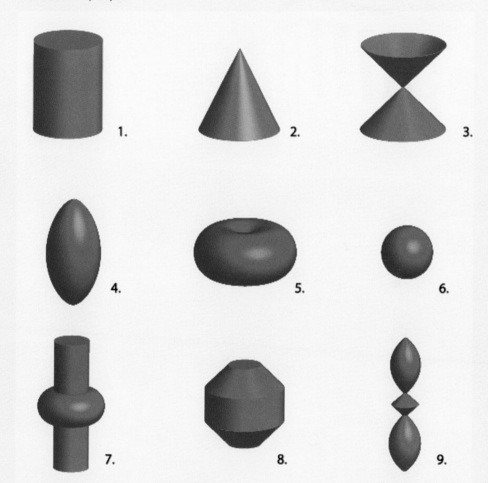

1. 2. 3.

4. 5. 6.

7. 8. 9.

CHAPTER

PREPARING A DOCUMENT FOR PREPRESS AND PRINTING

1. Explore basic color theory.

2. Work in CMYK mode.

3. Specify spot colors.

4. Create crop marks.

5. Create bleeds.

CHAPTER 1
PREPARING A DOCUMENT FOR PREPRESS AND PRINTING

Illustrator is so widely praised for its excellence as a drawing tool, it's easy to forget that the application is also a top-notch page layout solution. Illustrator CS is a powerhouse print production utility, a state-of-the-art interface with the world of professional prepress and printing. Everything that you need to produce an output-ready document is there—crop marks, trim marks, reliable process tints, the full PANTONE library of non-process inks—all backed by a sophisticated color separations utility. If you are new to the world of prepress and printing, Illustrator CS makes for an excellent training ground, with straightforward, easy-to-use palettes and dialog boxes. If you are experienced, you will admire how Illustrator seamlessly transitions from design and drawing to layout and output, thoughtfully and thoroughly encompassing the gamut of a printer's needs, demands, and wishes.

Tools You'll Use

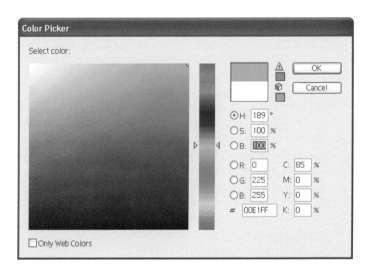

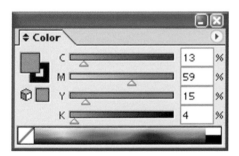

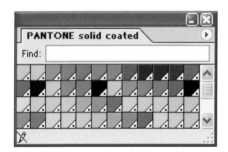

EXPLORE BASIC COLOR THEORY

What You'll Do

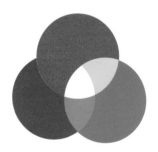

 In this lesson, you will learn basic color theory to gain an understanding of the role of CMYK ink in offset printing.

Exploring Basic Color Theory

All of the natural light in our world comes from the sun. The sun delivers light to us in waves. The entirety of the sun's light, the electromagnetic spectrum, contains an infinite number of light waves—some at high frequencies, some at low frequencies—many of which will sound familiar to you. X-rays, gamma rays, and ultraviolet rays are all components of the electromagnetic spectrum.

The light waves that we see in our world are only a subset of the electromagnetic spectrum. Scientists refer to this subset—this range of wavelengths—as visible light. Because this light appears to us as colorless (as opposed to, say, the red world of the planet Mars), we refer to visible light as "white light."

From your school days, you may remember using a prism to bend light waves to reveal what you probably referred to as a rainbow. It is through this bending, or "breaking down" of white light, that we see color. The rainbow that we are all so familiar with is called the visible spectrum, and it is composed of seven distinct colors: red, orange, yellow, green, blue, indigo, and violet. Though the colors are distinct, the color range of the visible spectrum is infinite; for example, there's no definable place in the spectrum where orange light ends and yellow light begins.

Colors in the visible spectrum can themselves be broken down. For example, because red light and green light, when combined, produce yellow light, yellow light can, conversely, be broken down, or reduced, to those component colors.

Red, green, and blue light (RGB) are the additive primary colors of light, as shown in Figure L-1. The term **primary** refers to the fact that red, green, and blue light cannot themselves be broken down or reduced. The term **additive** refers to the fact that these same colors combine to produce other colors. For example, red and blue light, when combined, produce violet hues. As primary colors, red, green, and blue light are the irreducible component colors

of white light. Therefore, it logically follows that when red, green, and blue light are combined equally, they produce white light.

Finally, you'll note that nowhere in this paradigm is the color black. That is because, in the natural world, there is no such color as black. True black is the absence of all light.

FIGURE L-1

Red, green, and blue are the additive primary colors of light

White light

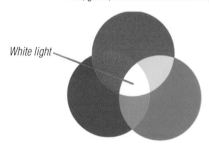

Understanding Subtractive Primary Colors

Three things can happen when light strikes an object: the light can be reflected, absorbed, or transmitted, as shown in Figure L-2.

Reflection occurs when light strikes an object and "bounces" off the object. Any object that reflects all of the light that strikes it appears as pure white.

Absorption occurs when light strikes an object and is not reflected, but instead is absorbed by the object. Any object that absorbs all of the light that strikes it appears as pure black.

Transmission occurs when light strikes an object and passes through the object. Any object that transmits all of the light that strikes it becomes invisible.

There are no truly invisible objects in our world (only some gasses are invisible). Nor are there any purely white or purely black objects. Instead, depending on the physical properties of the object, varying amounts of light are reflected, absorbed, and transmitted.

If an object absorbs some light, it logically follows that not all the white light that strikes the object will be reflected. Put another way, red, green, and blue light will not be reflected in full and equal amounts. What we perceive as the object's color is based on the percentages of the red, green, and blue light that are reflected and the color that that combination of light produces.

An object appears as cyan if it absorbs all of the red light that strikes it and also reflects or transmits all of the green and all of the blue light. An object that absorbs all of the green light that strikes it and also reflects or transmits all of the red and all of the blue light appears as magenta. An object that absorbs all of the blue light that strikes it and also reflects or transmits all of the red and all of the green light appears as yellow, as shown in Figure L-3.

Cyan, magenta, and yellow are called **subtractive primary colors**. The term subtractive refers to the fact that each is produced by removing or subtracting one of the additive primary colors, and overlapping all three pigments would absorb all colors.

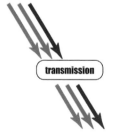

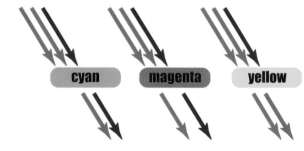

Understanding the Theory of Four-Color Process Printing

Color printing uses the three subtractive primary colors (plus black) to produce a color image or tint. To understand this, read the two points below carefully:

- The standard color for paper is white. The paper appears as white because it is manufactured to reflect RGB light in equal amounts.

- Cyan, magenta, and yellow inks are transparent—they are manufactured so that light passes through them. For example, cyan ink is manufactured to absorb red light and transmit green and blue light.

Here is the key to the whole theory: The color that you see when you look at a printed page is *not* reflected off the inks; it is light reflected off the paper. The light that is reflected off the paper is that which has not been absorbed (or *subtracted*) by the inks. Figure L-4 demonsrates this concept.

FIGURE L-4

The color of the printed image is reflected off the paper, not the inks

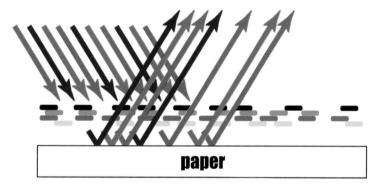

paper

Creating a rich black

For many designers, black is the most powerful "color" in the palette. No other color can provide such contrast. Black can be used to trigger emotions. Black is neutral, but it's never silent. Use black ink (K) for text and lines and small areas of your artwork. When you have designed artwork with large black areas that you want to be dramatically black, keep in mind that black ink alone may not be enough to produce the effect. To produce deep blacks, printers create a process tint that is 100% K plus 50% C. The cyan ink overlapped with the black produces a dark, rich black . . . which is why printers refer to this tint as a "rich black." Keep the idea in mind when you are working with black, but remember also that rich blacks are never used for text or lines.

Understanding CMYK Inks

CMYK inks are called process inks. Process inks are manufactured by people, so by definition, they're not perfect. For example, no cyan ink can be manufactured so that it absorbs 100% of the red light that strikes it. Some is reflected, and some is transmitted, as shown in Figure L-5. Perfect magenta and yellow inks cannot be manufactured either. In addition, an ink's ability to transmit light is not perfect. That same cyan ink should, if it were a true cyan, transmit both blue and green light. Manufactured cyan inks actually absorb a small percentage of blue and green light.

These imperfections become crucial when you try to use cyan, magenta, and yellow (CMY) to print dark areas of an image. In theory, if you overlapped all three inks, the area would appear black because each would absorb an additive primary, and no light would be reflected off the paper, as shown in Figure L-6.

FIGURE L-5

Cyan ink in theory vs. reality

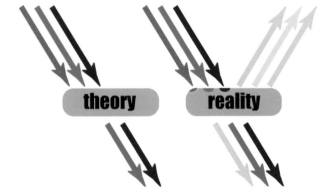

FIGURE L-6

If "perfect" inks were overlapped, no light would be reflected; the area of the overlap would appear black

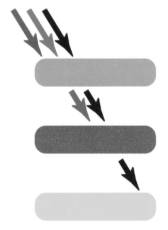

Because, in reality, the inks are unable to achieve 100% absorption and some light gets through and is reflected off the paper, CMY inks are unable to produce satisfactory shadows and dark areas of an image, as shown in Figure L-7.

To compensate, black ink is used to produce deep shadows and fine detail. Printers refer to black ink as "K." They do not refer to it as "B" because "B" could be confused with blue, and blue could be confused with cyan. Also, printers have long referred to

black as the "key" for aligning (registering) the four colors. Thus, the K in CMYK, though not a subtractive primary, is nevertheless essential to the subtractive printing process, as shown in Figure L-8.

FIGURE L-7

In reality, CMY inks are insufficient to produce black areas

FIGURE L-8

The image on the left was printed with only CMY inks; black ink adds contrast and depth to the image on the right

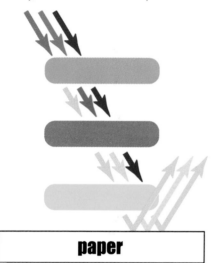

Coping with color confusion

If all of this color theory talk is making your head spin, don't worry about it. Working in Illustrator and producing a printed project *does not require* that you have these theories in your head. As you become more experienced with the printing process (and if you generally like this kind of stuff), these concepts will make more sense. Until then, remember the two essential points of this discussion: The offset printing process uses transparent CMYK inks; the color you see on a printed page is reflected off the paper, not the inks.

WORK IN CMYK MODE

What You'll Do

In this lesson, you will use Illustrator's Color Picker, Color palette, and print options in CMYK Color mode.

Understanding Color Gamut

RGB, CMYK, and HSB are all known as **color models**. The **color mode** determines the color model used to display and print Illustrator documents. Illustrator offers two color modes for documents: RGB and CMYK.

As we've discussed, offset color printing is based on the CMYK color model. All light-emitting devices, such as your television or your monitor, produce color based on the RGB color model. If you flick a drop of water at your television screen, you will be able to see that the image is composed of very small red, green, and blue pixels. The full range of color that you perceive when you watch TV is the result of the additive properties of light; the red, green, and blue light are combining to produce the image.

Color gamut refers to the range of colors that can be printed or displayed by a given color model. A good monitor, based on the RGB color model, can produce a color gamut of more than 16 million colors. However, the spectrum of colors that can be viewed by the human eye is wider than any man-made method for reproducing color.

Setting up color management

For the print and prepress professional, Illustrator's Color Settings dialog box simplifies the goal of setting up a color-managed workflow by bringing most of the standard color management controls to a single place. The predefined configurations offer a set of color management options that are designed to achieve color consistency in a production workflow. In most cases, the predefined color settings will provide enough color management controls to meet the demands of a prepress environment.

The CMYK color model is substantially smaller than the RGB color model. Therefore, when you are creating computer graphics, remember that some colors that you can see on your monitor cannot be reproduced by the CMYK printing process.

Illustrator addresses this reality in different ways. For example, if you are working in RGB mode and choosing colors in the Color Picker or the Color palette, Illustrator will warn you if you have chosen a color that is "out-of-gamut"—that is, a color that cannot be printed. Also, if you have created an image in RGB mode and you convert to CMYK mode, Illustrator will automatically replace the out-of-gamut colors applied to images with their closest CMYK counterparts.

As shown in Figure L-9, the colors in RGB that are out-of-gamut for the CMYK color model are the brightest, most saturated, and most vibrant hues.

Don't despair. As you have certainly noted from looking at art books, posters, and even some high-quality magazines, the CMYK color model can be used to reproduce stunning color images. (Note: Because this book is a printed product and therefore based on the CMYK color model, we are unable to show you examples of out-of-gamut colors.)

FIGURE L-9
CMYK color model is unable to reproduce the brightest and most saturated hues that you can see on your screen

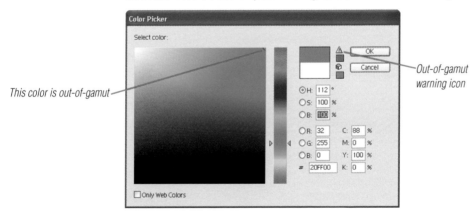

This color is out-of-gamut

Out-of-gamut warning icon

Specifying CMYK Tints

Tints are, quite simply, colors that you print by mixing varying percentages of CMYK inks. The lightest colors are produced with small percentages of ink, and darker colors with higher percentages. You can purchase process tint books that show you—with a high degree of fidelity—a large number of the color combinations available in the CMYK gamut.

In Illustrator, you specify CMYK tints by entering percentages in the Color Picker and the Color palette, as shown in Figure L-10. If this idea is setting off alarms in your head . . . good for you! All the color produced by your monitor is based on the RGB color model. By definition, you cannot "see" the CMYK color model (or real CMYK tints, for that matter) on your monitor.

In the early days of desktop publishing, this contradiction generated enormous fear in the hearts of print professionals and created an entire cottage industry of color calibration hardware and software. Despite the dire

FIGURE L-10
Specifying a process tint in the Color palette

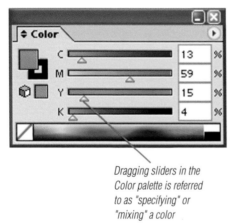

Dragging sliders in the Color palette is referred to as "specifying" or "mixing" a color

warnings, however, color calibration problems turned out to be a phantom menace; simply put, the majority of print work produced is not so color-critical that variation in color is a problem (if the variation is even noticed).

Practically speaking, you must accept that the colors in your illustration on-screen will *never* be an exact match to the printed version. However, the numbers that you enter when specifying percentages of CMYK are *exactly* the percentages that will be output when the illustration goes to the printer. Therefore, if you *must* have a specific tint, find the color in a process tint book, and enter the percentages as specified.

Then, don't worry about how the tint looks on your screen. If it looks close, that's great. If not, it doesn't matter. The printer is contractually responsible to be able to reproduce the tint that you specified.

Printing transparent artwork

Whenever you have a document with transparent objects (objects whose opacity is set to less than 100%), you should be sure to check the transparency preferences before printing the file. When you print or save artwork that contains transparency, Illustrator performs a process called flattening. When flattening, Illustrator identifies transparent artwork, then isolates the areas that are overlapped by the transparent object by dividing the areas into components. Illustrator then analyzes those components to determine if they can be output with vector data or if they must be rasterized (converted to pixels). The flattening process works very well in most cases. However, if you are unsatisfied with the appearance of the high-resolution output, you may want to step in and rasterize the artwork yourself. Before outputting the file, you can use Illustrator's Overprint Preview mode (found on the View menu), which approximates how transparency and blending will appear in color-separated output.

Specify process tints in the Color Picker

1. Open AI L-1.ai, then save it as **Oahu**.

2. Select the placed image, then hide it.

3. Double-click the **Fill or Stroke button** in the toolbox to open the Color Picker, then type **189** for the hue, **100** for the saturation, and **100** for the brightness.

   The out-of-gamut warning icon appears, as shown in Figure L-11.

4. Click the **blue square** under the out-of-gamut warning icon.

   The closest process color is specified as the new fill color.

5. Click **OK** to close the Color Picker dialog box.

6. Add the new color to the Swatches palette, then name it **Maverick**.

You chose a color in the Color Picker that was out-of-gamut for CMYK. You chose the process match that the out-of-gamut warning offered as a new fill color, then added it to the Swatches palette.

FIGURE L-11

Out-of-gamut warning in the Color Picker

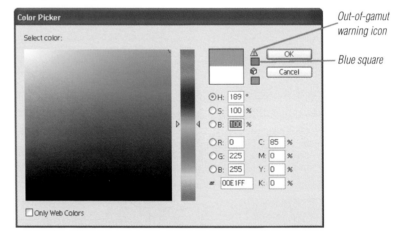

FIGURE L-12

Applying process tints to the artwork

1. Click **Window** on the menu bar, then click **Color** to show the Color palette, if necessary.

2. Click the **Color palette list arrow**, then click **CMYK**, if necessary.

3. Using the sliders on the palette, mix a process tint that is 5C/70M/100Y, then press [**Enter**] (Win) or [**return**] (Mac).

   In standard notation for process tints, zero is not specified. As there is no black in this tint, the K percentage is not noted.

   > TIP You will not see the new color in the Color palette if the cursor is still flashing in the last text box that you entered a new value in. Pressing [Tab] advances your cursor to the next text box.

4. Add the new color to the Swatches palette, then name it **Living**.

5. Mix a new process tint that is 5C/40M/5Y.

6. Add the new color to the Swatches palette, then name it **Amazing**.

7. Mix a new process tint that is 30M/100Y.

8. Add the new color to the Swatches palette, then name it **Twist**.

9. Apply the four new tints that you have added to the Swatches palette to the artwork, as shown in Figure L-12.

10. Save your work.

You mixed three different process tints in the Color palette, saved them in the Swatches palette, then applied the four tints you have created so far in this chapter to the artwork.

SPECIFY SPOT COLORS

What You'll Do

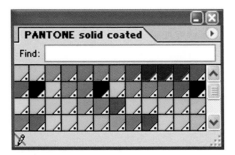

In this lesson, you will create and apply spot colors.

Understanding Spot Colors

Though printing is based on the four process colors CMYK, it is not limited to them.

Imagine that you are an art director designing the masthead for the cover of a new magazine. You have decided that the masthead will be an electric blue, vivid and eye-catching. If you were working with process tints only, you would have a problem. First, you would find that the almost-neon blue that you want to achieve is not within the CMYK gamut; it can't be printed. Even if it could, you would have an even bigger problem with consistency

issues. You want that blue to be the same blue on every issue of the magazine, month after month. But process tints will vary on press; as the cover is printed, the blue color in the masthead will shift in tone, sometimes sharply.

Designers and printers use non-process inks to solve this problem. Non-process inks are special premixed inks that are printed separately from process inks. The color gamut of non-process inks available far exceeds that of CMYK. Non-process inks also offer consistent color throughout a print run.

Tabbing through the Color palette

The easiest way to mix process tints in the Color palette is to start out by double-clicking the C text box to select the current value, then enter the percentage of cyan that you want for the new tint. Press [Tab] to advance to the next text box, enter the new percentage, and so on. After you have entered the percentage in the B (black) text box, be sure to press [Tab] again. If you want to reverse direction, press and hold [Shift] while tabbing.

The print world refers to non-process inks by a number of names:
- Spot colors: Refers to the fact that non-process inks print on the "spots" of the paper where the process inks do not print.
- Fifth color: Refers to the fact that the non-process ink is often printed in addition to the four process inks. Note,

however, that non-process inks are not necessarily the "fifth" color. For example, many "two-color" projects call for black plus one non-process ink.
- PANTONE color: Pantone is a manufacturer of non-process inks.
- PMS color: An acronym for PANTONE Matching System.

Loading Spot Colors

In Illustrator, you use the Swatch Libraries menu item to select from a range of color systems (or libraries), including PANTONE, the standard library for non-process inks. When you import the PANTONE library, it appears as a separate palette, as shown in Figure L-13.

FIGURE L-13

PANTONE solid coated library appears as a separate palette

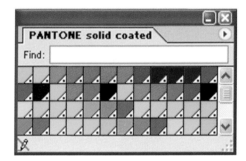

Rasterizing artwork

Illustrator is a vector-based drawing program; the graphics you create are called vector graphics. However, Illustrator is not exclusively vector-oriented, nor are Illustrator graphics limited to vectors. For a number of reasons, you may wish to convert a vector graphic into a bitmap graphic, a process called rasterization. If your Illustrator file is very complex, rasterizing it will convert it to a simple bitmap image. Output devices sometimes have trouble with complex objects and effects, such as gradient meshes and transparent objects. If you rasterize the graphic, you will see immediately if the effects translated properly. If so, the artwork is ready to print, as a simple, standard bitmap image. When rasterizing a vector graphic for output, whether for high-resolution printing or to appear on the Internet, you must determine the resolution (the number of pixels per inch) that the resulting bitmap will contain. You can input the desired resolution for the resulting bitmap file using the Document Raster Effects Settings dialog box. Click Document Raster Effects Settings on the Effect menu.

Outputting Documents with Spot Colors

All spot colors in the PANTONE library have a process match, which is of course a misnomer: if the process tint *matched* the spot color, there would be no need for the spot color in the first place. Some process tints—especially in the yellow hues—can come close to matching a spot color. Others—especially deep greens and blues—don't even come close.

When a four-color document is printed on a printing press, each of the four colors is printed separately: first yellow, then magenta, then cyan, then black. When an Illustrator document is output for printing, the document must be output as separations. Separations isolate each of the four process colors on its own "plate."

Clarifying resolution issues

The reckless misuse of the terms "resolution" and "DPI" by designers, printers, and even software programmers has resulted in widespread confusion over this concept and countless dollars and hours lost in struggling with files whose resolution settings are incorrect. And despite all of the confusion, the concepts are surprisingly simple and easy to understand. In general, when the term "resolution" is used, it is in reference to the number of pixels per inch in a bitmap image, or PPI. Unfortunately, seemingly everybody uses the term DPI instead of PPI; PPI is the only correct term for the resolution of a bitmap image. DPI stands for "dots per inch," which is the resolution of an output device. Dots are dots, and pixels are pixels; they are mutually exclusive. The resolution of your laser printer is probably 600 DPI or 1200 DPI, which is a satisfactory number of printing device dots to print text and lines that appear to be smooth. For bitmap images and blends, a minimum resolution of 2400 DPI is required for the output device to produce the smooth transitions of tone. Add to this confusion a third type of resolution, the resolution of a printed document. Lines per inch, LPI, or "line screen" is the number of lines of halftone dots (ink dots) in a printed image (professionally printed, not output from a desktop printer). Many printers refer to this resolution as, you guessed it, DPI, which is wholly incorrect. Lines are lines, and dots are dots. LPI is the only correct term for the resolution of a printed image. Standard line screens for color printing are 133 LPI and 150 LPI. A fluency with resolution terminology will help you in Illustrator when you want to rasterize a vector graphic (convert it to a bitmap image). When doing so, you must determine the resolution of the resulting bitmap image, the PPI. The PPI for a bitmap graphic that is to be used on the Internet is 72 PPI. The PPI for a bitmap graphic that is to be printed is twice the LPI.

Preparing a Document for Prepress and Printing

When a color document is printed with four colors and a spot color, the spot color requires its own plate on the printing press so that the non-process ink can be laid down separately from the process inks.

In Illustrator, all spot colors that you use in a document will automatically be converted to their process match when separated, unless you *deselect* the Convert to Process option in the Separation Setup

dialog box, which you access through the Print dialog box. See Figure L-14.

FIGURE L-14
Spot colors are converted to their process match when seperated

Understanding the output resolution of a vector graphic

Curved lines that you draw in Illustrator are, in terms of output, defined by small straight lines. "Curves" are made up of lines so small that your eye blends them together to create the appearance of a smooth curve. Therefore, the smaller the line segments, the smoother the curve. Of course, if the line segments are smaller, more of them are needed to draw the curve. Therefore, vector graphics have an output resolution, the number of line segments that will be used to draw the curve. Yet another term comes into play, and that is "flatness." The output resolution determines the flatness of the curve. A lower output resolution results in longer and fewer line segments to draw a curve. A higher output resolution increases the number of line segments and the file size. Sometimes, you will get a printer error if a document contains many long curved paths, simply because the file information is too much for the printer's processor to handle. In that case, you may want to reduce the default output resolution. Illustrator's default output resolution setting is 800 dots per inch (DPI). You can modify the flatness setting in the Graphics windows of the Print dialog box. In the Paths section of the window, drag the slider toward Quality for a lower flatness setting and a higher quality.

Import and apply spot colors

1. Click **Window** on the menu bar, point to **Swatch Libraries**, then click **PANTONE solid coated**.

   A new palette appears with small sample colors of each color in the library, as shown in Figure L-15.

   > TIP You can purchase PANTONE swatch books from the Pantone Web site at *www.pantone.com*.

2. Click in the Find text box in the PANTONE solid coated palette.

   > TIP If the Find text box is not available, click the PANTONE solid coated palette list arrow, then click Show Find Field.

3. Type **663** in the Find text box.

   Color number 663 C is selected in the PANTONE solid coated palette.

   > TIP To display the number for each PANTONE color, click the PANTONE solid coated palette list arrow, then click List View.

   (continued)

FIGURE L-15
PANTONE solid coated palette

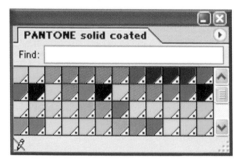

Preparing a Document for Prepress and Printing

FIGURE L-16

Spot color applied to the artwork

4. Click the **OAHU letters**, then click the **PANTONE 663 C color swatch**.

   The PANTONE 663 C color swatch is added to the standard Swatches palette.

5. Double-click the **PANTONE 663 C swatch** in the standard Swatches palette.

6. Note that Spot Color is listed as the Color Type in the Swatch Options dialog box.

7. Note the CMYK values.

   The CMYK values represent the values you would use to create the closest possible match of PANTONE 663 C with process inks.

8. Click **Cancel** to close the Swatch Options dialog box.

9. Change the fill of the red frame to PANTONE 663 C.

10. Show all, then send the placed image to the back.

    Your work should resemble Figure L-16.

11. Save your work, then close the Oahu document.

You displayed the PANTONE solid coated library of swatches. You then applied a spot color to artwork.

CREATE CROP MARKS

What You'll Do

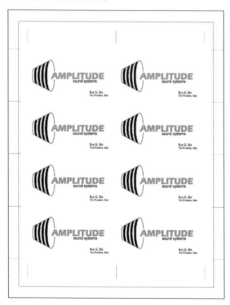

 In this lesson, you will set up documents to print with crop marks and trim marks.

Creating Crop Marks

The **trim size** of a document refers to the size of the finished document. **Crop marks** are short, thin lines that define where the object is trimmed after it is printed. Figure L-17 shows crop marks around an image.

You can create custom-sized crop marks on the artboard by drawing a rectangle that is precisely the same size as the document's trim size. Then, keeping the rectangle selected, click Object on the menu bar, point to Crop Area, then click Make. Crop marks will replace the rectangle.

When the trim size and the document size (the size of the artboard) are the same, you don't need to create your own crop marks. In this case, you can add crop marks in the Pring dialog box. Go to the Marks and Bleeds window in the Print dialog box, then check All Printer's Marks in the Marks section.

Editing Crop Marks

Once you've created crop marks, you cannot directly select them to edit them. Instead, you release them using the Release Crop Area command, edit the rectangle that defined the crop marks, then reapply the Make Crop Area command.

Using the Create Crop Marks Filter

Crop marks define where a printed image should be trimmed. You can create multiple marks using the Create Crop Marks filter on the Filter menu. For example, when printing business cards, printers use a standard-sized 8.5" × 11" sheet of paper. Printing a single business card on that size paper would be an absurd waste, so printers position multiple

copies of the card, usually eight or ten, on the same sheet. Each of those copies must be trimmed as shown in Figure L-18.

To create multiple crop marks, select the object whose size represents the trim size, then apply the Create Crop Marks filter. Use the same method to apply crop marks to the remaining artwork on the page, one at a time.

FIGURE L-17

Crop marks define the trim size of the artwork

FIGURE L-18

Create Crop Marks filter creates marks for multiple cuts

Lesson 4   Create Crop Marks

Create crop marks

1. Open AI L-2.ai, then save it as **Crop Marks**.

2. Click **View** on the menu bar, then click **Business Card**.

   The view of the artwork is enlarged.

3. Select the 2" × 3.5" rectangle. Switch to Outline mode if you have trouble selecting the rectangle.

   2" × 3.5" is the standard size for business cards.

   | TIP   Switch to Outline mode if you have trouble selecting the rectangle.

4. Click **Object** on the menu bar, point to **Crop Area**, then click **Make**.

   The rectangle is converted into crop marks that define the trim size as that of the rectangle. Your screen should resemble Figure L-19.

5. Save your work, then close the Crop Marks document.

You selected a rectangle, then you applied the Make Crop Area command.

FIGURE L-19
Applying crop marks

Roy G. Biv
Vice President, Sales

FIGURE L-20
Applying crop marks

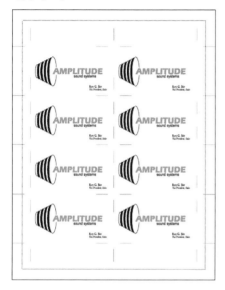

FIGURE L-21

Delete crop marks that lie on trim lines

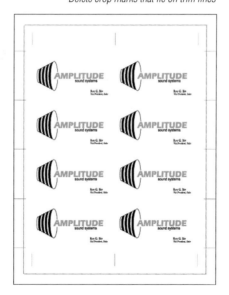

Use the Create Crop Marks filter

1. Open AI L-3.ai, then save it as **Multiple Crop Marks**.

2. Select all, cut the objects, then paste them.

   | TIP   Cutting and pasting artwork centers it on the artboard.

3. Switch to Outline mode, deselect, then select the rectangle of the top-left card.

4. Click **Filter** on the menu bar, point to **Create**, then click **Crop Marks**.

   Unlike the Make Crop Area command, when the Create Crop Marks filter is applied, the selected rectangle is not deleted and the trim marks can be selected.

5. Delete the rectangle only.

6. Select the next rectangle down, click **Filter** on the menu bar, click **Apply Crop Marks** at the top of the menu, then delete the rectangle.

   The last filter used always appears at the top of the Filter menu.

7. Repeat the instructions in Step 6 to create crop marks for the six other business cards.

8. Switch to Preview mode, then compare your screen to Figure L-20.

9. Use the Direct Selection Tool ▶. to delete all of the crop marks that are positioned on the inner trim of the business cards, leaving only the outer marks, as shown in Figure L-21.

   Crop marks should be positioned only "off the artwork."

10. Save your work, then close the document.

You applied crop marks to eight objects.

CREATE BLEEDS

What You'll Do

In this lesson, you will modify artwork to accommodate bleeds.

Creating Bleeds and Safety Guides

Artwork that extends to the trim is referred to as a "bleed" element, or simply a **bleed**, based on printer lingo meaning that to print correctly, the ink must bleed off the page.

Imagine that you have designed a business card that shows white lettering against a black background. You have used the Make Crop Area command so that the marks define the "live area" as 2" × 3.5". When the cards are trimmed, if the cutter is off by the slightest amount, $\frac{1}{10}$ of an inch, for example, your black business card will have a white line on one edge.

To accommodate variations in trimming, a printer will ask you to "build a bleed." What he or she is asking you to do is to extend bleed artwork so that it exceeds the cropped area by a minimum of .125". Artwork can bleed off any one or all four sides of the trim. Two of the most straightforward ways of doing this are to create a bleed object with the Offset Path command, or to extend the existing artwork off the artboard using the Move command for precision. Figure L-22 shows an example of using bleeds.

In addition to bleeds, as a designer you should be conscious of your safety margin. All elements that aren't designed to bleed should be kept a minimum of .125" from the trim edge. This practice is known as maintaining safety or type safety. As with bleeds, safety guides anticipate variations in the trim cut and are designed to keep artwork from being accidentally trimmed off the page.

FIGURE L-22

Bleeds extend the crop marks to accommodate variations when trimming

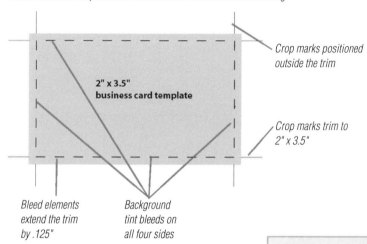

2" x 3.5"
business card template

Crop marks positioned outside the trim

Crop marks trim to 2" x 3.5"

Bleed elements extend the trim by .125"

Background tint bleeds on all four sides

Exporting Illustrator files to QuarkXPress and InDesign

Throughout this book, we have been regarding Illustrator as a drawing tool—software that you can use to create an illustration. Adobe has designed Illustrator to also play the role of a page layout application. However, despite Illustrator's excellence, Adobe InDesign and QuarkXPress hold the distinction of being the preeminent page layout applications. Both InDesign and Quark import Illustrator files easily. Because InDesign, like Illustrator, is an Adobe product, InDesign will import an Illustrator file in its "native" Illustrator ".ai" format. To save an Illustrator file that is to be placed in QuarkXPress, save the Illustrator file as an Illustrator EPS (Encapsulated Post Script). QuarkXPress recognizes Illustrator files only in the Illustrator EPS format. If you have used spot colors in the Illustrator file, Quark will recognize this and automatically list the spot colors in its own color palette.

Create a bleed using the Offset Path command

1. Open AI L-4.ai, then save it as **Oahu Bleed**.

2. Select the frame of the artwork that is filled with PANTONE 663 C.

3. Click **Object** on the menu bar, point to **Path**, then click **Offset Path**.

4. Type **.125** in the Offset text box, then click **OK**.

   The Offset Path command creates a new object, in this case, a bleed object that extends the artboard .125" on all sides. Your artwork should resemble Figure L-23.

5. Verify that the new bleed object is still selected, then send it to the back.

6. Save your work, then close the Oahu Bleed document.

You used the Offset Path command to extend the edges of a bleed object .125".

FIGURE L-23
A bleed object created with the Offset Path command

.125" bleed

Preparing a Document for Prepress and Printing

FIGURE L-24

Three sides of the blue rectangle must bleed

.125" bleed

FIGURE L-25

The rule, too, must bleed

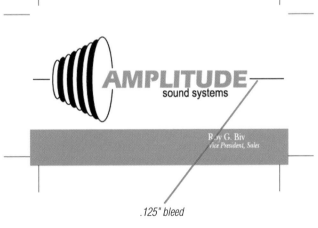

.125" bleed

Create a bleed using the Move command

1. Open AI L-5.ai, then save it as **Three Sided Bleed**.

2. Click **View** on the menu bar, then click **Business Card**.

3. Select the black-stroked rectangle, click **Object** on the menu bar, point to **Crop Area**, then click **Make**.

4. Click the **Direct Selection Tool** , then click the bottom edge of the blue rectangle.

5. Click **Object** on the menu bar, point to **Transform**, click **Move**, type **0** in the Horizontal text box, type **-.125** in the Vertical text box, then click **OK**.

6. Select the left edge of the blue rectangle, then move it -.125" to the left.

7. Select the right edge of the blue rectangle, then move it .125" to the right.

   The blue rectangle bleeds on all three sides, as shown in Figure L-24.

8. Select *only* the left anchor point of the black line, then move the point -.125" horizontally.

9. Select *only* the right anchor point of the black line, then move the point .125" horizontally, so that your work resembles Figure L-25.

10. Save your work, then close the Three Sided Bleed document.

You extended individual lines and anchor points outside the crop marks as bleeds.

Explore basic color theory.

1. List the seven distinct colors of the visible spectrum.
2. What are the three additive primary colors?
3. What are the three subtractive primary colors?
4. When red, green, and blue light are combined equally, what color light do they produce?
5. Explain the term "subtractive" in terms of the subtractive primary colors.
6. Explain the term "transmission" in terms of light striking an object.
7. Which additive primary color would be 100% absorbed by a perfect cyan ink?
8. Which additive primary color would be 100% absorbed by a perfect magenta ink?
9. Which additive primary color would be 100% absorbed by a perfect yellow ink?

10. What is the fourth color in the four-color printing process, and why is it necessary?

Work in CMYK mode.

1. Open AI L-6.ai, then save it as **Sleep Center**.
2. Using the Color palette, create a new process tint that is 55M/100Y.
3. Save the process tint in the Swatches palette as **Headline**.
4. Fill the words THE SLEEP CENTER with the Headline color.
5. Save your work.

Specify spot colors.

1. Click Window on the menu bar, point to Swatch Libraries, then click PANTONE solid coated.
2. Type **2622** in the Find text box of the PANTONE solid coated palette.

3. Select the object with the gradient on the artboard.
4. Select the black color stop on the gradient slider in the Gradient palette.
5. Press [Alt] (Win) or [option] (Mac), then click PANTONE 2622 C in the PANTONE solid coated palette.
6. Save your work.

Create crop marks.

1. Copy the rectangle with the gradient fill, then paste in front.
2. Select the copied rectangle, click Object on the menu bar, point to Crop Area, then click Make.
3. Save your work.

Create bleeds.

1. Click the left edge of the rectangle with the Direct Selection Tool.
2. Click Object on the menu bar, point to Transform, then click Move.
3. Type **-.125** in the Horizontal text box, type **0** in the Vertical text box, then click OK.
4. Select the top edge of the rectangle.
5. Open the Move dialog box, type **0** in the Horizontal text box, type **.125** in the Vertical text box, then click OK.
6. Select the right edge of the rectangle.
7. Open the Move dialog box, type **.125** in the Horizontal text box, type **0** in the Vertical text box, then click OK.
8. Save your work, then compare your illustration to Figure L-26.

FIGURE L-26
Completed Skills Review

You work in the computer department at a small print shop. Your boss brings you an Illustrator file for a business card for USAchefs, an Internet company that works with the top chefs and restaurants in the city. Your boss asks you to create a print proof, which she will show to the customer. She asks you to create a rich black, add crops, and build a bleed, then says, with a wink, "But not necessarily in that order." You realize that she's challenging you to figure out the right order in which to get all three processes accomplished.

1. Open AI L-7.ai, then save it as **USAchefs**.
2. Copy the black rectangle, then paste in front.
3. Use the copied black rectangle to make crop marks.
4. Select the new black rectangle, then use the Offset Path command to offset the path .125".
5. Keeping the new object selected, increase the cyan portion of its fill color 50% to create a rich black.
6. Delete the original (smaller) black rectangle.
7. Save your work, then compare your illustration to Figure L-27.
8. Close the USAchefs document.

FIGURE L-27
Completed Project Builder 1

You own a design firm in a small town. A new client delivers his logo to you on disk, telling you that it has two colors: PANTONE 255 and 70% PANTONE 5767. He tells you, "It's all set to go." You know that this client knows only enough to be dangerous. You open his file and, sure enough, you note immediately that all of the tints are process tints. You must change the fills and strokes to the proper PANTONE colors. Because this is a complex logo, and because you know that your client's knowledge of Illustrator is limited, you are aware that you must be very careful not to miss any elements.

1. Open AI L-8.ai, then save it as **City Square Associates**.
2. Apply the Show All command, just to avoid any potential surprises.
3. Delete the green letters.
4. Display the PANTONE solid coated palette.
5. Select the letter C in the center.
6. Click Select on the menu bar, point to Same, then click Fill Color.
7. Apply PANTONE 255 C to the fill, then hide the selection.
8. Select the top white rectangle.
9. Click Select on the menu bar, point to Same, then click Stroke Color.
10. Apply PANTONE 255 C to the stroke, then hide the selection.

11. Click the green square in the center, then change the black stroke to PANTONE 255 C.
12. Click Select on the menu bar, point to Same, then click Fill Color.
13. Apply PANTONE 5767 C to the fill.
14. Display the Color palette, if necessary, then drag the slider to 70%.

FIGURE L-28
Completed Project Builder 2

15. Hide the selection.
16. Select all and note that all the remaining items have a white fill.
17. Show all, save your work, then compare your illustration with Figure L-28.
18. Close the City Square Associates document.

You are the assistant art director for OAHU magazine. The art director tells you that, at the last minute, the editor in chief has changed the cover photo. You place the new photo in the Illustrator file and realize immediately that the colors that worked so well with the previous photo no longer work with this new photo.

1. Open AI L-9.ai, then save it as **Oahu 2**.
2. Choose a new PANTONE color for the title and the frame.
3. Mix a new process tint, then apply it to the word "living".
4. Mix three new process tints, then apply them to the three subheads.
5. Save your work, compare your illustration with Figure L-29, then close Oahu 2.

FIGURE L-29
Completed Design Project

You are the head of the film output department for a small printer. You receive an Illustrator file for the business card for USAchefs. The file is complete with a rich black, crop marks, and bleeds. With so many years' experience, you know how best to lay out and print standard-sized business cards for maximum cost-effectiveness. However, you have a group of six new workers whom you hired for the third shift, and you realize that the issues involved with preparing this job would make for a great lesson.

1. Open AI L-10.ai, then save it as **Chef Output**.
2. Have two group members discuss the most cost-efficient layout for the card on an 8.5" × 11" sheet. How many cards can be positioned on the sheet while still keeping a minimum .25" margin on all sides?
3. Once the group has calculated the number of cards that can fit on the page, ask them to calculate the size of the total area (without bleeds) covered by the artwork.
4. Note for the group that a bleed and crop marks have already been created in the file. Ask two group members to explain why both will need to be removed for the new layout.
5. Ask two other group members to study the parameters as listed above and then to explain to the group the best strategy for creating the bleed once the cards are laid out and the crop marks are in place.
6. Position 12 cards (4 across, 3 down) on the 8.5" × 11" page, then add crop marks and bleeds.

FIGURE L-30
Completed Group Project

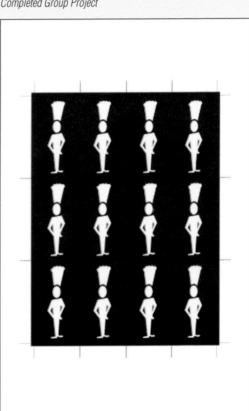

7. Change the document size to 11" × 17"
8. Save your work, then compare your document to Figure L-30.
9. Close the Chef Output document.

CHAPTER M

PREPARING GRAPHICS FOR THE WEB

1. Create slices.

2. Specify slice type and slice options.

3. Use the Save for Web dialog box.

4. Create an image map.

CHAPTER M
PREPARING GRAPHICS FOR THE WEB

Illustrator CS represents a giant step forward for creating Web graphics. We have all become familiar with the standard look for a Web page: headline across the top, a colored margin with links on the left, standard typefaces, and large blocks of HTML text flowing down the page. Illustrator CS shatters this standard and introduces nothing less than a new concept for a Web page: an artboard! Illustrator CS offers you the freedom to create a Web page entirely in Illustrator, with all the power and sophistication that the application has to offer. You can then save your artwork—export your document—as a Web page, complete with links, HTML text, and bitmap images. Illustrator has defined a new approach for Web design, one that is free from the constraints of producing a page from scratch with HTML code. For the designer, this approach offers a dramatic advance for originality and personal expression on the Web.

Tools You'll Use

Slice Tool — Slice Selection Tool

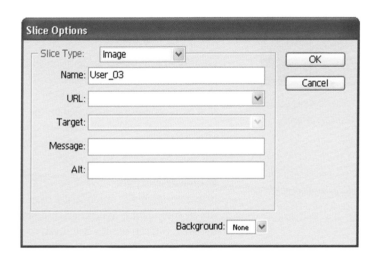

CREATE SLICES

What You'll Do

 In this lesson, you will create slices using guides. You will also combine slices.

Understanding Web Graphics

When you create graphics for the Web, you will need to pay attention to different considerations than you would when designing graphics for print. The Web is an entirely different medium, and you will be required to become familiar with, if not fluent in, many issues.

Color is an essential consideration when producing Web graphics. Since a computer's monitor functions as a light source, it produces color based on the additive model; color is created by combining light. Thus, graphics that you create must be saved in RGB mode.

For the designer, this is good news: The RGB color gamut is much larger than the CMYK color gamut. When designing for the Web, you can use the brightest, most saturated colors. However, the colors you see on your artboard aren't necessarily the colors that will appear in your Web browser. Color choices, file formats, and the degree of compression all affect the appearance of color.

Resolution is an essential consideration when using bitmap graphics on the Web. If you place a bitmap graphic in your Illustrator file, remember that 72 pixels per inch (PPI) is the standard resolution for bitmap graphics on the Web.

Two essential considerations when choosing the correct file format for your Web graphics are file size and display characteristics. Two standard compression file formats for bitmap graphics—JPEG and GIF—both reduce file size significantly, but through dramatically different processes. Knowing which to choose, and then choosing the degree to which each compresses the file, require understanding and experience.

Understanding Sliced Artwork

When you create graphics for the Web, file size is a fundamental consideration. Smaller file sizes enable Web servers to store and transmit images more efficiently, and allow viewers to download images more quickly.

When creating graphics for the Web, you often find that the file size of the entire document is far too large to be acceptable. For this reason, Illustrator allows you to divide your work into slices: You literally divide the artwork into areas to be output as individual—and therefore smaller—files.

Imagine a 100-piece puzzle whose pieces are all rectangular. Imagine that the entire puzzle, when put together, weighs exactly one pound. It would stand to reason that each of the 100 pieces weighs far less than one pound. This is a good analogy for understanding sliced artwork. Each slice is like a piece of the puzzle, smaller in area and—more importantly—smaller in size.

The analogy is not apt in one area: When a puzzle is completed, you can see the lines between the pieces. With sliced artwork, the slices in the work are invisible when it is viewed in a Web browser.

Slices provide another important function. Web pages can contain many different kinds of elements, such as HTML text and bitmap images. In Illustrator, if you use slices to divide the different elements, you can then output them differently. For example, if you create a slice that contains a bitmap image and another that contains HTML text, you can output the bitmap slice as a JPEG file and the text slice as an HTML file.

Creating Slices with the Make Slice Command and the Slice Tool

The Make Slice command creates a slice whose dimensions match those of the bounding box of the object. This command also creates a slice that captures text with its basic formatting characteristics. With the Make Slice command, the object is the slice, and vice versa. If you move or modify the object, the slice automatically adjusts to encompass the new artwork.

The Slice Tool allows you to draw a rectangular slice anywhere on the artboard. Slices that you create with the Slice Tool are independent of the underlying artwork. In other words, if you move the artwork, the slice does not move with the artwork.

Whether you use the Make Slice command or the Slice Tool to create slices, Illustrator generates automatic slices that cover the remainder of the artboard. Illustrator does this to create a complete HTML table, in case the document is saved as a Web page.

In Figure M-1, slice 3 was drawn with the Slice Tool. Slices 1, 2, and 4 were generated automatically.

Put quite simply, automatic slices are cumbersome, tricky, and hard to work with. Every time you add or edit slices, Illustrator must regenerate automatic slices; thus, the slice pattern on the artboard continues to change.

FIGURE M-1

Slice 3 was created with the Slice Tool; slices 1, 2, and 4 were generated automatically

Creating Slices from Guides

You can use standard ruler guides to define how you want artwork to be divided into slices. Figure M-2 shows three guides that were positioned so as to isolate the graphic of the dog.

By definition, guides extend across and beyond the artboard. Therefore, when you use guides to define areas to be sliced, the

length of the guide can get in the way. For example, the two vertical guides in Figure M-2 extend up beyond the dog area into the headline. Thus, the headline is unnecessarily divided into three sections.

This problem can sometimes seem extreme. Figure M-3 shows two additional horizontal guides positioned on the artwork to isolate each of the three photos

and their corresponding text on the right. Each will be used as a link that will take the viewer to a different page. Therefore, it is necessary to create a slice for each link. Note, however, that the horizontal guides extend across the dog area, dividing that artwork into three parts.

FIGURE M-2
Guides isolate the dog graphic into its own area

Horizontal guide   *Two vertical guides*

FIGURE M-3
Two additional horizontal guides divide the dog graphic into three sections

When you apply the Create from Guides command, Illustrator generates slices for each area defined by a guide, as shown in Figure M-4. Twelve slices are unnecessary to save this artwork for the Web. For example, slices 04, 07, and 10, if combined, could be saved as a very small file. Also, one might want to try to save the dog graphic as one file. Breaking the dog artwork into three slices runs the risk that each slice might vary slightly in color because of the file format and the compression that is applied.

FIGURE M-4

The Create from Guides command generates only slices—no automatic slices

Note, however, that each slice . . . is a slice! The Create from Guides command generates only slices—no automatic slices. Each slice can be selected with the Slice Selection Tool. Therefore, slices can be easily combined, as shown in Figure M-5.

Of the three main ways that Illustrator offers for making slices, using guides and then combining excess slices is the simplest, most straightforward, and hassle-free method.

FIGURE M-5
Slices can be combined easily

Make slices

1. Open AI M-1.ai, then save it as **SDS**.

2. Close all palettes except for the toolbox.

3. Change the style of the guides to Dots and the color of the guides to Yellow.

   TIP If you are using Macintosh OS 10, your preference settings are on the Illustrator menu.

4. Show the rulers, then position a guide on all four sides of the photo, as shown in Figure M-6.

5. Position a vertical guide to the left of the three text buttons, then position another guide to the right of the three text buttons.

6. Position a horizontal guide above the purple text as shown in Figure M-7.

7. Position a horizontal guide above and below the "purchase show tickets" button, as shown in Figure M-8.

8. Verify that your guides are unlocked.

9. Select all, click **Object** on the menu bar, point to **Slice**, then click **Create from Guides**.

   Thirty slices are generated, as shown in Figure M-9.

   TIP The View menu has commands to hide and show slices.

You positioned guides, then used them to create slices.

FIGURE M-6
Positioning guides on all four sides of the photo

FIGURE M-7
Positioning a guide above the text

Horizontal guide above text

FIGURE M-8
Positioning guides above and below the "purchase show tickets" button

Purchase show tickets button

FIGURE M-9
Thirty slices generated from guides

FIGURE M-10

Slices 06, 11, and 16 selected

Slices 06,
11, and 16

FIGURE M-11

Three slices combined into one

Newly combined
slice

FIGURE M-12

After combining slices, 14 slices remain

Combine slices

1. Click the **Selection Tool** , then click any-where in the scratch area to deselect the slices.

2. Click the **Slice Selection Tool** .

   TIP The Slice Selection Tool is hidden beneath the Slice Tool.

3. Using [Shift], select slices 06, 11, and 16 as shown in Figure M-10.

   TIP The easiest way to select a slice is to click the slice number.

4. Click **Object** on the menu bar, point to **Slice**, then click **Combine Slices**.

   The three slices are combined into one slice; all of the slices are renumbered, as shown in Figure M-11.

5. Hide the guides.

6. Using the same method, combine the four slices that contain the purple text.

7. Combine the six black slices on the right-hand margin.

8. Combine the three slices that contain the photo.

9. Combine the five slices that contain the logo in the spotlight, so that your slices corre-spond to Figure M-12.

10. Save your work.

You combined slices to create single slices for specific areas of the artwork.

SPECIFY SLICE TYPE AND SLICE OPTIONS

What You'll Do

 In this lesson, you will specify slices as Image or No Image, and you will add URL links to image slices.

Specifying Slice Types

A slice's type and the options assigned to it determine how the artwork contained in the slice will function on a Web page. A slice must be selected in order for you to assign a type and apply options to it. The Slice Options dialog box allows you to specify one of three categories for a slice's type. Basically, a slice's type defines its content.

The Image type is used when you want the content of a slice to become a linked image file on a Web page.

The No Image type is used when you want the area to contain text or a solid color. You enter the text or the color information directly into the Slice Options dialog box. You cannot view No Image slice content in Illustrator; you must use a Web browser to preview it.

Choosing between Image and No Image is not always as straightforward as it would at first seem. Consider slice 2 in Figure M-13, for example. It contains no artwork, and

certainly would not function as a link. However, it does contain a background color—the same background color that is shared by all of the slices.

If you were to define the slice type of slice 2 as No Image, it would by default have no background color. If you saved the file for the Web, the content of slice 2 would appear white on the Web page. You could apply a background color in the Slice Options dialog box, and specify the color to have the same RGB values as the background color in the Image slices. This solution may work well. However, you also have the option of specifying slice 2's type as Image—a single color image with no links. In this case, slice 2 would be output using the same file format as the other slices, logically a safer bet for color consistency.

The third type of slice is HTML Text, which you use if you want to capture Illustrator text and its basic formatting. You can only create this type of slice using the Make Slice command.

Generally, you will use Illustrator to create display text—text that is intended to be used as a design element, such as a headline. Rather than saving display text as text for the Web, it is a smart decision to simply save a version of your artwork with display text converted to outlines and defined as an image. With this method, you know for certain that your text will appear exactly as you designed it, with no risk of its being modified by or being in conflict with a browser's preset preferences.

Setting Options for Image Content Slices

When you specify a slice as an Image slice, you have the following options in the Slice Options dialog box:

- **Name:** By default, the slice name is used as the file name when you save the Web page. By default, the slice is named with the slice number. It is a good idea to rename an important slice with a name that is more descriptive of its content.
- **URL:** Specify a URL to make the slice a hotspot on the Web page.
- **Target:** If you've specified a URL, the target specifies the frame that you want the link to target. You can enter the name of a target frame, or you can use one of the standard targets in the pop-up menu. If you are unfamiliar with frames, note that _parent and _blank are the most common. _blank means that a new browser window will be opened, or "spawned," to show the linked page. _parent, the more standard of the two, means that the current window will change to show the linked page.
- **Message:** The information you type in the Message text box is what will appear in the status bar of a browser window when you position your cursor over the corresponding image slice. Messages usually convey information about the current image, or information about what the image links to.
- **Alt:** Think of Alt as an "alternative" to an image. Alternative text is for sight impaired Web surfers. They will hear the alt text rather than see the image.
- **Background:** If you are saving a bitmap image with a transparent background, you can specify a color for the background behind the transparent areas.

FIGURE M-13

Slice 2 could be specified as an Image or a No Image type

Setting Options for No Image Content Slices

In the Slice Options dialog box, you can set the following options:

- **Text:** In the Text Displayed in Cell text box, you can enter text that will appear in the slice. You can format the text using standard HTML tags. Be careful not to enter more text than can fit in the slice. If you do, the overflow will extend into neighboring slices. Because you cannot view the text in Illustrator, you will need to save the file for the Web and open it in a browser to view your work.

- **Alignment:** Use the Horiz and Vert list arrows to specify the horizontal and vertical alignment of the text.
- **Background:** Choose a background color for the slice.

FIGURE M-14

Slice Options dialog box for slice 03

Message text box

Alt text box

Slice Type
list arrow

1. Click the **Slice Selection Tool**, then click **slice 03**, if necessary.

2. Click **Object** on the menu bar, point to **Slice**, then click **Slice Options**.

3. Click the **Slice Type list arrow**, then click **Image**, if necessary.

4. Type **Susan's Dance Studio** in both the Message and Alt text boxes, as shown in Figure M-14.

5. Click **OK** to close the Slice Options dialog box.

6. Click **File** on the menu bar, then click **Save** to update your slice numbers.

7. Click **slice 14**, click **Object** on the menu bar, point to **Slice**, click **Slice Options**, specify it as an Image slice, type **Fall registration** in the Message and Alt text boxes, click **OK**, then save.

8. Click **slice 01**, define it as No Image, click the **Background list arrow**, click **Black**, click **OK**, then save.

   The black background will be coded in HTML. If you wanted to use the underlying black object as the black background, you would specify the slice type as an image, just as you did the logo.

9. Repeat Step 8 to specify slices 02, 04, 05, 11, and 12 as No Image slices with a black background, one at a time.

   TIP   You cannot apply Slice Options to multiple slices simultaneously.

You used the Slice Options dialog box to specify slices as Image slices and No Image slices.

Set options for image content slices

1. Click the **Slice Selection Tool** 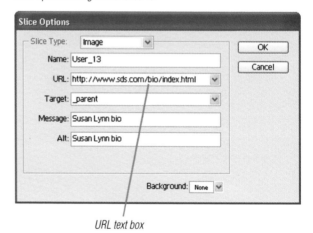, if necessary, click **slice 13**, click **Object** on the menu bar, point to **Slice**, then click **Slice Options**.

2. Click the **Slice Type list arrow**, then click **Image**, if necessary.

3. Type **http://www.sds.com/bio/index.html** in the URL text box.

   In a Web browser, clicking slice 13 will link to an HTML biography page.

4. Click the **Target list arrow**, then click **_parent**.

   In a Web browser, clicking slice 13 will change the current window to the HTML biography page.

5. Type **Susan Lynn bio** in the Message and Alt text boxes, as shown in Figure M-15, click **OK**, then save.

   > TIP   Each time you make changes to a slice or combine slices, the slice numbering is thrown off. Saving your work reapplies the correct slice numbers to the slices.

   (continued)

FIGURE M-15
Slice Options dialog box for slice 13

URL text box

Slice Options dialog box for slice 07

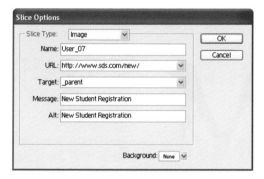

Slice Options dialog box for slice 09

Slice Options dialog box for slice 10

6. Click **slice 08**, open the Slice Options dialog box, repeat Steps 2–5 so that slice 08 contains the same slice information as slice 13, then save.

7. Click **slice 06**, open the Slice Options dialog box, verify that the Slice Type is set to Image, click **OK**, then save.

8. Click **slice 07**, open the Slice Options dialog box, type the information shown in Figure M-16, click **OK**, then save.

9. Specify the slice options for slice 9 as shown in Figure M-17, then save.

10. Specify the slice options for slice 10 as shown in Figure M-18, then save.

Because the target for slice 10 is _blank, slice 10, when clicked, will open a new browser window for the photo album page.

You used the Slice Options dialog box to specify URLs to which the image slices will link when clicked in a browser application.

Lesson 2   Specify Slice Type and Slice Options

USE THE SAVE FOR WEB DIALOG BOX

What You'll Do

In this lesson, you will optimize slices for the Web, using the Save for Web dialog box.

Optimizing Artwork for the Web

Most artwork, even when sliced, requires optimization. **Optimization** is a process by which the file size is reduced through standard color compression algorithms.

Illustrator CS offers a number of optimization features to save artwork in different Web graphics file formats. Your choice of a file format will have the greatest effect on the optimization method that is performed on the artwork.

The Save for Web dialog box presents unprecedented options for previewing images. The tabs at the top of the image area define the display options. The Original display presents the artwork with no optimization. The Optimized display presents the artwork with the current optimization setting applied. The 2-Up display presents two versions of the artwork—the original and the optimized version—side by side, and the 4-Up display presents the original beside three optimized versions.

Optimizing with the GIF File Format

GIF is a standard file format for compressing images with flat color, which makes it an excellent choice for many types of artwork generated in Illustrator. GIFs provide effective compression; for the right type of artwork, GIFs maintain excellent quality with crisp detail. In many cases, the compression has no noticeable effect on the image.

GIF compression works by lowering the number of colors in the file. The trick with GIFs is to lower the number of available colors as much as possible without adversely affecting the appearance of the image. Generally, if the number of colors is too low, problems with the image are obvious, as shown in Figure M-19.

Optimizing with the JPEG File Format

JPEG is a standard file format for compressing continuous-tone images, gradients, and blends. JPEG compression relies on "lossy" algorithms—lossy referring to a loss of data. In the JPEG format, data is selectively discarded.

You choose the level of compression in the JPEG format by specifying the JPEG's quality setting. The higher the quality setting, the more detail is preserved. Of course, the more detail preserved, the less the file size is reduced.

When JPEG compression is too severe for an image, the problems with the image are obvious and very unappealing, as shown in Figure M-20.

JPEG has emerged as one of the most used, if not the most used, file formats on the Internet. As a result, many designers ignore GIFs in favor of JPEGs, though many times GIFs would be the better choice.

FIGURE M-19
A GIF file with too few colors available to render the image adequately

FIGURE M-20
Problems with JPEGs are obvious and very unappealing

Optimize a slice as a JPEG

1. Click **File** on the menu bar, then click **Save for Web**.

2. Click the **Optimized tab**, if necessary.

   The Optimized view shows you the artwork with the current optimization settings applied.

3. Click the **Slice Select Tool**  in the Save for Web dialog box, click **slice 03**, click the **Settings list arrow**, then click **JPEG High**.

   The selected slice is updated.

4. Click the **4-Up tab**.

   The image area is divided into four views of the artwork. The upper-right window is selected.

5. Click the **Hand Tool** in the Save for Web dialog box, then drag the upper-right window until all of slice 03 is visible, if necessary, as shown in Figure M-21.

6. Compare the file size of the original to the other three.

7. Compare the download times and quality settings, as listed in the upper-right and bottom windows.

8. Examine the three images.

   The quality of the lower-right image is unsatisfactory. Distracting pixels are visible at the edges of the logo and on the legs.

9. Click the **lower-left window**, click the **Quality list arrow**, then drag the **slider** to 40.

10. Keep the Save for Web dialog box open.

You used the 4-Up view of the Save for Web dialog box to compare three optimized JPEG files, each with different settings.

FIGURE M-21
Save for Web dialog box

File size

Download time

Quality setting

FIGURE M-22
Slice 14, optimized as a GIF using 8 colors

Color Table

Change in file size

Optimize slices as GIFs

1. Click the **Optimized tab**.

2. Click the **Slice Select Tool** , click **slice 06**, press and hold [**Shift**], then click **slice 13** to add it to the selection.

3. Click the **Settings list arrow**, then click **GIF 32 Dithered**.

4. Remove the check mark from the Transparency check box.

5. Deselect, click **slice 06** only, then click the **Color Table tab** to the right of the image window.

   The Color Table shows the 32 total colors that are used to represent the artwork.

6. Click **slice 14**, click the **Settings list arrow**, then click **GIF 32 No Dither**.

   Note the change to the swatches in the Color Table. Though the setting is for 32 colors, only 17 colors are required to reproduce the artwork.

7. Note the file size in the lower-left corner.

8. Click the **Colors list arrow**, then click **8**.

   Note the change in the Color Table and the change in file size, as shown in Figure M-22. Note also the high quality of the artwork with only eight colors.

9. Remove the check mark from the Transparency check box.

10. Keep the Save for Web dialog box open.

You optimized a slice as a GIF. You lowered the number of colors available to draw the image, noting the changes in image quality and file size.

Compare and contrast JPEG vs. GIF formats

1. Click the **Slice Select Tool** 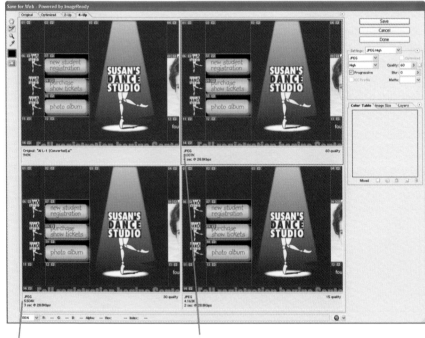, if necessary, click **slice 07**, press and hold [**Shift**], then click slices **09** and **10** to add them to the selection.

2. Click the **Settings list arrow**, click **JPEG High**, then click the **4-Up tab**.

3. Compare the quality of the three JPEGs to the original.

   The High quality JPEG in the upper-right window is the only version with acceptable quality. Note that the file size is over 9K, as shown in Figure M-23.

4. Click the **Optimized tab**.

5. Click the **Settings list arrow**, click **GIF 128 No Dither**, then remove the check mark from the Transparency check box.

6. Click the **4-Up tab**, then use the Hand Tool, if necessary, to see as much of the three buttons as possible.

(continued)

FIGURE M-23

Slices 07, 09, and 10 optimized as a high-quality JPEG

Change in file size

File size is large

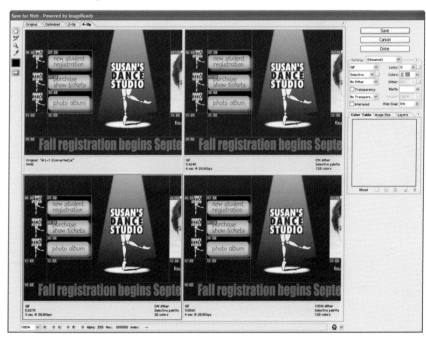

7. Click the **lower-left window**, then note that its Selective palette is 64 colors, one-half that of the image in the upper-right window.

8. Click the **Colors list arrow**, then click **32**.

   The Selective palette of the image in the lower-left corner is reduced by half, yet the quality remains acceptable.

9. Click the **Colors list arrow**, then click **16**.

   The reduced palette does not contain enough colors to represent the buttons' drop shadows smoothly.

10. Click the **Colors list arrow**, then click **32**.

    The file size is around 6 kilobytes—⅔ that of the acceptable JPEG—and the quality is almost indistinguishable from the original, as shown in Figure M-24.

11. Keep the Save for Web dialog box open.

You experimented with optimizing a slice as both a JPEG and GIF, comparing file size and image quality. You found that the GIF format was able to optimize the slice with higher quality at a lower file size than the JPEG format.

Create photo effects with a GIF

1. Click the **Optimized tab**.

2. Click the **Slice Select Tool** , if necessary, then click **slice 08**.

3. Click the **Settings list arrow**, then click **GIF 32 Dithered**.

4. Click the **Color Table tab**, if necessary.

   The Color Table shows the 32 total colors that are used to present the photo in slice 08.

5. Click the **Colors list arrow**, then click **16**.

   The number of colors in the Color Table is reduced.

6. Click the **Colors list arrow**, click **8**, then note the effect on the photo and the file size shown in the lower-left corner of the dialog box.

7. Click the **Colors list arrow**, click **4**, click the **Dither list arrow**, then drag the **slider** to 0%.

8. Click the **Settings list arrow**, then click **GIF iMODE 1-bit**.

9. Click the **Dither list arrow**, then drag the **slider** to 90% so that the photo resembles Figure M-25.

10. Keep the Save for Web dialog box open.

You specified an Image slice as a GIF, then lowered the number of colors available to reproduce the image, noting the effect on the image. You then specified a GIF 1-bit setting, which created the effect that the image was created with small black dots.

FIGURE M-25

An effect created by optimizing a photo as a 1-bit GIF

FIGURE M-26

Web page shown in a browser window

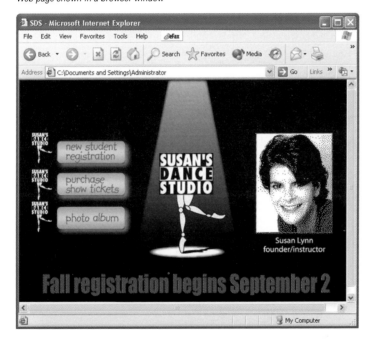

1. Click **Save**, name the file **SDS.html**, then click **Save**.

2. Launch your Web browser, such as Netscape or Internet Explorer.

   | TIP If you do not have access to a Web browser, proceed to the next lesson.

3. Open SDS.html in your Web browser application.

4. Point to different images and note the messages that you entered in the Slice Options dialog box, in the status bar of the browser window.

   Your screen should resemble Figure M-26.

5. Close (Win) or Quit (Mac) your browser, then save and close the SDS document.

You saved the file with the optimization settings that you specified in the Save for Web dialog box. You then viewed the HTML file in a Web browser application.

CREATE AN IMAGE MAP

What You'll Do

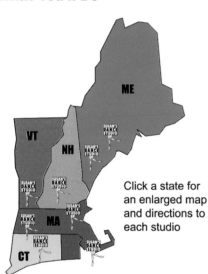

Click a state for an enlarged map and directions to each studio

In this lesson, you will change the colors in an illustration to Web safe colors and create polygonal image maps with URLs attached to them for use on a Web page.

Working with Web Safe Colors

Given all of the variables that might affect color display on the Internet—different monitors with different settings, different Web browsers with different settings, among many other conditions—you can never be certain that the colors that you specify in your document will appear the same way when viewed as a Web page. You can't even be certain that they'll be consistent from computer to computer. To alleviate this problem to some degree, Illustrator offers a Web Safe RGB mode in the Color palette and a Web swatch library. The Web swatch library contains predefined colors that are coded so as to be recognized by most computer displays, and by the common Web browser applications. When color is critical, it is best to think of the Web safe gamut as a safe bet for achieving reasonable consistency, understanding that a guarantee is a bit too much to expect.

Creating vector-based Web graphics

Though bitmap images are the most common graphics on the Web, vector-based graphics make for excellent Web graphics. Unlike bitmap graphics, which tend toward higher file sizes and lose quality when enlarged, vector graphics are scalable, compact, and able to maintain their image quality at different resolutions. The Macromedia Flash SWF file format supports vector graphics for the Web. SWF also recognizes symbols in your artwork. When the artwork is saved or exported as an SWF, each symbol is defined only once, which can substantially lower the file size. The SWF format also provides excellent support of complex Illustrator artwork, such as gradients, mesh objects, and patterns.

Understanding Image Maps

Image maps allow you to define an area of an illustration as a link. In a Web browser, when a user clicks the area of the image defined as a link, the Web browser loads the linked file.

Unlike using slices to create links, using image maps stores the artwork and the links in a single file; using slices causes artwork to be exported in different files. Another main difference is that slices are always rectangular, while image maps enable you to create links from polygons and odd-shaped objects, as shown in Figure M-27.

Image maps are quite simple to make in Illustrator. The Attributes palette contains an Image Map list arrow, which allows you to choose a shape for your image map. You can then enter the URL for the link. The resulting image map is not visible—not in Illustrator and not in the browser.

FIGURE M-27

Image maps enable you to define odd-shaped areas of an image as links to a URL

Choose Web safe colors

1. Open AI M-2.ai, then save it as **New England Map**.

2. Show the Color palette, if necessary.

3. Click the **Color palette list arrow**, then click **Web Safe RGB**.

4. Verify that the Fill button is in front of the Stroke button in the toolbox, click the **Selection Tool** , then click the **state of Maine**.

   The Color palette, as shown in Figure M-28, shows the current fill color, the Out of Web Color Warning button, and the In Web Color button. The In Web Color button shows the closest possible Web safe color to the green fill.

5. Click the **In Web Color button** in the Color palette.

   The object's fill color changes to a Web safe color.

6. Click the **state of New Hampshire**, then click the **In Web Color button** in the Color palette.

7. Using the same method, replace the fill colors of the remaining states, except for Connecticut and Massachusetts, with Web safe colors.

You used the In Web Color button in the Color palette to change objects' fills to Web safe colors.

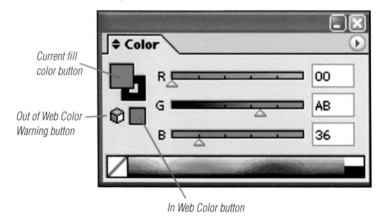

Current fill color button

Out of Web Color Warning button

In Web Color button

FIGURE M-29

The image map artwork, optimized as a GIF

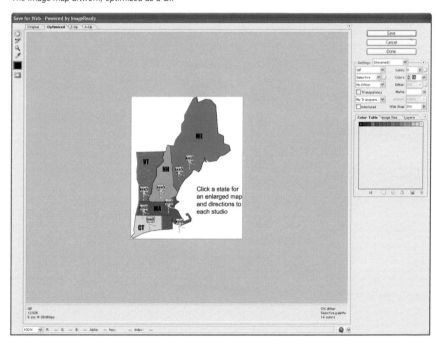

Create hotspots

1. Select the state of Maine, click **Window** on the menu bar, then click **Attributes**.

2. Click the **Image Map list arrow** in the Attributes palette, then click **Polygon**.

   An invisible hotspot that closely follows the outline of the selected object is created.

3. Type **http://www.sds.com/map/me** in the URL text box.

4. Select the state of New Hampshire, click the **Image Map list arrow**, then click **Polygon**.

5. Type **http://www.sds.com/map/nh** in the URL text box.

6. Add polygon hotspots and the following URLs to the remaining four states: **http://www.sds.com/map/vt**, **http://www.sds.com/map/ma**, and **http://www.sds.com/map/ct**.

7. Click **File** on the menu bar, click **Save for Web**, then click the **Optimized tab**, if necessary.

8. Click the **Settings list arrow**, then click **GIF 32 No Dither**.

9. Click the **Colors list arrow**, then click **16**.

10. Remove the check mark from the Transparency check box. Your screen should resemble Figure M-29.

11. Click **Save**, accept the current file name, then click **Save**.

12. Save and close New England Map.

You created six polygonal image maps with corresponding URLs. You then used the Save for Web dialog box to specify the artwork as a GIF file.

Create slices.

1. Open AI M-3.ai, then save it as **Hana**.
2. Show rulers, then place a horizontal guide just above the five photos. (*Hint*: Change your guides to a darker color.)
3. Place a horizontal guide just below the five photos (above the blue text).
4. Place a vertical guide between each photo and the next, for a total of four vertical guides.
5. Verify that your guides are unlocked.
6. Select only the six guides, click Object on the menu bar, point to Slice, then click Create from Guides.
7. Deselect all.
8. Click the Slice Selection Tool.
9. Select slices 01 and 02, click Object on the menu bar, point to Slice, click Combine Slices, then save.
10. Combine slices 02, 03, and 04, then save.
11. Combine slices 08 and 09, then save.
12. Combine slices 10 and 11, then save.
13. Save your work. (*Hint*: It's important that you save after Steps 9, 10, 11, and 12.)

Specify slice type and slice options.

1. Select slice 01, click Object on the menu bar, point to Slice, then click Slice Options.
2. Define slice 01 as an Image slice, click OK, then save.
3. Select slice 02, click Object on the menu bar, point to Slice, then click Slice Options.
4. Define slice 02 as a No Image slice, click the Background list arrow, click White, click OK, then save.
5. Select slice 08, define slice 08 as a No Image slice, click the Background list arrow, click White, click OK, then save.
6. Select slice 09, click Object on the menu bar, point to Slice, then click Slice Options.
7. Define slice 09 as an Image slice, click OK, then save.
8. Select slice 03, define it as an Image slice, then type **http://www.hana.com/photo1** in the URL text box.
9 Click the Target list arrow, then click _blank.
10. Type **Explore by car** in the Message and Alt text boxes, then click OK.
11. Save your work.

Use the Save for Web dialog box.

1. Click File on the menu bar, then click Save for Web.
2. Click the Slice Select Tool, if necessary, click slice 01, click the Settings list arrow, click GIF 32 Dithered, then remove the check mark from the Transparency check box.
3. Click slice 09, click the Settings list arrow, click GIF 32 Dithered, remove the check mark from the Transparency check box, click the Colors list arrow, then click 8.
4. Click slice 03, click the Settings list arrow, then click JPEG High.
5. Click the 4-Up tab, click the Hand Tool, then drag the Hand Tool over the selected window until slice 03 is visible in all four windows.
6. Compare the quality and file sizes of the three optimized images.
7. Click Done.

Create an image map.

1. Click Window on the menu bar, then click Attributes, if necessary.
2. Click the Selection Tool, then click the purple diamond in slice 01.
3. Click the Image Map list arrow in the Attributes palette, then click Polygon.
4. Type **http://www.hana.com/car** in the URL text box in the Attributes palette.
5. Click the gold diamond.
6. Click the Image Map list arrow in the Attributes palette, then click Polygon.
7. Type **http://www.hana.com/horse** in the URL text box.
8. Click the green diamond.
9. Click the Image Map list arrow in the Attributes palette, then click Polygon.
10. Type **http://www.hana.com/foot** in the URL text box.
11. Click the blue diamond.
12. Click the Image Map list arrow in the Attributes palette, then click Polygon.
13. Type **http://www.hana.com/bike** in the URL text box.
14. Save your work, then compare your window to Figure M-30.
15. Close the Hana document.

FIGURE M-30
Completed Skills Review

You work in the online department of *OAHU* magazine as an art manager. Every month, when the magazine hits the newsstands, you update the magazine's Web site with the new online issue. The top page always features this month's cover of the magazine (reduced 50% to fit on the page). The print department sends you an Illustrator file. Your job is to prepare the file to be used on the Web. You dislike this month's cover choice—a dark, busy, and out-of-focus image—and note that the subheads must remain bright when they are converted to Web safe colors.

1. Open AI M-4.ai, then save it as **Oahu Online**.
2. Click File on the menu bar, point to Document Color Mode, then click RGB Color.
3. Click Window on the menu bar, then click Color, if necessary.
4. Click the Color palette list arrow, then click RGB.
5. Select the word OAHU. (*Hint*: The magazine cover frame is grouped to the Oahu text.)
6. Click the In Web Color button in the Color palette.
7. Select the word "living."
8. Click the In Web Color button in the Color palette.
9. Change the colors for the three subheads (TWIST & SHOUT, A-MAZE-ING, and MAVERICK) to Web safe colors.
10. Click the Color palette list arrow, then click Web Safe RGB.
11. Select the word "living."

FIGURE M-31
Completed Project Builder 1

12. Drag the G slider in the Color palette all the way to the right.
13. Save your work, then compare your document to Figure M-31.
14. Close the Oahu Online document.

You work in the online department of *OAHU* magazine as a Web master. Every month, you receive the color-corrected version of this month's cover, which you position on the top page of the Web site. The cover is one of your favorite features of the *OAHU* magazine Web site: Users can click the three featured cover stories and go immediately to the online article. You create the slices and specify the slice options.

1. Open AI M-5.ai, then save it as **Oahu Magazine**.
2. Show the rulers, if necessary, then place a vertical guide between the A and H in OAHU.
3. Place a horizontal guide beneath the word "*living*."
4. Place a horizontal guide above the word A-MAZE-ING.
5. Place a horizontal guide above the word MAVERICK.
6. Use the guides to make slices.
7. Combine slices 5 and 7, then save.
8. Define the options for slice 5 as follows:
   Slice Type: Image
   URL: http://www.oahu.com/twist
   Target: _blank
9. Save your work.
10. Define the options for slice 6 as follows:
    Slice Type: Image
    URL: http://www.oahu.com/amazeing
    Target: _blank

11. Save your work.
12. Define the options for slice 7 as follows:
    Slice Type: Image
    URL: http://www.oahu.com/maverick
    Target: _blank

FIGURE M-32
Completed Project Builder 2

13. Save your work.
14. Define slices 1, 2, 3, and 4 as Image slices.
15. Save your work, then compare your document to Figure M-32.

You work in the online department of *OAHU* magazine as an art director. Every month, you personally optimize the cover image for the Web site. You feel strongly that the process of compressing a cover image demands a critical eye to maintain image quality. You note that you'll be able to optimize the image substantially: the photo is so busy and out-of-focus that it will be hard to see any flaws created by compression. Your goal is to compress each slice to approximately 8K or less, while maintaining acceptable quality.

1. Open AI M-6.ai, then save it as **Oahu Cover**.
2. Click File on the menu bar, then click Save for Web.
3. Click the Optimized tab, if necessary.
4. Select all seven slices.
5. Click the Settings list arrow, then click JPEG High.
6. Click the 4-Up tab.
7. Note that the quality of the JPEG with the quality setting of 30 is unacceptable, then click the Optimized tab.
8. Note the file size and download time of the total image.
9. Deselect by clicking outside the magazine cover, then select each slice, noting the file size of each one in the lower-left corner of the window.
10. Select all of the slices.

11. Click the Settings list arrow, then click GIF 64 Dithered; note the file size.
12. Change the Colors to 32, as shown in Figure M-33.
13. Note any changes in quality.

FIGURE M-33
Completed Design Project

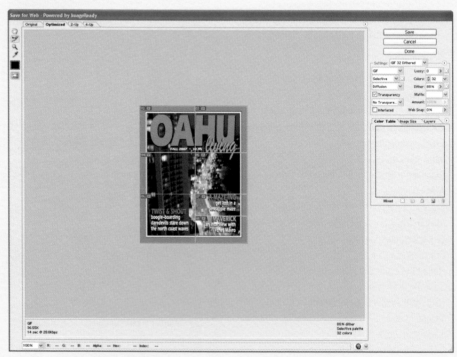

14. Deselect all, then select each slice, noting the file size of each one.
15. Click Done, then close the Oahu Cover document.

You work for a design consulting group. Lately, your company has enjoyed much new business from Internet companies who want your team to assess the design quality of their Web sites. Your newest client is USAchefs, a national Web site for chefs and the restaurant industry that features high-quality food photography.

1. Connect to the Internet, go to *www.course.com*, navigate to the page for this book, click the Online Companion link, then click Link 1 for this chapter.
2. Print the Web page, make copies, then distribute them to the group.
3. Have each member of the group draw lines on his or her copy that represent guides to be used as slices.
4. Collect the copies, then lay them out on a table.
5. Have the group come to a consensus as to the best grid for slices.
6. Have the group discuss the quality of the graphics on the page—all the graphics, not just the picture of the food.
7. Poll each group member, asking if he or she thinks the food slices are JPEGs or GIFs.

FIGURE M-34
Completed Group Project

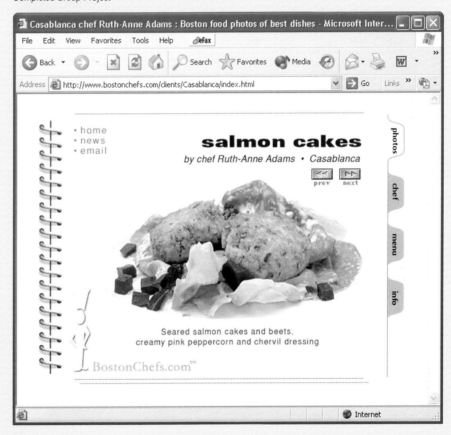

Topic Area	Objectives	Chapter
1. General Knowledge	■ Describe the major features of Adobe Illustrator.	A – M
	■ Describe the native file format used by Adobe Illustrator.	A
	■ Given a scenario, explain when you would use Adobe Illustrator to complete a task versus when you would use Adobe Photoshop to complete a task.	A
2. Laying Out a Document	■ Describe the different components of the work area.	A
	■ Given a document, determine the appropriate document settings for the art board.	A – M
	■ Given a scenario, select and configure the appropriate settings in the Document Setup dialog box.	A – M
3. Working with Shapes and Objects	■ Given a shape or object, determine which tool should be used to create the shape or object.	A & C
	■ Transform shapes by using the Transform tools or the Transform palette.	A & D
	■ Transform shapes by using 3D effects.	K
	■ Create spot colors and add them to the Swatch palette.	B & L
	■ Apply colors, strokes, fills, and gradients to objects by using the Fill box, Stroke box, or Appearance palette.	A, B, H
	■ Create and modify masks, including clipping masks.	D
	■ Create, use, and customize brushes.	F
	■ Modify overlapping objects by using the Transparency palette.	H
	■ Change the appearance of objects by using the Styles palette and Effects menu.	H
	■ Create, use, and edit symbols by using the Symbols palette and Symbols tools.	J
	■ Create and modify compound shapes by using Pathfinder palette.	D
	■ Select objects by using the selection tools.	A
4. Working with Type	■ Add type to a document.	B
	■ Modify type by using the Character and Paragraph palettes.	B
	■ Transform type by using setting options for scale, rotate, reflect, and shear.	B
	■ Change the look of type by using the Create Outlines command.	B
	■ Change the look of type by using the Envelope command.	G
	■ Insert special characters by using the Type menu and the Glyph palette.	B
	■ Manage the composition of text by using palettes, menus, and preference settings.	B
	■ Create, apply, import, and modify styles by using the Character and Paragraph palettes.	B
	■ List and describe the advantages and disadvantages when using OpenType, TrueType, or Type 1 fonts.	Online Companion

Topic Area	Objectives	Chapter
5. Creating and Working with Layers	■ Discuss layers, and how they can be used to help create and manage objects in a document.	E
	■ Change the attributes of objects in a layer by using the Layers palette.	E
	■ Explain the process, and guidelines associated with creating clipping masks.	D & E
	■ Explain the considerations associated with importing and exporting an Adobe Photoshop file with layers and an Adobe Acrobat file with layers.	E
6. Managing Color	■ Discuss the color management workflow process that is used in Adobe Illustrator.	Online Companion
	■ Set up color management in Illustrator by using the Color Settings dialog box.	Online Companion
7. Outputting to Print	■ Set crop marks and trim marks in a document.	L
	■ Prepare a document for printing by choosing and configuring the appropriate resolution and rasterization settings.	L
	■ Explain guidelines associated with printing gradient mesh objects and color blends.	L
	■ Prepare and output a document to be used for color separation.	L
	■ Explain guidelines associated with printing transparencies.	L
8. Saving and Exporting	■ Given a file type, describe the options available when exporting an Illustrator document to that file type.	L
	■ List and describe the options available for saving Illustrator documents by using the Illustrator Legacy Options dialog box.	L
	■ Describe the differences, and explain criteria for when you would output an Illustrator document to various file formats. (formats include: PSD, JPEG, GIF, PDF, SVG)	Online Companion
9. Publishing for the Web	■ Discuss options and considerations associated with preparing graphics that will be used on the Web.	M
	■ Export Illustrator images that are optimized for publication on the Web.	M
	■ Output symbols to SWF and SVG formats.	M

Read the following information carefully!

Find out from your instructor the location of the Data Files you need and the location where you will store your files.

- To complete many of the chapters in this book, you need to use the Data Files provided on the CD at the back of the book.

- Your instructor will tell you whether or not you will be working from the CD or copying the files to a drive on your computer or on a server.

- Your instructor will also tell you where you will store the files you create and modify.

Copy and organize your Data Files.

- Use the Data Files List to organize your files to a zip drive, network folder, hard drive, or other storage device.

- Create a subfolder for each chapter in the location where you are storing your files, and name it according to the chapter title (e.g., Illustrator Chapter A).

- For each chapter you are assigned, copy the files listed in the **Data File Supplied** column into that chapter's folder.

- Store the files you modify or create in each chapter in the chapter folder.

Find and keep track of your Data Files and completed files.

- Use the **Data File Supplied** column to make sure you have the files you need before starting the chapter or exercise indicated in the **Chapter** column.

- Use the **Student Creates File** column to find out the filename you use when saving your new file for the exercise.

Files used in this book

Chapter	Data File Supplied	Student Creates File	Used in
A		The Lay of the Land	L1
	AI A-1.ai		L2
		Basic Shapes	L3–L6
	AI A-2.ai		L7
		Funky Flag	Skills Review
	AI A-3.ai		Project Builder 1
		Iris Vision Bid	Project Builder 2
	AI A-4.ai		Design Project
	AI A-5.ai		Group Project
B	AI B-1.ai		L1–L6
	AI B-2.ai		L2
	AI B-3.ai		Skills Review
		La Mirage	Project Builder 1
	AI B-4.ai		Project Builder 2
		Vanishing Point	Design Project
		Firehouse	Group Project
C	AI C-1.ai		L1
	AI C-2.ai		L2
	AI C-3.ai		L2
	AI C-4.ai		L3–L4
		Snowball Assembled	L5–L6
		Montag	Skills Review
		Peppermill Vector	Project Builder 1
		USAchefs Logo	Project Builder 2
		Sleek	Design Project
		Shape	Group Project
D	AI D-1.ai		L1
	AI D-2.ai		L1
	AI D-3.ai		L1

Chapter	Data File Supplied	Student Creates File	Used in
	AI D-4.ai		L2
	AI D-5.ai		L2
	AI D-6.ai		L3
	AI D-7.ai		L3
	AI D-8.ai		L4
	AI D-9.ai		L4
	AI D-10.ai		L4
	AI D-11.ai		L4
	AI D-12.ai		L5
	AI D-13.ai		L5
	AI D-14.ai		L5
	AI D-15.ai		Skills Review
	AI D-16.ai		Skills Review
	AI D-17.ai		Project Builder 1
	AI D-18.ai		Project Builder 2
		Ties	Design Project
		Dartboard	Group Project
E	AI E-1.ai		L1–L4
	AI E-2.ai		L1–L4
	AI E-3.ai		Skills Review
	AI E-4.ai		Project Builder 1
	AI E-5.ai		Project Builder 2
	AI E-6.ai		Design Project
	AI E-7.ai		Group Project
F		Checkerboard	L1
	AI F-1.ai		L2
	AI F-2.ai		L2
	AI F-3.ai		L3
	AI F-4.ai		L4
	AI F-5.ai		L5
		Polka Dot Pattern	Skills Review

Chapter	Data File Supplied	Student Creates File	Used in
	AI F-6.ai		Skills Review
		Shower Curtain	Project Builder 1
	AI F-7.ai		Project Builder 2
	AI F-8.ai		Design Project
		Original Plaid	Group Project
G	AI G-1.ai		L1
	AI G-2.ai		L1
	AI G-3.ai		L1
	AI G-4.ai		L2
	AI G-5.ai		L2
	AI G-6.ai		L3
	AI G-7.ai		L3
	AI G-8.ai		L3
	AI G-9.ai		L4
	AI G-10.ai		L4
	AI G-11.ai		L4
	AI G-12.ai		L4
		Filter Skills	Skills Review
	AI G-13.ai		Skills Review
	AI G-14.ai		Skills Review
	AI G-15.ai		Skills Review
		Tidal Wave	Project Builder 1
	AI G-16.ai		Project Builder 2
	AI G-17.ai		Design Project
		Saint Claw Flag	Group Project
H	AI H-1.ai		L1
	AI H-2.ai		L1–L3
		Triple Fill	L3
	AI H-3.ai		L4
	AI H-4.ai		Skills Review
	AI H-5.ai		Project Builder 1

Chapter	Data File Supplied	Student Creates File	Used in
	AI H-6.ai		Project Builder 2
	AI H-7.ai		Design Project
	AI H-8.ai		Group Project
I	AI I-1.ai		L1–L5
	AI I-2.ai		L6–L8
	AI I-3.ai		Skills Review
	AI I-4.ai		Skills Review
	AI I-5.ai		Project Builder 1
	AI I-6.ai		Project Builder 2
	AI I-7.ai		Design Project
		Sales	Group Project
J	AI J-1.ai		L1–L4
	AI J-2.ai		L4–L5
	AI J-3.ai		Skills Review
	AI J-4.ai		Project Builder 1
	AI J-5.ai		Project Builder 2
	AI J-6.ai		Design Project
	AI J-7.ai		Group Project
K	AI K-1		L1
	AI K-2		L2
	AI K-3		L2
	AI K-4		L2
	AI K-5		L2
	AI K-6		L3
	AI K-7		L4
	AI K-8*		L4
	AI K-9*		L4
	AI K-10*		L4
	AI K-11		Skills Review
	AI K-12		Skills Review

*artwork is copied from Files K-8, K-9, and K-10 and pasted into Tea Can file. Students do not save these files.

Chapter	Data File Supplied	Student Creates File	Used in
	AI K-13		Project Builder 1
	AI K-14		Project Builder 2
		T-Shirt Text	Design Project
	AI K-15		Group Project
L	AI L-1.ai		L2–L4
	AI L-2.ai		L4
	AI L-3.ai		L4
	AI L-4.ai		L5
	AI L-5.ai		L5
	AI L-6.ai		Skills Review
	AI L-7.ai		Project Builder 1
	AI L-8.ai		Project Builder 2
	AI L-9.ai		Design Project
	AI L-10.ai		Group Project
M	AI M-1.ai		L1–L3
	AI M-2.ai		L4
	AI M-3.ai		Skills Review
	AI M-4.ai		Project Builder 1
	AI M-5.ai		Project Builder 2
	AI M-6.ai		Design Project
			Group Project

Absorption
Occurs when light strikes an object and is absorbed by the object.

Additive primary colors
Refers to the fact that Red, Green, and Blue light cannot themselves be broken down but can be combined to produce other colors.

Ambient light
Determines how an object is lit globally.

Art brushes
A brush style that stretches an object along the length of a path.

Attributes
Formatting which has been applied to an object that affects its appearance.

Bevel
The angle that one surface makes with another when they are not at right angles.

Bevel join
Produces stroked lines with squared corners.

Bitmap images
Graphics created using a grid of colored squares called pixels.

Bleed
Artwork that extends to the trim and must extend the trim size by .125" to allow for variations when trimmed.

Blend
A series of intermediate objects and colors between two or more selected objects.

Blend Steps
Controls how smoothly shading appears on an object's surface and is most visible in the transition from the highlight areas to the diffusely lit areas.

Blending modes
Preset filters that control how colors blend when two objects overlap.

Brightness
The degree of lightness of a color.

Butt caps
Squared ends of a stroked path.

Calligraphic brushes
Brush style that applies strokes that resemble those drawn with a calligraphic pen.

Caps
The ends of stroked paths.

Clipping mask
An object whose area crops objects behind it in the stacking order.

Clipping set
Term used to distinguish clipping paths used in layers from clipping paths used to mask non-layered artwork.

CMYK
Cyan, Magenta, Yellow, and Black; four inks essential to professional printing.

Color gamut
Refers to the range of colors that can be printed or displayed within a given color model.

Color mode
Illustrator setting determining the color model of a document: RGB or CMYK.

Color model
A system used to represent or reproduce color.

Color Picker
A sophisticated dialog box for specifying colors in Illustrator.

Combination graph
A graph that uses two graph styles to plot numeric data; useful for emphasizing one set of data in comparison to others.

Compound path
Two or more paths that define a single object. When overlapped, the overlapped area becomes a negative space.

Compound shape
A term used to distinguish a complex compound path from a simple one. Compound shapes generally assume an artistic rather than a practical role.

Corner point
An anchor point joining two straight segments, one straight segment, and one curved segment, or two curved segments.

Crop marks
Short, thin lines that define where artwork is trimmed after it is printed.

Custom graph design
Artwork used to replace traditional columns, bars, or markers in Illustrator graphs.

Direction lines
Emanating from an anchor point, they determine the arc of a curved segment.

'Drag & drop' a copy
Pressing [Alt] (Win) or [option] (Mac) when moving an object; creates a copy of the object.

Effect
A type of appearance attribute which alters an object's appearance without altering the object itself.

Envelopes
Objects that are used to distort other objects into the shape of the envelope object.

Extrude
To add depth to an object by extending it on its Z axis. An object's Z axis is always perpendicular to the object's front surface.

Extrude & Bevel effect
A 3D effect that applies a three-dimensional effect to two-dimensional objects.

Flatten Artwork
Consolidating all layers in a document into a single layer.

GIF
A standard file format for compressing images by lowering the number of colors available to the file.

Gradient / Gradient Fill
A graduated blend between two or more colors used to fill an object or multiple objects.

Graph
A diagram of data that shows relationships among a set of numbers.

Graph type
A dialog box that provides a variety of ways to change the look of an Illustrator graph.

Graphic Styles
Named sets of appearance attributes.

Highlight Intensity
Controls how intense a highlight appears.

Highlight Size
Controls how large the highlights appear on an object.

Hue
The name of a color, or its identity on a standard color wheel.

Image map
A graphic with areas defined as links for the Internet.

Imageable area
The area inside the dotted line on the artboard which represents the portion of the page that a standard printer can print.

Joins
Define the appearance of the corner where two paths meet.

JPEG
A standard file format for compressing continuous tone images, gradients, and blends.

Kerning
Increasing or decreasing the horizontal space between any two text characters.

Keyboard increment
The distance that a single press of an arrow key moves a selected item; editable as a preference.

Layers
A solution for organizing and managing a complex illustration by segregating artwork.

Lighting Intensity
Controls the strength of the light on the object. The range for lighting intensity is 0-100, with 100 being the default.

Linear gradient
A gradient which can fill an object from left to right, top to bottom, or on any angle.

Menu bar
At the top of the Illustrator window; a bar which includes all of the Illustrator menus.

Mesh lines
Paths that crisscross a mesh object, joined at their intersections by mesh points.

Mesh object
A single, multicolored object in which colors can flow in different directions and transition gradually from point to point.

Mesh patch
The area between four mesh points.

Mesh points
Diamond shaped points which function like anchor points, with the added ability of being able to be assigned a color.

Miter join
Produces stroked lines with pointed corners.

Miter limit
Determines when a Miter join will be squared off to a beveled edge.

Multiply
An essential blending mode in which the colors of overlapping objects create an effect that is similar to overlapping magic markers.

Non-process Inks
Special pre-mixed inks that are printed separately from process inks.

Offset
(noun) The distance that an object is moved from a starting location to a subsequent location.

Offset path
A command that creates a copy of a selected path repositioned at a specified distance.

Opacity
The degree to which an object is transparent.

Optimization
A process by which a file's size is reduced through standard color compression algorithms.

Outline stroke
A command that converts a stroked path into a closed path that is the same width as the original stroked path.

Outlined text
A command that changes text in a document to standard vector graphics.

Palettes
Windows containing features for modifying and manipulating Illustrator objects.

PANTONE
The standard library of non-process inks.

Pathfinders
Preset operations that combine paths in a variety of ways; useful for creating complex or irregular shapes from basic shapes.

Pattern brushes
A brush style that repeats a pattern along a path.

Pattern fill
Multiple objects used as a fill for an object; the object is filled by repeating the artwork.

Pica
12 points, or $\frac{1}{6}$ of an inch.

Pixel
Picture element. Small, single-colored squares which compose a bitmap image.

Point
$\frac{1}{72}$ of an inch.

Point of origin
The point from which an object is transformed; by default, the center point of an object, unless another point is specified.

Process tints
Colors that can be printed by mixing varying percentages of CMYK inks.

Projecting cap
Produces a squared edge that extends the anchor point of a stroked path by a distance that is ½ the weight of the stroke.

Radial gradient
A gradient which fills an object as a series of concentric circles.

Reflection
Occurs when light strikes an object and 'bounces' off the object.

Resolution
The number of pixels in a given inch of a bitmap graphic.

Resolution-independent
Refers to a graphic which can be scaled with no impact on image quality.

Revolve
Another method that Illustrator CS provides for applying a 3D effect to a 2D object by "sweeping" a path in a circular direction around the Y axis of the object.

RGB
Red, Green and Blue; the additive primary colors of light.

Rich black
A process tint that is 100% Black plus 50% Cyan; used to print deep, dark black areas of a printed page.

Round cap
Produces a stroked path with rounded ends.

Round join
Produces stroked lines with rounded corners.

Saturation
The intensity of a hue.

Scatter brush
A brush style which disperses copies of an object along a path.

Scratch area
The area outside the artboard where objects may be stored for future use; objects on the scratch area will not print.

Slice
Divided artwork to be output as individual—and therefore smaller—files.

Smart guides
Non-printing words that appear on the artboard and identify visible or invisible objects, page boundaries, intersections, anchor points, etc.

Smooth points
Anchor points created by clicking and dragging the Pen Tool; the path continues uninterrupted through the anchor point.

Snap to point
Automatically aligns points when they get close together.

Stacking order
The hierarchy of objects on the artboard, from frontmost to backmost.

Status bar
A utility on the artboard that contains a list arrow menu from which you can choose a status line with information about the current tool, the date and time, the amount of free memory, or the number of undo operations.

Subtractive Primary Colors
Cyan, Magenta and Yellow; the term subtractive refers to the concept that each is produced by removing or subtracting one of the additive primary colors and that overlapping all three pigments would absorb all colors.

SWF
Macromedia Flash file format that supports vector graphics for the Web.

Symbol instance
A single usage of a symbol.

Symbol instance set
Symbol instances created with the Symbol Sprayer Tool.

Tick marks
Short lines that extend out from the value axis of a graph and aid viewers in interpreting the meaning of column height by indicating incremental values on the value axis.

Tile
Artwork, usually square, used repeatedly in a pattern fill.

Tiling
The process of repeating a tile as a fill for a pattern.

Title bar

At the top of the Illustrator window; contains the name of the document, magnification level, and color mode.

Toolbox

A palette containing Illustrator tools for creating, selecting, and manipulating objects in Illustrator.

Tracking

The process of inserting or removing uniform spaces between text characters to affect the width of selected words or entire blocks of text.

Transmission

Occurs when light strikes an object and passes through the object.

Trim marks

Like crop marks, define where a printed image should be trimmed; trim marks are used to create multiple marks for multiple objects on a page that are to be trimmed.

Trim size

The size to which artwork or a document is to be cut.

Tweaking

Making small, specific improvements to artwork or typography.

Type area select

An Illustrator preference which allows the user to select text simply by clicking anywhere on the text.

Vector graphics

Resolution-independent graphics created with lines, curves, and fills.

Visible light

Light waves that are visible to the human eye.

White light

Refers to the concept that natural light on Earth appears to people as not having any dominant hue.

Zoom text box

A utility in the lower-left corner of the Illustrator window that displays the current magnification level.